2001

Managing Internationally:
A Personal Journey

Managing Internationally:
A Personal Journey

GARY R. ODDOU
Utah State University
San Jose State University

C. BROOKLYN DERR
University of Utah

The Dryden Press
Harcourt Brace College Publishers

Fort Worth   Philadelphia   San Diego   New York   Orlando Austin   San Antonio
Toronto   Montreal   London   Syndey   Tokyo

Publisher:	George Provol
Acquisitions Editor:	John R. Weimeister
Executive Market Strategist:	Lisé Johnson
Developmental Editor:	Jennifer Sheetz Langer
Project Editor:	Tamara Vardy
Art Director:	Biatriz Chapa
Production Manager:	Anne Dunigan

ISBN: 0-03-006852-5

Library of Congress Catalog Card Number: 98-87748

Address for Domestic Orders
The Dryden Press, 6277 Sea Harbor Drive, Orlando, FL 32887-6777
800-782-4479

Address for International Orders
International Customer Service
The Dryden Press, 6277 Sea Harbor Drive, Orlando, FL 32887-6777
407-345-3800
(fax) 407-345-4060
(e-mail) hbintl@harcourtbrace.com

Address for Editorial Correspondence
The Dryden Press, 301 Commerce Street, Suite 3700, Fort Worth, TX 76102

Web Site Address
http://www.hbcollege.com

THE DRYDEN PRESS, DRYDEN, and the DP LOGO are registered trademarks of Harcourt Brace & Company.

Printed in the United States of America

8 9 0 1 2 3 4 5 6 7   039   9 8 7 6 5 4 3 2 1

The Dryden Press
Harcourt Brace College Publishers

To Jane and Jill

The Dryden Press Series In Management

Anthony, Perrewé, and Kacmar
*Human Resource Management:
A Strategic Approach*
Third Edition

Bereman and Lengnick-Hall, Mark
*Compensation Decision Making
A Computer-Based Approach*
Second Edition

Bergmann, Scarpello, and Hills
Compensation Decision Making
Third Edition

Boone and Kurtz
Contemporary Business
Ninth Edition

Bourgeois, Duhaime, and Stimpert
*Strategic Management:
A Managerial Perspective*
Second Edition

Calvasina and Barton
*Chopstick Company: A Business
Simulation*

Costin
*Readings in Total Quality
Management*

Costin
*Managing in the Global Economy:
The European Union*

Costin
Economic Reform in Latin America

Costin
*Management Development and
Training: A TQM Approach*

Costin
*Readings in Strategy and Strategic
Management*

**Czinkota, Ronhainen, and
Moffett**
International Business
Fifth Edition

Czinkota, Ronhainen, and Moffett
Global Business
Second Edition

Daft
Leadership: Theory and Practice

Daft
Management
Fourth Edition

Daft and Marcic
Understanding Management
Second Edition

DeSimone and Harris
Human Resource Development
Second Edition

Foegen
Business Plan Guidebook
Revised Edition

Gatewood and Field
Human Resource Selection
Fourth Edition

Gold
*Exploring Organizational Behavior:
Readings, Cases, Experiences*

Greenhaus and Callanan
Career Management
Second Edition

Hodgetts
Modern Human Relations at Work
Seventh Edition

Hodgetts and Kuratko
*Effective Small Business
Management*
Sixth Edition

Holley and Jennings
The Labor Relations Process
Sixth Edition

Holt
*International Management: Text and
Cases*

Kirkpatrick and Lewis
*Effective Supervision: Preparing for
the 21st Century*

Kuratko and Hodgetts
*Enterpreneurship: A Contemporary
Approach*
Fourth Edition

**Lengnick-Hall, Cynthia, and
Hartman**
Experiencing Quality

Long and Arnold
*The Power of Environmental
Partnerships*

Morgan
Managing for Success

Oddou and Derr
*Managing Internationally: A
Personal Journey*

Ryan, Eckert, and Ray
*Small Business: An Entrepreneur's
Plan*
Fourth Edition

Sandburg
*Discovering Your Business Career
CD Rom*

Vecchio
Organizational Behavior
Third Edition

Weiss
*Business Ethics: A Stakeholder and
Issues Management Approach*
Second Edition

Zikmund
Business Research Methods
Fifth Edition

Preface

Teaching International Management: Why a Journey?

We need to innovate, to find better and more interesting ways to teach our students. It is perhaps even a moral imperative of the teaching profession. Innovation, however, does not always mean better or more effective. So why a story or journey format?

A story has characters, a plot, and a point. Such a venue allows for creating a real-life context in which the reader follows the characters over time through their eyes, decisions, and interactions. The story can be used to help the reader, as in this book, live through the difficult moments of expatriate life, sense the frustration of confronting the subtleties of Japanese culture in an organizational context, and celebrate the success of finally understanding French hierarchy. The story in this text is a compilation of different parts of individuals' lives and companies with whom we, the authors, are familiar. In that sense, the people, events and issues are very real.

We often learn best when we learn first-hand through our own experiences. Vicarious learning is also a powerful tool as theorists such as social psychologist Albert Bandura and others have adequately shown. In this book, each chapter in the story is like a case study that allows for vicarious learning. As such it allows the instructor to ask the student to put her- or himself in a particular situation and to explain what she/he would do or have done and why. It requires the student to think, to apply conceptual information, and to justify the decision as much as possible.

In short, to communicate the reality of international management, this book must treat the topics at a personal level. At the same time, broader cultural values and business operations are described and will be the context for the individual, personal interactions as each of the characters does business.

Real Life Comes in Integrated Scenarios

Most international management texts treat the discipline topically and separately: communication, motivation, strategy, human resource management, organizational structure, and so forth. Within each topical area, studies are cited that contrast different countries' approaches with respect to that topic. Another common approach is covering a topical content area by relevant theories (as it is often in the U.S. management texts) and then looking at studies to see if the theory is valid in other cultures. For example, using the leadership topic again, the chapter might cover situational leadership theories such as Fiedler, House's Path-Goal, and so on. Studies related to Fiedler's theory are compared with others done in several other foreign countries, maybe Germany, Italy and Hong Kong, for example. Then the student moves on to Path-Goal leadership theory. Here, the applicable comparative studies might come from Japan, South Africa, and France.

If the same countries were consistently contrasted across topical areas, this approach could be very useful and help the students form a more integrated picture of various cultures and better understand the relevance of theories and topics in their cultural context. However, this is not the case and is unlikely to be the case for decades due to the lack of systematic research across topics in various areas of the world. The body of knowledge is far from being robust and vast enough to allow this kind of consistent cross-cultural comparison. Instead, as stated, the field is currently taking a shotgun approach, citing one study about motivational issues in one country, another about a certain theory in another country.

The net effect is that at the end of the term, students have been exposed to so many disparate pieces of information that their ability to integrate and apply the information can be difficult and fragmented.

Traditional textbooks also organize information sequentially and around a common conceptual theme. Life, on the other hand, comes in what seems to be simultaneous events with multiple issues or topics embedded in them. And so in our text, Part I, the story is basically a real-life story, with issues around leadership, communication, and gender, for example, occurring in the same chapter (and in some cases, in multiple chapters).

Presenting the material in more life-like reality, however, increases the challenge to help the student understand the material. There are several things we do to address this:

1. We include provocative discussion questions both inside the chapter and at the end of each chapter. These questions address the different topical areas introduced in each chapter.
2. We include in the student text a "Conceptual Lessons" section in Part II. This section addresses in a more traditional way the major topics/subject areas that are to some degree addressed in each chapter. There is one important difference again in how we treat the traditional material we select to present. Typically, we also integrate in the discussion that material and how it applies to the characters and story line in Part I.
3. The first two items above address content issues. We also have tried to provide an array of ways for the instructor to teach the chapter material in the instructor's manual. In fact, unlike most instructors' manuals, we have spent as much time developing a practical, useful resource manual to the instructor as we have spent developing the student text.

A Primarily Two-Country Focus: An Indepth and Coherent Picture

To remedy this problem, although others are created in their stead (but of a less serious nature in our opinions), our story primarily focuses on cross-cultural management issues between the United States and Japan and the United States and France. To avoid focusing solely on two countries in the world, however, we also deal with regional cultures. In the section treating primarily the contrast between the United States and Japan, a complete chapter on Vietnam is included, representing many of the typical issues that characterize entering emergent markets; in addition, cultural information about Hong Kong, Singapore, and Malaysia is also presented, partly reinforcing general Asian cultural patterns but also illustrating some of the differences between Asian countries.

Further, when MedTech is bought by a German firm, the two firm's cultures are contrasted as a way of symbolizing the larger cultural values that differ between the United States and Germany. In addition, when the focus in the story turns to France, other countries and cultures in Europe, Eurasia, and Africa are also dealt with to broaden the cultural context as well as to develop other topical issues, such as strategic planning.

We Learn through Repetition

As discussed earlier, many texts present material sequentially with little attempt to integrate material in previous chapters. Students are presented material about one topic, are tested on it, move on to the next chapter topic, mysteriously supplanting the previous material they "learned." To avoid this trap, we have purposely built in redundant cultural information across changing contexts from one chapter to another. For example, material on acculturation is introduced in four different chapters, part of it with regard to moving to Japan, then to France, and finally when returning to the United States. To avoid simple repetition, though, there are important variations in the redundancy. For example, in Chapter 4, acculturation concepts are presented; in Chapter 5, the student is asked to apply some of those concepts to the characters' experiences in Japan. In Chapter 14, the context changes to France and the material on acculturation is new material about the same topic. (Remember, though, each chapter focuses on multiple topics, so in these chapters acculturation is only one of the topics treated).

As a result of this focus, and from our experience teaching from "The Journey" over the last two years, students can demonstrate a clear, sound knowledge about Japanese and French management culture as well as the general business environment. Very importantly, they also feel much more confident about their knowledge. Probably most importantly, they have been exposed to different ways to analyze cultures and have ample opportunity to later apply these frameworks not only to Japan and France but also to Vietnam, Germany, Russia, and Burkina Faso. The overlap they experience between using the frameworks, answering the chapter discussion questions, and discussing the topics addressed in the student text (Part II) and the *Instructor's Resource Manual,* serves to reinforce and refine their knowledge about cultures and topics. Students still derive the conclusion that cultures can be different in their motivation, leadership styles, methods of organizing, and so forth, but now they have the additional advantages of having solid content knowledge about some major cultures in the international business arena and, very importantly, they feel confident in their ability to use frameworks to understand a new culture.

In conclusion, in writing this type of book, we have made a serious attempt at improving the pedagogy of international management. Although there are also costs in doing so, such as not covering the breadth of a typical text, we believe the overall learning benefit far outweighs such costs.

We're excited about this text.

Our students are, too:

"I feel the issues, whether theoretical or concrete, have become more personal because of the way they are presented. Specifically, I find it much easier to relate to Matt and Jan's experiences than I do the Ulriche models and concepts."

"Reading *International Management, A Personal Journey* was beneficial to me because of its significant practical worth. For instance, since the book was based on the real-life international experiences of the authors, rather than on theory, its business principles were easy for me to internalize and conceptualize. Further, compared to the theoretical articles which are often difficult for me to become motivated to read, the book's unique novel format made the information enjoyable and interesting. Finally, I also found the business principles of the book relevant to today's business environment."

"Overall, I found the format of this text to be very useful. I think that having the contrast of Japan, France, and the United States specifically favor a good understanding of the differences that as managers we can realistically expect to encounter. The differences in culture and approach to work are significantly different in each country and it was very interesting to see how Matt adapted to after-hours work and few vacations in one country and long lunches and month-long vacations in another. It was also very useful to be able to know Matt's thoughts and frustrations of working in each culture."

"The coverage of cultural issues are rich in the text. Deep levels of understanding of foreign culture are possible in the context of *International Management: A Personal Journey* that might not be possible in a textbook format."

"The greatest strength of the text is the in-depth exploration into multiple cultures such as Japan, Eastern Asian countries, France, Russia and Africa. It is also evident that the authors are either very knowledgeable about the particular customs of each of the discussed countries, or they did an appropriate amount of research. The customs and cultures in the text are discussed in a personal and in a business context which I found very interesting and informative. The reader is able to gain insight into the intricacies of Japanese culture as if they were living there themselves."

"This approach has the obvious advantage of providing realistic and internalizable instruction, which while necessarily falling short of actually having the international experience, is still much more credible and personally applicable than a theoretical approach limited to charts and lists of cultural issues and management principles never reduced to practice. It provides real examples of and context for the academic framework introduced in lectures."

Acknowledgments

Acknowledging other peoples' help is always very enjoyable for two reasons: First, it's a way of sharing in the credit (or the blame) for a work that has taken a significant part of our lives these last couple of years; second, it means the lengthy process from conception to print is largely finished!

Thank you, Butch (Gemin), for being our sponsor for such a project. We're still not sure how you sold it to management. Ruth (Rominger), you allowed us ample freedom to conceptualize in our own minds what we were trying to do. Your encouragement was always helpful. John (Weimeister), you became our voice in the wilderness when we thought no one was out there. And Jennifer, you have been our constant companion (i.e., a kind "boot in the pants" when we needed it) over the last several months to make sure we weren't going skiing too much or hanging out in the garden when we needed to be working. Thanks to all the others at Dryden, Debbie K. Anderson, Lise' Johnson, Biatriz Chapa, Sandy Walton, Tamara Vardy, and Anne Dunigan who have helped get this into print.

We also thank the reviewers for their time and their comments. Our appreciation goes to Mary Louise Lockerby, College of Du Page; Nancy Napier, Boise State University; Cam McLarney, Illinois State University; and Allan Bird, California Polytechnic State University. Allan (Bird) you were especially helpful, both as a critical eye to ensure accuracy in the Japanese section and as a cheer leader for our pedagogy. We hope we responded to your input.

We would both like to thank our colleagues and universities for their encouragement and support to help give us the time to complete this undertaking. We want to especially thank our students over the last several years, who have universally encouraged our effort to be both informational and interesting and whose feedback has really helped us refine our concept. We are grateful to various research assistants, editors and secretaries who helped prepare parts of the manuscript. Grant Madsen, Peg McKensie, and Nguyen Ngoc Hoang helped craft and edit several of the chapters, Peg using her Peace Corps experience in Berkina Faso and Russia, Nguyen his personal and journalistic experience in Vietnam. Kristen Rogers, Sylvie Rouissillon, Frank Bournois and Eugenie Draper were careful readers. Lori Wadsworth provided research assistance and Anh Phan and Lorna Jenkins secretarial services. Yvette Derr Ison wrote the poems in Chapters 12 and 14 and, along with Danielle Derr Kennington, helped edit the Instructor's Resource Manual.

Finally, we want to thank our wives, Jane and Jill, for their tremendous support through this seemingly never-ending process.

About the Authors

Gary Oddou is currently the department head of the Management and Human Resources Department at Utah State University. Professor Oddou completed his doctoral work at Brigham Young University. He has received various teaching awards including participation in a federal grant for MBA Course Curriculum Change to Increase MBA Student Community Involvement in 1997. Previously Professor Oddou has been affiliated with the International Institute for Management Development (IMD), Lausanne, Switzerland; Ecole de Management-Lyon in France; Monterey Institute of International Studies; Ecole Superieure de Commerce, Lyon, France; and the University of Sarajevo in the former Yugoslavia.

His primary search and consulting interests relate to international human resource management and outdoor management development. He is internationally known for his work in expatriation and repatriation.

Professor Oddou is the author of several books and supporting supplements. His research has been published in journals such as Academy of Management Review, Human Resource Management Journal, Employment Management Association Journal, International Journal of Management, The Journal of Management Education, European Management Journal and Columbia Journal of World Business.

C. Brooklyn Derr is Professor of Human Resources Management and the Knowles Faculty Scholar at the University of Utah. Professor Derr completed his doctoral work at Harvard University. His areas of special interest are management development, work–family issues, conflict management, cross-functional and cross-cultural teams, and internationalizing top management. Currently he is also the Director of Global Business Programs and the Co-Director of the Brigham Young University-University of Utah Center for International Business Education and Research (CIBER). Previously he has taught at Harvard, UCLA, the International Institute of Management Development (IMD), Lausanne, Switzerland; Ecole Superieur de Commerce in Lyon, France and INSEAD in Europe.

Professor Derr has written 3 books and published over 30 articles. He is currently writing a test on international management development and conducting studies on cross-cultural conflict management orientations, and work–family conflicts. He has been a consultant to international corporations and government organizations in Europe and North America. Professor Derr's consulting specialties are in management development, high-potential management, internationalizing managers and conflict management.

List of Important Characters (in alphabetical order)

Name	Role	Chapters
Charles Caussé	Director of Sales and Marketing at Transfusions, French, poses cultural problems for Matt and Jennifer Stewart	15
Ron Clancey	International Vice President at Plasmatec	15, 17, 19
Karl Davidson	Former UCLA professor of Matt and current mentor from whom Matt receives career guidance	2–4, 11–14, 19
Lan Phan Tran	Manufacturing expert in MedTech	2–4
Gisèle	Jennifer's French language instructor and close French friend	16
Ian Hughes	British, President of Pathway in Vietnam. Educates Matt about business in Vietnam	9
Heathery Irsay	Jan's friend, former law school buddy and roommate, in environmental law, still a friend and confidant for Jan	11, 12
Tom McDonald	CEO of Plasmatec	11–13, 17
Mr. Satoh	Japanese contact in Muhashi for MedTech. Principal character representing Muhashi	2–4, 6–7
Melanie Sierra	Marketing assistant to John Solt	2–4
Doc Silverman	Matt's boss and mentor at Plasmatec	11–13
Jennifer Stewart	High potential in Plasmatec. Expatriate to France for development. Matt's assistant in Grenoble and remains an ally when Matt is VP of International Operations	16, 17, 19
Matt Sumner	Jan's husband and principal character in text	1–19
Jan Sumner	Matt's wife and main character in text	1–8, 10–12, 14–19
Jeff Sumner	Son of Jan and Matt	3, 6–8, 11, 18
Michelle Sumner	Daughter of Jan and Matt	5–8, 11, 18
Jeff Thompson	CEO and founder of MedTech	2–4, 6–8, 10

Names of Companies Most Represented

MedTech	Start-up medical supply company; main firm in Chapters 3–10; located in Santa Cruz, CA
Muhashi	Japanese firm that creates a joint venture with MedTech, in Chapters 3, 4–9; located in Tokyo, Japan
Oberfeldt, A.G.	German firm that buys MedTech out, Chapter 10
Plasmatec	Pharmaceutical/biotech firm that hires Matt after he leaves MedTech; located in Scotts Valley, CA
Transfusions	French branch of GTS that has the joint venture with Plasmatec; located in Grenoble, France
GTS	French parent company of Transfusions; located in Paris, France

List of Minor Characters (in alphabetical order)

Name	Role	Chapters
John Bishop	British banker who tried to set up first bank in Vietnam but failed because of political incorrectness	9
Henri-Claude de Brie	Matt's French boss in Transfusions	15
Sean Connolly	Dragon Exploration's director in Hong Kong	
Mary Gorman	Jennifer's friend and business associated in Burkina-Faso	17
Thanh Huong	Vietnamese who developed perfume and credit business in Vietnam	9
Mr. L'Inspecteur	A member of the Cabinet du Prefet of Grenoble who ensures policy adherence to French law	15
Prof. Paul Jenu	INSEAD professor, expert on French culture and business	12, 14
Mr. Liu	MedTech contact in Hong Kong	8
My	Pathway's interpretor for Ian Hughes	9
Carl Nolan	Matt's replacement when Matt goes to Japan	4, 7, 10
Irum Rangwala	Controller for MedTech	2, 4
John Rosenford	President of Dragon Exploration, Inc., parent firm of Pathway, a distribution co. in a joint venture with Pharmthuco in Vietnam	9
Corine Salvay	High-potential employee in Transfusions (GTS) Counterpart to Jennifer Stewart	16
John Solt	Marketing head in MedTech Gets fired for poor performance	2, 3
Ba Thoi	An expert on foreign direct investment in Vietnam who was an advisor to Pathway's Hughes	9
Sau Tung	Vice chairman of DEER, a powerful local government official who had influence to approve of Pathway's and Pharmthuco's activities	9
Nguyen Van Thanh	Director of Planning in Pharmthuco, joint venture partner of Pathway in Vietnam	9
Mr. Wibowo	MedTech contact in Malaysia	8
Dr. Tran Van Xuan	Director of Pharmthuco, joint venture parther with Pathway in Vietnam	9

Note to Reader:

Some students wonder why Jan so often accommodates her career to Matt's career. There are several reasons why we decided to feature a more traditional international couple in this story. First, one of the purposes of this text is to explore the complexities and realities of an international career. Typically, the international move requires that one partner temporarily subordinate his or her career to that of the internationalist. It is often not possible, for example, to obtain work visas for both partners in the assignment country. In addition, the first six moths is a period of demanding intensive

Contents

List of Minor Characters (in alphabetical order)

Name	Role	Chapters
John Bishop	British banker who tried to set up first bank in Vietnam but failed because of political incorrectness	9
Henri-Claude de Brie	Matt's French boss in Transfusions	15
Sean Connolly	Dragon Exploration's director in Hong Kong	
Mary Gorman	Jennifer's friend and business associated in Burkina-Faso	17
Thanh Huong	Vietnamese who developed perfume and credit business in Vietnam	9
Mr. L'Inspecteur	A member of the Cabinet du Prefet of Grenoble who ensures policy adherence to French law	15
Prof. Paul Jenu	INSEAD professor, expert on French culture and business	12, 14
Mr. Liu	MedTech contact in Hong Kong	8
My	Pathway's interpretor for Ian Hughes	9
Carl Nolan	Matt's replacement when Matt goes to Japan	4, 7, 10
Irum Rangwala	Controller for MedTech	2, 4
John Rosenford	President of Dragon Exploration, Inc., parent firm of Pathway, a distribution co. in a joint venture with Pharmthuco in Vietnam	9
Corine Salvay	High-potential employee in Transfusions (GTS) Counterpart to Jennifer Stewart	16
John Solt	Marketing head in MedTech Gets fired for poor performance	2, 3
Ba Thoi	An expert on foreign direct investment in Vietnam who was an advisor to Pathway's Hughes	9
Sau Tung	Vice chairman of DEER, a powerful local government official who had influence to approve of Pathway's and Pharmthuco's activities	9
Nguyen Van Thanh	Director of Planning in Pharmthuco, joint venture partner of Pathway in Vietnam	9
Mr. Wibowo	MedTech contact in Malaysia	8
Dr. Tran Van Xuan	Director of Pharmthuco, joint venture parther with Pathway in Vietnam	9

Note to Reader:

Some students wonder why Jan so often accommodates her career to Matt's career. There are several reasons why we decided to feature a more traditional international couple in this story. First, one of the purposes of this text is to explore the complexities and realities of an international career. Typically, the international move requires that one partner temporarily subordinate his or her career to that of the internationalist. It is often not possible, for example, to obtain work visas for both partners in the assignment country. In addition, the first six moths is a period of demanding intensive work involvement in a new assignment but also demanding intensive parental support for children entering not only a new community, but a new culture. Second, while this is a story about both Matt and Jan, the story follows the international career of Matt. Finally, even though Matt and Jan are supportive dual career partners, they have different career success orientations. Matt is more typically a "getting ahead" careerist and Jan has more of a "getting balanced" profile. Jennifer Stewart, on the other hand, is a professional woman less encumbered by family relationships than Jan. With her own "getting ahead" orientation, she more single-mindedly pursues her international career.

Topical Contents

Contents

PART

I

Matt and Jan

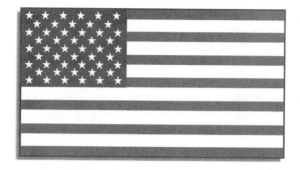

CHAPTER 1

Beginning a Journey

MATT

I grew up in Berkeley when there were only stories about the sixties and seventies—student riots at the university, police barricades, boycotted classes, marijuana growing in the botanical garden, and so on. Born just after things quieted down, there was still a lot of abnormalities back then if judged by the rest of the nation. Drugs seemed a way of life for many, a way of exploration for others; to an insider, sometimes it seemed almost everyone had some use for drugs, regardless of their age, position, or stature in the community. Of course, in reality, there were more that didn't do drugs than did—but the image lives on beyond reality. Debates on the merits of national policies took place in various forms—intellectual discussions in university classrooms or on the campus, demonstrations in the community, and essays published and handed out on the street corner. Diversity became a way of life—different colors, different ideas, different causes. There was unity in diversity. It was a special time in the history of the Bay Area, even the United States—at least this is what my dad has told me. I was too young at the time to really know what was happening.

El Monte High School was a memorable experience for me, although I missed my junior year while I was studying in Aix-en-Provence, France. Aix had diversity, too—students from all over the world. In my first week, I had met North Africans, other Americans, Turks, Germans, black Africans, British, and even a few French! I spent many evenings discussing—or trying to discuss—politics, religion, and the "American" way of life, sometimes in French but often in English. *Je ne parlais pas très bien français à ce moment* (I didn't speak French very well at that time). Foreign students were anxious to talk about the U.S. role in Nicaragua, about U.S. support of the shah in Iran, and a host of other issues that I was more or less familiar with. I know these things are ancient history to college students now, but they were the talk of the world back then. One of the first expressions I learned from classmates was "*Non, non, je ne suis pas de votre avis*" (No, no, I don't share that opinion). My debate and negotiation skills were honed immensely that year.

My experience in Aix was the realization of some aspect of one or more of my childhood dreams. At the age of 12, I had three dreams: own my own sailing yacht, circumnavigate the world, and discover a lost city in South America. I think there was a common theme there somewhere.

With El Monte High School diploma in hand and Berkeley and Aix in the past, I headed off to Renssaeler Polytechnic to study engineering. Although not a brilliant quantitative mind, I was smart and liked challenges. I had won first place in the high school egg-dropping contest, the first in school history to drop an egg off the gym ten times without its breaking. Of course, we didn't drop the egg by itself; we could wrap it in something, build a parachute, or fashion something else to keep it from breaking. There were a few limits to what materials could be used, the size of the box, and that kind of thing, but basically it was the most creative or ingenious creation that won. I was also the first person to pull the school's fire alarm twenty times in twenty days without getting caught. These were things I couldn't exactly put on my résumé, though.

After Renssaeler, I worked for a couple of years with Hewlett-Packard (HP) as a member of a design team for instruments that measure the density of molecules in space above the earth's atmosphere. It was a neat little instrument that was installed in small orbiting satellites, but I had to admit, it wasn't what I had envisioned doing as a career. I had always dreamed of being part of something really important. HP was a great company, but I just wasn't excited about what I was doing. It was important to me to have a real impact on things.

With this HP instrument, the technical challenges were there, but nothing else. I was just one member of a small team of scientists and engineers. The instrument itself was a very small volume, high-priced product that only a few so-called companies bought, like NASA or telecommunications firms. The average person on the street didn't even know the instrument existed. That was a downer. People would ask you what you did, and I'd have to tell them, "I help design an instrument that measures molecular density of space above the earth's atmosphere." They'd always respond, "Oh," and then move quickly to another topic. My job was a real conversation piece, all right.

My wife, Jan, was born on Martha's Vineyard, an island barely off the coast of Massachusetts. When she was 10 years old, her family moved. Her father had become ill and could no longer take care of the grocery store and small farm on the island. They sold it and moved to Bangor, Maine, to join Jan's grandparents. There, in the big city, Jan's mother was able to find work and help the family stay afloat. Although Jan had developed a deep love for the sea and all it meant to her and generations of her family, she seemed to adapt her love of the sea to a genuine appreciation for the woods, rivers, lakes, and mountains the mainland brought. She was a natural backpacker, spending every spare moment during the summers and winter vacations in the backwoods of Maine with friends and her grandfather, a retired clocksmith. Jan received her first pair of randonnée skis when she was 13 years old—a used pair of Kahrus with Silvretta bindings. By the time she was 18, she had climbed and toured all of the major peaks in Maine many times.

It was difficult for her to leave Maine and venture off to Texas where she had received a scholarship that would pay her four years of college tuition. Given her family's financial situation, she felt obligated to accept the generous offer from UT-Austin over other offers. There she studied American literature, and her favorite authors were Henry David Thoreau, Friedrich Paulsen, and Samuel Clemens (Mark Twain). She had spent many evening hours on her front porch in Maine reading the great literature of the birth of the United States—especially of the frontier. Bedtime reading for her was books about the Lewis and Clark expeditions and John Muir's writings. She knew early on what she wanted to study at the university—what she called "environmental literature." I think she was the first to coin the term. I've never heard it since either.

During her time at UT-Austin, Jan became involved with several environmental groups—a real oddball according to prevailing business thought. Austin was becoming a center of residential development and commercial growth at the time because of the attractiveness of its lower cost living, tax incentives, and very skilled work force. Like some others, Jan became concerned that the natural environment was being destroyed only for the sake of money. Although her studies were very important to her, she found time to write leaflets to pass out in the community and to participate in weekly environmentalists' meetings. She enjoyed the cosmopolitan group that met in the community center and didn't realize a few of the friendships would last over time.

Before graduating, Jan had trouble deciding what she wanted to do. She had been offered a position as an editor for a small publisher, but her heart was really in causes rather than jobs. She really wanted to go on to graduate school but wasn't sure what she wanted to study and whether her family needed her help financially. With her family's encouragement, though, she applied to several law schools and eventually decided to study at UC-Berkeley. Her exposure to environmental issues at UT-Austin made her realize that her days hiking in the Mahoosuc range of Maine and New Hampshire had left a deep impression.

On our first date we talked about where Jan was from and about her interests. Hiking and backpacking were her favorites.

"Sometimes the mosquitoes were so thick, you'd think it was dusk at two in the afternoon," she'd say. "I liked it because it kept the 'weaker' ones away," she added, referring to other backpackers.

I especially remember that last line. I knew it told me something about Jan that distinguished her from any other woman I had met. I liked that kind of spirit.

Her occasional run-ins with the law in Austin during some picketing demonstrations had led her to appreciate the complexity of environmental issues. She became convinced that the best way she could protect the environment was through understanding the laws, pursuing its enforcement, and, where necessary, trying to create legislation where none existed. Jan was passionate about the environment, but she seemed completely rational and reasonable in her approach. In this way, she was often different from the others picketing with her. Jan had internalized the cause. Many of the others picketed because it was a way to channel excess energy.

Berkeley was an ideal place to study, so that's where she went. While in her third year of law school, we met at a Halloween party at a mutual friend's house. Jan had come as an astronaut, me as a frontiersman, wearing my real coonskin cap I had bought in Jackson, Wyoming, on a ski trip. I still have it. At that time animals didn't yet have rights and it seemed like the "manly" thing to do. I mean, I thought all real men wore coonskin caps. Jan wasn't as impressed.

Despite showing a certain insensitivity to animals, Jan seemed to look "underneath" my cap and become interested in me. We enjoyed each other's company, shared similar values, and had a lot of long discussions while hiking in the nearby Redwoods up the coast and near Santa Cruz. Eventually I got up the courage and asked her to marry me. By this time, Jan had graduated and had just begun working at a law firm in San Francisco that specialized in environmental issues, focusing on pro-environment clients. She had clerked for them during her second and third year of law school, working with many of the major well-known environmental groups: the Sierra Club, the Wilderness Society, and others. After getting married, we moved to a small, barely affordable house in San Bruno, not too far from my work at Hewlett-Packard and an easy commute to San Francisco for Jan.

We both worked hard at our careers our first couple of years. I enjoyed the professional experience I was getting at HP and Jan was passionate about her work at the law firm. Every case taught her about the complexities of the reasonable balance between the needs of humans and nature. Her cases were not all local; in fact, most of them were in nearby states—Nevada, Oregon, Washington, Utah, and Colorado. Sometimes her work involved traveling, which she enjoyed—the first year.

I worked long hours that first year also, often coming home at 7 or 8 o'clock at night after having put in ten- to twelve-hour days. I can't say it was totally because I was passionate about my work—I did really enjoy applying what I had learned in school to something real—but I think it was also because I was following the unwritten law of advancement: getting ahead meant impressing the boss and my colleagues. Neither Jan nor I seemed to have much energy for each other by the time we got home—the honeymoon was over. Weekends were spent recuperating from the week, going shopping, mowing the lawn, changing the oil, paying the bills, and doing other necessary evils.

It didn't take too long before I realized that Jan and I needed to take more time for our relationship. Jan agreed our careers had taken over. She realized also she was losing intimacy with what had made her so passionate about the environment and her work in the first place—her feelings for the animals, the peaks, the wind, the snow, the rivers, all the wonders of nature she had grown to feel a part of. It had been a year since she had even taken a walk in the mountains. The environment to her was more than winning legal games.

"Sometimes I feel like an animal out of its natural element—trapped in a "game" much bigger than I am," she said to me once. She had been filling her vacation time with phone calls and reading to continue her case strategies. Too, I had seen a few young engineering friends at HP suffer from troubled marriages and, in a few cases, from divorces. I know it sounds sentimental, but Jan and I loved each other and didn't want that to happen to us.

After three years at HP, I began to feel a little restless. My interest in the projects began to wane a bit and I think I suffered from the "grass looks greener" syndrome. Several of my co-workers had left HP for smaller start-up firms and seemed to be having a great time. Although I had gained solid experience at HP and the company had some of the characteristics of a much smaller firm, I wanted to get some experience working in a start-up entrepreneurial firm. I also realized that although I enjoyed the challenges of technical problems, eventually I wanted to take on roles that would give me greater decision-making authority in the company. I was struggling with the idea of getting an MBA. Although I knew I could find a position in a small start-up without the degree, I had always been told an MBA increases one's options. As I looked around me at HP, almost all of the people above lower level managerial jobs and under 40 had MBAs or PhDs. I knew sooner or later an MBA would come in handy. As I examined my options—staying in engineering or getting into general management—I knew an MBA would help avoid a technical-only route to the top. It almost always meant more money, and even though I didn't yet know why I would need more money (after all, Jan and I were pretty happy), intuitively I knew it would come in handy—a ski trip to Les Trois Alpes in France, a safari in Kenya, or even a house with a white picket fence and kids if we were really desperate!

Marketing had always been attractive to me, and I had even considered majoring in it instead of engineering. I also enjoyed working with people. Now with school and some experience behind me, I was better able to discern my long-term interests.

By this time, Jan and I had built a more solid relationship. Although we talked about having children, nothing had yet come of it. Neither of us seemed to have time for anything else but our work; not that this was by design, it had just happened. I must admit I was a little uncomfortable about what a new job with a start-up might mean for our marriage. Here I had begun to settle into a more reasonable workload and now was seriously considering seeking a position that I knew would require a greater commitment than I was currently giving to HP. "Am I out of my mind?" I asked myself. "How is Jan going to feel about it? How do I really feel about it? An MBA program might be a better route right now." Just then the telephone rang, so I just tucked some of these thoughts away in my mind for a rainy day.

That rainy day kept getting postponed—an unusually long drought it seemed! It took me six months to resolve it within myself—not an easy feat, let alone to bring it up to Jan. Fortunately for me, though, I have an unusually discerning wife. She had sensed I was wrestling with something and one day just came out and asked, "Are you really happy at HP or is something else going on?"

Being the courageous soul I was, that kind of opened the door for me and I told her what I had been thinking. Jan questioned me about my motives, about what I wanted to get out of a career, what path I wanted to take to get there, and how I thought it would affect our marriage and someday our family when children came along. At first I felt a little on the spot, like a secret agent being interrogated by the enemy. How did I know the answers to all of those questions? I just knew how I was feeling. After a few minutes of hemming and hawing, I realized she was right; we needed to consider all the implications of a such a change. And so we did—until about three in the morning, finally falling asleep from sheer tiredness.

It was Saturday morning, fortunately. I would have hated to have had to go in to work that day. I woke up feeling like I was somewhere between this world and the Land of Oz, my eyelids only half open that morning as I prepared breakfast while Jan was still asleep. When Jan did finally awake, it was to the smell of one of my famous omelets. She dragged herself out of bed, grabbing her bathrobe, and wandered into the kitchen. Coming off a difficult night's discussion, I wanted the morning to go more smoothly. I had the table set and was just cutting the omelet in two, making sure I didn't scrape the Teflon, as Jan slipped into her chair, hands over her eyes. It was 10 A.M.

Dropping her hands and looking up groggily, Jan said, "Just keep one thing in mind when you start applying to MBA schools. I have a job I am committed to. I don't want to move, and this whole idea is yours, not mine. Don't assume that my job is part of the package to be negotiated," she added.

Question 1:   What would your reaction be if you were Matt?

For that and other reasons, I struggled with where to apply. The major considerations were reputation of the MBA program, location, and expense. After doing some research, I applied to three schools: UCLA, Berkeley, and Northwestern. Northwestern had a particularly strong marketing program, considered the best in the United States. UCLA was an excellent school in all areas as was Berkeley. Berkeley represented the familiar to someone who had grown up in the Bay Area, but most importantly, it made sense to try and stay close to the City (local vernacular for San Francisco). Stanford was just too expensive and didn't have the reputation in marketing that attracted me to apply to Northwestern—another $25,000 institutional investment!

Staying in the Bay Area didn't seem to be in the cards anyway—at least not for both of us. I was accepted to Northwestern and UCLA. The decision was really difficult. I wanted to go to Northwestern for its marketing program but I recognized it would put a real strain on our marriage, and without any scholarship the tuition was just too much. UCLA, however, would allow for the possibility of a commuter marriage if we decided that was a better alternative than Jan's leaving the firm. Also, Jan's firm had a quasi partnership with two firms in LA. There was a chance she could work for one of those firms.

After some initial research, though, that possibility didn't materialize. They were overstaffed as it was and would probably be letting someone go before they hired someone new. Jan seemed depressed about the reality of the whole situation. "I don't know," she told me. "It seems like we've worked so hard to get to where we are and now this. I wish you had been happy at HP."

"Are you reconsidering your support for the MBA?" I asked, shaking my head. Jan didn't say anything for what seemed like hours.

"I don't know. It's just depressing," she said. "I guess I just wish life could stay the same. But I don't think I can leave my job, and that means being apart for the two years. It's more than I want to think about right now," she added, her energy trailing off.

Question 2:   How do you think Matt and Jan should handle their conflicting needs and goals?

I think neither of us really wanted to confront the issues head on. Jan thoroughly enjoyed her work, was learning a great deal, and had a partner who had taken particular interest in developing her career. I really wanted to go to Northwestern, but couldn't financially and didn't want to be so far from Jan if she stayed.

In the end, I decided it wasn't fair for me to ask Jan to give up her dream when she had so generously agreed to support my leaving HP and going back to school. So with great reluctance on both sides, Jan stayed in the Bay Area and I headed south to UCLA.

The first months were incredibly difficult for both of us. There were a lot of telephone calls, some questioning about whether we had lost our minds—or more specifically, whether I had lost mine—and a number of weekend visits. After a while, reality set in. We knew we couldn't continue wishing the situation were different. In addition, I was becoming increasingly occupied by my studies. The intensity of missing each other waned some as we settled into the routine of being separated.

After a few months, we usually saw each other only one weekend a month during the first year, although there were times when Jan couldn't get away for several weeks because of an impending case she was working on. My courses were killers that first year, so actually it was a blessing in disguise sometimes when Jan was too busy to get together. It gave me a chance to give a few more hours to what seemed like a never-ending pursuit. MBA school was quite competitive. Everyone was trying to outdo the others. I got tired of it after a while, but I had to just keep going.

I figured something good had come out of our visits, though, when Jan announced she was pregnant. We were ecstatic, and yet I think after the initial euphoria wore off, we both felt a little empty knowing we wouldn't be sharing much of the pregnancy. I still had three months of school left in my second year. I was a little depressed, to say the least. Our first baby and I was going to be an absentee father right at the start. Jan had it even worse, suffering from my absence, which wasn't even her choice.

The last few months of the second year, we did see each other a little more. My courses were mostly electives. The workload was less routine; there was less group work, and the courses were more interesting so I got through everything a lot faster. The bottom line was I didn't have to spend so much time on them. Besides, it finally dawned on me that school had always just been a means to an end for me. It was a way to a career that I was in search of.

When I finally graduated, we swore we would never have a commuter marriage again. Up to then, those were the roughest years of my life, and I think Jan felt the same. Frankly, we loved each other and didn't enjoy the separation. Both of us had a chance to reflect on our strategy of career first, marriage second, and we decided that only once in our marriage could that choice work. We loved each other more than we did our careers.

We named the baby Jeffrey, after Jan's favorite uncle who had passed away a few years earlier. It had been really exciting during the pregnancy feeling Jeffrey kick and turn and listening to his heartbeat with a stethoscope Jan had borrowed from a doctor friend. Jan would update me by phone as "historical" moments occurred—his first move, his first kick—and would report on what the doctor said after each visit.

Jan's parents kept in close contact with her while I was gone. Jan's dad was hilarious. He even bought a cellular phone to have with him out in the garden just in case Mom was gone and Jan had an emergency. Dad's hearing wasn't great and he didn't trust he could hear the phone ring if he was outside.

My parents were in New York where my dad had made his last career move up the corporate ladder. He was still in his mid-fifties, so he figured he had a good shot at a senior vice president job in his firm. This was their second move from the Bay Area after I finished high school. First they went to Arizona for four years, and then he was promoted to a corporate position in New York. Dad had been an engineer and was of the so-called old school. You showed your loyalty above everything else and stuck with the firm through thick and thin. He had turned down a number of offers from headhunters for sometimes as much as a 40 percent salary increase. In Silicon Valley this is almost unheard of for my generation. If you don't change jobs every three to five years, you stagnate and end up making a lot less money. Those are the two important values in the valley—growth and money.

We saw Mom and Dad once or twice a year. It wasn't easy for Dad to get away, and Mom didn't like traveling without him. Those first few years were tight for us, too, timewise and moneywise, so we didn't have much opportunity to go to New York either.

QUESTIONS FOR DISCUSSION

1. Based on the descriptions of Matt and Jan, what appear to be their individual values? Which are shared? Which, if any, are in conflict?
2. Based at least partly on your answer in question 1, what would you say are Jan and Matt's career orientations (those values that drive their career choices)?
3. How would you describe Jan and Matt's relationship in terms of personal and professional issues? How does each respond to the other, sense the other's concerns? Have they developed a relationship that would form the basis of integrating their personal and professional values into a "whole"? Finally, how would you predict they would manage their careers and marriage if one were to accept a position in a foreign country?

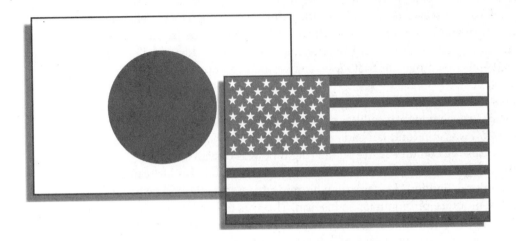

CHAPTER 2

Seeking Markets: Meeting Up with Japan

MATT

It was an average year for job recruitment at UCLA. Most graduates had at least one solid offer; the best had two or three. A few had to really dig. I interviewed with General Electric, IBM, Apple, and several other large firms, although I interviewed mostly out of courtesy to the School of Management's Placement Center. I had already decided I was looking for the excitement and challenge of a small start-up firm. I wasn't looking for bureaucracy. I wanted a roll-up-your-sleeves-and-get-it-done-any-way-you-can kind of a job.

A few months before graduation, I contacted a few small companies I respected to see what was out there and to leave my résumé. I also called some of my friends who had left HP to see what they had going or knew about. Eventually, the list narrowed to three companies. But after the first interview, with Jeff Thompson, founder of a really small start-up, called MedTech, I knew this was the firm. It was gut—pure gut feeling in this case. Of course, if anything said had been obviously dumb, a warning sign would have surfaced immediately. But it hadn't, and I didn't need to do any detailed analysis. Some decisions are best made on what your instincts tell you. Over the years, I had learned to trust my instincts.

I met with others at MedTech too. John Solt, the marketing director, seemed sharp and kind of cocky as well. A Harvard MBA, John had been in the work force about six years. He had been with MedTech since its inception about a year ago. Tall, slightly balding, and well built, he took about an hour with me to talk a little about MedTech, but mostly about my background. He was interested in why I wanted to leave HP in the first place and what I thought I could bring to MedTech. I remember John's office was attractively decorated. Nicely matted original pen and ink drawings of sailing vessels hung on the walls. John also had a stack of *Wall Street Journals* on the table next to his desk. These were symbolic of a chink in John's armor that I describe later on.

I also interviewed with Irum Rangwala, the controller. She had about 10 years' experience in accounting and some in finance, working for two different high-tech firms in the Bay Area. She was recruited by Jeff, who had known her from a brief stint he had done at a biomedical firm. He had been really impressed with her, and so were others. She had a superb reputation in the industry as someone who grasped details quickly, sized them up, and conceptualized a solution, and then, most importantly, could get results.

Finally, I interviewed with the senior engineer, Lan Tran, an individual in his late 40s, who seemingly had been around, done everything, and knew everyone. He wasn't a braggart. In fact, you would have never known about all of his accomplishments except everyone else talked about him. The guy was of average height, a little overweight, dark complexioned with thinning jet-black hair. We walked around the facility as he talked me through what they were trying to do. He spoke of the problems they were confronting in terms of the manufacturing process design, which was why I was being interviewed. There was too much work to do. MedTech needed someone who could give the design process full-time attention. Tom would work with me on it, but he had too many other problems to follow through on it.

I liked him a lot. The guy was humble, yet intelligent. Any other engineer would have been interested in having someone else take care of all the details about materials supply, vendors, and so on, that were taking up too much of his time. The design aspect is much more interesting and glamorous. He was willing to let me work on it and he would consult with me on what I would be doing. Structurally, we would be equals on the chart. I would be senior engineer over the design process and Tom would manage the materials supply and quality control side. In essence, we would have overlapping responsibilities to some extent but would also have individual duties that would consume the largest part of our time.

After the interviews, I canceled one of the other two appointments without knowing for sure whether I had the job with MedTech. I realize some would say that was rather foolish, but I again had to follow my instincts. In this case, it worked out. Jeff, the president, called me the next day, and I started work the day after. We got along great from the start. We were "kindred spirits," I would often tell Jan. Plus, I had a really good feeling about the rest of the people at MedTech with the exception perhaps of John Solt, the marketing honcho. But with Jeff, Irum, and Lan, it all went very smoothly. I liked all of them—their styles, knowledge, and so on. That doesn't mean we were clones of one another. As time passed, differences in our styles and in how we approached problems did emerge. But we were all open to hearing the other side and then discussing it—sometimes with a bit too much emotion, but in the end, we complemented each other nicely and were able to come to a consensus despite some initial differences. I think we made a successful team because we implicitly trusted each other. Somehow, even though we hadn't known each other long at all, we knew in spite of our differences that we all wanted our company to be successful.

Jeff later admitted that the reason he hired me wasn't for my "obvious" design and management skills but more for the enthusiasm, energy, style, and confidence I had shown during the interview and walk-through tour of the facility. After the interview, Jeff said, he was convinced I had the right combination of talents to do the job. Apparently so were the others. Out of the four engineers they had interviewed, I was the only one they all agreed on. They might have overestimated me a bit, and certainly I have been thrust into situations since then that have more than tested whatever talents I have. One of the most important lessons I have learned thus far is that a willingness and openness to learning are the most important keys to being successful.

MedTech was capitalized to develop disposable surgical instruments that were recyclable (e.g., scalpels, scissors, various kinds of surgical knives, etc.), a market niche that hadn't been fully exploited. Initial research indicated that this new market had few entrants and would mature over the next few years. MedTech had a chance to make a significant impact in this market, so Jeff was eager to put the management team together as quickly as possible. The marketing manager was an old friend of one of the venture capitalists and seemed to be capable from all

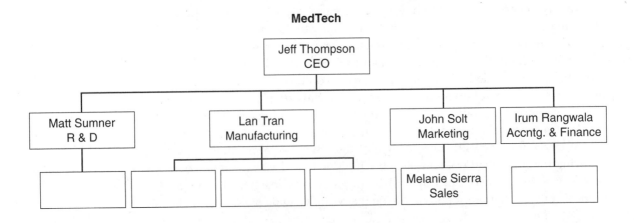

appearances, Jeff and I thought, but neither of us liked the idea that he was a friend of one of the venture capitalists. Hiring someone on that basis always leaves an uneasy feeling that it isn't your person. In this case, though, I wasn't sure if what I was feeling was a premonition or just a natural intolerance to feeling somewhat "imposed upon." It became clearer as time passed what that feeling meant.

With a new disposable surgical products concept, a potentially hot market, and a strong venture capital group behind the company, the future looked bright for everyone involved. Sometimes during lunch we would joke and talk about how we were going to spend our millions after the company went public and our shares were actually worth something. Our shares were in lieu of higher salaries, although we were getting paid typical start-up salaries—usually somewhat low and requiring you to demonstrate your willingness to sacrifice and work hard to make the venture succeed. Below Jeff, the management team was earning about $60,000 to $70,000 a year. That wasn't too bad at the time.

Our dream was to have a beautiful but rustic mountain cabin where Jan and I could spend the weekends and vacations, and maybe someday retire there. I envisioned a large rock fireplace built of local shale, a balcony overlooking a falling river, and taking long walks with Jan along its banks. I also dreamt of having a very successful career as a start-up champion, being full or part owner of several successful companies, and later doing something completely "off the wall."

Irum dreamt of finally being able to achieve harmony in balancing her career, family, and church responsibilities. Her best energies, she felt, were always spent at work, and although she was a driven person, she wanted to do more with her family and in her church. Her kids were 7 and 5 and she didn't want to be one of those moms who had abandoned her kids. Of course, she wanted her seaside house when she retired, somewhere along the Mendocino coast of California, perhaps close to Bodega Bay or farther north near Trinidad.

These kinds of lunchtime conversations—and daydreams—were mixed with new thoughts on the design process, ways of reducing costs, and strategies to improve product quality and marketing. It was therapeutic to talk this way because we were all putting in 12-hour (or more) days. Keeping the dreams alive sometimes kept the energy going just when we needed it.

We were all convinced MedTech had the potential to make those dreams come true. One of the distinct marketing advantages of the disposable surgical products was the price. Instead of paying a hefty sum for a good quality scalpel that had a fairly long shelf life, the price was a measly $1.50. For other surgical instruments (e.g., forceps, etc.), the price differences were even greater. Our disposable instruments could be made with a largely paper handle with an extremely thin covering of a recyclable plastic. The paper was processed so it took on hardened qualities much like a petrified wood but without the weight. Our pricing was a particular advantage to financially strapped hospitals or HMOs that were doing everything they could to cut costs. The dollar outlay would be considerably less—even as much as a quarter of a million dollars less depending on the necessary initial outlay. That, in a nutshell, was our products' primary advantage and determined how we were going to position it in the medical markets. "Our marketing strategy is fairly simple," Jeff would tell us: "Offer a high-quality, differentiated product at a much lower price than existing competitive products in a market where prices are escalating and hospitals' number one priority is to control costs. We can't lose."

I knew it was folly to be overly confident, but I also knew the power of positive thinking.

About two and a half years after the inception of MedTech, we were still in the process of bringing the product to market. We designed a new handle for MedTech's disposable instruments and made some other improvements. The doctors were ecstatic about the products—if they were willing to try. Although the doctors who had initially been consulted were totally sold on the new products, I also discovered that doctors can be quite conservative. Maybe it is an effect of suit-happy people or maybe it is just doctor mentality. Even though there was absolutely no indication that a doctor could not perform as well with recyclable instruments, some doctors expressed the fear their hospital could be held responsible if the instruments' quality was ever in question.

It was difficult to alter the perceptions of some doctors we talked to. And our new design, which was more ergonomic than the present surgical instruments, wasn't always seen as a plus. They were used to holding the instruments in a particular way that was comfortable to them. When you're performing delicate operations, it is difficult to have to adjust the way you have always held your instruments—even if the adjustment is very slight.

As I began to look into the marketing research that had been done before I had come on board, I realized it had been far from adequate. There had been no focus groups and no in-depth field or secondary research. The whole concept was based on the enthusiasm of several doctors who were convinced from the beginning this would be an advantageous design and product. I couldn't believe it as John Solt, our senior marketing person (and good friend of one of MedTech's initial investors), explained to me the research basis on which the whole company had been funded.

"I believe in following hunches," I told him, "but not when *other* people's careers depend on it!"

I was livid and left John's office before I said or did anything I would regret. I didn't want to have to call Jan from jail! It wasn't long after that, though, that I realized part of my anger was from my own naiveté about joining a company whose main product concept was based on a handful of doctors' opinions—and I didn't even know it or ask to find out. It wasn't as though I had done thorough research on MedTech before joining. I operated on a gut feeling and I guess that's what MedTech was doing. It bothered me a little that I didn't have a problem with my own so-called research methods, but I did with MedTech's.

The lack of sound research was only one of MedTech's problems, though. In addition, over the two-year period MedTech had been operating, the market had matured much more quickly than MedTech had expected. Other, larger firms with already existing distribution networks had gotten into the market. Even though I thought our instruments had a superior design, their distinction was less than before. Plus, we could not compete well with these large international and multinational firms that gave discounts for bundle purchases from hospitals and medical centers and spent lots of money wooing physicians by sending them to medical conventions, supporting research, giving donations to their universities, and so on. These discounts really dug away at what made our product especially distinctive from others—the price. With these bundle discounts, the lower price we could offer was now only a fraction of the original difference between the price of disposable and nondisposable surgical instruments.

I told Jeff that John was exploiting us as a result of his friendship with one of the investors. John couldn't care less if we sunk. Instead of being out of the office, talking with doctors, trying to locate distributors, researching other potential markets, John could usually be found out on the golf course or in his office reading the *Wall Street Journal.* John's typical line was "When you bring me a product, I'll sell it." In other words, he had no marketing strategy. He was a salesman, not a marketer and certainly not a strategist. It was frustrating to deal with such incompetence on the management team. That gut feeling Jeff and I had about this guy was right on. He never should have been hired for the job and we knew it. When Jeff and I found some time to think it through, our plan was to figure out some way to get John out.

Our needed market strategy was clear to me: the market had changed. The same opportunities that were there two plus years ago weren't there now—at least not accessible in the same way. We needed to align ourselves with a large well-known medical products firm that already had a well-established distribution system. We simply could not compete on our own. We were just too small. In addition, I began rethinking the completely disposable instrument concept and began snooping around a few hospitals, asking questions, doing my own marketing research—while John was reading the *Wall Street Journal* with his feet up on his desk.

After nosing around and talking to people for a few months, I was sure we needed to modify the completely disposable instrument concept to a semi-reusable concept. In fact, my calculations based on the actual costs of product development, manufacturing costs, and value added (yes, my finance classes at UCLA did actually come in handy) indicated that disposable surgical instruments would be nearly as expensive as reusable ones relative to a specified number of operations. Our products were increasingly becoming an advantage only in the initial investment. That was narrowing our market more than was necessarily healthy. It meant we were going to have to go outside the country increasingly to cash-poor hospitals if we didn't get the product to market soon.

Only some of the increased costs were production costs. The other part was costs to market the products in a now more complex, and therefore costly, environment. "Thank you, John!" The more I thought about it, the more I fumed, and between work and my drive home that evening, I had figured out at least seven different ways to get rid of the "Wall Street Man" (a name Jeff and I had given John of late). Usually, I am not indecisive, but I have to admit, in this case I wasn't sure whether bamboo up his finger- and toenails and a complete body "stretch" from his present 6′1″ to 8′6″ were in order, or if we should just hang him off the Golden Gate Bridge and drop him just before the Coast Guard arrived. It was food for thought.

I think Jeff and Lan had their own dreams of what to do with him, but we all tried to keep a lid on it so our objections to him didn't become too obvious. Because John was a good friend of one of the investors, it didn't pay to make waves unless they were really necessary.

But before the situation reached that point, a promising breakthrough occurred. A Japanese surgeon had attended one of our earlier product demonstrations and together with a veterinarian they had used the instruments in some animal surgeries in Japan. He was very enthusiastic and totally convinced these instruments would sell well in Japan and possibly other Asian markets. We were really excited. This time, though, we were going to do some decent market research I told the other engineers. "We're not going to make the same mistake in Japan that we did here," I said. Lan agreed. "One doctor does not necessarily speak for the whole group—even if they do wear basically the same color suits and have the same hair," I continued. That comment was made before I was sensitized to the insensitivities of stereotypes about the Japanese.

I had great admiration for the Japanese and what they had achieved, but my understanding of the Japanese and their markets didn't extend much beyond what exposure to the media had given me. What I did know was that their clear penchant for quality products and their reputation for closed markets would make Japan a tough nut to crack. I was looking forward to the challenge and figured if we could do it in Japan, we could do it anywhere. I did wonder whether we were getting in over our heads, though. Was Japan really the best place to start?

Lately, however, Jeff and I had been wondering if MedTech was going to be able to pursue its strategy at all. Through the grapevine, Jeff got word that the venture capitalists were getting impatient with the time it was taking to get the product to the market. With operating costs running at $400,000 a month for the last eight months, MedTech was burning up a lot of money just getting the last bugs out of the production process. We were worried we might not see the product through to market.

One day later, just after I arrived at the office, I got a call from Jeff. "A Japanese firm contacted me," he said. "They're interested in what we're doing. I gave them a rundown of our current product line, but they already seemed to know every-thing I told them. These guys seem serious and they're here in the States now," Jeff continued. "The 'Wall Street Man' is going to be out of town and won't be back for two weeks. We ought to set up a meeting anyway. What do you think?" Jeff asked me. I jumped at the chance—even more so because John was going to be out of town. Tom didn't think it would look good setting up the meeting without our marketing director. But he didn't really think John would add anything substan-tive to the meeting either.

"I suppose if we get Melanie to meet with us it wouldn't look too bad," Lan stated. "Maybe John wouldn't suspect too much," he added.

Melanie was John's underling. She had excellent qualifications—a degree in marketing from San Jose State University with seven years of solid sales and mar-keting experience in the biotech industry. She had three years of outside sales and had been the top salesperson in her company every year in a row. She had then moved into sales management for a year before she left to go to another firm in the biomedical engineering field. There she became involved in sales management and some lower level marketing strategy development also. Her employer rated her top-notch and had tried to entice her to stay with a 20 percent bonus. She elected to come to MedTech, however. I think she was a bit like the rest of us who signed on—an entrepreneur at heart and wanting to be a big fish in a little pond. I liked her. She was professional and personable. Jeff and I were both afraid we were going to lose her if John didn't let go and give her more responsibility. But John didn't want to let go and he didn't want to really do much, either, is how we saw it. Our best hope was that John would quit.

The following Tuesday, four middle-aged Japanese came to MedTech. On Friday I made a call to Karl Davidson, a professor and mentor of mine at UCLA, to get some tips on dealing with the Japanese. In the brief time we had, he told me the most important thing was to work toward building a long-term relationship, not to move too fast. He also mentioned that the exchange of business cards is an important ritual and it is customary to have a gift to present, such as some California wine, fine chocolates, or distinctive designer ties. He told me bowing wasn't necessary, that most experienced Japanese businessmen shook hands with no problem.

When the Japanese arrived, they were all dressed impeccably—dark gray business suits, well-groomed hair, polished black shoes. One, older looking than the rest, stood in front of the others. His name was Mr. Satoh, a slight gentleman about 5´6˝ with a broad, tanned-looking face. One of the others was quite stocky, but they were all under 5´8˝ or so. It was Mr. Satoh who presented Jeff with a superbly wrapped gift. It was a beautiful but simple crystal figurine that could decorate Jeff's office or the small foyer of MedTech. We then offered them our gift, some very fine Napa Valley wine, also beautifully wrapped. They seemed pleased and bowed gently to thank us.

In looking back, I was amused at some of their other behaviors. They seemed fairly well versed in American business practices, but maintained some Japanese customs too. They bowed slightly when they shook our hands, Mr. Satoh doing so first and the other three following in what appeared to be a particular order. I felt a little awkward but I leaned a little forward too as I shook hands. Immediately after, Mr. Satoh handed us his business card, holding each side of this tiny 2×3-inch card paper with two hands, bowing slightly once again. He gave a card to each of us, starting with Jeff, then Lan, me, and then Melanie. It was as if their cards were a gold platter that was to be handled with great care. I remembered what Professor Davidson had told me about it being an important ritual.

"It was just a piece of hard paper," I thought to myself. Professor Davidson had warned me about the importance of this ritual to the Japanese. Yet I hadn't anticipated the exchange of cards so early in our meeting. I fished mine out of my front coat pocket. I quickly counted five of them—what luck! One left over. Each Japanese bowed slightly and looked at my card for what seemed an eternity—as if there was something unusual about it. I thought maybe there was a misspelling. Karl Davidson had told me the Japanese expect everything to be perfect and that they can make judgments about a firm based on really unimportant things—to us—like a typo in a proposal.

I had once heard that a Japanese company canceled an order from an American company for electronics equipment just because the color was gray instead of black as they had requested—and it wasn't even a piece they would show to the end consumer. It worried me that they might decide not to do business with us just because there might be a misspelling on my business card. After we had all shared cards, the atmosphere seemed a little more relaxed. The whole ritual took what seemed like an eternity for eight people to exchange cards.

When I got a minute alone in the bathroom at the restaurant, I pulled out my last business card, just to double-check it for errors. I was relieved to see everything was in order. Worrying about such a seemingly small thing seemed to be overreacting, but Jeff and I both literally felt the investors breathing down our backs, watching every move we made—or didn't make that we should have. And with what Karl had told me about the appearance of perfection so important to the Japanese, I couldn't help myself. It was clear that the West and the East— at least Japan—didn't share the same value on appearance. We're definitely more oriented toward functionality—does the thing work? does it perform its duty?— than we are toward its looks. If it works right, it's beautiful. If it doesn't, it stinks, no matter what it looks like.

Of course, as I learned later on, the Japanese seem to value both aesthetics and functionality.

Speaking of aesthetics, we took the Japanese to the Trading Post, a very Western-looking building. Saddles hung on from the ceiling. Buffalo-style rifles hung on the walls along with cowboy hats and other Western paraphernalia. The choice of meals was also decidedly Western—different steaks, roast beef, and various forms of chicken plates. The Trading Post was a well-known restaurant in town where visiting dignitaries were often brought—despite its unsophisticated name and appearance. It was either the Trading Post or Chez Philippe, a well-known French restaurant downtown. We thought the Trading Post would be different for them and maybe impress them in some Western way! The food was well prepared and the decor interesting, especially the buffalo head attached to the massive rock fireplace—"No one quite knows where the buffalo head came from," Jeff told the Japanese. "Some of the environmental groups had on occasion even boycotted the restaurant," I mentioned. Relatively tame stuff compared to growing up in Berkeley.

The time at the restaurant passed rather enjoyably, trading stories and biographies about their companies and some of the personnel, interspersed with grunts the Japanese would sometimes make before speaking. I ordered my usual herbal tea and the others ordered coffee. The typical small talk ensued as we finished. We returned to the company in Jeff's 450 SEL and Lan's Honda.

"You probably should have borrowed a Lexus or Infiniti for the day," I joked with Jeff in privacy—"or borrowed a Harley hog from a friend. I hear the Japanese are really nuts for those things. Couldn't you picture Mr. Satoh hanging on to you, driving down El Camino Road?" (I was glad Jeff had a sense of humor, and I usually took advantage of it too.) Jeff gave me one of those looks to let me know I had gone far enough.

Besides the exchange of cards, the only other real awkward part related to Melanie. They almost never talked to her or made an effort to acknowledge her presence. If it weren't for her questions to them, I think they might have ignored her entirely. Between John's reluctance to delegate meaningful responsibilities to her and the Japanese tendency to ignore her, I could believe her self-esteem might be suffering a little.

Later, back at the office during some of the discussions in Jeff's office, two of the Japanese, the younger ones in their mid- to late 40s, kept punching away at their calculators when they talked about prices and product numbers. The Japanese would occasionally talk to each other in Japanese and make those same grunting kind of noises when we would ask them questions. I had expected some cultural differences because of my experience in France, but this behavior seemed kind of strange nonetheless. I had read some articles in *Fortune* about Japanese etiquette, but even then, you're never quite sure what to do—whether the others will try to change their behavior or they expect you to pretend you're one of them. I feel like I got caught somewhere in between.

Question 1:   *If you were Jeff or Matt, how would you gauge the level of interest by the Japanese? What would your next step be at this point in the relationship?*

Muhashi was just the kind of company we were looking for. It had a large distribution network, including hospitals and clinics, not just in Japan, for it even had clients and contacts in China, Thailand, and Vietnam. It was well experienced in the medical products manufacturing and distribution business. Muhashi was the pharmaceutical-medical products arm of a large Japanese conglomerate that had virtually every major industry represented in its portfolio—heavy industry, including steel and iron products; glassware, including everything from windshields for cars to windows for apartment buildings to glasses for the dinner table; rubber products, including tires and all kinds of rubber derivatives. It was a typical "family" firm in Japan. As one of the most profitable industries in the industry "family," Muhashi had a moderate to strong amount of influence on the parent firm.

After Mr. Satoh and his assistants returned to Japan, unbeknownst to us, their typical research began. Satoh told his assistants to look into MedTech. "Find out who MedTech's investors are and other ventures these investors have participated in. Find out the success rate of these investors and their motivation for investing. Learn where 'Mr. Jeff' and 'Mr. Matt' grew up, the universities they went to, who their previous employers were, the quality of work they are known for, and anything else we should know. Oh, yes, and don't forget to get information about the other company officers, especially the chief financial officer and the engineering department head," Satoh told his team.

Two months later, except for asking several of us for our résumés and acknowledging our "hospitality," as they put it in a courteous letter, we still hadn't heard from the Japanese about a possible business deal. I couldn't imagine what they wanted with our résumés unless it was to do a job background check.

"I feel as if I'm interviewing for a job," Jeff told me.

I had the same feeling.

"That's more positive than I felt," Melanie mentioned. "They didn't even consider me as a candidate! I can't believe how antiquated some cultures can be, especially considering how advanced they are in everything else."

Jeff became a little uneasy, figuring the Japanese weren't interested and just didn't want to say so. They hadn't really responded to our follow-up faxes or phone calls except to acknowledge their receipt and say, "We are still studying the possibilities." I had expected the long drawn-out process because Prof. Davidson had told me the Japanese take a long time before making decisions. "They like to know who they're dealing with, so expect a long courtship," he had told me in our last phone call.

Question 2: If you were Jeff, what would you do now if you were MedTech—put some pressure on Muhashi, turn your attention elsewhere, or ?

But I was eager to get things going because I knew Jeff was under some heat from the venture capitalists to see some visible progress with potential markets. Then early one evening about 6:30, Jeff burst into my office with that big grin of his: "They want us to come visit them," he said—I mean he *yelled*. We were ecstatic. Our whole management team celebrated that night with our spouses.

The next day Jeff, John Solt, Lan, and I met with several surgeons from Stanford Hospital for a prearranged meeting. The meeting was important because we were going to introduce our products to another group of doctors, some from Europe. This would be a helpful beta test for MedTech Products because these doctors were some of the leaders in their field in orthopedic, heart, and cancer surgery. The meeting was a long one—from 9 A.M. to about 3 P.M. I got out just in time to beat the traffic headed south on 280 to stop by Western Mountaineering off Winchester and pick up some ski brakes Jan had ordered.

A week after our meeting, informal feedback indicated that the doctors generally liked our products. They liked the design and they seemed to like the feel of the instruments. We had arranged for several cats that had been euthanized by a local animal shelter to be there for the doctors to try out various instruments.

The next morning, I got off the phone with Jeff. Everything was prepared for our visit to Muhashi. Originally, the same team that met them on their visit to MedTech was going to go. After some thought, though, between the expense of tickets and a few vendor problems that had risen unexpectedly, Lan stayed behind. There was no way John was going to stay in California and let Melanie go, so we were stuck with him for this trip.

It had taken numerous phone calls and faxes to specify all the details for the visit and figure out exactly what the Japanese wanted out of the visit. It seemed a little like a tug of war, and Jeff and I began to wonder whether there was anything substantively to be gained by going to Japan more than another getting-to-know-you "party." Even though intellectually we knew this meeting could still be important even if it turned out to be mostly social, emotionally we were ready for something much more concrete and promising.

We all went coach class in an attempt to save some money. The difference of more than $1,500 round trip per person could be better put to use than for better drinks, softer reclining seats, and more "bennie." We wanted to do what we could to show our investors that we were trying to make the buck stretch. Besides, we figured it wouldn't hurt to show the Japanese that we are cost conscious too.

Jeff took out his planner. "We also have that meeting with the board and the venture group in two weeks," he reminded us. "Something's got to break—something."

Excluding Satoh, the same Japanese were waiting at the airport when we arrived. Apparently they almost thought that we had missed the plane because we hadn't deboarded with the business class passengers. They acted glad to see us, shaking hands while bowing ever so slightly a couple of times. I told myself that one of these days I've got to ask someone how you know how many times to bow and how far to bow. It was kind of fun for a change, but I really didn't have a clue about the intricacies of bowing. Work had been so hectic the last several months that I hadn't really had any time—or taken time—to read up on Japanese customs. You get so busy in the day-to-day business that sometimes you lose sight of what should take priority. Because you never know exactly what's going to pan out, you put your energy into a lot of different directions. When something works out, you just hope you're ready.

In the airport I was also amused at the televisions set up in the area for those waiting to board their plane. The Japanese were intently listening to politicians speak before the upcoming election. I jokingly told Jeff I wanted to get a closer look at the TV manufacturer to see if any American company had any of the television airport market. Call it a gut feeling, but I don't think the Japanese would have appreciated my humor.

After the ritualistic hellos, bows, and handshakes, we followed the Japanese through the airport maze to the curbside parking. Two very impressive Mercedes-Benzes were waiting for all of us. When we asked about our bags, they told us, "All that has been taken care of. Your bags will be taken to the hotel."

I thought, "I could handle a few more trips like this to Japan!"

I asked what the young Buddhist dressed in a light orange robe, head shaved and bare feet was doing in the airport as we began driving away. I had seen Buddhist priests dressed like that on television programs but hadn't expected to see them in an airport. I could see John shaking his head out of the corner of my eye, evidently thinking, "What kind of a question is that!"

"It is a young Buddhist trainee who allows passersby to give him money," responded the senior Japanese. "Most priests do not have other means of living. Also, they need money for temple restoration and other projects. The government helps financially, but maybe not enough," he added.

"Besides," I thought—joking to myself—"what else would they do if they didn't have an 8 A.M. to 6 P.M. job?"

Once at the office, we were met by Mr. Satoh, who greeted us very warmly. Another exchange of cards ensued between John and those he hadn't met before. The original four Japanese were joined by an engineer and another marketing person for the discussions. The day was well spent, and we felt the Japanese must be sold on the products.

"Why else would they spend this much time with us?" John whispered to Jeff.

After leaving the firm that evening to go to our hotel, the Japanese picked us up a couple of hours later and took us to a great restaurant with entertainment. There were fewer people on the streets now than earlier in the day. I couldn't believe the number of people on the sidewalks. Streams of cars seemed more like a train—one hooked up to the other in a long line. Most of them were white—a favorite color I guess. I don't recall seeing anything outlandish, like a yellow, red, or green car. I'm sure they must have been there, but I didn't remember seeing any. Some Japanese were on bikes and others on small motorbikes. They say this is one of the most crowded cities in the world and I believe them.

At the restaurant, we ate and drank until nearly midnight. I kept to my non-alcoholic drinks, but that was no easy feat. In another conversation with Karl Davidson, he had warned me that the Japanese can drink most Westerners under the table and to be prepared. He told me the best thing to do if the Japanese insist is to tell them, "It would be very difficult for me to drink alcohol." That was supposed to tell them to "lay off" in polite terms.

We were all somewhat surprised by the more jovial mood of the Japanese compared to when they were at the Trading Post. I was doing my best to be accommodating while at the same time not fall asleep. The jet lag was starting to win the battle, and I kept wishing I could leave graciously and go back to my hotel room. We had meetings the next morning about 10 o'clock and I wanted to make sure I was at least half awake. If the Japanese spent this much time and drank this much with all their potential business partners, I figured either they had stainless steel livers or they were on the road to national alcoholism, at least among the men. This kind of entertainment went on for the next two evenings. Each successive morning it became more difficult for us to get up on time for the meetings.

That Thursday, close to midnight, I called home to check in with Jan and make sure everything was all right on her side of the Pacific. With 17 hours' difference between Japan and California, partly because of crossing the international date line, it was Wednesday, about 7 o'clock in the evening. We didn't talk long, but it made me realize how much I missed her even though I had only been gone for a few days. I think subconsciously it brought back memories of our brutal separation while I was at UCLA. I longed to get home and get back into a normal routine of going to bed by eleven and getting up around six, refreshed and more or less ready to go. Although I enjoyed the experience in Japan, all-day meetings, extended luncheons, and all-evening meals with late-night entertainment were not my idea of the good life.

Our conclusion at the end of the entire visit was that the Japanese seemed impressed with the products and that they felt MedTech was a serious firm, albeit tiny—no, minuscule—compared to the Japanese giant. The conversation had ranged from product characteristics and quality, to manufacturing processes, to distribution, to personnel within MedTech. The Japanese team seemed satisfied on all accounts and genuinely appeared to agree with us on many of our ideas. But then at this point, there was no real negotiation of points going on, just trading of information, I thought. The next day, we met for a few hours. To my surprise, Jeff decided before we left he was going to ask them if they had made a decision and, assuming it was positive, if they would be ready to sign a contract.

Jeff, John, and I met at breakfast early to decide on a plan of attack before meeting with the Japanese.

Question 3:   *If you were MedTech management, what would your next move be?*

Friday morning, Jeff was eager to pop the big question and ask what kind of deal Muhashi might want to cut. We were going to be leaving early the next day, and Jeff really wanted to bring some closure to our mission. I felt like a diplomat sent on a strategic mission to bring peace to two different nations. That's just a euphemistic way of saying I had all the rice, fish, Japanese veggies, and tea I could handle—at least with a smile. My stomach just wasn't used to that kind of diet. By the third evening my stomach felt and sounded like bulldozers in a demolition derby. I had been told by my UCLA buddies that international business was going to be really exotic! It was, but not in the way I had expected.

After a brief discussion, they picked us up as usual and thirty minutes later we were at Muhashi headquarters. When Jeff asked the Japanese if they were ready to talk numbers, the Japanese seemed uneasy and even a little surprised at our question. After what seemed a century-long moment of silence, Mr. Satoh finally said something characteristically evasive: "We think things will work out for both companies and we want to continue our discussions."

They didn't say "No" and they didn't say "Yes." In fact, it was difficult for us to interpret what their response meant. Had we just spent several thousand dollars on a trip that had permanently rearranged my stomach? Why would they have wined us and dined us if they didn't want to make a deal?

Jeff was really annoyed at the lack of closure on the whole thing. So much depended on our finding a partner and having a large contract to get the support of the venture capitalists.

"What was the problem?" Jeff asked us, not really expecting an answer. "Muhashi had had all of the projections and figures more than two months ago. They've seen our product and the manufacturing process, and they spent a day and a half with us at MedTech."

"What more could they need to make a decision?" I blurted out. We had assumed the visit to Japan was probably to close the deal and, if not sign a contract, at least agree in principle that they would propose something to us to consider. Sure, we had anticipated more talks in the near future as we hammered out details toward a marketing strategy and possible product modifications necessary for the Japanese market, but this was really a surprise—and even more so a disappointment—to us despite Professor Davidson's warning to expect a prolonged "engagement," as he had put it.

John reminded us that from the start he thought the whole trip would be a waste of time.

"If the Japanese haven't moved any faster than this so far, they aren't really serious," he said.

"Besides, if they are and this [pace] is any indication of how quickly they move, none of us will see it in our lifetime," he added.

Jeff told me an interim meeting with the board was upcoming and he had to begin scrambling to get things ready to present. "The trip to Japan was both a blessing and a curse," he told me personally. "It is something that we can present to the investors as a solid potential outlet for their surgical products, but it has also taken time away from getting everything in order for the meeting. Plus, we can't present anything concrete on the Japanese trip. On top of it, I've got a significant personnel problem to deal with. John Solt, 'Wall Street Man' and head of marketing, is totally worthless as far as I'm concerned. He doesn't do anything constructive; he's a 'downer.' The more I've thought about it, the more I've decided I'll have to push for John's resignation—that or fire him."

I knew Jeff didn't like to talk about the situation. He had always felt there wasn't much he could do, given that John was a good friend of one of the major investors in MedTech.

I never thought the next morning would come, but it did. After the long trip I was looking forward to seeing Jan. Although we hadn't closed a deal, the trip to Japan was a great experience in many ways, but I was exhausted and glad to be going home. Fortunately, I had a weekend ahead of me to recuperate physically before going back to work.

When I finally arrived home, I hugged Jan, gave her the short version of the trip, and rolled—rather fell—into bed. The next morning came too early, but I had to get up sometime. Eventually, I struggled out of the grasp of my covers, put away my clothes from the trip, and got rid of my boarding pass to San Francisco with my usual 10-foot jumper to the wastebasket in the corner of our bedroom. I rarely missed, which gave me a kind of dumb sense of pride—at least for a minute or two. I had always figured with another 8 inches and an additional 40 pounds of muscle, I could have competed one on one with people like Michael Jordan or Shaque.

I think I was beginning to feel better already.

QUESTIONS FOR DISCUSSION

1. Should MedTech enter the international marketplace before having developed its reputation and product expertise in the domestic market? Does the traditional organizational life cycle model fit today?
2. From how Jeff and Matt have handled things so far, do you think MedTech has the business and cultural savvy to develop a relationship with a major Japanese firm? Why or why not?
3. What are some of the differences in Japanese *expectations* in terms of a business relationship as directly or indirectly portrayed in this chapter?

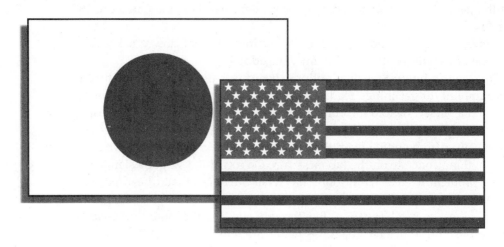

CHAPTER 3

Negotiating a Partnership: An International Perspective

MATT

Jeff handed me the memo, making it all official:

Memo

To: Jeff Thompson, CEO
From: John Houston [principal investor]
Re: Continued funding of MedTech

Congratulations! As you know from our telephone conversation, the investors have approved MedTech for a third round of funding. The amount we have approved is $2 million for this next cycle.

We are pleased with the progress you have made in pursuing a partnership with Muhashi and expect this to bear good fruit. We expect you to continue to pursue other markets as well, of course, as discussed in our meeting with you on February 7.

The details of the disbursement of the $2 million will be forthcoming.

Keep up the good work. The investors are eager to see some return on their investment.

As Houston mentioned, we had already learned by telephone of the decision to reinvest. The good news arrived two weeks after we got back from our trip to Japan. The investors were pleased with the interest from the Japanese firm and were persuaded it would be the boost MedTech needed to bring things to fruition. Although the meeting with the investors was only an interim report, the results were more than expected. Jeff had done a good job of presenting our case with supporting presentations from John and me. I was thrilled and happy for Jeff—for all of us. I knew Jeff had been really sweating it. The official word of the funding spread fast among the 26 employees, and that afternoon we all celebrated. I had reason to celebrate even more. Jeff had talked to two of the three major investors and convinced them that the "Wall Street Man" was not their boy for the marketing position.

"I told them you and Melanie would get more done than John ever thought of doing," Jeff said with a smile.

"What do you mean 'me' and Melanie?" I asked with a great deal of interest. "Melanie's the one in marketing," I added, searching for some clarification.

"I know," Jeff said, "but I also know the design process for the instruments is nearly finished. I also know that the reason you got your MBA is because you eventually want to get out of the technical area and into marketing."

"Yeah, that's true," I said, "but . . ."

"I know," Jeff said. "You're worried about how Melanie's going to take this and how I'd position you two. I'd like to talk to you both about that because I think it's critical you both agree and that you both see the logic to the repositioning.

"Besides, for the moment, I need you to continue with the design process until it's pretty much perfected. We'll be hiring another engineer or maybe promoting Jack [a junior engineer] to take over some of Lan's current responsibilities that are really beneath Lan's level of experience and expertise, anyway. Lan can take over the design elements with no problems. Fortunately, he has enough experience to make him extremely versatile. That's his unique value to us as a start-up. You're part of the key to the partnership with the Japanese firm, and right now that's the most promising future MedTech has. Plus, you have something Lan will probably never have to the same degree—your energy and ambition. Lan's gotten to where he is comfortable with his expertise based on his incredible natural talent. I think he lacks the drive, though, that would really make him a superstar.

"Melanie is top-notch but doesn't have the strong technical skills you do. You know the products and their design backward and forward. You would serve as our boundary spanner from the engineering side to the marketing. Melanie would serve in a pure marketing function, getting involved in some strategy but also working with the salespeople to generate some more leads. If this Japan venture takes off, we'll also need to—or maybe I should say be able to—hire a few more salespeople to try and aggressively market some of our products stateside. That will all keep Melanie busy and involved," Jeff commented.

"Well, if none of this poses a problem for Melanie, I'd be ecstatic," I told Jeff. "But I really don't want her to think with John gone that I'm stepping in and filling his void without any consideration for her," I added.

"No problem," Jeff stated confidently.

I wasn't so sure, though, but I guess my anxiety was unfounded. Jeff talked to Melanie about his ideas and she was excited about it all. I think she was most relieved to get rid of John, so any alternatives must have seemed better than that. She and I always worked well together and shared a similar outlook, so I imagine that was a plus. Melanie would get a promotion, too, taking over some of John's responsibilities. My move would be a strange one. For the moment, I would work directly under Jeff, with kind of a dotted-line responsibility over Melanie. My primary role would be to interface closely with marketing and engineering.

A week later MedTech finally let John Solt go with a respectable severance package—six months of his salary while he looked around for another job (about seven months more than he was worth in my humble opinion!).

On the promise of a healthy salary increase, Jan and I celebrated by going out to our favorite restaurant—Le Jardin, a small family-owned French restaurant in the City. *Les cuisses de grenouilles* (frog legs) were my favorite, but certainly they weren't enough for anyone with much of an appetite. Quality was one thing, but there had to be a certain amount of quantity also or "a guy could starve to death eating at French restaurants," I would sometimes say. Jan preferred *lapin* (rabbit) with a very rich cream sauce with sautéed mushrooms. "Not exactly a health food kind of meal," I kidded Jan. She was normally one of those Brussels sprouts and salad types—you know, the kind that make you feel like saying, "Eat some real food!" Soups and salads are great during the summer, though. Well, after le meal, le vin, le dessert, et le tip, we left the restaurant approximately $178.15 lighter.

The weekend went fast. Worked around the house, replaced a broken sprinkler, changed the oil on the two cars, stopped by Lucky's to get some yogurt, and so on—the usual mundane weekend activities that make you wonder why you worked so hard during the week.

Come Monday, though, you could tell there was more energy at work than usual, a little more excitement in people's voices. It was great. We needed the lift.

Three weeks later, Jeff burst into my office waving a fax: "The Japanese are coming back. And this time, they're bringing the senior engineer we met in Japan," Jeff continued. "I think they're getting serious now."

Several faxes later, a date was set for their arrival. The only problem was we weren't sure what the visit was for. Melanie, Jeff, Lan, and I met together to discuss what we might do to get ready for the visit. It was tough to think of anything out of the ordinary, though, because we didn't really know what they hoped to accomplish that they hadn't already in our previous visits together.

Question 1: *If you were Jeff, what would your primary objectives be for this visit? What do you believe the Japanese are coming to do?*

Muhashi seemed only to say that they wanted to come and they would be bringing one of their engineers who had experience with designing surgical products. That gave the only clue. They were probably going to scrutinize our production process and quality control. Either that or they were going to suggest an alteration to our design. I wasn't ready for that, but Melanie's position was the typical marketing perspective: "If that's what they want, that's what we'll have to give 'em. We don't really have a choice."

Of course, she was right.

Question 2: *If you were Melanie, what do you think your primary role should be in this meeting?*

The Japanese arrived on time and we spent the next four days in various meetings with them. There was Mr. Satoh, Mr. Aihara, the design engineer, and Mr. Takasawa, a marketing-product development guy. Mr. Aihara had been with one of Muhashi's suppliers—part of the Muhashi family—since his graduation from Kyoto University, twenty years ago. He had moved up the ranks slowly, as most Japanese do, to his present position managing a design team for some biomedical products.

Mr. Takasawa had graduated from Satoh's alma mater, Tokyo University's medical school. He had never practiced medicine but hired on with Muhashi as a medical adviser for the products they distributed. He was one of their sets of eyes and ears to help understand the medical field's needs. He was a slim fellow who spoke very good English and was probably in his late 30s or early 40s.

I think we could have sped things up had we got right down to business and been more efficient. They spent a lot of time asking about our backgrounds, our interests, our experience, and so on. Somehow, though, I had the gut feeling that they already knew a lot of the answers before we gave them. This time they seemed more interested in Melanie and her role in the company. It was as if they hadn't wanted to believe they were going to have to deal with her. Lan seemed to get along very well with them. This was his first in-depth meeting with them. They seemed to have a great deal of respect for Lan. Maybe it was his age or something; otherwise, I don't know how they would have known enough about him to give that respect—which he deserved. Then again, maybe I was just imagining things. It was tough to know what they were thinking.

Finally, when we did begin talking about the real issue of our product, they seemed to focus on the manufacturing process as it related to the quality of the instruments. They had been satisfied with the quality of the ones we had shown them in Japan, but apparently they wanted to make sure those weren't going to be flukes. Basically, all my time and a lot of Lan's was taken up by their visit. I had phone messages that didn't quit, an in-basket of work that rivaled the Sears Tower, and general exhaustion had set in. By the time Friday had come, about all I had energy to do was sit in my chair and stare at the work to do.

Melanie remained involved, often accompanying us as we visited the production part of MedTech, trying to ascertain what their interests and concerns were. She also made some excellent suggestions and asked some pointed questions as different issues arose around the product design and potential markets in the United States. The Japanese seemed more responsive to her by the end of the visit.

Unfortunately, after such a time- and energy-consuming visit, I couldn't look forward to a quiet weekend. Jan was going to be gone to meet with government officials in Washington about a case her firm was working on. I always missed her and her absence meant I had to set my schedule around the baby. Usually I looked forward to Saturday morning, waking up around 10 or 11 in the morning, getting a leisurely breakfast, catching the UCLA-USC game on TV, maybe taking an afternoon nap . . . that's the life.

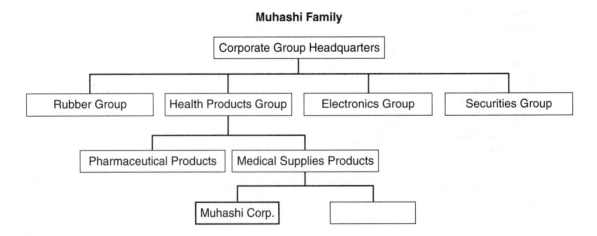

Muhashi Family

Monday arrived too soon. The four of us—Jeff, Lan, Melanie, and I—had a long talk about how the meetings went. It was the first time we had had a chance to sit down together since they left. Lan got a call and had to leave early—some problem on the production floor related to a new plastic supplier we had just signed on. Anyway, from our own sense of the meetings, the Japanese had again seemed pleased with their visit—but that wasn't anything unusual. They were by nature polite and seemed to smile often. And, also as usual, there still was no promise of anything more by the end of the meeting. "We will contact you. We must talk further," they would say. I wondered what Muhashi's travel budget was like. I couldn't imagine an American firm spending so much money on travel. Everything we've done in three meetings and more would normally be done in one in the United States. It was as if this was the most important decision they had to make and as though they had all the time in the world.

We didn't, frankly.

JAPANESE BUSINESSMEN

On the plane back to Japan, the Muhashi officials discussed their impressions. "What concerns me the most," said Satoh, the head of the group, "is that they are like the other American firms our parent company has dealt with. They want to sign an agreement right now. They want to specify everything in writing right away. They want to discuss products, pricing, and contracts before we can agree on some fundamental points. They have never even asked us one question about how long we have been in business."

"The Americans seemed complacent maybe," said Aihara. "The hotel was nice and they met us at the airport, but only once during the several-day visit did they arrange to get together after business hours," he added. "I'm not convinced they are that ready to do business with us. They say they're serious but they act another way."

The younger Takasawa thought to himself, "This is the old way of thinking. This is why Japanese are slow to change. Sometimes if the price is right and the product is good, we maybe don't need a relationship. I had hoped the Americans would show us around San Francisco and maybe go to a ballet or opera, but not because we need to develop a relationship. San Francisco is a very interesting place. I have never been there. Everyone in Japan wants to come and visit San Francisco. But maybe we shouldn't be that concerned about their hospitality. They behave fairly typically. It would be different if one of our customers visited. I might be embarrassed. I think we need to change."

Question 3: **What are the Americans focused on and what have the Japanese been focused on? What do you think is the basis for the Japanese concern? Why the difference in the older and younger Japanese perspective?**

Mr. Aihara added, "I remember my father explaining to me that a business relationship is like an arranged marriage. The two families have known each other for many years. They can trust each other. They are confident that both families will work hard to make a success. It has been slowly changing in Japan—even among the big companies. I'm not sure how much we should expect now. American firms are different. There are few rules. There is little respect for seniority by itself. Look at the Americans who lead MedTech. They are very young—including the CEO. But I suppose we should not be bothered by this. Even in Japan seniority has become less important. Some family businesses are beginning to be run by younger members of the family. New Japanese firms are sometimes led by men in their 20s and 30s."

The other Japanese nodded in agreement.

"We must anticipate questions about MedTech, their personnel, and their products when making our presentation to our parent company," Satoh added.

MATT

As far as how we saw the meeting, Jeff and I were both puzzled about the drawn-out, expensive, time-consuming talks over the past eight to nine months. We both felt the Japanese must be interested or they would not continue the contact—unless they were trying to steal our technology under the guise of a potential partnership. That was something we hadn't really considered. We had a patent pending, but even I knew that in international business, one country's patents aren't necessarily honored by another's legal system. And sometimes it isn't really a legal issue in the foreign firm's eyes; it's a cultural issue. I had heard that some cultures don't perceive property as something for which one can claim sole proprietorship. Whatever the situation was with the Japanese, I thought what we were doing with Muhashi was just a risk we were going to have to take.

In fact, as Jeff and I continued to talk about this over lunch, I recalled that one of the Muhashi managers had made the statement that such a partnership would suggest a future exchange of technology of other products that MedTech developed. Were the Japanese going to exploit us? And what would happen if the Japanese had the technology and then severed the relationship? Who had more to lose? The more we thought about it, the more it concerned us. But really, we didn't know what to do except check around with other companies that had partnerships with Japanese firms to see if Muhashi's long courtship was typical.

If we didn't continue pursuing the relationship, we would never survive another request for funding. On top of that, nearly nine months had passed since we started negotiations with the Japanese. If after a year we had to start all over again . . . neither of us wanted to even think about that.

Melanie wasn't as pessimistic as we were. She knew the Japanese are very slow compared to Americans in making decisions. She understood from talking to other marketers who deal with the Japanese that silence is not a bad sign. Karl Davidson had told me the same thing, but realizing it intellectually and accepting it fully psychologically or emotionally isn't as simple. When you've been socialized into thinking a certain way for your whole life, it's not easy to change.

"The fact that they have continued to show interest is a very good sign," Melanie stated. "I think it's just a matter of time," she said matter-of-factly. My mind told me what she was saying is true. In a recent conversation with Davidson, he had told me there's a network of individuals involved in making important decisions in Japanese companies. "It's not the straightforward process it is in most Western firms," he said. "So don't expect quick decisions!" he added, understanding my frustration.

In the meantime, over the next couple of months Melanie and I worked together to pick up where we had left off before our Muhashi visitors came— energetically pursuing other possible distributors—giant American and European hospital companies like Becton-Dickinson, Johnson & Johnson, American Hospital Supply, and Manheim-Bollinger. We needed to get all the exposure we could, but so far we hadn't gotten any solid bites from any American equivalent like Johnson & Johnson. At the same time, Melanie was busy setting up product demonstrations in Finland, England, Germany, France, and Italy to introduce our products to doctors in Europe.

Unbeknownst to us, Muhashi management had been making the necessary presentations to parent management and conferring with all those to be affected by the possible acquisition of a partner in this new venture. Satoh and the rest of the marketing group had to come to an agreement on whether they could market the disposable surgical instruments.

"We need to make sure our Japanese customers will not perceive these disposable instruments as inferior to the traditional fine steel ones used in hospitals. We can never underestimate their perception of quality," Satoh told his staff. "I don't think there will be the same problem in other Asian countries," he stated. "They have already seen Muhashi's products and think they are quite good and will work there."

The engineers at Muhashi needed to confer with one another to decide whether MedTech's manufacturing process seemed adequate to produce consistent quality. Mr. Aihara, the senior engineer that visited MedTech, had taken careful notes and had personally inspected the process to be able to give detailed information to the rest of the engineering staff.

Satoh's boss, Mr. Takasaki, represented the possible venture with MedTech to Muhashi's parent firm. Resource allocation was always an issue that had to be carefully studied. Within the parent firm, the information had to be distributed to several key people who oversaw general operations and whose responsibility it was also to ensure "safe" business practices to ensure the company's stability and good reputation. Each of these individuals, in turn, had to talk to their workers to try to anticipate any unforeseen implications.

The process was definitely complicated. Engineering had to be consulted. Marketing and sales became heavily involved. And, of course, Muhashi's financial personnel had to be informed and their opinion solicited about the financial advisability.

In turn, each of the heads of these departments discussed the idea with their subordinates and any other employees who might be affected by the decision to join forces with MedTech. The process was obviously long and drawn out by the time all the connections had been made—typically Japanese we learned later. In our case, Muhashi management received approval from parent management and consensus within its own ranks in well under one year, apparently a fairly quick turnaround for a Japanese firm!

The long awaited news came on a Wednesday afternoon. Muhashi wanted to meet "to discuss the kind of business partnership that would be most mutually beneficial," Satoh said in his fax. It seemed incredible after all these months of visits, faxes, and telephone calls. The bottom line, though, was we were over the hump. Now we knew they meant business. They weren't just after our technology. They wanted to be partners. This certainly called for a celebration. "I know where there's some discretionary money to pay for catering service," Jeff said with a big grin. We all celebrated that Thursday at—you probably guessed it—the Trading Post.

Muhashi invited the MedTech management team to come to Japan to talk about the particulars of the business arrangement we each had in mind. Of course, the Japanese knew exactly what we wanted. Between what we had told them during their first meeting and the extensive questioning and research we later learned that Muhashi had done, no stone had been left unturned. We had assumed Muhashi was in basic agreement with us on the arrangements—and "basically" they were. The particulars of who would run the operation in Japan, what authority MedTech would have in terms of decision-making power, the pricing and distribution of the products, and so on, were still to be negotiated.

None of us was looking forward to late nights and long meetings again in Japan. I knew it would be particularly awkward for Melanie. I mean, if I were the only male in the whole place and was not recognized as much as my female counterparts, I think I'd feel resentful and out of place. Even as a male, having nonstop meetings until late and then going out to a bar wasn't my idea of an enjoyable time—different, yes, but not particularly enjoyable.

In preparation for the trip, all of us were extremely busy and would be for the next three weeks. We were going to be out of the office a lot still trying to make other contacts, and Melanie was still heavily involved in the process of setting up demonstrations in Europe. In a small start-up, assistants are lacking and everyone has to do a lot of the so-called grunt work that in a larger organization would be done by assistants and secretaries. "I'm already exhausted just thinking about it," Jeff sighed.

"Me too," Melanie added.

Of course, we did what we had to do to maintain the deal with Muhashi. We were not about to lose the deal after all our investment. It was another expensive trip, though. Airfare alone for the four of us was almost $5,000; the hotel, another thousand plus a night for the four of us—ridiculously expensive, but that's the way it was for a decent hotel in Tokyo.

We left San Francisco one of those afternoons when the fog was just starting to roll into the Bay and swallow up the lower half of the Golden Gate Bridge. I already missed Jan and Jeffrey. Jeffrey had turned 2 and had been walking for some time. We were so glad to have him. I had really gotten into the child-raising stuff—warming the bottle, spooning the carrot puree, and—yes—even changing the diapers. But that was a while ago. It seemed like in the last six months I hadn't been spending much time around the house or helping out as much with Jeffrey.

I knew Jan would be very busy while I was gone, so we asked whether Jan's mother could come and stay with her to help with Jeffrey. Jan's parents had recently moved to the Bay Area from Maine because the doctor told her dad he needed a warmer climate. Personally, I think most of all they wanted to be near us and our growing family.

Jan had been working on a case between a well-known local developer and a community of citizens opposing the construction of 600 homes in a rural part of El Dorado County near Sacramento. The 200 acres had been home to coyotes, raccoons, squirrels, an occasionally sighted wild boar, and various other birds and animals. Sacramento had been growing, however, and developers were hungry for relatively inexpensive land for bedroom communities. Jan was in charge of the case, her first important case that would determine her real potential in the eyes of the firm's partners. Of course, Jan was more interested in "doing what was right" (i.e., stopping the developers) than she was in impressing the partners, but I think she wasn't naive about what the project could mean for her career at the firm. She had been absorbed in the project now for a month, often not getting home until 9 o'clock at night. I had to try to get home by 6 to pick up Jeffrey from day care, but that didn't always work out. So it seemed as though we hadn't been together much lately, and certainly hadn't been a family.

I reclined in my seat and listened as the words to the Beatles song sung at our marriage came to my mind:

Who knows how long I've loved you?
You know I love you still.
Will I wait a lonely lifetime?
If you want me to, I will.

Love you forever and forever
Love you with all my heart
Love you whenever we're together
Love you when we're apart.

And when at last I find you
Your song will fill the air.
Sing it loud so I can hear you
Make it easy to be near you
For the things you do endear you to me
. . . you know I will.

"Yep, can't beat the Beatles," I said to myself as I tried to clear my mind of everything to get some rest.

Upon arrival in Japan late in the evening, Mr. Satoh and the others were there to greet us. I had an additional greeting—from Jan. She had faxed a note to me at Muhashi. She was pregnant. I was so excited. Without thinking, I let out one of those yells I used to make at the UCLA basketball games when we went up by two points with about ten seconds left on the clock (but I probably shouldn't compare babies to basketball games). It took the translator some time to convey the meaning of my emotional outburst to the Japanese. I'm sure the Japanese were surprised—and embarrassed. At the time, I didn't notice and probably wouldn't have cared, though. I asked where the nearest phone was to call Jan until I realized it would be about three in the morning. I was really disappointed I had to wait.

The meetings the next day went well, although I was so full of tea I had to discipline myself to concentrate solely on the meeting agenda. Also, my mind was really on Jan and the baby. This was going to be a hard few days. The Japanese talked about the importance of product distribution, the effective use of suppliers and low inventory, and knowing your customer. Usually, they said, to develop this kind of relationship takes many years of working together. We asked about the promotion and pricing of the product in Japan. They simply responded that pricing was different from that of the United States. Instead of adding up the costs and tacking on a profit margin, the Japanese typically based the price on the market share desired; costs were then assigned to the suppliers and manufacturers, costs that usually were largely nonnegotiable.

Promotion, for these kinds of products, was closely tied with the distribution, the Japanese felt. It all tied back to knowing your customer, they said. Muhashi had a distribution network that was very efficient and had worked for over 75 years. They knew their customers, how they operated, and they knew the competition, they told us in their usual indirect, humble manner. Basically, we got the message that Muhashi knew what it was doing and probably didn't need a lot of help from MedTech. That might have been a wrong conclusion; we weren't really certain.

That night, Jeff and I talked about our reactions to the discussions so far. I think we both had similar gut feelings about the negotiations. For sure, we wanted—and desperately needed—a partner to help distribute our products. Still, we didn't want to give up all control to a partner we didn't know that well. We felt it would benefit MedTech to be an active partner in the whole process rather than leave everything to Muhashi.

"No one is going to have MedTech's best interest at heart except MedTech," Jeff reminded us.

At the same time, the potential advantages of a joint venture were clear.

"We'll gain international market experience that we can take to other foreign markets. In the short term, though, Japan is a very promising market and could bring us the success that we promised our investors," Jeff added.

We were all eager to see some tangible progress for all of our efforts. At the same time, we wanted some control over the sale of the surgical instruments.

"It's not that I don't trust the Japanese," Jeff told me. "I would just feel more comfortable if we had a clear role in distributing, promoting, and pricing our products."

I agreed with Jeff. It was important to make that clear to our future Japanese partners.

Question 4: What do you think of MedTech's concern? If you were the CEO, how would you ensure some control over the issues of promotion, pricing, and distribution?

The next morning we met with the same Muhashi officials. We presented our situation as directly but diplomatically as possible. The Japanese did not disagree; Satoh acknowledged, "MedTech might want to post someone in Japan to be a liaison between the two companies. And we could possibly send one of our engineers to MedTech to better understand your products technology for better distribution," Satoh added. This proposal left some ambiguity in what role the MedTech employee would play and whether MedTech would really have much control over the promotion and pricing of our products. Plus, he knew we couldn't afford an extra person's salary. Jeff asked Satoh if Muhashi would be willing to pay the engineer's salary and asked some clarification on what specific role Satoh saw this person playing at MedTech. In typical fashion, Satoh replied, "Of course, these are things that can be worked out in the future."

Under some pressure, though, and without too many alternatives (we certainly were not in a power position), Jeff felt it would be an act of good faith to agree to this plan. So he did. Further, he hoped the Japanese company was acting in good faith and would pursue a plan that would accommodate MedTech's interest. We all agreed, at least in principle, on the general terms of the agreement, including forecasted shipments and ballpark numbers and prices. As we understood our role beyond providing the products, we would be in the discussions concerning the promotion and the pricing of the products. Muhashi would be solely in charge of any legalities, the importation and distribution of the products, and would have first rights over any other products developed by MedTech to be sold in Japan. In the future, Muhashi could also suggest engineering and manufacturing improvements.

Although the proposed pricing seemed quite high—in the Japanese market 50 percent over what they would be sold for in the United States, the Japanese reassured us that this was in line with Japanese distribution costs, cost of competitive products, and buying potential of hospitals and clinics in Japan. Plus, they were quick to add, "Although it may be 50 years, probably one of your largest markets in Asia will be China. We have distributors who can sell your products there. The pricing will be much different, of course. The main obstacle for this kind of business is still Beijing. The Ministry of Health must give their approval," Satoh mentioned, "but we have connections there," he added.

Thus far, negotiations seemed to go quite well despite a few vagaries in the "agreement." We just hoped we had the same understanding of our discussion and its unstated implications. There wasn't much we could do to push them to be more specific. Every time we tried to push a little, the discussion basically turned back to rehashing points already covered earlier. Either we just weren't communicating or they didn't want to communicate more specifics at this point. In any case, we were all leaving the next morning and had to bring some closure to the talks rather than leaving them open. We needed to make progress, and this was the only way it was going to happen it seemed.

QUESTIONS FOR DISCUSSION

1. What appear to be the different approaches MedTech and Muhashi are taking in entering into a partner relationship? In their negotiation style?
2. What appears to be the basis of trust between the two firms from Muhashi's and MedTech's perspectives? Are they the same?
3. How should MedTech ensure its interests are being taken care of? Is posting a MedTech employee in Japan the best way for MedTech to oversee its interests?

CHAPTER 4

The International Assignment:
Selecting the "Right" Candidate

MATT

Once home, Lan and I began working more closely with the junior production and design engineers to ensure the quality of the product for the numbers that had been proposed in Japan. Although the manufacturing process was already quite good, we worked for 12 weeks straight to hone the process in order to avoid production errors. Lan solidified our supplier relationships to ensure the best supplies possible. In the several years MedTech had now been operating, we had changed resin suppliers for our plastic three times because of inconsistent quality.

With a firm from North Carolina, we finally got some resin that seemed to give us a consistent and homogeneous reaction to the heating and forging process. There were also a number of visits to Seattle, where we bought our paper, to iron out a few problems in the paper quality. We were fortunately able to work with them to get us the quality and exact materials we needed. But for a while we kept having a slight variation in blade resistance. It was caused by a heating fluctuation from a bad fuse in a switch that had partially corroded because of too much humidity in the air. We had a dehumidifying system installed, which seemed to take care of that problem.

During this time the nagging question of who might be the "overseer" of operations in Japan kept haunting Jeff. He never really brought it up directly to me, but I could tell it was preoccupying him some. I guess it would have me too. First of all, it wasn't even clear what role this person would be playing. And the Japanese didn't seem to be able to or want to clarify the role. And on top of that, it wasn't clear how important this person or role was to the Japanese.

Just about then, I showed up in Jeff's office. I could see the frustration written all over his face. "What's up, Jeff?" I asked.

"Oh, just thinking about something," Jeff said in a low tone. I learned later that Jeff didn't want to involve me in the decision in any way. It was his way of being objective.

That same day Jeff drove out to Santa Cruz to have lunch with some old school buddies. On the way over, his mind naturally came back to the most pressing problem on his mind.

JEFF

"I guess another possibility would be one of the junior design engineers," Jeff thought to himself. "If I just knew how important this position in Japan is and what the person would be doing—if it's operational and our guy would really be able to have an impact, I might be more inclined to send Lan or maybe Matt or . . . , and if it ends up being a symbolic gesture on our part, then I'd send someone totally different—one of our junior engineers probably. I really question whether it merits tying up one of our best people. I can't see Muhashi sending us one of its most valuable employees over to us if roles were reversed," Jeff thought aloud as he crossed over the summit.

He turned right into the parking lot and found a spot next to O'Neil's shop. "It was one of those beautiful sunny days in Santa Cruz when your high school memories came back, one of those days you cut classes 'cause an overhead northwest swell was breaking at the Point or the Lane," Jeff later told me. Seeing his friends waiting in front of the Crow's Nest temporarily brought Jeff out of his reverie.

Normally Jeff could turn these things off well while he concentrated on other things. He was barely part of the conversation during the meal, though, as the others talked about "old times." The time passed quickly and Jeff had hardly said a word. "What's up, Jeff?" one of his friends queried. "Problems on the home front?"

"Nah," Jeff answered. "Just something preoccupying my feeble brain," he continued. They all threw a couple of bucks on the table for a tip and headed out the door.

"Keep in touch," Jeff said as he opened his door to climb into his new Infiniti 4 × 4.

"As much as I don't want to, I have to consider Matt," Jeff continued his one-way conversation, turning onto Highway 17. "Matt has an engineering background and has done most of the design work on the initial product. He's the one who's probably most familiar with the whole process from production to distribution. Plus, with his marketing training and familiarity with the Japanese partners . . . ," Jeff's thoughts trailed off as he pulled into Safeway to pick up some ice cream for his daughter's birthday party that night.

Monday morning, Jeff began a more serious process of considering all those who were potential candidates.

"Melanie could be a logical choice, too," he thought. "She's got good solid marketing and sales experience, which will be the primary function of the Japanese partnership. She's extremely professional and seemed to get along well with the Japanese. With Matt's training and involvement in marketing, he could pick up the slack here. Maybe the actual sales side would suffer some, but . . ."

Jeff moved on to the next candidate, Lan.

"Lan's just a great all-around get-it-done type of guy," Jeff observed. "He would make an excellent 'coordinator' because of his strong technical and manufacturing background. And even though the operation in Japan and Asia would be focused on marketing, in reality the Japanese seemed most concerned about the product design and manufacturing process. Lan knew those cold, probably as well as Matt. And I'm not sure how much we really need Lan at MedTech now. It's true, he's the only one who really knows our suppliers well, and that's key. But now that all 'the ducks seemed lined up' in that area, I don't anticipate that it's going to be a major issue. Lan doesn't have any marketing experience, though . . .

"We could get someone from the outside, too, someone who speaks Japanese, maybe knows Japanese culture really well. That could be a real advantage to us. But then we'd have to train him at MedTech for at least six months first, get the person familiar with MedTech's operations. Even then, just how loyal the person would be to us is a question if it came to an issue that was pro Muhashi and against us. Would we be well represented?"

Jeff's frustration began to show to himself as he tossed in the wastebasket another paper with the old "pro-con" list he had drawn up.

Question 1: *If you were Jeff, who would you send over to Japan? What principal role(s) would this person play?*

"I hate this," Jeff said to himself. "Those 'gray' decisions are always the most difficult. I think I need to just let the thoughts sift a little now . . . see if in a few days something hasn't come clearer," he thought. "If I press it too much now, it'll all block. Nothing will happen. I need to let a little 'free flow' happen."

One morning Jeff called me into his office. I sensed what the topic was about as he leaned forward in his high-back leather chair, fidgeting with the pencil on his desk. He looked up at me and said, "Matt, I've thought about this for two weeks solid, and no matter how much I keep trying to push it away, your name keeps coming back to me as the right person for the Japan job."

"You are one of the few who knows the Japanese at Muhashi. You've been involved in all the negotiations, know the product backward and forward, and you're also someone I feel I can trust 100 percent. You've got the marketing background to cover that side of things, too, in case that's helpful. That, in fact, is one of the main problems I've been struggling with. Without knowing exactly what the Japanese are looking for in this person—or if they're even looking for anything—you're the safest bet. I know that doesn't sound clear, but when you're grabbing for straws and have to make a decision sooner or later, you make the best decision under the circumstances. Plus, I have to admit, my gut feeling says 'you.'"

MATT

"How well I knew those words," I thought to myself. This time they represented the start of something I really didn't want to face. Jeff and I talked for a few more minutes before I was called out to the production line. Thinking about Jeff's feeling and the implications of it made the day go by very slowly. As I drove home that evening, the old wheels began turning. Setting aside the more precarious part of the decision about my going to Japan—what would Jan think?—I mulled over in my mind the second part: who would take my place? It's interesting that I really didn't even seriously consider the question at the time whether I wanted to go or not. I don't know if that was reflective of the adventurous part of me or the "corporate man" mentality. Was I my own person or just going along with it because it was expected?

On the more concrete side of the situation, I began thinking about who would replace me. Lan could certainly take over the manufacturing side and do it at least as well as I could. The design aspect is basically taken care of, but even that I could do from Japan to a certain extent. Melanie is a pro at the marketing and sales side, so maybe I don't need a replacement. Maybe this is the natural evolution of things—growing out of my present position and into another.

But Jeff also knew I might not accept the position. I didn't have to pressure myself to do this. There was a lot at stake and Jeff knew it. He knew Jan's career was and would be a major concern as well as my own career. It had only been a few years since UCLA. This whole situation brought up all those feelings about careers, individuality, family, and so on. Still, I knew Jeff's job was to make decisions that were the best for the firm.

In any case, I asked for a few days to talk it over with Jan.

I also gave Professor Davidson a call. He is really approachable and gives you the feeling he's genuinely interested in you. He asked me a lot of questions and finally told me what I didn't necessarily want to hear but needed to, I guess.

"It sounds as though you've already made up your mind, Matt," Karl Davidson said matter-of-factly. "You want to go. I can understand that. It's part of your makeup—reach for the challenge, the exciting new opportunity. And that's great because you'll grow ten times more than someone else who prefers to stay in his comfort zone. From what executives are saying, people with international experience are going to be more and more valuable in the future. On the one hand, whether practices have caught up to the talk is questionable. There are still a lot of expats that are left hanging after they return. In the end, I'm sure there are a few that would have made a different decision had they to do it over again. On the other hand, I'm sure none regrets the personal growth that kind of experience brings.

"One thing, though, Matt. If you decide to go, remember, someone with your enthusiasm for new experiences can easily bowl over someone else with a weaker personality or a weaker commitment. I know your wife is a strong individual from what you have told me. She isn't about to let you ride rough shod over her, and you shouldn't anyway. But you're going to need to approach this with diplomacy and give her time to assimilate the idea. Make sure that she understands how important it is to you, but also make sure she has an important say in this whole thing. You know I've already told you about some of my mistakes—those career versus family decisions that eventually led to my divorce. It isn't worth it. And this can be a critical decision for your career and your marriage," he added.

I appreciated his advice and it usually confirmed what I was thinking myself but hadn't yet realized. It was that old mind versus heart battle that sometimes kept me from seeing clearly. He typically laid the fundamental issues in front of me and without pushing me one way or the other helped me see things more clearly.

On the "pro" side, certainly it would be a tremendously enriching experience personally for all of us. We would learn a great deal about Japan and probably about our own culture as we confronted a lot of differences in how we do things. Going to France was a real eye-opener and Japan is a lot different from France. Professionally, I'm sure I would learn a great deal about working with people very different from me, which in Silicon Valley can be a real asset. There's so much diversity here [in Silicon Valley]. If ever I worked for a company later on that dealt with Japan; this experience would be very helpful. Even if I didn't, the broader business perspective I would gain would be invaluable.

But moving to Japan would interrupt Jan's career and we'd lose the close and frequent association with Jan's parents for a while. They wouldn't be around the kids and vice versa. For me, well, I'd miss the Warriors games, but I guess I could handle that! Professionally, Karl Davidson warned me that it is common for the expatriate to experience an "out-of-sight-out-of-mind" phenomenon. I don't think that would happen at MedTech. We're so small and this looks like our big opportunity in the marketplace. I don't think Jeff is going to forget me. It is possible that technology will be changing rapidly enough to antiquate me a bit, but if I make regular trips back to the United States, any technological changes should be learnable. Besides, I'd have to worry more about that if I were in the electronics and computer fields.

I'm not sure why I was going through this detailed analysis of the whole thing. Deep down, I wanted to go and I knew I would—Jan allowing. It probably didn't matter if there were ten cons and one pro. Some things you just knew were to happen. You don't always know why—just got to go with that gut instinct.

A day went by, and another, and I still hadn't found a good moment to ask Jan what she thought. In fact, I guess I was so afraid this moment might actually arrive that I hadn't even mentioned to Jan about MedTech's situation other than we were going to get someone to oversee the operations in Japan. If I had said much more, Jan is intelligent enough that it wouldn't have taken much for her to figure out I was probably going to be the one asked to go. Rather than face that and her disappointment when it wasn't clearly fact yet, I had avoided the whole thing by only telling her a little bit of the picture.

Now I had to tell her. Waiting for a "good moment" wasn't a very good strategy because I realized there wasn't probably going to be a good moment. I knew I had to bring it up as soon as possible. Her reaction was predictable, I guess.

Question 2:   *If you were Jan, what would your reaction be in this situation? What would the issues be for you?*

"You've got to be kidding," Jan said. "Japan?"

I think she felt betrayed at first. I used the stun gun approach without realizing it. The fact that I would even consider it was asking a lot.

"This time there's not just our careers to consider," Jan added. "There's also Jeffrey, the new baby, and our parents."

Although initially the stay was supposed to be a year or so, I knew that would depend on how things were going. I wanted to be honest about that with Jan. I reassured her that it was "our" decision and not mine alone; I would do whatever we thought best.

"How could you even ask? I'm just getting my career under way, working for a firm that represents everything I feel strongly about, and you want me to just throw it all away?" she continued. She dropped the knife and potato she had been cutting and went outside. Things were a bit tense, to say the least. I could have picked up the knife and cut designs in the air it felt so thick.

When I told Jeff of her initial reaction, he suggested we take the weekend to think about it, go down to Monterey or Carmel, one of our favorite spots, to reflect and just take time out.

"The company will pick up the tab," Jeff mentioned encouragingly.

It was a fairly long three days before the weekend for Jan and me. I sort of tuned in and out of work that Thursday and Friday; Jan had a difficult time concentrating on her case at work. We were both kind of quiet at home. Later, Jan's parents said they sensed a little rift, too, when they came for dinner that Friday evening.

The trip down to Monterey was a little tense for a while, and about all we could talk about was the weather and countryside. We passed the stacks at Moss Landing and still hadn't said much more than how great the weather was. It wasn't until we hit Fort Ord that we were actually able to start talking about going to Japan.

"I know this whole thing sounds really one-sided," I said to Jan, "but just hear me out for a few minutes. On the positive side, I think the assignment would be a super career opportunity for me. I would gain valuable international experience, and I would become even more critical to MedTech because of the importance of the Japanese market to our success. I also think it would be really personally enriching for both of us. And frankly, I'm ready for a new, different challenge," I commented. "On the other hand, I know for you it poses a lot of negatives."

"Yeah, I'd say so," Jan mentioned matter-of-factly. "It would pull me out of my career track and distance me both physically and intellectually from environmental law. I like my job. I'm devoted to the causes I represent. How many people can say that?" Jan asked emphatically.

"Maybe you could become involved in similar cases in Japan," I wondered out loud. "I've been reading about Japan the last few months and according to the articles, they're fairly environmentally conscious." I knew I was just throwing darts indiscriminately, hoping something would land. Jan must have thought the same thing.

"Come on, Matt," Jan said. "Be realistic for once. The Japanese aren't going to let some American lawyer walk in and take over. You don't even know if there are any firms that represent environmental issues. And I don't speak Japanese," Jan's voice trailed off.

"I know," I said. "I'm sorry I have gotten myself into this situation so that you feel all the pressure. I just can't seem to let it go. I guess this is kind of a cause for me—going after new situations that will challenge my skills—maybe even sink me. It's probably a weakness, but . . ."

I shared these thoughts with Jan and, to her credit, she listened carefully. We also talked about our future family with the new baby arriving. Jan wasn't afraid of having the baby in Japan. She was logical enough to know that Japan is a modern society and the survival rate is as good as or better than in the United

States. It was more the psychological and emotional aspect that bothered her. Jan, especially, felt it was important for the grandparents to be around the baby and to have their support when starting our new family.

There were also questions about the financial terms of the position.

"How much would you make and how would we be compensated for the loss of my income . . . and the loss of my career?" she added quietly. "What kind of medical and dental benefits would we have, and how does that work in Japan? Would you still be able to maintain your retirement plan with MedTech? Would you even still be a MedTech employee?" she continued.

"Yeah, and I'm not sure about the schooling situation," I said under my breath. "Tuition for American schools must be expensive, but I assume they're good schools," I thought to myself.

Jan had other concerns as well. "Would our finances allow me and our kids to return home occasionally? Would I be able to maintain connections to the law firm? Just how isolated would we feel and be in Japan? We don't have any idea what it would be like to live there," she added.

I had to admit I also had questions about my job. What exactly would I be doing in Japan? Would I be able to influence things the way Jeff is expecting me to? The assignment was supposed to be for about a year. What if it made business sense to stay longer—two or three years? Would Jeff expect me to stay? Would I feel trapped into staying? What would Jan think? Would she have gotten involved in her profession in Japan by then? If she knew we might be there more than a year, would that make a difference in her decision now? Is it fair to subject her to that possibility at the outset?

One thing we both had decided from our experience when I was at UCLA: our careers would not separate us. We would stay together in the future. Now this "opportunity" was going to test that resolve.

Despite the ambiguities that remained, the weekend passed relatively well. There were still some unanswered questions, but then some would never be answered unless we went to Japan.

"At least Jeffrey would be young enough that we wouldn't have to worry about the schooling situation," I said. "And you would be home with him and our new baby when it was born. That's an opportunity you wouldn't have if we stayed here," I added, trying to point out any positives I could.

When I started on Monday, I talked to Jeff about the financial situation and benefits. Jeff assured me that I would be taken care of and would live at least at the level Jan and I did in the States. On Jan's side, she talked to Anh Phan, one of the partners at the law firm, and told her about the dilemma. Anh was understanding and thought there might be some way Jan could still remain involved if there were a good English law reference library in Tokyo.

"Perhaps at least in a limited way, you could remain involved in the research end of the case strategies," Anh told Jan. "And unless things changed drastically, you would be welcomed on board when you returned and we'd give you a period of time to get up to speed."

Anh advised Jan, however, that the rupture would definitely set back Jan's progress toward becoming a partner, that some attorneys might see her willingness to go to Japan as a lack of commitment to the firm and to Jan's own career. For Jan, being a partner was only important in that she would have more influence in the cases the firm accepted and the strategies they would use to argue their cases. Jan had never lost sight of the reason she became an attorney—to further social causes she fiercely believed in. Being a partner for the extra income and prestige held relatively little value for her.

In the end, Jan knew the decision was hers. I would never come out and say she should put her career on hold, even though in retrospect that's exactly what I was doing. But, she knew I felt I should go and so my decision was made. I know that was unfair for her to have that pressure, but there was nothing I could do short of turning down the position myself. Whether I should have or shouldn't have, I just couldn't do that. Jeff, the rest of MedTech, and I had worked too hard to get things to this point. This was our chance for success, and I felt strongly I had to do my part.

Jan told me flat out, "You know you're putting me in a no-win situation. If I say 'yes,' I probably kill my career—at least I kill my real chances for partnership at this firm, and partnership means more influence in the direction the firm takes, and the cases it takes on, and so on. So much that I've pushed hard for goes down the drain if we go. If I say 'no,' your career and all you've worked for at MedTech might be in jeopardy. It's not fair to you if we stay and it's not fair to me if we go."

Jan was right, but I didn't know what else to do. I couldn't—or at least I felt I couldn't—just let go of this opportunity, yet I felt for Jan too. In looking back at it, what I was asking Jan to do wasn't fair. It was being self-centered—a cheap shot, really. But I didn't see it that way at the time and didn't know what else to do. So, in essence, I left Jan with the decision, deep down knowing that if it came between her career and mine, she would probably willingly give up her career for mine. Even admitting this now hurts a little.

Finally, on a Sunday evening, nearly three weeks later, we reached a decision—or rather Jan did. She would go, "but I want it to be clear that if there's a next time, my career choices take priority should there be an either/or situation," Jan said matter-of-factly.

I agreed and apologized again about how this was all working out. Inside I have to admit I was elated, though.

Once the decision was made, I think Jan felt okay about it. Sometimes the stress created by not coming to a decision is worse than the decision itself—regardless of the decision outcome. I was both relieved and, in reality, kind of scared. I still was unsure of what I would be doing in Japan and how successful I would be, but I was probably equally anxious about the possible negative consequences on Jan's career. Still, I learned that right or wrong, you can't stay forever in the state of mind wondering whether the right decision was made. You just have to make a decision and then move on. Once we both made this mental adjustment, there was a kind of release and we could actually get excited about the challenge. We both had the feeling it would turn out okay.

Going to Japan was a once-in-a-lifetime opportunity. I mean, how many people with only a few years of experience and in their early 30s have this kind of opportunity offered to them? I would have the kind of responsibility that most who stay stateside have at the age of 40 or even 50. What a feather in my cap! At a time when the marketplace was truly becoming global, this kind of experience would increase my own marketability should I leave MedTech. But actually, I wasn't looking much beyond MedTech right now. I wanted to do all I could to make it work. I thought with my experience in France and my natural open-mindedness that I would be able to adapt well enough to Japan to become effective. I couldn't wait for the experience and was on the telephone to my MBA friends from UCLA and a couple from Renssaeler to tell them the great news.

Although it took a while for Jan to psychologically let go of her job, she, too, began to get excited as she focused on going to Japan. Jan was naturally an adventurous person, and seeing a different part of the world, viewing the beautiful countryside, having other unique experiences like skiing inside the famous ski dome near Tokyo, hiking Mount Fuji, and so on, began to appeal to her.

JAN

I'll bet you didn't know I am a great fan of haiku poetry. It was among my favorites in one of my poetry courses at UT-Austin. I especially recall one because it reminded me so much of summer evenings I spent on the Maine shoreline:

Constant crashing waves,
On the dike in the evening
Waving to the stars

I also took a world religion course at Berkeley as an elective. I found Buddhism and other aspects of ancient Japanese life really fascinating—very different from my American Protestant upbringing. Buddhism was like haiku poems—close to nature and revealing the interconnectedness of all things. I guess I really liked it because it paralleled my basic philosophy of life; there was such a close kinship with the environment in its teaching. Ever since my days in Maine, I have loved and respected all that was natural around me. I admired the Native Americans for their keen understanding of this similar Buddhist concept. And I have to admit, at times I hated the white imperialist fortune seekers who saw nothing but achieving their own profits at the sacrifice of others' way of life. I admired the balance between people and their environment that the Indians had achieved. I think we're still struggling to rediscover this balance, and it is an uphill battle all the way.

"But I must not be too extremist . . . I married you!" I told Matt.

"Besides," I added, "it could be exciting to be in Japan and study more about Buddhism and other religions there—the Buddhist temples, their beautiful architecture with their interesting colors and storytelling-surrounding gardens. One of the other attorneys visited Japan and told me the famous Kiyo-mizu-dera Temple in Kyoto is a must visit. And Mount Fuji—wow—what beautiful natural architecture. And there's the world-renowned Tokyo ballet, operas, the classical Kabuki drama theater."

I didn't say it to Matt, but I kept having to tell myself these things to hide some of the emptiness of leaving my causes temporarily behind. As I did, though, I think I genuinely began to develop an interest in going to Japan. There is much in life to experience, and this could be a significant part of that partaking.

Much of my excitement was soon replaced with some anxiety, though, as the reality of the whole move began to settle in for both of us. Matt and I made out our agendas for the next two months. It was crazy.

Matt had to transfer the necessary information to Carl (Matt's assistant) and at the same time try to make all the necessary preparations at home to leave. In fact, he had to meet with Carl almost every day to bring him up to speed on everything Matt had been doing—the product planning, the contacts in the United States and Europe, the medical associations and hospital administrator groups, the doctors who were acting as informal sponsors for MedTech, the coordination between production and their "office" that was critical, the people Matt would be working with in Japan, and on and on. It wasn't just Matt and I who were feeling the effects of the transfer. Carl complained about feeling overwhelmed too. Matt admitted to me that over the last year or so he hadn't delegated as much as he should have or included Carl in as many meetings as he could have.

"Hindsight always has the answers," Matt mumbled to me one evening.

That was simply the effects of a small firm, I think—everyone had a lot of responsibility but not much overlapped. Sometimes Matt wondered if it was all worth it. "You get so caught up in the process that you lose sight of why you're doing it," he complained.

For me, making preparations to leave was still somewhat emotionally traumatic despite the fact that I tried to keep focused on the advantages of going to Japan. "Sometimes I have second thoughts about all this," I said to Dad over lunch one day. "But," I continued, "it really will open up other opportunities that I might otherwise not have had the courage to create. You know I have always wanted a career to fight for causes I believe in, and I have always been willing to work hard to achieve things. But you probably know better than anyone that I've also wanted children," I told him.

Realistically, I was probably kidding myself that I could give the same intensity to my career if I were really serious about children. I don't believe in sacrificing children to a career, despite the fact that some women say it isn't a choice between one or the other. You only have so much energy and so much time.

Sooner or later I was going to have to face that decision. Maybe in some ways, this just forced the issue and made a cleaner break. "You're the one who taught me to trust my feelings on things that otherwise seem rather confusing," I told my dad.

"That's why you're my favorite girl," Dad said with confidence. I laughed and told him, "Dad, I'm your only girl."

In the next few days it became apparent to Matt and me that the professional preparations were only part of the story. Personally, the amount of preparation seemed equally incredible. We decided to rent our house instead of selling it. Given the circumstances, we weren't sure we would be able to come back and buy an equivalent home. Renting our house meant we had to leave it totally functioning. That meant repairing part of the sprinkling system, fixing the plumbing in the bathroom sink, replacing some of the tile on the kitchen counter that had pulled away from the grouting, putting a drip mist system in the backyard to try to ensure the health of our roses and canna lilies we had planted last year, and so on. Of course, these were all chores we were going to have to do sometime, but we had to do it all in two months now. Procrastination, it seems, is no respecter of persons.

I contacted the mortgage company to find out the options of paying the mortgage from Japan. Finally, we decided we would mail the check from Japan and keep our account open with Citibank in the United States. That meant we would have to wire money to our account or Matt could talk to Irum Rangwala, the financial officer at MedTech, to determine whether part of his salary could be sent directly to our U.S. account and the rest sent to Japan. Neither of us wanted to have to depend on the tenants to pay their rent in order to pay our mortgage. I would ask the tenants to send the check to my parents; they could then deposit it in our account. From time to time, they said they would stop by the house to see if everything looked okay. I didn't want to burden them, though, with anything extra—Dad had arthritis and was diabetic. I would try to take care of the Visa billing while we were gone, and the Discover card we had just started would have to be canceled, and on and on it went.

Both of us had to shop for some clothes too. Winters are colder in Tokyo, and clothes more expensive. Both of us had good shell coats with warm fleece linings and down vests, but neither of us had everyday clothes for a colder climate than San Francisco.

Nearly everyday from 5 A.M. to 11 P.M. we both worked to leave our jobs in some semblance of order while trying to prepare ourselves to go to Japan. Finally, we made a quick trip to Japan to find an apartment, hopefully, not too far from where Matt would work. We would be living on an expatriate contract because

Matt would not technically be an employee of Muhashi. Muhashi could have left us alone to do the nearly impossible—find a suitable apartment—but that wasn't the Japanese way it seemed. They knew it was difficult for foreigners to find a place without going through one of the English-speaking agencies that specializes in accommodating foreigners. So Muhashi gave us the name of such a company and had already called it to let the agency know we would be coming to ask them to help us find a suitable accommodation. The agent told Matt it's very important where we live and that his rank in the company should be considered when choosing a location. This was kind of amusing because we were used to living in our small starter home in a very middle-class neighborhood in San Bruno. I wasn't used to what I began to think of as a kind of "class-conscious" society, but it was something Matt could probably get used to, he chuckled to me.

Our initial exposure to prices was catastrophic. With the recent recession in Japan, I had heard the real estate prices had really nosedived. Somehow, it didn't seem to be affecting rental prices much from what I could see. We were still looking at a rent of $3,000 to $4,500 for a very small one-bedroom apartment in the Meguro or Azabu districts, where a good-sized expat community lived. Although these weren't the equivalent of more expensive areas, they still had an element of prestige attached to them that told others a great deal about you without knowing you. We had set out looking for a three-bedroom apartment for when the baby comes, but soon decided that for the cost of the extra room, we could probably both figure out some other arrangement and save a lot of money in the interim, possibly providing for trips back to the States for me and the children. That was the goal anyway.

We finally decided that in spite of the thought of being "stars," we could do with a somewhat less prestigious area that was less expensive too, and still a bit international, somewhat like the neighborhoods of the Ginza district. Even in these areas, to buy a very small basic apartment hovered around $400,000 at the time of the exchange rate. I was told that in the Shinjuku district, a 1-foot-square plot of land cost about $15,000. We figured at that rate, we could probably afford a 5-square-foot home, including the price of the land! And with new construction, we were assured of having a flush toilet, which we were told a lot of rural Japanese living in older homes still did not enjoy.

I began thinking about that—a 5-square-foot home with a flush toilet. "We could always cook on top of the toilet with our cookstove," Matt told me, "and set the television on top of it when we were through cooking and eating. It would be an all-purpose toilet," he chuckled.

And, of course, there was the economic crisis in Japan that some had predicted because of huge loan defaults on the part of some of the largest Japanese banks. That could certainly lower prices a bit. Regardless, we quickly realized the salary MedTech was going to pay Matt would probably be about half of what we would really need to live at a standard comparable to what we had in California. We could certainly live less luxuriously in Japan even though in the States we had a very simple place in a quiet middle-income neighborhood in San Bruno. Still, $75,000 and medical and dental benefits just weren't going to be enough if we were going to live in a more central part of Tokyo, which I insisted on, since I would be without a career or a car. I wanted to be close to a subway or train station and not spend a lot of time traveling to get there.

It was difficult for a small foreign firm like MedTech to compete financially with Japanese firms in Japan, especially since it was the large powerful Japanese firms that directly or indirectly dictated much of the living conditions in Japan. In talking to the agency we were working through to find an apartment, we learned some interesting facts about salaries in Japan. Salaries were often much lower in Japan than in the United States, especially during the first ten to fifteen years of one's career. To compensate for the lower salaries, the agency's reps told us the large Japanese companies typically supplemented the "salaryman's" wages by giving extensive benefits to their employees: heavily subsidized living quarters; the equivalent of about six months' salary in the form of bonuses two or three times a year (depending on how good a year it was); for upper management, there was a large entertainment budget allowances, golf club membership fees easily totaling $25,000 a year or more, and other great benefits.

For the professional employee, the Japanese "salaryman's" pay had traditionally been supplemented with extra pay according to the number of family members, the particular housing needs, the commuting cost from the employee's home to the work site, and other individual factors like extra pay for no absences and even in some cases a dating allowance (although officially we were told it was referred to as "entertainment" expense) given to select young, single males. I reminded Matt that he was married and told him that except for not being eligible for the dating allowance, he should have worked it out to be a Muhashi employee instead of being on MedTech's payroll while we were here. With the financial concerns in Japan, it was hard to know whether it was best to be paid in yen or in dollars. Unfortunately, no one could predict the future with any kind of real assurance, and we weren't totally sure how long we would be in Japan, even though it wasn't supposed to extend much beyond a year. The way the exchange rate seemed to be going before the crisis, within a few months we might have had to live on rice alone and in the back of our car if Matt's salary had been in dollars.

During an economic recession in Japan, like the recent one, we were told that Japanese firms do modify some of their generous benefits, cutting off some of those perks or reducing bonuses. Unlike U.S. companies, when salary cuts first happen in Japan, it is the management ranks that suffer cuts before skilled employees' wages and benefits are tampered with.

"That would go over really well in the United States," I thought to myself.

Matt and I both noticed as we trekked through Tokyo that there was a remarkable homogeneity. To the uneducated eye—and we were definitely uneducated when it came to Asians—nearly everyone seemed to have the same black hair, same color skin, same dark suits for men, interspersed with women and students, many in uniforms going to work or school, others doing their shopping. But as time passed, we also began to discern the less-than-obvious differences you don't see right away. We had been so used to the Bay Area where differences among minority groups are obvious to even the untrained eye. In Japan, immigrants represented less than 1 percent of the total population!

In the subway, older Japanese seemed to stare into space or read the newspaper, carefully folded to allow the maximum reading in the littlest amount of space; younger, male Japanese seemed to have rather blank looks on their faces as they read their comic books, newspapers, or just stared, waiting for their stop; young schoolchildren often chattered softly with their friends or listened to their Walkman. It reminded me of subways in Paris. I learned later from some American women (you almost always heard the extremes from the Americans who lived there) that although it probably rarely happened, younger woman were occasionally groped in the subways and, until recently, women seemed to outwardly accept this as part of men's right in Japan. Apparently, some Japanese women are embarrassed to bring attention to themselves by crying out and simply endure such treatment even though they, too, find it unacceptable; in the coming years, that will probably change, we were told—the only question is when.

"I think I'd be tempted to kill the first Japanese who did that to me," I told Matt.

MATT

I think it surprised Jan to hear herself say that and actually half mean it. She had always been driven about causes and could become very passionate. "I think I have always approached life with a very logical, but thoughtful perspective," she stated. "The last time I remember reacting emotionally was when a 400-pound hungry brown bear wandered into our camp on a hiking expedition in the Moose Lake area of Maine. I was about 7 and just the night before my dad had been telling us some bear stories about people being mauled or killed from bear attacks. I had been primed, to say the least," Jan added.

I think Jan keenly sensed the plight of the Japanese woman where men were still typically the businesspeople, the engineers, the doctors, and so on, and the women were still usually the assembly-line workers, the teachers, the nurses, and the part-time employees. These were messages about who traditionally has had what place in society, but they, too, have been changing as more women have entered engineering and other traditionally male professions.

"American women are still fighting their own battles too," Jan reminded me— "like when the man's career supersedes his spouse's because he thinks it's more important," she said, smiling.

That was a hit below the belt, but probably well deserved.

To bring the conversation back to something I could deal with better, I told Jan if she ever had a problem with a man to be sure she could describe him. She told me, "No problem. I could do it now—black hair, kind of round face, slightly dark complexioned, about 5-feet-six, wearing a conservative suit and tie." We both laughed, but I have to admit, the sting of her earlier comment lingered some.

It doesn't take a long time in Japan before realizing that it really is a different place. Physically, all the neon lights at night vying for attention, the crowds, the predominantly white cars, the uniforms on schoolchildren, and a host of other differences rang loud and clear that this was not San Bruno. Jan and I had decided that we should have rented an apartment in Chinatown in the City (San Francisco) before coming. That might have eased the transition!

I noticed differences at work too. The bows and an occasional handshake, the singing of company songs by the employees—although it happened infrequently— the white shirts and ties, the open rooms with desks clustered neatly to identify work groups, and even just the sheer size of the company compared to MedTech— all this seemed quite strange, and I wondered how easily I was going to fit in. Although many Japanese at the company spoke English, their accents sometimes made it very difficult to understand. Having lunch last week with Mr. Satoh and three other Japanese posed some difficulties for me. I began to get a glimpse of the experience I was in for. "Most of the time," I told Jan, half serious and half joking, "I pretend I understand what they say and hope I'm not nodding my head or saying yes to something that I can't deliver on—like if we can manufacture scalpels with the doctor's name engraved on them! I realized this potentially could be dangerous if I misrepresented myself or MedTech. I have the most problem understanding Mr. Satoh, but fortunately, I won't be working with him all that often."

I rationalized that I would get used to Satoh's accent soon. I certainly wasn't going to ask him to repeat nearly everything he said. It's especially embarrassing when I'm with several Japanese and someone says something in "English"—and everyone but me is laughing.

Once back in the States—and somewhat relieved to be so—I discussed some of my thoughts concerning the salary with Jeff. Jeff talked to the board and managed to negotiate for a subsidization of our housing expenses. MedTech would pay for three-fourths of our housing costs. This was a difficult negotiation for Jeff because to date, MedTech was all expenses and no revenue. If the Japanese venture did not pan out, that was it. And we both thought about that once in a while.

With a couple of weeks left before packing up for good, we began to really feel the strain. We felt like we would never be ready, and the stress of it all began to tell on us both. We saw each other less than before and had strained conversations sometimes when we did. Jan tired much faster than before she was pregnant, which made it difficult too. While she fought the traffic on 101, she also wondered about the challenges she would have to deal with in Japan.

"I worry about how I am going to function in a country where I don't speak the language at all," she told me. "My high school and college French would not be of much help there," she added. Jan had always prided herself on her ability to communicate well. It was certainly one of the skills that had served her well as an attorney and as a writer in her university days. Without an ability to speak Japanese and without her work, I think she had already begun to sense some isolation. I think it was as if a major part of herself would be inaccessible. I think she thought of herself as a disabled person.

Time would tell how we both dealt with our challenges in Japan. Neither one of us was totally immune from our fears.

The day before our departure from SFO (San Francisco Airport), I met with Jeff to discuss last-minute details about what Jeff wanted me to accomplish while in Japan. Basically, it was my job to make sure the product got to market. From MedTech's perspective, I would have responsibility for coordinating with MedTech, overseeing product quality, distribution, and customer satisfaction in Japan. I thrived on responsibility, but I would be less than honest if I didn't admit I also felt a little overwhelmed. How was I going to control product quality from Japan for one? Here I had dumped so much onto Carl and his assistant. I had set things up as well as I could, given the circumstances. I versed Carl thoroughly on problems in the past, discussed the new manufacturing process with the current design and production engineers, and had personally talked to the surgeons who had used their instruments to seek any additional feedback on the most recent production runs.

Everything seemed in place. Plus, I would be making regular visits to MedTech to help coordinate and report personally to Jeff what was going on in Japan. Jeff mentioned in a somewhat embarrassed way that we'd have to travel coach class until we got things going. About a third of the seats on Nippon Air are for businesspeople going first class or business class, so I'm not sure Jeff was referring to the limited number of coach seats or the idea that we weren't going to be situated in the business section.

Jan's parents drove us to the airport the next day and wished us their best. You could tell it was especially difficult for Jan's dad to say goodbye, knowing he would not see Jan or Jeffrey for a while or be there as the baby developed. And I think it was hard on Jan too. Jan and her dad have an especially close relationship. They had spent many summers together over the years, most recently doing some day hikes in Yosemite and in the Trinity Alps area west of Shasta. Her dad always liked to tell the story about their hiking in the Hetch Hetchy reservoir with three days' provisions. They had gotten into camp too late to find a good tree to hang their food on and settled for a rock that her dad foot-lifted her up onto enough that she could get foot- and hand-holds for the rest. She placed the food about 11 feet high, taller than any bear they had ever seen, especially the smaller black bears that inhabit Yosemite. Unfortunately, the tree next to the rock was too close.

About midnight the first bear came, shimmied up the tree, and lunged over onto the rock. Jan's dad stayed up all night watching the bears eat their food, making sure they weren't going to come for human flesh. The only thing the bears didn't eat was the tuna in the non-poptop cans. Tuna wasn't Jan and her dad's first choice for breakfast. They hiked out the 7 miles the next day in 90-degree weather.

A sudden jolt from air turbulence 32,000 feet up brought me back to reality. About three more hours before arrival. I started to mull over some plans for MedTech's objectives in Japan, and shortly thereafter, Jan kind of crashed—which I could never do sitting up like that, especially when the turbulence hadn't completely stopped.

What seemed like long hours later, the pilot's voice announced our approach into Narita Airport. We had left on Thursday, and crossing the date line, arrived on Friday. Muhashi officials were waiting for us; two of the them were Japanese I had worked with before. They drove us to our hotel because the apartment wouldn't be ready for another two weeks. Passing a lot of drab tiny homes along the way made me realize how lucky we were to have even a modest—but comparatively much larger—home in San Bruno.

The hotel we stayed in, the Ana, was in the Roppongi district, a place fairly popular among foreigners. I wasn't expected in to work until Monday, so we used the time to explore Tokyo. We also slept a fair amount that weekend, recovering from jet lag. Although traveling from east to west wasn't nearly as hard as the other direction, we had exhausted ourselves the last several weeks from getting ready to go. Jan had stayed up until 2 A.M. the morning we left for Japan. I had quit at midnight and said we should have hired a maid to do the cleaning. Jan agreed. I don't know how she did it all while being five months pregnant.

In the Roppongi district, we found Domino's Pizza, Dunkin' Donuts, and other decidedly Western symbols of civilization. What surprised Jan most, though, were the very visible neon signs of the different stores and restaurants. Many of the signs hung far out into the street so you could see what restaurants and stores were down the street. Of course, you couldn't see more than ten or fifteen at any one time. But they sure lit up the night—reds and yellows and whites, some blinking and others not. Jan thought it was a bit garish, she told me later on in the hotel room.

JAN

Our hotel restaurant offered western, Japanese, and Chinese food. Some of the Japanese names seemed unpronounceable next to their English equivalents. We met a British couple with two small children, ages 3 and 18 months. They were at the hotel waiting for their apartment too. At first we often saw them eating at the hotel. After that, they began eating out at fast-food restaurants. They told us they were embarrassed because the 3-year-old kept throwing silverware on the floor and would often spill her juice or knock over her cup of hot chocolate— apparently on purpose. It bewildered the couple because it was totally out of character for the little girl to do that. The stress of the situation wasn't worth the convenience of eating at the hotel. They found a couple of decent fish 'n' chips places in Tokyo, apparently catering to the British contingency there.

I told Matt it was probably just her way of dealing with the unsettling of the move to Japan. "Kids have the right to feel stressed, too," I thought. So far, Jeffrey had been behaving fairly normally, but that could change.

For us, being at the hotel sheltered us from some of the realities of living in Japan. We assumed housing costs would be high. Then, as we began shopping, we realized just how expensive Japan was: $3 for a liter of milk, $25 for a kilo of beef, and the list went on. At least we wouldn't have to cut out our daily yogurt entirely, but because we weren't big meat eaters, losing out on the beef didn't bother us. Rice wasn't very expensive but we had heard that because of climate changes that year there was less rice to go around than usual. I don't know if it was just for that, but more and more Japanese were eating bread now, anyway— sandwiches for lunch and that sort of thing. Apparently, the only rice the Japanese were willing to import was American short grain rice to make up for the unusually lower recent Japanese yields. Most of it was imported from California. The Japanese looked for certain qualities in their rice and most other countries' rice did not qualify!

Later on we did find out, by accident from wandering around the store, that in some large department stores the basement floor had ready-made food items, even western-style bakery goods and other foods. They were actually pretty good—definitely better than McDonald's and not as expensive as eating out at decent restaurants.

Matt and I had a few days to settle in because we arrived on a Thursday and he wasn't expected to be in his office until Monday. We used that weekend to just relax and get our breath back. It had seemed as though we had done nothing but run the last few months, and frankly, we were both ready for a vacation—even a three-day one.

We finally found an affordable apartment in the Meguro district. It was going to cost us $3,500 a month. It was a two-bedroom, one-bath furnished place, architecturally typical Japanese. There was the entryway to slip off one's shoes and put on "house" slippers. There was a small room with a "kneeling" table in the center, and our small bedroom had mattresses on the floor. The bathroom seemed large relative to the total space in the apartment.

The neighborhood was typical also, a mixture of different looking buildings, none with an address we would recognize. In fact, we didn't seem to see street names either. We were told the Japanese typically identify a house's location by the name of the neighborhood and its date of construction or by other identifying buildings nearby. This was apparently a vestige of the fact that neighborhoods, many many years ago, were fairly self-contained entities. You didn't have to travel outside your neighborhood to get the necessities to live, and everyone knew everyone else. There was apparently no need to identify a home with a number. I guess it was like the old western towns in the United States. Everything—stores, post office, houses—usually were built up along the main street, so locating everything was not difficult.

Now some modern housing developments have numbers assigned, and we began recognizing that neighborhood names were often marked on pedestrian overpasses or a block number within a neighborhood was indicated also. Sometimes we also saw the names on utility poles.

QUESTIONS FOR DISCUSSION

1. Is Matt the best choice to represent MedTech in Japan? Who from MedTech would you send over to Japan to oversee the operation (consider personal qualifications, background, personality, etc.)? What are the pros and cons of your choice?
2. Does it make sense for Matt and Jan, personally and professionally, to take the position in Japan? Why or why not?
3. What would you say about Jan and Matt's relationship based on their discussions about and their final decision to go to Japan? Discuss the career-family balance reflected in their decision to go.
4. To those who have never traveled and worked internationally, the experience is only seen from a glamorous perspective—seeing new, interesting places. To those who have experienced the preparation, move to, and settling in the foreign country, there is quite another practical side. What were some of the things Jan and Matt experienced personally and professionally as they went through the stages of first impressions of going to Japan, preparing for the departure, and initial settling in?
5. What differences can you detect between Japanese and Americans as you see through the eyes of Matt and Jan during their initial experience?

CHAPTER 5

West Meets East: Adapting to Japan

JAN

During the first months while Matt tried to figure things out at work, I busily explored Tokyo, including several famous Buddhist temples and Shinto shrines. I also enjoyed just walking down the typical streets of Japanese commercial areas and neighborhoods. It was good exercise for me, too, during my pregnancy. It was really interesting to see the Japanese restaurant window displays of their meals with elaborate ceramic models showing every detail of the fish or whatever else you might order. Some of the restaurants had their meals in movable glass window displays on wheels that they could roll out onto the sidewalk and back into the restaurant at closing time. Others displayed the food models in the restaurant windows.

September 1 came and I started an early labor with our second child, Michelle. This time, instead of going to the States, we coaxed my parents to come and stay with us for about a month. It wasn't a hard sell job, though. Mom couldn't wait to come. Dad had already set aside some money. Initially they were set to come the week following the birth because my due date wasn't until September 8. I had been going to an English-speaking Japanese gynecologist who came highly recommended by an American orthopedic surgeon we knew from the expat community. Office visits were sometimes interesting, trying to understand his assistants, but to make a long story short, the pregnancy went well and the baby arrived just fine. In Japan it is apparently the custom to give the doctor a very generous tip for his service, so we did—reluctantly. Unfortunately, it wasn't until later that I found out it was mostly the older Japanese people who gave tips. This is on top of the fact that doctors have their own pharmacies as well. I began to think maybe I should have gone to med school instead of law school!

Matt was home as much as he could be, but if it weren't for my parents, I don't know what I would have done. Jeff was in preschool, so Dad went to pick him up every day at 2 o'clock and Mom stayed to help take care of the house. I could already tell life was going to be a lot more complicated with one child and one baby in the house—well, let's make that two babies—Michelle and Matt! Kidding aside, there were times when I thought Matt was completely helpless. With our second child here, though, Matt seemed to be picking things up a little faster—changing diapers, feeding, and so on.

The month went by quickly and there was a definite emptiness to the house when Mom and Dad left. The best remedy for that was just to get back into the swing of things as quickly as possible, which I did.

In October I even did some skiing in the Tokyo ski dome. I had brought my skis with me from the States, anticipating having time to get some skiing in while I wasn't working. Having the ski dome so close was great. It's really an interesting place, basically a 17-story refrigerator on stilts. The brochure promoting Lalaport Ski Dome "SSAWS" (English translation for Spring, Summer, Autumn, Winter Snow) boasts you can experience powder all year long and enjoy the equivalent of a European mountain resort, promising to evoke the "ocean, forests, port towns and glaciers" of Scandinavia. There's something to be said for PR.

The first shock was the price: the equivalent of $70 for a three-hour ski jaunt. But the length of the dome is decent, about a 1,500-foot vertical drop on a slope close to 100 yards wide. And the service is typically Japanese. I was greeted by five Japanese who led me inside. The first woman sold me a ticket, the second put the ticket into the automated turnstile, and the third took the ticket as I passed through and then handed it back to me. Then two men pointed me to a door 5 feet away as if I might have trouble finding it. In their fastidiousness, they even publish a trail map even though there is only the one run and the run's boundaries are fairly obvious—the two walls on both sides. Authenticity, I discovered, or at least the appearance of it, is important to the Japanese.

At the rental desk, you can rent skis, boots, and poles, a video camera, long underwear, a various array of designer skiwear, and swimsuits and towels for an après-ski swim. After I got past the rental desk without any incident, I was sent to the lobby to wait for my lift pass number to appear on a giant screen. The limit is 2,000 skiers at any one time. While you're waiting, you can look at smaller screens that show people skiing in the dome. I only had to wait a few minutes. The lift line doesn't last long and the time to get up the slope is very short. Once on the slope the ski levels are clearly marked—the right side is for the "experts," the left side "intermediates," and the bottom of the slope is for the beginners. I had heard that the slope is good enough for competition slalom skiing and surprisingly enough, it was really enjoyable. The expert side consisted of small moguls, not as challenging as Killington, but fun enough to feel like maybe it was worth the money. Besides, when the nearest skiing is several hours away, it serves its purpose.

Matt and I thought we'd go together once in a while and then maybe take a week's vacation to Mount Fuji and have a real ski vacation. Matt had brought his Dynastar Vertical Assault "team" as he called them. They were great cruise-'n-bump skis he said, but unfortunately, the ski dome specialized in groomed skiing. The bumps he would encounter would be mostly with other skiers or when he fell, which he did more often than I.

While I was visiting temples, walking the neighborhoods, and skiing once in a while at the dome, Matt tried to get connected at work. The first few days on the job consisted mostly of introductions.

MATT

My Japanese colleague took me from one person to the next, including engineers and managers. What I remember most singularly was that they all seemed to have a similar smile and demeanor—reserved and polite. Some of them I had already met from previous visits to Japan, but by the end of the week, I still had a pocketful of new business cards. I couldn't remember whom more than half of the cards represented—in fact, I really only remembered three or four of the fifteen or so Japanese I had met—those that I had met personally, anyway. I'm sure they expected me to remember each person with whom I exchanged business cards. There was only one of me, so they clearly had the advantage!

Each time I was brought into a work area to meet the manager or senior engineer, all the employees also stopped their work, stood up, smiled at me, and bowed courteously. I had rarely felt more uncomfortable. You'd think I was the next emperor of Japan. Ceremony was clearly important to these people. Of course, I smiled back and bowed to them. I'm not sure they expected me to bow, but I wasn't up to going around shaking everyone's hand individually. Coming from a country where ceremony doesn't count for much, I often felt out of place.

Actually, it wasn't a total surprise to me—the bowing, smiles, and all that. I had remembered reading in the *San Jose Mercury News* before leaving California about a large Japanese multinational. Senior management felt that the younger generation of workers had begun to lose some of the traditional notions of courtesy that had preceded them. So they published a 40- or 50-page manual on courtesies, everything from the degree of bow to where to sit in a mixed hierarchical group. I kept thinking to myself that either the Muhashi employees had read the same manual or they maybe had one of their own. One of my Japanese "informants" told me that these manuals are typically for receptionists and salespeople because they have the most direct contact with clients, and companies want to make sure they give the "right" (i.e., most respectful) impression.

Unlike the other Japanese, who all shared a large office space, the Japanese gave me an office of my own, which later I really appreciated in one sense—it gave me a place to "hide" and rejuvenate when I became totally frustrated.

My office was in the same building as those with whom I worked, but I had to walk down a short hall to see my primary work group that had overall responsibility for MedTech's product distribution. I wasn't sure what that meant in terms of my relationship with the others involved in the joint effort. It could have been a compliment to me because I learned later that only senior managers had individual offices, but it could have also been a way of subtly excluding me from conversation—not that I would have understood anything in Japanese anyway. But the Japanese around me might have felt constrained to speak English and that probably would have been tough on them—and me—to try to understand. I imagine I was enough of an enigma to them already, a little over 30 years old and yet a senior manager in MedTech.

They wouldn't have had to exclude me by putting me in an office down the hall. The language and cultural barriers were sufficient to exclude me from most of what went on. Among themselves, their office setup was really open. There was one big room with perhaps as many as 50 desks, each clustered in smaller groups to indicate who worked with whom. They were typically facing the manager's desk or else perpendicular to it. I don't know how I would have liked that. Everyone could hear basically anything anyone else said to another person in that work group. Granted, it made communication easier, and you surely learned things that you otherwise wouldn't have. And you didn't have to pick up the phone to call the person in a nearby office because here the colleague was maybe 3 to 10 feet to your right or left or in front of or behind you. There was no such thing as an "open door" policy with the manager, either. I mean that notion didn't seem to apply—open or closed door. He was sitting there in front of you with no doors to open or close.

This openness was obviously linked to their mode of decision making. It certainly made gathering information much easier. Having these work groups bunched so closely together almost gave it an informal meeting atmosphere all the time. With the work group to which I had been kind of informally attached,

I figured regardless of where I was, I would be consulted as decisions needed to be made. In the ensuing months, as I relate later on, I realized how naive that was.

Question 1:   *How does the Japanese office setup differ from the usual one in your culture? What values or beliefs do these differences reflect about each culture?*

While I was acclimatizing to the work environment at Muhashi, Jan visited Tokyo and regularly went to the Tokyo American Club as a guest of some of the women. We were really surprised at the lavishness of the club. It was definitely set up for recreation, with tennis, basketball, racquetball, and squash courts. There was a formal reception room and other facilities. Being a member was helpful to develop connections for possible professional reasons and for Jan to talk to other expatriate wives to learn the "ins" and "outs" of being in Japan. The club consisted primarily of a group of expatriates and their wives, including Europeans and even Japanese, who met regularly to discuss everything from Japanese bathhouses to world politics and the various experiences their kids were having in the international or Japanese schools. Only a few Americans had put their children in Japanese schools—private ones that allowed foreign students who didn't speak Japanese. Even in as large an international city as Tokyo, you could count those schools on your hand.

Before we left the States, Jan and I figured we wouldn't have to confront the issue of schooling for our children because of their ages. Now, though, Jan was getting a little restless and was eager to start doing some professional work. The issue of who would take care of the children if she were working came up. We had the option of hiring someone to be in our home to take care of both kids or taking Jeffrey to one of the academic nurseries that are so popular in Japan and having someone watch Michelle. One of our friends told Jan that we had come at a good time if we were going to put Jeffrey in a Japanese school. Some Japanese elementary schools were actually encouraging kids to ask questions and express their own opinions. This was a quiet revolution we were told.

Despite such apparent encroaching changes, Japanese schools are amazing, Jan told me, even the pre-kindergarten. It seemed that everyone wants their kid to go to Tokyo University or one of the other elite schools in Japan (I'm sure a lot of parents don't really care, but that was the hype you heard at the Tokyo American Club). To get there, you have to make sure your 3-year-old is admitted to the best prep schools—for kindergarten, that is. Some of these kindergartens are supposedly owned and operated by private companies, although I was told by some Americans that there is often just an "informal" connection to a large Japanese company. More often, the best kindergartens are actually vertically integrated all the way up to the best universities. Muhashi operated a day-care center that resembled a kindergarten and so I think that's where the misunderstanding might have originated.

I had the impression that's where everything starts in Japan—at the pre-kindergarten level. Of course, before entering pre-kindergarten, your mother preps you to be able to score well enough to get in. And these schools are not cheap. A six-week summer program for a 3- or 4-year-old, Jan learned from one of the mothers in the American Club, can easily cost from $5,000 to $8,000 or more. I had always heard that the Japanese are really education oriented. I knew it then. That's what you call putting your money where your mouth is. Unbelievable— $5,000 to $8,000 or more for a six-week class for a 3-year-old! I hate to use the word "insane," but I think that does describe it pretty well.

Confucius believed that social order is ensured with a highly educated population. I'm not sure which came first in Japan—the desire for social order or the value on education, but both are clearly present now. Education seems more a way to get ahead and ensure a comfortable future than for any value in itself.

The intense preparation to get into the best kindergarten, to get into the best elementary school, to get into the best junior high, and so on, continues until the national university entrance exam. If you have successfully matriculated from a kindergarten associated with one of the top universities through the system into high school, and you are one of the top students in the high school, apparently your entrance into the "sponsoring" university is greatly facilitated.

Confucius had another impact on Japan during these formative educational years. Despite the increasing signs of westernization, moral education seems to be taught at all levels. Values like hard work, cooperation, and abiding loyalty to the family (i.e., the parents) are extolled. This can be seen in even the elementary schools. Kids are organized into small "teams" with a designated rotating leader. These "teams" are responsible for sweeping floors, emptying wastebaskets, wiping the chalkboard, cleaning bathrooms, and so on. Typically, the leaders are eventually asked how their teams did. The expected answer is typically filtered through the other team members to the leader and invariably is a modest "We could have done better" type of response. Sometimes I wondered if this stoic humility is really learned or if it is genetically patented in the Japanese.

Everyone receives the same education across Japan. The curriculum comes down from on high (Ministry of Education in Tokyo) and showers the country, we were told in loosely translated Japanese.

Starting in junior high and high school, students regularly study until midnight. This long day usually includes attending a *juku,* an after-school cram school to prepare students for the national university exam. This is perfectly normal and expected. Even though the younger generation has begun to "question" their parents' traditional ways, I didn't get the impression many Japanese kids question their rigidly scheduled lives—whether it is good or right for them. "That's just the way it is . . . because [all] Japanese want to go to the best university to get the best jobs in the best companies," a Japanese told me. The only problem is, even after all those years of studying so much, only about 40 percent of the students pass the exam. And of those, only the top scorers are admitted into the best universities. The "failures" either have to study full time for another year in another cram school to try to pass the exam the second time around, go to a less prestigious university, or settle for a terminal high school degree, which also puts a termination to any likelihood for career success—as defined by the Japanese.

One day I picked up the *Japan Times* (the most popular English edition of Japanese news) and learned that the Japanese Ministry of Education had passed a law that schools should close on Saturday. Maybe this was because enough younger Japanese complained their kids were too stressed. Maybe it was because the kids read too many articles about how the rest of the world's kids go to school much less than they do, especially kids in the United States. I guess that's one of the by-products of becoming an industrial power. You open yourself up to what's happening in the rest of the world and people start realizing there is more than one way to do things and that some values are relative.

In this case, I really do think the Japanese found out that American students only study until six in the evening, party on Friday nights, sleep in on Saturday, play some more Saturday, lounge around on Sunday, and start to think about school again Monday morning. I studied seven days a week myself (and if you believe that . . .). Anyway, closing schools on Saturday would still keep the Japanese kids way ahead of their American counterparts. Ironically, though, the Ministry of Education did not reduce the number of hours of school required—only the number of days—so most schools basically have kept their Saturday habit.

I think this whole situation illustrates the contrast between the Japanese and American work ethic. Ten- to twelve-hour days, six days a week—that's the norm for most white shirt and tie Japanese. That's not to say it isn't done in other countries either. Some high-tech start-ups, small business owners, or sometimes top-level executives in the United States live that kind of pace too. But here it's a societal thing. It's no wonder the Japanese are beating us in the trade game. All they ever seem to do is work except for their long coffee and smoke breaks, occasional golf rounds, and so on. But even then, their chitchat over coffee and their other "nonwork" activities seem to be all a part of their system of networking, connecting with each other, learning how the others think, being better able to work with one another. They might not be on the phone talking to a client or having brainstorming sessions related to a product quality problem, but they, in their Japanese way, are still learning things that will be useful "on the job."

I was talking to an American working for Applied Materials Japan who said most of the Japanese managers he knew in Japanese companies take off a day or two during the year; a few hadn't taken vacations for several years. Their lives revolve around the needs of their companies, and some have been known to die for their companies—literally.

I read in *Time* magazine several years ago that a Japanese wife sued her husband's company (totally unJapanese) because he allegedly died of a heart attack in a hotel room from being overworked.

In the preceding week her husband had been all over the world, not stopping for any breaks, having long meetings, experiencing jet lag and time zone changes nearly every day. The whole story got international press, probably because he died outside Japan. Afterward some Japanese companies started imposing vacations on their older employees, those who especially tended to work through vacations. Can you imagine—having to *impose* a vacation on an employee? Of course, it might end up being like the school "mandate." On paper and even by word, vacations are imposed, but no one probably will monitor it to see if anyone actually takes a vacation.

I mean who would be the first? If I were a Japanese employee, unless everyone else took longer vacations, I wouldn't do it. They're so "Don't be different" that it really baffles me as an American. How does anything new ever happen if they're all so "follow tradition," "maintain expectations," "do what's best for the company"? And even when they rebel à la Japanese, it seems to be in carefully orchestrated group demonstrations. I called them "self-controlled revolts."

I should add about Japanese and vacations that I wasn't always sure that what I was told by other Americans or what I read in the English press was accurate. I recalled seeing a lot of Japanese at tourist spots in the United States. If they weren't on vacation, it was one great way to work!

Little did Confucius know what an impact he would make on the Japanese when he taught the principles of total loyalty to one's superior, obedience to authority, and a keen reverence for education.

Still, despite all these strong traditions, the weakened Japanese economy and increasing exposure to the west is beginning to weaken some of this kamikaze spirit. Fewer companies are hiring. College grads from decent universities are taking jobs as bookkeepers, clerical workers, and other 'low-level" job categories. Women and nonfemale part timers are being displaced to make room for them.

This reminded me a little of the "big company-small town" phenomenon in the States, where the local mining company or auto company kind of dictated life for the town's inhabitants. I was glad this wasn't the norm, though, in the States. It was at these times when it was particularly enjoyable to have a "little America" in Japan via the community of expatriates and their families—something to remind us of "normalcy." It was especially therapeutic for Jan, I think, but I have to admit, it was really helpful for me to be able to drift mentally and emotionally among "my own." You could talk freely and even though there was a lot of diversity, in opinions and perspectives, there was a common value we shared around freedom of speech. Plus, we didn't have to know each other for 20 years to be able to speak openly.

Members of the American Club represented a variety of professions and levels of achievement. There were entrepreneurs, high-level managers, salespersons, mid-level engineers acting as technical advisers, and diplomats and their spouses. Many of these professionals, themselves, participated in club activities organized mostly by the spouses—which were 95 percent women. Picnics, walkathons for charities, museum visits, an occasional formal dinner, and other activities were planned for those interested. There were the usual nonstop talkers in the group whose lives centered totally around their kids and the problems with their kids' teachers and some of their schoolmates—that otherwise impeded their children's genius from coming through. Still others liked to talk about how the Japanese are too conformist, too competitive, too isolationist—too Japanese! And many talked about current events in the States.

I suppose in a way our community of expats coalesced faster than a normal group in the United States would simply because in a strange way there was almost a perceived "threat" from the outside (i.e., the Japanese). In those situations, though, it is never really clear whether we isolate ourselves or whether they exclude us. I'm sure that quickened the "friendship" development among us—we had to rely on one another for things we normally might expect from the outside community.

JAN

Being part of the Club sometimes also made information too easy to share, I thought. I got tired of the complaining by some of the expats and their spouses.

One woman couldn't stand the fish market smell, so she moved apartments to get away from it.

Fish markets are not my favorite place to visit either. But Japan's a fish paradise—I could find so many more kinds of fish here than I could in my store market in California. In fact, there are so many here I had no idea what three-fourths of them were or if any American had ever eaten them.

I was used to the displays in the Safeway near us, presenting the usual salmon, trout, and a few other fish in attractive displays—usually dead except for the lobster swimming in the aquarium. In the Tokyo markets, I could find everything from eel to tuna—and fresh! I mean the fish were often still flopping when the fishermen would grab them to chop off their heads in preparation for a filet. I was amazed at the speed and precision at which they could work with their large meat cleavers without cutting off their fingers in the process.

Despite some of the unpleasant things like fish market smells, I was so glad there were a few others in the American Club who shared my enthusiasm for new experiences and seemed open to changes and trying to understand a foreign culture. I tended to do spend time with these women and avoid those who seemed eternally caught up in outdoing each other for who could tell the worst story. I really felt sorry for their husbands, who probably had to listen to that every day.

After having been in Japan for a couple of months, I got some great news. A contact I had made through Matt at the American Club paid off. He expressed an interest in discussing several legal cases the firm was currently considering. Eventually, if there was a mutual interest, the firm might hire me on a case-by-case basis. Although the cases involved patent law, which that normally doesn't interest me much, I was so eager for any professional involvement that I was elated at the prospect. I had hoped to remain active as a researcher for the firm I had previously worked for. Unfortunately, in Japan I couldn't find an English law library that had adequate coverage of environmental law. I had also already tried to identify active environmental groups I might join in Tokyo, but either there was no real organized association or as an American I was seen as more of an intruder. I'm not sure it would have bode well with Muhashi, either, not that I cared entirely about that. It bothered me to care at all, though, which wouldn't have happened when I was younger. I wasn't sure if I was maturing or simply losing focus.

MATT

Ironically, I think it was Jan's curiosity about Japanese businesses and society that developed my own interest in understanding the Japanese. The information she discovered made me realize that I had been far too passive a player up to now. Except for my Japanese friends and co-workers I really had grown close to, I realized I had not taken much initiative to understand the Japanese. I told Jan I consciously decided that although I wasn't going to be as effective as I wanted to be in Japan, at least I was going to try to learn as much as I could about the Japanese. If ever I had to come back to Japan after this stint, I was going to come back with my eyes wide open.

I began asking questions and doing some research that I should have done long ago. I visited the embassy, talked to the commerce people, asked some of the Americans that had already been working in Japan for some years—some of whom had actually received some training before coming to Japan (those were usually associated with the large multinationals, like IBM, HP, GE, and so on).

Japan's ability to produce such high-quality products is in part, I discovered, due to its having adopted Deming's principles on manufacturing processes. Although U.S. industry had rejected people like Deming, Japan had eagerly embraced his ideas. It was a game of catch-up for them and they did not like being behind. But it also is part of their spiritual heritage. Friends told us that for centuries the Japanese believed that high-quality fine art works such as paintings, calligraphy, and pottery reflect the spiritual quality of their works and draw the admiration of all those who witness this quality. Jan wondered if today's Japanese even realized this is the origin of their quality orientation. It's like asking Americans why they want to achieve something. I don't think most ever think about it. They're brought up that way and each generation repeats itself. Just like I doubt the average Frenchman would be able to tell you why food is so important there. It just is, right?

Given the Japanese work ethic and their penchant for quality, Jan couldn't understand why the Japanese had neglected their environment for so many years. The answer, of course, was in the country's focus after World War II. Japan had set almost all its efforts on rebuilding its industry that had been destroyed in the war—not on maintaining its environment. A lot of rivers and the surrounding seas had been polluted as a result. As a country, though, Japan began to pass strict laws in the 1970s to regulate industry to avoid further destroying the environment. Depending on the industry, however, not all of the laws were consistently enforced. And just like in the United States, sometimes it was less expensive to get fined than to correct the problem. The Japanese people sacrificed and learned to work hard and improved their standard of living, but their environment has suffered because of it.

It didn't help that Japan's main religions no longer reinforce in a substantial way the interdependence between humankind and nature. Buddhism and Shintoism have held little more than a ceremonial place in Japanese society for some time. Shintoism is still practiced in Japan, but apparently in urban areas it is more a formality than anything else—a sign of respect for tradition. It is a religion that focuses on the natural powers and living things—wind, water, earth, and fire. It was the indigenous religion of the rural people of Japan. Jan witnessed a Shinto priest conducting a ceremony one day while she was walking to the Tokyo American Club. A small crowd was gathered in a store with a few people out on the sidewalk. Jan stopped to see what was going on. Being half a head taller than the Japanese, she could see a man dressed in ceremonial clothes touching an altar of fish, fruit—and she couldn't tell what else—with what looked similar to a small pompom. As he did so, he spoke some Japanese. The ceremony did not last long, and so Jan went on her way. Later, she learned that it was a Shinto priest blessing the opening of the store. This kind of ceremony was apparently customary when Japanese opened new stores or manufacturing sites.

In the rural areas, though, Shintoism is occasionally still practiced as a serious belief system. Instead of going to the doctor for ailments most would diagnose as medical problems, some very rural people seek out an exorcist to expel the evil spirits from the individual. Potions are concocted, sayings written, songs chanted, and other "medieval" cures are pursued in order to cure and bless. Most, however, would first turn to herbal medicine, acupuncture, chanting Buddhist sutras, massages, or other ways to be healed.

But it was not only Shintoism that has seemingly taken on only a ceremonial role in Japanese society. Buddhism, too, seems to no longer play a visibly important role in the daily lives of the Japanese. Yet, like Confucianism, it seems to underlie much of Japanese culture. One of the basic tenets of Buddhism is that of interdependence—everything depends on something else. There is no total isolation or total power one thing has over another without serious consequences for the lack of harmony in relationships. This whole notion of harmony and interdependence are pillars of Japanese culture.

This is interesting because Western society is at least partly based on the assumption that we humans can conquer everything—become a controller over nature and over other human beings if necessary. Japan, too, it seems had once brushed aside some of its belief that nature is an important part of human living. In the 1960s and 1970s, during the push for industrialization, instead of being concerned about the rivers and its sea it was polluting, Japan seemed to confine its respect for nature to its beautiful, but isolated gardens it has become so famous for. Some of the most beautiful gardens are at the Buddhist temple sites. Those gardens represent an efficient way of incorporating some of Buddhism into society. They're like our monuments to war veterans—an easy way to celebrate our value of liberty and life, regardless of whether we are becoming subtly indifferent to these values.

"Japan is going to do what it is going to do and as much you would like it to be different sometimes, you're not going to be able to change it," Jan told me one day, awakening me from a bit of reverie and complaining.

Although that was a depressing thought to an idealist like Jan, I think—for good reasons—she rarely dwelled on the negative. Instead, she turned her energies to her legal research, a part-time endeavor that was good for several reasons.

"It keeps me active in my profession, which is good for my morale," she said to me, "even if it's not very interesting work," she added. "It has also come at a time when I was ready to be challenged in a different way."

"Being a tourist was fantastic for the freedom it brought," she reflected to a friend of hers. "And being a mom has called on talents and skills that are incredibly important and challenging to develop. In looking back at it though, even though I don't think I would have admitted it then, I can now see signs sometimes of having been slightly depressed from the lack of professional growth and stimulation. Plus, moving from a highly structured kind of life as an attorney to one of complete lack of structure was really difficult sometimes. Of course, being pregnant and maybe not totally accepting this huge stomach you develop probably added to it! Then, too, there's the extra fatigue, not having your family around to help out. In fact, I think in reality what I missed a lot was just the absence of the 'familiar.' Japan is different, very different. Practicing law again has brought back some familiarity to my environment—a kind of security blanket," she admitted to her friend.

QUESTIONS FOR DISCUSSION

1. What can we learn about the Japanese from knowing something about their school system and their work expectations?
2. What appears to be the function of religion in Japan, especially Shintoism and Buddhism today? How are they manifested in present-day Japan as discussed in this chapter? What changes have occurred in your own culture in the last 30 or more years that perhaps reflect changes in cultural values?
3. How would you describe the stage of adaptation Jan is in now? What are the issues she has been able to deal with so far and what does this reflect about her personality?

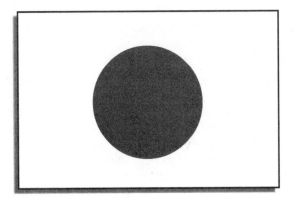

CHAPTER 6

Managing Relationships in Japan: Being Part of a Japanese Family

MATT

At Muhashi, we continued to have meetings as we strategized how we should promote MedTech's products within Muhashi's distribution network. It became evident to me that often the meetings were only a symbol for what had preceded them or what was to follow. The direction of conversation led me to believe that informal discussions or meetings to which I wasn't invited were being held to further discuss or refine what we talked about in our meetings. I assumed this because sometimes the follow-up meeting to which I was invited took a very different direction from the previous one—as though some new information between meetings had changed the previous discussion. Of course, I was gleaning information at our meetings through a translator or through their somewhat proficient English when English was spoken. Having thought about the open office spaces, though, I could see how information could easily be exchanged affecting the development of a particular issue. The topic could come up quite naturally in the course of conversation, and if you weren't there to hear the information or discuss it, a gap was created. But, in my case, I didn't speak Japanese so I wouldn't have understood the group discussions anyway. There were lots of gaps in my information sometimes. As long as I remembered that, I kept myself from making some unfair stereotypes.

The actual meetings themselves were different for me too. Sometimes there were periods of complete silence—probably less than 10 seconds, but it seemed like an eternity at times. And the Japanese would sometimes close their eyes as though they were pausing before moving on to the next point. Later I was told that this is common among the Japanese. It is probably their way of thinking through the issues that had been discussed up to that point—a moment of reflection.

At Muhashi they did not always bring papers to the meetings—at least not always to the staff meetings—as part of the ceremony that is almost always the case in the United States. It wasn't all that common for someone to take notes either at staff meetings. And I never did see what we would call a secretary at a meeting. I wondered how they had any record of what was discussed, who was to do what by when, and so on. Oral communication was definitely the rule, and I guess the Japanese were expected to listen well and remember what they heard. I felt kind of stupid sometimes sitting there, the only one with a pen and pad of paper. These were not like the negotiation meetings we had with them at MedTech. They came with a lot of papers and took copious notes, except Mr. Satoh. He just listened most of the time, speaking only on rare occasions to one of the other Japanese. I think they were taking notes word for word sometimes! But not at the staff meetings. Here within Muhashi, I had the impression they all already knew most of what was going to be said and so they usually didn't need to be reminded with notes. It almost seemed as though the real meeting had already occurred and this was just a formal symbol of something. There were hardly ever any follow-up memos to summarize the meeting or clarify tasks that were delegated, either—at least not many that I saw. When memos did float, they were typically in Japanese anyway, so I couldn't understand them unless I got a translator. Occasionally I was given a letter in English that went to a potential customer outside of Japan. After a while, if it were a two-page letter, I skipped all or most of the first paragraph. I might be exaggerating a little, but typically the first page was nonsensical to me. It was usually at best indirectly related to the meat of the letter. It was certainly not the "Let's-get-down-to-business-and-not-beat-around-the-bush" approach. I wondered if the Japanese actually read the first part either. Maybe it was part of the ceremony.

Muhashi representatives had been meeting with their network of people who acted as distributors for their other pharmaceutical products. Besides deciding how to promote the instruments, they were discussing how best to package the surgical instruments. Meetings were being held with both the distribution agencies and with hospitals and clinics. High-ranking officials in Muhashi had also been meeting with their cohorts in the Ministry of Health. It was important for the Japanese to maintain a close working association with their counterparts in government, but from another practical point of view, approval was needed for certain issues regarding domestic businesses entering into agreements with foreign business. All this activity on Muhashi's part was an indication of the importance of this venture to Muhashi. They wanted to ensure success as they saw a potentially large market for such instruments and as the pharmaceutical industry was becoming more competitive.

American giant Johnson & Johnson, Britain's BOOTS, the German multinational Manheim-Berringer, and the Swiss medical technology engineering firm SULZER were making inroads into Japanese hospital supply markets. Even though the Japanese firms monopolized the medical supplies distribution market, Muhashi figured it was only a matter of time—albeit perhaps 100 years—until foreign firms began to be serious competitors in some of Muhashi's product lines.

I found out later that serious competition to the Japanese meant a company that had the potential to get more than 6 to 7 percent of an established Japanese market where Japanese firms already had a solid and loyal distribution network. I'm only half joking too. Of course, there were always the Knorrs and Levis that had the lion's share of their markets. But that was typically because there had been no existing competition from Japanese firms in those markets.

Loyalty to business relationships in Japan is more important than loyalty to price or product, even at a financial cost sometimes. Cooperation and trust will always beat out the competition is their underlying philosophy.

As time passed, I learned indirectly of decisions being made without my input regarding the distribution, pricing, and promotion of the product. As I mentioned before, often no one told me anything, but I could just tell from things said in our meetings that this was going on. At first, I couldn't believe it. I went home totally depressed. I complained to others at the American Club. I moaned to Jan. I even cussed at the fish in the fish market one day because no one else would listen!

At first it took me several days to *recuperate* psychologically—to function normally. Here I had been invited to many meetings, some of which were held in English, and I thought I knew what developments were occurring. What seemed to really puzzle me was that during the "official" meetings (i.e., the ones I had been invited to), my ideas seemed to be well received. They assured me that my input would be seriously considered and had merit. They would "get back to me after they had discussed it with others." Usually I wasn't sure who those "others" were and wondered if it was a polite front.

In any case, they rarely did get back to me—at least not directly. Sometimes I would get my answer in that they would inform me of a decision—and the decision wasn't one I had suggested. Other times they would say it was still "under discussion." I later figured out either a decision really hadn't been made or—my guess is—it was bad timing for them to tell me.

This happened rather often. Despite the occasional reminders that Japan was changing and the economic conditions were leading up to some potentially drastic changes, I felt sometimes as though I had just stepped into the twilight zone. "I was in ninja land," I would mutter to myself when it just got to be too much. I had learned to expect the unexpected, despite the fact that one of my professors at Renssaeler had talked to us about Japanese management style. Unfortunately, that class was one of those memorize-regurgitate-forget experiences in which really understanding Japanese management didn't figure prominently in the class. It really began to sink in, though, that I was on my own in a culture I really didn't understand in the slightest.

I recall one specific issue I raised with my Japanese colleagues that illustrates some of the frustration I experienced on a regular basis. One of my ideas was to use a price skimming strategy going into the market with our products. It was perfect. There was no one else in the market and MedTech needed to recoup its R&D costs—classic pricing conditions for price skimming. I remember clearly Mr. Satoh and the others nodding in agreement with their "Japanese grunt" as I called it. Sometimes it reminded me of a dog with that long low growl just before barking. Only the Japanese never barked. They only smiled or would say after the "grunt," "This is an idea we can think about. This is something we can discuss with 'the others.'"

Question 1: If you were Matt, what would you do to increase your influence in Muhashi?

Although the Japanese did seem willing to consider my ideas, they seemed to do whatever pleased them. It—and I don't mind saying it—teed me off. They seemed two-faced sometimes—one was American and the other Japanese. But in their defense I learned one thing as time went on: If you can't understand a system, you certainly can't influence it strategically. And for the first year I certainly didn't understand the Japanese well enough to influence them meaningfully.

When I confronted Mr. Satoh on the issues of pricing and distribution, I was told that this (the Japanese way) was how all their products were distributed and priced and that Muhashi had been profitable for more than 100 years selling this way. Mr. Satoh reassured me that this venture would be another profitable one for Muhashi—and MedTech. To be honest, during the first months I wasn't quite sure what to tell Jeff when he would call to get an informal progress report. If I had any details, I would tell him. If not—which was more often the case—I would usually say something like, "It's all coming along, but I need to clarify a few things with Muhashi to give you any specifics." I'd tell him I'd get back with him just as soon as possible. It killed me to say that because I realized it sounded exactly like what the Japanese would often tell me when I asked them about something. The difference probably was that when the Japanese said it, they actually did have some specific ideas on it; I didn't. But in fairness to the Japanese, it's possible—even likely—I learned later that a decision simply hadn't been made. Decisions, I learned in Japan, cannot be rushed. A French expat at the American Club told me only half jokingly, "Decisions in Japan are like wine in France—the longer they take to develop, the better they are."

The Japanese must love good decisions.

One day Jeff told me he needed some solid figures soon to give to the board in order to satisfy them that the venture was everything we had promised. Four months had passed and "the board is eager to find out if we were just playing them for more money or what," Jeff stated. This was probably what I needed, because up to that point I had basically avoided confronting the Japanese on most issues. Now I had to do something. Jeff was expecting a solid answer and I didn't want to let him down.

I went to Mr. Satoh and told him I was expected to know when the next product would be shipped, what the expected shipments were over the next year, and what expected revenues were for this year. Mr. Satoh told me he would have all the information he could get in my office by that afternoon. And he did. At first I was really proud of myself. I had finally demanded the Japanese do something and they responded! Then I realized that they had probably already had the information and just hadn't thought to share it with me. It seemed like I was always doing that—guessing about motives or behaviors I wasn't sure about.

Despite the economic downturn in Japan, the news was quite good. Projected sales revenues were a clean $3 "mil." Granted this wasn't much in the grand scheme of things, but it was even slightly beyond what MedTech had figured for the first year based on information traded with Muhashi earlier. MedTech's share of that was $1.8 million, which seemed a little under what it should have been, I thought. But the Japanese drive a hard bargain.

I remember when we were negotiating with Muhashi back home. The Japanese asked a lot of questions during the initial meetings. But I had the distinct impression they already knew half the answers—how I don't know, but they're extremely resourceful. That was one thing I did remember about Japanese management from one of my marketing classes at UCLA which was confirmed by our experience with them. The Japanese want to know everything they possibly can about a firm and its key decision makers before entering into an agreement. They ask a lot of questions to find out what the other side is interested in. They even do research to find out about the firm's reputation with its current customers, how long it has been in business, and so on. I even learned that before entering a foreign market, Muhashi usually sends one or two employees to study the people, their habits, and the competitors for as long as one year before making a decision to enter the market or strike up a relationship with a foreign firm. How they justify the time for all that on their budget I'd like to know. They must have a keen dislike for "unnecessary" risks.

So I called Jeff and told him the good news and set up a tentative production and shipping schedule with him on the phone. Jeff wanted me back in the States to oversee the quality on this first major production run and to help get set up for overseas shipping. That was fine with me. Jan was scheduled to fly back with me to the States with Jeff and Michelle soon. They would spend time with their grandparents and I could combine a little pleasure with mostly business. Jan and the kids were going to fly back to New York to spend a week with my parents also. That's a long trip—Tokyo to New York—so they were planning on spending about three weeks in the Bay Area before making the hop to New York.

I was glad they were going to spend time with my parents. We were never very close. When my dad accepted a promotion to New York, I had just graduated from high school. I didn't want to leave the West, so I stayed. Dad was so wrapped up in his career and Mom was the loyal IBM wife. We had just grown apart over the years, and after high school, it was a natural separation. Jan had a hard time understanding all this, and I was glad she wanted our kids to know their grandparents on both sides.

For other reasons, I looked forward to being back in the United States and also doing something concrete for the joint venture.

The plane ride over the Pacific gave me a chance to reflect on what had happened early on in the negotiations with Muhashi, which helped me understand why things were how they were now. In retrospect, I think what the Japanese had done was to know exactly what our tolerances were and then push us to that limit. We had asked for 70 percent of the revenues, given the fact that we had done the work and incurred the product R&D expenses and all the other start-up costs. If we didn't supply the product, Muhashi wouldn't have anything to sell. Muhashi took the tack that they knew the Japanese market very well, had all the necessary contacts to get the product approved—no easy feat they said—and that distributing the product would be easy because their distribution network was one established well over four generations. I thought it interesting that they used the term "generations" and not just referred to the number of years. They stressed how long they had been in business, that their name was trusted in the hospital products market.

They also said they could protect us from other Japanese companies that would try to copy the product. That way, the joint venture would not be considered a foreign firm. Mr. Satoh said it would "be very difficult for MedTech to penetrate Asian markets by itself." By now I learned that "very difficult" meant nearly impossible to impossible. Other things I learned were interesting to me from the perspective of doing international business. For example, in Japanese patent law, U.S. patents are not necessarily honored. For example, Japan does not recognize music patents after 20 years. Japanese patent law, we learned from them, can have very broad implications. You don't really patent a product in the same way as you can in the United States, Mr. Satoh said. "In the United States, it is more of an umbrella patent," he explained. This protects U.S. firms from competition. "It is an exclusionary kind of approach," he added. Mr. Satoh continued, "In Japan, we can patent very narrow aspects of a product. This allows Japanese competitors to enter the same markets with novel characteristics—albeit very narrowly novel sometimes."

Mr. Satoh explained that among Japanese firms, the patents are usually mutually respected, but this is not always the case between Japanese and foreign firms. For example, Mr. Satoh told me of a British firm that had come to Japan with a new, more efficient way to measure various characteristics of a person's blood. The method was patented and quite soon the firm noticed that a Japanese pharmaceutical company began getting patents for various aspects of an instrument that operated similarly. There were no illegalities because there were novel differences between the two methods. The British claimed the differences were trivial, though, and that essentially the Japanese firm had taken their instrument and made small changes to warrant the patent. Eventually, the British firm formed a partnership with the Japanese company to avoid an eventual loss of market share and profits.

Without claiming genius, I think what Muhashi was trying to say politely to us was "There's no way you're going to succeed on your own. Your only chance is to join us." They never did come right out and say it—and especially that way—but it was a fairly obvious message. And they were probably right. But this is general business strategy everywhere—not just in Japan. If you have an advantage, you exploit it to some degree. Their clear advantage was in their connections—with the government for approvals and with their customers they distributed to.

This is why most successful American companies that have been in established Japanese markets for years still only hold a meager 5 to 8 percent of the market. They try to go it alone. Of course, there are the exceptions. Companies like Borden and L'Oréal dissolved their partnership with a Japanese firm because of too many restraints. They seem to be successful on their own.

In our case, Muhashi knew we were desperate to find a partner and get some sales going if we wanted to remain solvent. Who told them this I don't know. But they knew it. So we ended up with 49 percent and they with 51 percent. I later learned that in industries considered to be of national interest, Japanese law prohibits foreign companies from owning more than 49 percent of a joint venture anyway. The question was this: Would it have been better to have complete control over pricing and promotion and 100 percent of the profits, whatever they would be, or to join Muhashi and have little control over the promotion and pricing and receive about one-half the profits?

I later learned that recently there were some "counter-Japanese" elements in Japanese business that bucked the current system in larger firms—which probably would have been quite intolerable only a decade or more ago. Some of these Japanese sought foreign businesses that wanted to bypass the typical Japanese distribution network; others sought professionals and managers who might be interested in switching jobs. Although these strategies sound perfectly normal in a "free" market system, they are still not wholly accepted by the larger Japanese firms.

Question 2:   *Knowing what you know now, would you have joined Muhashi in a joint venture, partnered with one of the "renegade" Japanese firms looking to bypass the typical distribution network, or have "gone it alone"?*

Fortunately, I became friends with a few Japanese co-workers after I had been in Japan about four months. I got most of my revelations about what was going on during some of the "after work-before going home" sessions at one of the local bars my Japanese colleagues visited almost nightly. After I had been in Japan about four months, I was invited to go with them to their local hangout. At first, I politely turned them down. Going to bars wasn't what I was used to doing after work. I felt guilty if I left Jan alone more than I already did, given the fact that it was her career that was on hold and not mine. Eventually, however, I learned from some other Americans that being invited to go with the Japanese to the bar was a critical invitation, one that indicated I was accepted by the members of that particular group, an invitation I shouldn't refuse, they said.

This advice was very sound because being part of this small group was critical to helping me understand the Japanese better. It was during these bar talks that I learned a lot about Mr. Satoh. He was an interesting character, apparently typical of the Japanese who reach the top of an important subsidiary or senior management of the conglomerate's headquarters. The eldest of three children, and male, his parents expected the most from him. He was to set the example for his little brother, the third child. And so Satoh set his goals high and did not stop until he had accomplished what his parents had set out for him.

Beginning with junior high school, he attended one of the infamous Japanese *jukus,* an after-school cram school. Studying several hours after the *juku* helped him pass the stiff university exams and score well enough to enter perhaps Japan's most prestigious university, Tokyo University. An engineering graduate of Tokyo University, he had come into Muhashi along with over 80 of its other graduates. They all knew each other. They had entered Tokyo University at the same time, moved through their courses together, and finished together—four years of eating, sleeping, singing, playing, drinking, and yes, sometimes studying together had created a genuinely cohesive group. Of course, not all of them had done all of these activities together, but they all knew of each other and shared this kind of lifestyle, university heritage, and hopes of their parents.

The closest phenomenon we have in the States to this kind of cohesion I am told by my bicultural friends is a fraternity, but often even those tend to dissipate after graduation. Not even Harvard or Stanford has alumni groups as tight as Japanese university graduates, especially the top Japanese schools, I was told.

So Satoh, like his compatriots—all males—entered Muhashi at the same time. Nearly all of them lived in company-supplied dormitories to formally begin the building of close personal relationships necessary for success in Japanese companies. Although this helped ease the necessity for the new Muhashi recruits to find and pay for lodging themselves, the more I learned about the Japanese system in general, the more I began to believe this was one more practice that subtly built a dependence on Muhashi.

The first month or so of employment consists of orientation sessions. The first meeting is presided over by top-ranking officials and the president of Muhashi. Family members are often invited to these sessions that typically resemble pep rallies more than anything else. Here they often learn and sing company songs and recite company slogans reflecting the moral philosophy of the founders of the company. This was all incredible to me—the idea of having your parents, say, at your work orientation and singing company songs together. This seemed more like what you would do when being inducted into some secret cult or maybe the Hall of Fame. After talking to others, I found out that Muhashi is somewhat more traditional than other companies. I also learned that small Japanese companies do not share many of these traditions that working professionals have in the large Japanese firms—housing, transportation allowances, union representation, and so on.

New employees are also taught about company history, the product lines, their customers, the proper way to sell their products, the proper way to introduce oneself, the way to show respect to those at different levels in the firm and to those outside the firm, and on and on it goes.

After the orientation, the situation begins to only slightly resemble a work week like someone who's beginning a career in the States. Satoh's first assignment, typical of the university graduates, was to work in one of the production labs alongside high school graduates and a few other university graduates. Their apprenticeship consisted of learning the business from the ground floor and sharing responsibilities with those they would one day manage. In fact, during the first eight to ten years of their careers, these highly sought-after university graduates remain in lower-level management positions, learning the various facets of the business.

Can you imagine someone from Wharton in the United States or HEC in France staying in lower-level management for eight to ten years? I mean we're talking about two extremes here—the humble, maintain-your-place Japanese intelligentsia versus the stereotypically self-confident, self-centered, money-monger American elite.

Anyway, Satoh moved around in various marketing positions during those first years, gaining a broader view of the organization. As he moved from one position to another, his cohorts from Tokyo University moved around some also, often exchanging similar positions. All the while, Mr. Satoh, along with the others, was not only getting to know the business but deepening his working relationship with his cohorts and others who worked there. These networks became all so important as decisions had to be made and the necessary commitment gained.

After slightly more than four years with Muhashi, Mr. Satoh was given his first management position as a *kakaricho* (subsection chief) in the production area, equivalent to production manager in a U.S. firm. Up to this point, although informal evaluations are occurring, apparently almost no visible and explicit attempt is made to distinguish among employees' performance. In fact, I understand that although not everyone contributes exactly equally during the first ten to even fifteen years of service, it is considered dishonorable for employees to communicate in any way that they are working longer or harder or smarter than anyone else. Distinguishing personal performance from someone else's simply is not the Japanese way. "Sometimes it is discouraging," one of my Japanese business friends told me. "You know you are doing much better than some of your co-workers, but you all pretend as if you don't notice. You act humble. You perform so the team is considered good. You surrender yourself. But down deep, many of us wish we could say something. Fortunately, most of the time, things work out in the end, but you have to maintain a long-term perspective; otherwise, you feel as though you might never see equity," he added.

Most Japanese who are typed as "high potentials" à la Japanese university graduates like Mr. Satoh, are also treated very similarly salarywise and in their work conditions until they approach *middle* management, which sometimes does not occur until after close to 15 years with the company, depending on its size and the economic conditions at the time (which might "force" early retirements). At that point, the individual's performance begins to count for somewhat more than his or her alma mater. But even then, performance is noticed but not touted.

Despite the apparent slow promotional scheme, though, I was told that often within the first month of employment, the new hires know who the high potentials are as a result of very subtle differences. For example, even very small differences in salary, as little as 1,000 yen—almost nothing—can symbolize one's higher status in the cohort group.

For Mr. Satoh, his performance was noticed, and five years later, as retirements opened the way, he was given the title *kacho* (section chief) of a marketing group. By this time, Satoh had developed a reputation as someone who was very skilled in human relations and a very hard worker, probably the two most important ingredients for promotion at this point in his career. The manager he replaced was someone who had held several *kacho* positions, but who had never moved beyond this level. I was told this is not atypical, holding a Japanese manager at this position for an entire career. But as with other Japanese managers, Satoh didn't do it alone. He had the support of his peers who were also hard workers and who made the group look good. Plus, as is typical of Japanese firms, Muhashi had made sure Satoh had a mentor all along.

This *senpai-kohai* (senior-junior) relationship is critical for Japanese professionals. It is expected that one's "office senior" will help show his junior the ropes. This is an individual in whom one can confide and ask for help, not just for work-related problems but personal ones as well. Mr. Satoh's various *senpai* along the way often gave him advice about working with his employees, about marriage, and the importance of showing your company that you are faithful to your employer. In fact, it was Mr. Ito, Satoh's first section chief, who introduced Satoh to his wife, which is fairly common in Japanese corporations.

Up to his promotion to *kacho*, Mr. Satoh had also been moved to three different locations, two within the larger Tokyo area and once to Kobe, where Muhashi had an important production facility. Although Satoh was still considered in marketing, part of his company education was to understand the product from the ground floor.

The Japanese employee typically fills out a "wish" sheet, explaining the kind of experiences and position that he or she would like, which the company considers in making its assignments. This is very much like the "dream sheet" in the military in the States. You put down where you would like to be stationed with two alternatives. Of course, as with the Japanese firm, it is always the "needs of the service" that prevail if there is any discrepancy. Until very recently, apparently these decisions were always accepted with great humility. Now I am told that occasionally younger Japanese are beginning to evaluate such assignments with a more personal perspective and end up switching companies to find a more suitable position. This does not speak well of that Japanese, though, and often he or she is regarded as someone who cannot be completely trusted and, therefore, less employable by many Japanese corporations.

This of course is really different from the Silicon Valley culture where I began my career with HP. If you don't change employers every two to four years, you limit yourself. Changing companies is the fastest way to get a higher salary and better promotions. Talk about contrasts!

Well, to make a longer story shorter, Satoh became *bucho* (department head) at around 42 years old, I was told. This is a solid middle management position with liberal benefits: a generous expense account, travel opportunities, golf club memberships, and so on. Satoh was an avid golfer with a 5 handicap. He was out on the course at least once every two weeks. Besides personally enjoying it, it was an important way for him to entertain guests, often government employees, and maintain connections with former university graduates.

Being seen as a high performer (in the Japanese sense of "performing"), he moved from middle management to a directorship at age 47, where he is now. Of course, Satoh made his climb during a time when seniority was the most important criterion for advancement. This was during Japan's phenomenal growth after World War II up until recently. In a lot of companies, ability has become more important now than seniority alone. With slower growth, senior management positions are becoming limited. For Satoh, if he continues his progression, in several years he could well find himself in a managing director's position and then later as a senior managing director, sometimes mingling with the government ministers who form industrial policy. Of course, if Satoh isn't considered managing director or senior managing director material, he will likely be "retired" into a top management position of one of Muhashi's subsidiaries. But if he is considered superior management material, he might even be inducted into Muhashi's parent company. Even when this happens, though, because most of Satoh's associations are in Muhashi, he would still largely be considered a Muhashi employee in the minds of the parent firm's employees.

I also found it very interesting that someone can leave a government ministry position and enter a private company at a very high level of senior management. Then I realized that similar kinds of things happen in the U.S. defense industry, an industry very tight with the government. The practice of ministers moving into top-level firm positions is not uncommon in Japan, dating back to World War II if not before. At that time, Japan's sole goal was to rebuild and become independent of its conquerors—the United States and the Allied powers. Dependence on other countries does not characterize Japan's history as I have found out. Quite the contrary. After doing a little bit of reading, I learned that Japan had invaded China more than once and still held Korea hostage up to Japan's loss in World War II. But then, what goes around comes around. China attacked Japan a couple of times in China's early history too.

To this day, the Koreans apparently have very strong feelings against the Japanese, even though I understand the younger Japanese are much more tolerant and even welcoming to foreigners than were the World War II generation of Japanese. I guess the military was quite brutal in its takeover of Korea. In Japan Koreans are supposed to change their last name to appear Japanese if they remain as "foreign citizens." Koreans who were taken back to Japan after the war are still not considered Japanese and are not technically given citizen status, even if they are third- or fourth-generation Japanese-Korean children. Even second- and third-generation Japanese-born Koreans must register annually with their local government and they used to get their fingerprints taken. Obviously, most of these Koreans are limited in their ability to climb the social or financial ladder in Japan. "We are limited because of who we are and what our origins are," a Korean friend told Jan. "Many of us feel second class here. It is like being a non-communist in a communist country. You just don't get the same opportunities. The difference is, in Japan, you can't decide to become Japanese. It's not your decision. Maybe some day things will be different for our children," he said thoughtfully.

I wondered if most of the Japanese people themselves agree with the leftover policies and attitudes about the Koreans reflected by the old government leaders.

I was told by friends at the American Club that a long time ago the urban Japanese, especially those in Tokyo, felt superior to many of the rural Japanese, especially those whose families come from feudal families where animals were butchered and hides were tanned. Slaughtering animals is forbidden by Buddhist teachings and those who did so were considered unclean. I don't know if any of these notions linger on. My hunch is that many of the younger Japanese aren't even aware of these differences.

Question 3: What are some of the ethnic prejudices in your culture and what is their basis historically? How do these prejudices relate to fundamental values of your culture?

Knowing about some of these prejudices sometimes made us seem all the more strangers. I don't mean we don't have prejudice in the States—we certainly do—but Jan and I never have shared the view that any group of people is superior to another by birthright. The idea that whites are superior to blacks, that Chinese are superior to the Malays, or any other such notion seemed savage at the least and ignorant at best. Our Japanese friends personally felt the problem is minor and said those kinds of feelings are usually not a topic of discussion in Japanese society.

From these and other experiences, we learned a really important lesson from our stay in Japan. Those who have no insider's view cannot possibly judge a people. From many an after-work evening out with some of my Japanese co-workers, I learned the personal, caring side of the Japanese—not the stereotypes one hears from other Americans and the extraordinary events one picks up from the media. But then, whether you're Japanese or Korean, black or white, you don't have to overtly commit prejudicial acts to be held in contempt by someone. Doing nothing to help the less fortunate is also part of the problem.

Besides, however we felt about the Japanese views on social issues, we couldn't argue that this was one solid mass of industrious workers, accomplishing something probably no other people had in such a short time. The Japanese are fighters, and their recent history shows this. After World War II, the Japanese government led the strike toward economic independence. Workers put in very long days. Government officials developed policies for the sole purpose of becoming economically powerful. As industries grew, business leaders and government officials worked together. Politicians conferred with heads of industries on economic policy. The close-knit relationship between government and business created a kind of cohesive mindset that still pervades Japan today despite the occasional minister who steps down to repent symbolically of mismanagement. Most outsiders see these things as completely dependent on crises. If no crisis arises, there is no apparent shame to acknowledge, and no change occurs.

Groupings of the largest industrial concerns in Japan, such as Keidanren, which represents nearly 900 corporations and other business associations, have enough power to significantly influence the economic policy in Japan. It was this group, my Japanese colleagues tell me, that essentially put the Liberal Democratic Party into power in Japan. The LDP is actually a conservative group despite its name, and even though it has strong, broad representation from farmers, big business, and government bureaucrats, it has been primarily a tool for keeping big business in the forefront.

This kind of inbreeding has caused a few wrinkles in their system, though. The fact that the LDP party has been the overwhelming governing party since World War II has created a sense of invulnerability, I think. Although bribery is commonplace within the political parties in Japan, in the Japanese press, until recently, it has been rarely covered in the same way or to the same extent as in the American press. I can't remember the minister's name who was found with several million dollars of gold in the walls of his office—gifts over time from who knows how many companies. Although corruption has been a way of life in Japanese government for many years, it has only recently gotten a lot of exposure in the foreign press and has started to see more coverage in their own journalism. Prime ministers in Japan have come and gone in the last few years all because of embarrassments they brought on the government because of corruption. Heads of large corporations have also been shamed into resigning to take the symbolic blame of corruption within their firm. Elections in Japan have reflected that the Japanese themselves recognize this corruption looks bad—and is bad—and have deposed former LDP leaders with others who have promised reform.

In a country like Japan, where "bribes" or "favors" are a normal part of the exchange because you live in a society that is so interdependent, I think you simply have to accept that as a part of life. We all hope it is done for the greater good of the people, but reality is that it won't always be the case. You're not going to have just the advantages of interdependence.

Question 4:   *To what extent is there corruption in your national government? How is such corruption handled when it becomes visible to the populace? Is corruption relative to one's culture?*

My Japanese friends tell me nothing fundamental has changed, though, and that not much probably will in the near term at least. I am told radical changes will require a revolution by the younger generation! If it is radical change that occurs, though, I hope I won't be around if and when that happens.

In a sense, though, maybe it's already happening. Potential leaders like Ryutaro Hashimoto, who show a certain rugged individualism and non-Japanese style, are perhaps going to be the new generation of leaders. Although an experienced politician, Hashimoto is said to be a media junkie, showing up on television in everything from the traditional *kendo* dress as he practices ancient dueling with a bamboo sword to flashy clothes with his long sideburns. He's also known for his directness, quick temper, and arrogance, not exactly traits traditionally rewarded in Japanese society. Word has it that he's very popular with the ladies and that a former mistress even published an account of his amorous techniques.

Many Japanese question the true motives of their leaders and doubt they will bring the reform that has been promised. I think all this reveals the clear centralized power structure that still permeates Japan. No matter who the leader, change seems to come grudgingly. In a society built on the importance of connecting relationships, it would logically be unlikely that one individual could have a tremendous influence on anything.

I have learned a lot from living and working in Japan. But it's funny being an outsider. You go through those phases of feeling like you don't understand anything that's going on, then you gather a little information over time that seems to explain a number of things, and you—I—tend to hold on to that like the goose that laid the golden egg. Sometimes just when you think you're beginning to understand them, you see something that contradicts everything else. It's a cycle, for sure. And you've got to want to understand and be willing to live in total frustration at times, or you're doomed forever. I don't mean to sound overly pessimistic. But this is why it's so helpful to have friends in that culture who can explain things to you. Fortunately, I had a few Japanese co-workers who befriended me fairly early on. It's the key, I think.

I think in 10 or 20 years I might begin to really understand the Japanese. Until then, I hope I can just survive my term and do the best possible for MedTech. Whatever happens, though, Jan and I agree that we have seen and experienced things we never ever would have—or could have—had we stayed in the States. Besides, Japan is a beautiful country. The people are very polite and respectful. They all try to get along, even if it's on the surface. Americans, I've decided, are not much different. But I'm not sure it's all bad. Until the last few years, it appeared to me—admittedly, one of the majority group—that Caucasians, Asians, blacks, Hispanics, and others all got along fairly well in the United States. It's only been the last few years since events like the Rodney King beating that I have begun to realize the deep underlying hostilities which ethnic groups seem to have harbored against what they perceive as the dominant group—us.

QUESTIONS FOR DISCUSSION

1. What are five practices by the Japanese that indicate the importance of relationships?
2. How might Muhashi's relationship with MedTech be reflected in its relationship with Matt? What are the symbols of this relationship? What appears to be Matt's role in their partnership?
3. Do you think MedTech could be successful in the Japanese market without Muhashi? Why or why not?
4. The kind of recruitment and advancement system described here shows a very different approach from firms in most of the rest of the world. How does this cohort recruitment and the type of career development and advancement system Muhashi characterizes fit into the Japanese culture in general? Would it be effective in firms in your country?
5. What can we learn about the challenge of living in a foreign culture through the experiences and thoughts of Matt and Jan?

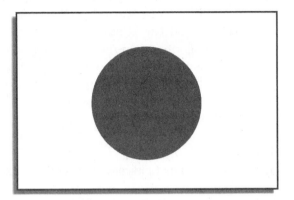

CHAPTER 7

Managing Relationships in Japan: Power and Hierarchy

JAN

It had been about two and a half years since we had left the United States, and I was wondering when Matt's job would end here. Jeff was 4 now and Michelle, 2. I really wanted Jeffrey to start kindergarten in the States if that could be worked out. The initial "agreement" between Muhashi and MedTech was for Matt to stay one year, and although I agreed to the indefinite extension, I was beginning to think we had spent enough time in Japan.

I don't know if Matt sensed my slight uneasiness or if he felt it himself. But it was now February and he announced one day that we should head off to snow country and take a break.

"I've already talked to Sue [an American friend in Tokyo] and she'll gladly watch Jeffrey and Michelle while we're gone for a week or so. I can talk to a few travel agencies and find a package that's fun and not too expensive," he said cheerfully.

Although we had originally thought of heading off to a resort around Mount Fuji, we both felt like going someplace where they speak English. After some research, we decided Whistler Resort was just the right place. About an hour and a half north of Vancouver, British Columbia, it was easily one of the best resorts in the world—huge, a vertical drop of over 5,000 feet, a couple of gondolas, a bunch of high-speed lifts, and some fantastic chutes and tree skiing. We paid for the package and couldn't wait to go. Psychologically, we were both ready for a break.

Landing in Vancouver was impressive—seeing the islands just off the coast, beautifully forested and so green, and then the contrasting "man"-made skyscrapers in Vancouver, surrounded by the more beautiful nature's green and white skyscrapers—the Coast Mountain range of Canada meeting the Cascade mountains of Oregon and Washington. It was really a sight. Vancouver itself is a fascinating city, very cosmopolitan with Chinese, Japanese, Vietnamese, and other cultural and ethnic groups mixing in. With only a week's vacation, we didn't have the time to explore the city like we wanted to, but we loved what we saw.

Five of the days we stayed on the mountain in a recently renovated log cabin lodge and had an absolutely great time. I didn't really care for the moose and elk heads that adorned some of the walls of the lodge, but it usually goes with the territory. Our room had its own gas-lit fireplace with a view of the mountain. Matt was loving and romantic. The whirlpool bath was totally relaxing after a full day of skiing. We both thought we had found paradise. We didn't want to leave. Most importantly, a low-pressure system combined with an arctic flow had dropped some of the best snow we had ever skied. Unlike the Sierra cement that often falls in the Sierra Nevada, this was light and dry stuff. By the fifth day, though, our thighs were just gone. There was just nothing left by midday.

When it came time to return to Japan, Matt offered to send me down to my parents for a couple of weeks to relax, drop in at my old law firm, and see some friends. I was a little concerned about the kids and missed them even after only a week, but Matt reassured me everything would be okay. I decided to take him up on his offer (you never know when those offers are going to come around!).

Upon returning to Japan, Matt arranged for the kids to stay at another friend's house while our friend Sue "recuperated," as he put it. And because Matt's Japanese colleagues knew he didn't have to worry about feeling guilty for staying out late, he went out more regularly with "the guys" to their favorite bar after work.

MATT

Working all day and then going with Ken and those guys to the bar afterward really wreaks havoc on my sleep schedule. I hated getting in around midnight or one in the morning. Sometimes I had a problem getting to work by 9 A.M.

After hanging up the phone with Jan one day, I thought again how different expectations were between spouses in Japan and the United States. Unlike some of my Japanese counterparts, Jan would not be waiting up for me until midnight or one—I wouldn't either if I were she. In fact, I wouldn't want her to. I'd have to look—and smell—pretty bad by that time.

I have to admit, though, the time at the bar was interesting. It was during these after-work sessions that my Japanese colleagues unbuttoned their shirts, so to speak, and actually talked frankly. I couldn't quite figure it out, though, why they would be so protective of information and so impersonal on the job and then slip in an occasional 'tell-all' statement or story at the bar. It wasn't like one of the employees was alone with me and this would only be his and my secret. We were always in a small group—three or four of us.

It was during these after-work sessions that I really became educated about how things worked in Japan. I learned that Muhashi's distribution arm had apparently been part of Muhashi for over 100 years—it was part of the family of firms representing nearly every industry in Japan and gathered under the wing of the parent corporation. That seemed almost unbelievable to me—100 years was a little under half the age of my country! Daiman Department Store is over 300 years old! Often, as it was with the Muhashi group, family members in the various industry groupings and networks within the conglomerate had known each other for generations. This was balanced by the fact that traditionally new college graduates were hired from the elite schools every year. And like most other *keiretsu* groups, as they called them, and which Muhashi's "family" resembled, it was a top-down organization, clearly indicating the role of hierarchy in Japan.

"Hierarchy is important in giving order to things," my friend Ken (short for Kenichi) told me. Ken was one of the few clear English-speaking Japanese I had met. "Several years ago," he continued, "when Muhashi was having financial difficulty in its antique glassware group, it went to its suppliers, all the way down to the individual families that gathered the most basic raw materials to make the glass, telling them how much Muhashi could pay for their work. It was basically the family's problem to figure out how to survive if the wage Muhashi was paying wasn't sufficient. Although this does not happen often, when it does, the big guy always wins. If one of these small family businesses threatens to sell—or does sell—to another company instead, the business can be blackballed. After all, if it is disloyal once, it could do it again. That leads to mistrust in a system which has been stable and dependable for generations, one that has absolutely depended on a system of interdependence." Mistrust in a society that has treated interdependence as its lifeblood is hari-kiri, I thought to myself.

In fairness, though, if it is one of the small firms that needs help and its larger, more powerful "parent" is able, it will always come to the small firm's aid. "It is very much like a father to a child," one of my Japanese friends mentioned.

My Japanese colleagues were always quick to add to these tidbits of information that Japan is changing. What was true "one hundred years ago may not be true in the next one hundred," they would say. I think there was a message there.

I remember another experience I had during one of these after-work "talks." In fact, I'll never forget it. I had been trying to learn some Japanese from a tutor, a single Japanese woman who had not found a job in a "good" company. So I got brave and asked the server for another round of drinks. As I was asking for the drinks, my Japanese colleagues all burst out laughing, after which one quickly spoke some Japanese to the hostess in an apologetic tone. Being tired and relaxed, I probably wasn't as embarrassed as I should have been; in fact, I started laughing too, not knowing what we were laughing about. Finally, one of my Japanese colleagues explained to me, laughing intermittently, that I had just more or less insulted the server.

Apparently, I used the "you" form to the hostess that you would use to address an elderly woman. I burst out laughing when I heard this, but I wasn't really laughing at what I had done so much as how crazy I thought this country was. If it wasn't one thing, it was something else. I rarely seemed to know what was going on. In English "you" is suitable for addressing *anyone*. Even in French, there are only two forms of "you." But in Japanese, there is a very clear distinction by age, gender, position, etc. You don't use the same word for "you" if you are talking to someone one generation older than you, and you also use a different expression when talking to a child or to an animal. I just couldn't believe people would want to complicate something seemingly rather simple. It wasn't until later, as I began to understand the Japanese better, that it all made sense.

Question 1: How does language reflect values or "perspectives" of your own culture?

In a society that is highly differentiated socially, speech is one way to indicate and acknowledge such social differences. I doubt it was a conscious strategy by whoever invented Japanese, but the extreme complexity also made it all the more difficult for a foreigner to integrate into such a society. Coming from a culture where "you" refers to everyone from the poorest, least educated child to the president of the United States and to animals of any kind, it was kind of comical to see all the different forms of address to fit the status of the person or thing you were addressing. I didn't know something simple could be so complicated. And then there was gift giving also. Knowing when to give gifts, whom to give them to, and what gifts were acceptable all served as built-in barriers to penetrating the Japanese culture.

All in all, those "nonwork" hours spent after work were really helpful to understand how things work here in Japan.

When Jan returned from her extended stay with her parents, she was really glad to see all of us. The caseload at her old firm had decreased because a falling out between partners had caused a division within the firm. Finally, one partner left and took some of the business and some of the attorneys with her. Jan's mentor stayed with the firm. "Right now the caseload wouldn't have justified hiring another attorney," Jan told me. I think she had ambivalent feelings about that—thinking about what might have been and what couldn't happen now even if we had been able to return.

We had both grown immensely from the challenging experiences in Japan even though those experiences were quite different. For Jan, it was leaving an absorbing career and learning to supplant that activity and redirect her energy to other things and explore a totally different culture. That can be really tough for a lot of people and some never do succeed. We saw many couples fail in Japan because of the difficult cultural experience. A few got divorced or separated, and some families just went home early. The families that make it become even stronger. Ours became stronger. Jan's a creative person and so she kept herself busy and, fortunately, just when she began to get itchy, the patent law job came along. Plus, she put a lot of energy into our kids and I think that was really rewarding for her. I know she got a lot of energy from her work, too, but I was really lucky that at least some of her fulfillment came from being a mother. At this stage of my life, I was still putting most of my energy into my job. Time would tell if it was more than a stage. I was glad Jan had more balance.

For me, the challenges were constant—sometimes boredom from not knowing what to do and so just not doing anything at all—and getting depressed from it—to having too much to do, to knowing that a lot was going on but not being in the network to know what it was or when it was going to happen. Either way, it was stressful. You do a lot of introspection during those rough times and really figure out who you are, what your values are, your tolerances, your strengths and weaknesses. And you find out whether, as a couple, you have the stuff to make it through life together. I know this sounds rather philosophical and maybe somewhat sentimental, but that's the way it is. There's no other experience like it. It's probably not for everyone, but I really believe everyone should try it. If you want to grow personally in a year or two what it would normally take five or ten, then take an international assignment to a really different culture.

Several more months passed and things progressed well on all fronts. The product was selling as expected and so we were all happy. Muhashi seemed to be doing a good job and so Jeff and the investors were happy. To them, it appeared as though I was very successful and they attributed much of the product's success in Japan to my efforts. I hadn't told them any outright lies to deceive them about what was going on, but I didn't want to say that I really hadn't had much to do with it—except I hadn't muddled things up, and maybe that was one of my greatest contributions to the joint venture—I hadn't alienated the Japanese in the process.

Muhashi was fairly typical of many of the larger Japanese firms. The longer I was in Japan, the more I learned. The mostly female work force at the production floor level was quite typical. As the economy had its ups and downs, these jobs were more flexible. Laying off women was not seen as negative as laying off men.

After all, this was a country in which a recent prime minister made a statement that women belong primarily in the home; that is where their skills and abilities are most needed and best applied, he implied. Admittedly, Muhashi was fairly typical of most Japanese manufacturing firms. Men held the engineering, marketing, and other jobs. Other Japanese firms, especially the smaller ones, are starting to hire increasing numbers of women in marketing and other areas.

But again, in fairness, many of these women who are let go are not technically laid off. Their contract simply ends and they are not rehired. Almost all larger Japanese companies have a certain number of female workers who are on three-to six-month contracts. These are the truly expendable employees. Others are on year-long contracts. Then there are the "regular" employees who are considered "permanent." It is rare, though, that any of the year-long contract employees are not rehired. Typically, the three- to six-month group provides enough buffer for a company to expand and contract without having to pull from their year-long employees.

We looked at this lingering attitude toward women as rather offensive and somewhat degrading. The Japanese seem to approach the gender issue more as a role specialization issue. Women are more to serve than to rule, some of my American friends would tell me. In reality, though, I believe most Japanese women who "serve" their husbands do it very willingly. It was an outsider's view that felt this was contemptuous. One thing that could not be denied, even by our critic friends: the Japanese family remains much more intact than the American family. Violent crime is almost unheard of except in truly exceptional cases. Streets can be safely walked at night in downtown Tokyo. I know this is going to sound old-fashioned, but I think there's a relationship between more family solidarity and these kinds of statistics.

I did learn that an equal job opportunity law was passed back in 1986 in Japan. Some thought this was done more in response to international pressure than as a reflection of any internal moral commitment within the Japanese ranks. In any case, minimal but some headway has been made. I read about a young female Japanese building inspector who ventured into a tunnel that was still being built to do an inspection. The construction crew didn't object, apparently because they were younger and weren't aware of or didn't care about the policy that women not enter incomplete tunnels. The policy originated from the belief that a mountain god caused bad things to occur if this happened. Nothing bad happened, at least not in the short term. So progress is being made!

Question 2:   What are the differences in attitudes and practices between genders in the workplace in your culture? What value(s) do such differences in your culture reflect?

Two women at Muhashi were let go because there had been no work for several months. They had to surrender their company uniforms. It was almost like a ritual when the women handed their uniforms over to their boss. It was as if their lives had just ended, and I suppose for a Japanese, in a sense they had. But I'm probably exaggerating it a bit as an outsider.

Muhashi's uniforms were blue and white, ones that mostly the assembly and skill-level employees wore every day. You could see them all walking to work or getting off the buses, filing out one by one in their "blue and whites" as I referred to them to Jan. It reminded me of parochial schools in the States, although Jeff reminded me that even public schools were beginning to adopt them in California to avoid gang identification. Whether a firm's employees in Japan or gangs in California, the uniformity of clothes serves the same purpose: identifying yourself with others who share the same interest. The difference is that in Japan it is real.

Of course, it wasn't just lower-level employees who wore these uniforms in Japan. Upper-level managers did on occasion, too, particularly when visiting the production-level employees. Either that or they wore white over smocks. The university grads also had their uniform at work. They all seemed to wear white shirts and dark ties, gray or black slacks, and black shoes. Japan was simply riddled with uniforms—part of that group-belonging thing. Schools that have cute uniforms are more popular among students. Private schools have asked famous designers to design uniforms almost as an advertising stunt to attract students. Pre-university school kids also wear them to their schools. It was interesting to me how symbolic the uniform is.

You couldn't get much more different between the Japanese and the Americans, at least on the West Coast in Silicon Valley firms. Hardly anyone wears dress shirts and ties except maybe the sales force and senior management. Even then, it's not absolute. Microsoft has no dress policy whatsoever, except that Bill Gates once said he would prefer people wear shoes or sandals in the hallways. I loved it. Individualism and informality are bedrock values where I come from.

In Japan, it was simply understood that you identify yourself with some larger group. In fact, your identity is found in the group you belong to. I sometimes wondered if the average Japanese kid ever gave it a second thought. Certainly it was more efficient and probably less expensive to have uniforms. You wouldn't have to decide what to wear every morning and you wouldn't have to have a large wardrobe. Efficiency. This was a Japanese staple.

Even the skilled employees at Muhashi—the backbone of the firm as far as I was concerned—reflected this efficiency. Enterprise unions, as they are called in Japan, are typically organized by the company—hence "enterprise" unions! There are no general trade labor unions that I was aware of such as plumbers, carpenters, and so on. Muhashi's union is self-contained. And first-level managers are part of the unions. I could see this system has many advantages. Although these first-level managers are destined at some time to move on to higher levels, they are constrained to identify somewhat with the manufacturing level of the organization. They are boundary people, with two "groups" they affiliate and identify with. This creates a unique psychological structure that crosses over the organizational structure lines. Unlike unions in the states, attorneys or other outsiders are not hired to arbitrate disputes or represent sides. There is not this adversarial relationship of union-management. Management is part of the union in Japan.

When there are problems, the workers' boss typically discusses concerns with them at length. He then goes to his boss and expresses the concerns of his employees. This kind of communication goes up the lines of management with different relevant parties being included until a tentative decision is made. Then the decision comes down the organization reaching the employees several weeks later—or more—sometimes. In the meantime, the employees continue working just as hard as before. There's no slacking, no complaining, no picketing, and no sabotaging. I saw this happen at Muhashi one time. It was over a pay issue. The company was willing to increase bonuses but not wages because that gave the company more flexibility to deal with economic downturns. Muhashi wouldn't be locked into a "permanent" higher wage. Because bonuses were typically tied to profits, bonuses could be adjusted to what would be best for the entire firm. The employees were very satisfied with this suggestion and that was the end of that. If they hadn't been pleased, they could have suggested an alternative and sent that up the chain via their boss for another round of discussions. The whole situation was much more amicable than we have in the United States or nearly anywhere else for that matter, except maybe in Germany and some of the Scandinavian countries. I think there was more of a partnership sentiment underlying the whole process in Japan and these other countries.

Question 3: *How are unions organized in your culture? How does this organization affect the relationship between management and nonmanagement?*

As I learned more about how companies treat their employees, I could see why employees rarely had problems with management. Thirty to 35 percent of their salary can be in benefits. Typical of other large Japanese firms, many of Muhashi's workers live in company housing—dormitories for single workers, low-rent apartments for younger married couples, and sometimes a small number of rentable houses for the professional employees. Most employees also receive a travel allowance to help pay for the habitual hour or more commutes on trains, buses, and so on. Plus, some companies still pay a family allowance based on the needs of the family. In short, it's tough to complain to your employer when it has its hand in so many aspects of your life. But then this is purely an American interpretation of a Japanese phenomenon. The Japanese might not view it the same way.

Unlike benefits, though, bonuses are based on the employees' actual take-home pay because that is more indicative of their relative worth to the company. Benefits are more circumstantial—based on an individual's situation, like how far he lives from the company, if he's married, for example.

I was once told that the president of Sony, Akio Morita, actually encouraged his employees to strike one time. Apparently, he wanted to make the point that Sony, without its production employees, would not be able to achieve its goals. He wanted to impress on Sony management that they depend on its production employees, both skilled and nonskilled, as much as those employees depend on Sony for their livelihood. I'm sure Sony could have picked up the equivalent of those employees somewhere else, but even if so, the story makes a clear point that Japanese managers do not think the same way managers do from most other countries.

Can you imagine the CEO in a U.S. firm encouraging his or her employees to strike? This kind of behavior is what sometimes makes me think I am in "never-never land," although it's not Disneyland.

So a few more months went by with the status quo kind of taking over. In August we'd turned the three-year mark in Japan and were glad to be heading back again to California for a combination of business and vacation to see family. Jeffrey was 5 now and really excited to be going. Michelle was 3 and had accepted life in Japan as her normal existence. Jeffrey was a little older and had grown very attached to Jan's parents, even though they didn't see each other often. He seemed to have a little more mature concept of what the "States" meant. I have to admit it was nice to think about going back and having the kids reconnect with Jan's parents. Her parents spoiled both the kids, but not with toys and Nintendo games. They spent time with the kids, taking them to parks and to the beach. Last time we were in the States, we all went whale watching off Monterey. We must have seen 30 whales. It was great and the kids loved it.

The gate stewardess's voice broke the silence, "Ladies and gentlemen, because of the dense fog in San Francisco, we have been asked to delay the flight two hours. Please accept our apologies for this delay." Then the Japanese announcement came. I told Jan the fog was just our welcome home call and the air traffic people shouldn't worry about that.

Finally, a little over two hours later, we boarded and taxied out to the runway. An hour later, one of the kids bumped my elbow and I woke up from a pseudo sleep. I still hadn't gotten to the point I could fall asleep completely sitting up in a plane, but I had made progress. Flying at about 35,000 feet above the ocean gives you a wonderful view of the miles and miles of sea below—at least when there isn't cloud coverage. That's the kind of perspective I needed in Japan and in my life right now—the never-ending one. I wondered if doing business internationally was as difficult—or different—in Europe as in Japan. At least the Europeans are mostly Western, I told myself. And despite the differences I noticed with the French during my college year there, the French seemed to share more similarities with Americans than the Japanese do, although they had no problems at all about telling you what they thought of your American politics—good or bad—or about the obesity they read about in the United States and see on television.

The French seemed both suspicious—and admiring—of the United States and they didn't seem to clam up or talk about superficialities as if to avoid discussing more serious issues—at least not when on a peer level and about impersonal topics—politics, economics, religion, and so on. They were sensitive to when you became too emotionally invested in the discussion, though. They were in it more for the intellectual exercise. Maybe if I had taken our discussions less personally they would have seemed less confrontational. But in general, I could ask them questions and they would seem to give direct responses, especially if the questions were about their own government. I would have loved to have been there to talk about the treatment of the Ministry of Health officials involved in the AIDS-contaminated blood that killed several hemophiliacs. Just like in the United States when important officials face criminal charges, it apparently was a whitewash in France. I'm sure the French people weren't happy with that. I could just hear François or Pierre (two of my best friends at Aix) . . . and then Jacques Chirac's gross miscalculation of the people's will that resulted in a new government—these were the kinds of stories every Frenchman loved to tell you about.

Once back in the States, we drove up to Rohnert Park, where Jan's parents lived. Sometimes I commuted from their house to work, but most of the time I stayed in a hotel near MedTech if I finished too late that evening. I really wasn't into three-hour plus commutes in traffic. Plus, recent storms had done damage to roads from flooding and mudslides, so that didn't help any.

The main problem at MedTech was my replacement hadn't really "picked up the ball and run with it." Although I had kept tabs on him while I was in Japan, I don't think he had been telling me or Jeff the whole truth. The bottom line was this: We had no really big customers in the nearly two years I had been gone. This only put more stress on me because I knew I could have advanced things more than they were, yet I was needed in Japan—or so Jeff and I thought. But for all the good I was doing in Japan, I might as well be back in the States. I decided to talk to Jeff about this and come totally clean with what was going on in Japan. We both came to the conclusion that I should trade places with Carl, the present director of marketing, my former assistant. He knew the product and MedTech well enough to basically represent our interests as much as the Japanese would let us, and I could do a lot more good in the States.

I called Jan to tell her what Jeff and I were thinking.

"Are you kidding, Matt?" she asked me. "That would be too good to be true."

She had been in contact with one of her good friends and had heard that work had picked up some at her old firm and thought maybe she had a chance. It really didn't end up mattering, though, because unfortunately, she was right. It was too good to be true.

We faxed Mr. Satoh our probable decision and received a fairly quick reply. Mr. Satoh told us it could be disastrous to change personnel at this time (he didn't use that word, but that was the message). More accurately, Mr. Satoh said I "was familiar with the necessary contacts within Muhashi and they knew me. I had already "invested three years in Japan and someone new would have to start all over. This would probably impede progress."

I told Jeff, "What does he mean by 'start over'? What had I really accomplished?" I wondered to myself.

Mr. Satoh also said they were getting ready to introduce me to others within their distribution network and that "This would be very difficult with someone new." He encouraged us to please reconsider and said that it might be time to meet together to discuss our partnership. Understanding at least some of the Japanese culture, I think I began to read the writing on the wall and suggested to Jeff that we reconsider. We decided that if Jan was willing to stay a little longer in Japan, we would stay.

I knew Jan would be so disappointed in the news, and I felt really guilty for having gotten her hopes up. I couldn't believe how dumb I was to have brought anything up before it was definite. But neither Jeff nor I had anticipated the Japanese reaction. I guess I hadn't internalized enough about Japanese culture. In retrospect, I should have predicted that probable response. In Japan, familiarity and consistency equals trust. And they trusted MedTech because they trusted me.

I was only partly right about Jan's reaction. Jan was disappointed, but she was also clearer on her position (maybe she had been before and I just didn't want to hear it).

"You realize this could go on forever, don't you?" Jan told me. I cringed as the gunfire continued: "I'm sorry, but I've given up three years of my career, taken care of our kids almost single-handedly and tried to stay current in my profession by performing a rather boring patent research job in Japan and taken a few correspondence law review courses. I've given all I can give, Matt. It's time to return," she stated in no uncertain terms. There was a moment of silence—maybe a gesture of a truce or the reloading of the artillery! It seemed like it was forever in any case. But then in a calm tone of voice, Jan graciously added, "We've had a tremendous experience in Japan—both of us personally and you professionally—but it's time to move on." She added, "The longer we stay, the more difficult it will be for our kids to integrate into the American way of life and to keep Jeffrey's English skills at his age level. You and Jeff have to learn to tell the Japanese 'No.'"

"Okay," I told Jan. "I can't turn around now and say 'No.' But we can decide how much longer we're going to stay in Japan. In the meantime, we can begin to focus on planning for our life back in the States." Jan seemed okay with that. At least she didn't say anything on the phone.

I was almost glad Jan was so clear cut about it all. It actually made it easier because part of my stress had been wondering just how much longer she could last—or I could last for that matter. It also made me realize that we needed to communicate better. It shouldn't have come to this. Either Jan should have told me her mounting frustration earlier or I should have talked to her more about it to give her the chance to do so. Adapting to a foreign culture is difficult enough when alone, but it necessitates even more effort to coordinate, to talk and share ideas and feelings when you're a couple.

In the short term, I would need to sit down with Jeff and explain to him the situation. I knew he would understand personally, but I also knew he would be disappointed about the risk that it might cause a slight rift between Muhashi and MedTech. That was going to be a risk we were going to have to take, though. I was also going to have to sit down with Carl and explain what we expected of him until I returned, that we were disappointed in the progress he had made to this point. Some goals would need to be set for the next quarter. The intimation was that if things didn't change, he would possibly be looking for another job. That hurt because we had invested a lot in him and had possibly misjudged him.

I spent nearly three weeks of 12-hour days in California trying to get things in order. I couldn't believe the hassle it was to ship something overseas. Although we had already shipped samples once, it never ceased to amaze me, all the paperwork—letters of credit, bill of lading, and on and on. Fortunately, we worked through Muhashi's affiliate bank to facilitate certain aspects of the shipment. I had about decided to hire an outside agency to do the shipping for us, but we were on such a tight budget. In the future I decided I'd look into "piggybacking" with another company. I had heard that was done fairly frequently—a small company shipped a like product with a larger firm's shipment. Then the shipment only became another item on the bill of lading instead of a shipment in and of itself.

Our other alternative, of course, was to set up a production operation in Japan with Muhashi. After talking to Muhashi about this, we decided against it for the moment. First, wages were somewhat more expensive in Japan than in the United States. Second, the yen's value made purchasing the instruments quite tolerable for the moment. But probably most of all, with a new product like this, it wasn't a good idea to start another production facility before declaring the setup in California a success. That would have just been asking for problems. So to keep the quality consistent, we opted for California production despite the exporting hassle.

The time passed so quickly from being totally busy. It seemed like we were back in Japan so soon. It was still hot and humid in September and we all wished we had been able to prolong our time in California more. The kids were growing up fast. Jan and I both sensed it was getting time to return to the States.

Several months later at one of our after-work get-togethers, I talked to Ken and my other Japanese business associates about leaving, about how Jan felt, and the best way to bring it up to Mr. Satoh. "You must let him know that this is your plan without telling him directly that you will be leaving," Ken said. "And be sure to not say anything about how your wife feels. Instead, suggest to him that MedTech might need you soon, that your American boss is troubled by your long absence."

By January I had mustered enough courage to approach Satoh and I did as my co-workers had suggested. It was hard to tell what Satoh's reaction was, as it is so often with the Japanese—at least for an American. But I believe his low "growling" noise meant he acknowledged what I had said and would reflect on it. I told him I had four more months, even though Jan and I had decided six would be the absolute maximum. I figured this way, if we stayed a little longer, Satoh would read it as a good-faith sign of our willingness to "do our duty." Telling Satoh that MedTech had given me this time put it in a context that a Japanese would understand. It wasn't necessarily something that "I" wanted. What "I" wanted wasn't important. It was what MedTech wanted that counted!

I think I was beginning to learn something about Japanese culture.

QUESTIONS FOR DISCUSSION

1. In a nutshell, what purpose do the after-hours bar sessions seem to serve? Would Matt's effectiveness have been limited had he not participated in this activity? Why?

2. How do the Japanese language, gender issues, and even the uniforms reflect Japanese culture? What do they tell us about Japanese values? Do similar traditions in language, dress, or other conditions exist in your own culture? How would the similarities or differences make adaptation easier or more difficult in Japan?

3. How is the way labor unions are organized in Japan different from your own country's labor union organization? What do the differences reflect in terms of cultural values in Japan?

4. Muhashi is reluctant to approve a replacement for Matt. Why? If you were Matt or MedTech, how would you have responded to Muhashi's objections about replacing Matt? Do you believe Matt approached Satoh properly in telling him about his impending departure? How would you have done it if you believe it should have been done differently?

5. What additional issues are raised in this chapter about expatriation, family communication, and successful adaptation?

CHAPTER 8

Exploring Other Asian Markets:
A Broader Cultural View

MATT

Several weeks later I got an e-mail message from Jeff saying that he had contacts in Hong Kong and Malaysia who were possibly interested in some of our products. There was apparently a small but growing market in other parts of Asia. In particular, although Chinese hospitals in Hong Kong and even in other parts of the Chinese mainland still maintained a traditional medicine of healing with herbs and acupuncture in their hospitals, for most serious illnesses, like a closed heart valve, they used Western surgical methods. Many Chinese doctors got their training from Western countries, so it was only natural that much of that training was applied in their own country. It wasn't like surgery was a new method, anyway. Ancient Egyptians and Greeks had performed surgical operations. They probably had disposable scalpels and forceps back then too!

Jeff sent me the name and contact information of this Chinese fellow in Hong Kong. I called him and he sounded interested in meeting with me and invited me to come visit him. I was looking forward to seeing another Asian country besides

Japan, so the invitation came at a good time. But what neither Jeff nor I had really thought through was if a deal is cut with this fellow, Mr. Liu, would we distribute the product directly from California or from Japan? We'd feel that one out if it came to such a decision. We had to be really careful, though, because Muhashi also had contacts in China, Thailand, and other places. If Muhashi thought we were trying to undercut them or do an "end run," that might compromise whatever trust they had in us. To cover our bases, we decided I should try to make contacts in other locations.

As long as I was going to Hong Kong, I decided I might as well try to set up some appointments in Singapore and possibly another nearby Asian country where Muhashi didn't have any presence. Singapore was extremely modern and developed enough to support a fairly good surgical market, so to speak. I faxed Jeff my idea of setting up additional meetings and asked him to work through his network, including the investors, to also find potential contacts in Singapore. If I was going fishing, I might as well make it a real fishing trip!

Within a month I had an appointment in Singapore as well as one in Malaysia. In Singapore I was to meet with a group of surgeons. In Malaysia I was going to meet with someone high up in the Ministry of Health. Apparently, one of the investors lived near a Malay doctor who was doing a residency at Stanford Medical Center before returning to Malaysia. His uncle was the Minister of Health and I might even have a chance to meet him.

When I told Jan about the visits, she wanted to come with me. That was okay with me; in fact, we could probably prolong the visit a bit and do some touring together. Hong Kong wasn't that big; neither was Singapore, and the meeting in Malaysia shouldn't take that long, so I figured I could probably be gone for two weeks and include some vacation in there with Jan.

After I let my colleagues in Muhashi know I would be gone to meet some contacts for potential future business, they were very interested and asked a lot of questions to which I didn't know many of the answers. I could also tell they were surprised I had initiated this on my own without including them because they had contacts they were developing in China and Hong Kong. It didn't look good, they told me in their indirect way, to present a segregated approach to potential customers. They were surprised I knew almost nothing before going to meet Mr. Liu. I assumed that's what the visit was for—to get some basic fact finding out of the way and see if a deal might be worth exploring. I got the vague impression they thought I should have studied an encyclopedia about this person, the company he represents, and so on. Then it dawned on me that this is exactly what they had done with us, which is why they had such an advantage when it came to negotiations. Unfortunately, time was against me and besides, I didn't really know how I could find out information about Mr. Liu or the Singapore contacts. Had I more time, I'm sure I could have found out more about the Minister of Health in Malaysia. Hindsight.

The plane touched down on a typical balmy Hong Kong day. The view from the plane just before landing was beautiful. We could see the harbor clearly and the mountainous terrain all around Hong Kong—it felt as though we were going to land right on top of apartment buildings. Jan was really excited to tour the place. Mr. Liu was at the airport to meet us and greeted us with typical polite Asian formality. We took a taxi to the hotel in Kowloon, a seaport section of Hong Kong where we were going to stay. On our way, we noticed large apartment complexes with clothes hanging on short lines out the windows. Armies of television antennas stuck out of the top of every apartment building. Many of the buildings seemed old and dirty from the outside. Roads were crowded, the air a bit thick from humidity and pollution, and horns honked regularly. What interested us the most, though, was the bamboo scaffolding the Chinese use to work on buildings. I couldn't believe it was really bamboo until Mr. Liu confirmed it. To see these guys 15 stories up with only bamboo shoots underneath them was incredible, but apparently it's as strong as steel and tied together with bands of some plant-like skin or something—I couldn't quite make out what it was from the car.

After a 20-minute ride, we were at the Imperial Hotel. (In 20 minutes of driving, you can see a lot in Hong Kong!) The hotel was beautiful and clean— marble floors, colorful flowers adorning strategic spots in the lobby, and a large tea-serving area for patrons to be served while waiting. The bellboy took our luggage and Mr. Liu quickly checked us in. Within a few minutes we were in our room, which overlooked some of Kowloon and the harbor separating us from Hong Kong Island.

My appointment with Mr. Liu was for 1:30 the next afternoon, so he suggested we all three get together for breakfast. He also invited us to visit a little of Hong Kong before our meeting later on that day. The brief excursion was a lot of fun and Mr. Liu seemed to know everything about Hong Kong. We crossed the harbor on a small ferry and then took a tram up the side of the mountain to view Kowloon and Hong Kong from above. It was beautiful and interesting. You could really see the mixture of the old and the new. Part of the harbor still tolerated many Chinese junks and very small traditional-looking boats, yet on land there were beautiful modern skyscrapers, from hotels to corporate offices of many well-known British, U.S., Japanese, Australian, and other companies. The harbor was actually becoming smaller because buildings were being erected over what used to be waterways.

Most of the buildings below seemed to be pointed in a northward (I think) direction. On the way up to the peak in the tram were large apartment complexes that had huge arches exposing the mountain. Mr. Liu told us this was so the spirits would not be trapped in the buildings and become angry.

"It's the Chinese belief in *feng shui*," he told me.

I'm not sure I completely grasped the concept, but basically, it has to do with energy flow and if the building isn't facing the "right" direction or otherwise positioned correctly, a kind of negative energy flows in and around the building. I'm sure there was more to it than that . . .

We had lunch at a restaurant in the business district, adjacent to the water. I can't remember what I ordered—and am not sure I want to. It was some kind of sea animal—good but different. Jan had bird's-nest soup. I didn't really want to ask what that meant, but Jan did. It is some kind of secretion from the mouth of a bird. That was it for me. I stopped asking questions and just let my imagination play on me instead. I'm not sure which was worse. Sometimes not knowing is better than knowing.

The meeting with Mr. Liu went well. He introduced me to two other businessmen that he had known for a long time. In China their families had done business with each other for over two generations. I left some of our surgical instruments and a professionally done video showing their use. He was to pass this on to some doctors and hospital administrators.

That evening, we went to dinner with Mr. Liu. We went through the usual small talk but also discussed a few really interesting things. His and his wife's lives reflected experiences most Americans and others in stable countries can't really conceive of. Around 1948 a civil war ensued because Mao Tse-tung, the leader of China, had a vision of returning China back to the people and away from the hierarchy of wealth that had accumulated under a more capitalistic economic system. Eventually Mao mounted enough resistance to isolate General Chiang Kai-shek and eventually chased him to Taiwan. Later, Mao had thousands of the wealthy and educated imprisoned or killed—the Cultural Revolution as they call it—around 1967. Rather than be killed, imprisoned, or otherwise disposed of, many Chinese tried to flee China. Most fled to Taiwan. Some located in the United States, Canada, or other countries, including the Hong Kong area—where Mr. Lui's and his wife's families fled. Mr. Liu also has a cousin who lives in Los Angeles, who had also left during the Cultural Revolution.

We talked some about Jan's and my families and our experience in Japan. It was an enjoyable evening and my stomach even seemed to tolerate the food! Mr. Liu offered to guide us around Hong Kong on our last day there, but we politely declined. He insisted a bit, and we probably should have accepted. I'm not sure if we goofed by declining or not. Jan and I just wanted a day to ourselves.

Our next stop was Singapore.

The flight on Singapore Airlines was enjoyable. The stewardesses were dressed in impressive Oriental gowns, and their service matched their dress. Upon deplaning, Dr. Chang was waiting at Changi Airport. He was holding a sign that said MATT SUMNER to make it easier to connect. As we approached the elevator to get to the car in the basement, an announcement came over the loudspeaker: "Ladies and gentlemen, we'd like to remind you that being caught with illegal drugs is punished by hanging."

The drive to Singapore was a stark contrast to Hong Kong. Instead of the airport being right downtown, it is outside the city in a lush area of the country. Palm trees, green plants, and grass line the two-lane well-maintained highway into the city about 15 minutes away. Once in the city, though, it reminded me much of Hong Kong except it is much cleaner and the sidewalks seem much wider. New buildings, ongoing construction, and the crowded streets underscored that this is a bustling hub of Southeast Asia. The weather was hot and humid. I could tell I was going to be well acquainted with our hotel shower before our visit was over. Clouds brought frequent short rainstorms, but nothing really violent while we were there.

Singapore is famous for its economic miracle. Lee Kuan Yew, the former head of Singapore, had instituted reforms and poured money into Singapore's development. Its seaport location is a natural stop for much of the world's sea transportation. It has developed a well-educated work force, particularly among the Chinese and the skilled laborers. But alongside the tremendous development came harsh laws and ethnic containment. Those who opposed the new government went to prison or were "disposed of." Laws were developed that ensured maintaining order and a clean appearance to Singapore. Littering was rewarded with a heavy fine. Tagging was punishable by a prison sentence. Selling drugs was a death sentence. Armed robbery was also automatically punishable by death if there was killing involved. There were no juries necessary to try such cases. The law was the law and it was enforced.

This kind of regime kept a lid on violent outbreaks. Protesting was not allowed unless you wanted to face imprisonment. Ethnic groups that felt discriminated against could do nothing. To shore up this kind of "military democracy," children in schools were taught ethnic tolerance and the importance of hard work and cooperation. Lee Kwan Yew ruled Singapore with the proverbial iron fist. Even though some of this is a little distasteful to many who consider freedom a right, I couldn't argue with what Singapore has accomplished. It is clearly one of the most advanced nations in the world. When Lee's son took over the situation was expected to remain pretty much the same.

That night I got a call from Jeff saying that we had a contact in Vietnam I should meet—a British fellow who had been doing business in Vietnam for several years. He was a good friend of a friend of one of the investors. "Just take a few days to check it out," Jeff urged me. Without really thinking about it, I said okay, got the contact information, and spent the last ten minutes chatting about business at MedTech. Although Jan really wanted to go with me, one of us had to return to Japan on time to get Jeffrey and Michelle. Our friends who were watching them had a trip of their own planned a day after our original return date. We couldn't ask them to postpone their trip. That night I went to bed wondering what Vietnam was like and glad that I hadn't been drafted like so many other Americans. I turned 18 and became eligible for the draft about the time the Vietnam War was winding down. Some of my friends had to go, but my draft number was too high. I thought how strange it would be to return to Vietnam now under such different circumstances. I'm not sure what my feelings would have been had I been there during the war. For most of the soldiers who returned it was a nightmare, a period of their lives that served little or no purpose, a couple of years that might have been better spent going to college or just spending time together at a local café.

The next day came early and I met with the team of doctors at 10 A.M. after Jan and I had a delicious continental breakfast. They were all of Chinese descent, the ethnic group that seemed to dominate over the more indigenous Malays and the Indians. Jan and I saw other ethnic groups too as we walked and toured different areas of Singapore. We visited the Old Market, which was absolutely impressive—lots of ornate glass ceilings and pillars, little shops everywhere, and a small musical group in the center of the main lobby. Having been a former British colony, many of the streets reflect this heritage: Thompson Street, Prince Henry, Bayshore, Orchard Street, and so on.

Although the different ethnic groups appear to live peacefully with one another, we learned there was a clear hierarchy. The Chinese are on top and the Indians and others in the middle, with the Malays picking up the bottom rung. At the National University of Singapore, as in the government, it is the Chinese who hold the most important positions. Indians, Malays, and others generally hold much inferior posts.

The different ethnic communities reflect their heritage in architecture and obviously in people. "Little India" has really interesting two-story buildings painted blue, green, pink, and other colors. Some facades have what looks like tree vines growing out of the wood and up the wall. We saw an old, wrinkled, tanned Indian sitting in yoga position on a sidewalk dealing cards to another man of similar age. The dealer was truly classic in his facial features and dress and I motioned to him whether I might take his picture. He shook his head "no," but I was nearly tempted to take it anyway. This was a chance of a lifetime—the kind of picture you only see in *National Geographic!*

But something kept me from taking it. Maybe it was that need to honor a human being's request, a feeling that transcended my intellectual enthusiasm for this great picture. Then again, maybe I was just afraid the police would jump out of the woodwork after I took the picture and handcuff me and throw away the key for taking an illegal picture—I'm joking, of course. Things were pretty squeaky clean, though. Not flushing a toilet in a public building, for example, is punishable by a large fine. If you are caught cheating in business, it is announced in the newspaper to warn others about doing business with you. Spitting on the sidewalk incurs a huge fine, as does littering. Jan and I decided to keep our hands in our pockets, our mouths shut, and to make sure we flushed all public toilets by double-checking each other.

Question 1:   *How well would you tolerate the level of strictness in Singapore? How does it compare to laws in your country? What are the advantages and disadvantages of such a legal system? What does such a legal system reflect about Singapore's culture? And your legal system about your culture?*

My meeting with the doctors seemed to go well. I showed them the sample surgical instruments and we viewed the video as we had in Hong Kong. They asked me some questions about liability and availability. I asked questions about how hospitals and doctors went about purchasing surgical instruments, any current need they might have, their perception about semidisposable instruments, who paid for such medical equipment, what the main obstacles might be in working through making a deal, and so on. My general impression was that there was interest but not any real commitment at this time, although it's always hard to tell after product discussions like this.

Getting out of Singapore was more harrowing than I had expected. First off, we had to have a departure card along with our ticket. I had forgotten mine. They led me to a special desk to get another one. Also, Jan and I had calculated our money fairly closely so we wouldn't have too much Singaporean money left over. When we got to the ticket counter at the airport, we realized we had forgotten to calculate enough money to pay for the airport tax of 12 Singaporean dollars that each passenger has to pay in order to board the plane. Fortunately, we had $27 total between the two of us. It wouldn't have been a big deal but we didn't have enough time to find an exchange in the airport before our plane left. We had also nearly miscalculated the time to get to the airport using the underground (which actually is above ground most of the time between the city and the airport). Believe me, international travel isn't always easy!

It was a short hop to Kuala Lumpur, one of those flights where just when you get to the top of your flight pattern you begin to level off and descend toward your destination. Your eardrums are confused and you spend the next couple of days as though you have earmuffs being turned on and off—another one of the glorious aspects of international travel!

An assistant to the Minister of Health, Mr. Wibowo, was waiting for us with a big smile. Any good friend of a friend of his nephew was almost part of the family here in Kuala Lumpur. We had planned to spend only a couple of days there, but Mr. Wibowo made it clear in the most diplomatic way that three or four days were a minimum to discuss business and to see their beautiful island. "Yes, you Americans are always in a rush to go here, to do this and do that. Here, we have problems typical of a growing economy in a region that hasn't reached a stable maturity yet, and we are becoming a major market in Southeast Asia. Still, we take the time to live," he said in a very gentle, unaccusing voice.

When I told him we would love to stay a day or two longer but our tickets were nonrefundable if we changed our departure, he told me very matter-of-factly, "In Malaysia, nothing is permanent if you know the right people. Malaysian Airlines is a government-owned company and I know the minister of transportation very, very well. We have lunch often. We all know each other in the government. It is a very tight family. I will make a telephone call."

Question 2:   Is it a positive thing that "In Malaysia, nothing is permanent if you know the right people"? Why or why not?

Somehow I had a very secure feeling with Wibowo as our "associate." I wondered if the decision to buy our surgical instruments was his alone or if he had to sell someone on it. I had a feeling this was going to be easier than I had thought.

We spent the day in his office with a little historical introduction to his country, then had a sumptuous feast at a local restaurant, drove around Kuala Lumpur to see the sights, and at a different restaurant had dinner that lasted well into the night. The only real distraction were the mosquitoes at night that tended to congregate in greater numbers in this highly humid environment. I thought of inventing a mosquito bat and selling it to the Malays, but they didn't seem too bothered by them.

Malaysia has an interesting ethnic mixture of native Malays, who run the government and the health and school systems, and the long-established Chinese, who control most of the important businesses and much of the banking system. Unlike Singapore, they have all gotten along fairly well without the same underlying force. Still, I wondered if this might complicate the situation in terms of getting market entry. Who was going to have more control over that—the businessmen, who are principally Chinese, or the government, composed of Malays?

The next couple of days were more of the same with a few times interspersed with another host while Mr. Wibowo had to attend to government business. He always left us with someone who spoke excellent English. Mr. Wibowo himself had attended college in the United States. He graduated with a master's degree in public administration from Harvard. Being part of the privileged class within the Malay people, he had been groomed for the position he holds now.

This was typical of the native Malays in power. Most of them are related in some way or another—first cousins, second cousins, uncles, nephews, or very good friends of first cousins, second cousins, uncles—you get the idea. Mr. Wibowo has two brothers and two sisters, which is fairly typical of the family size in Malaysia. One younger brother is in the United States studying engineering and the other in England. His sisters still live at home. Having gotten married three years ago, Mr. Wibowo has one daughter who is 1 year old. They live on the same large plantation about 3 miles from the center of town as their parents and other family members.

This is their way of life—a kind of tribal life. The center of the family is the patriarch. The elder brothers with the patriarch are the "government" of the family. The women run the day-to-day affairs of the home, though, and are held in high esteem by the male members of the family. Jan became quite interested in some of this and asked a lot of questions, probably more than she should have. Generally speaking, although held in high esteem, women in the privileged families do not get the same level of education as the men. They tend to stay in Malaysia to bring stability to the family. They are the mainstays, Jan was told, and have to provide the necessary continuity to the family that men cannot provide because of their career orientation.

The women are typically in colorful floor-length batik dresses. They wear scarves around their heads as Muslims, but without the veils typical of Muslims in most of the Middle East. The women run the indigenous open marketplaces and are an essential part of the basic economy of Malaysia. The city seems alive and dynamic, cars going everywhere (mostly Nissans and Toyotas) with motorcycles and motorbikes moving every which way. The roads in the city are good—paved and in good condition despite the heavy rains and hot and humid weather. Construction on the then tallest building in the world has been completed. And construction on the world's longest building is just starting. It is being built in downtown Kuala Lumpur and will have a canal running through the seventh floor, an artificial rain forest, shops, restaurants, offices and—my favorite part—an in-line skating area.

All this construction fueled by rich oil reserves and a booming manufacturing society hums along fairly well despite economic crises or other blips in their development. Walking the streets was definitely an experience. The downpours were incredible sometimes—but not to them. What would have forced us inside to wait out the rain seemed to have little effect on changing their stride. Everyone just carries umbrellas. Buildings have open rain gutters that let the monsoon rain gush into drains in ditches. Palm trees are everywhere and hold up miraculously under the occasional strong winds. It is an interesting backdrop—the lush tropical island look adds an obvious green hue to the city with a deceptive hustle and bustle of people and machines.

Shopping centers and stores seem very modern. Clerks hang out but are not much help. I wanted to buy a couple of shirts and never could figure out how to get their attention to let them know I had questions. Maybe that was why there were large groups around a booth inside the mall to sign up for English lessons. They figured they were losing out on a lot of sales!

When it came time for business talks, we never did really have any. We were shown a great time, driven around, superbly hosted, informed of the local culture, and generally treated like royal guests. But there was never any time reserved just to talk business. When I could see our time in Kuala Lumpur was coming to a close, I told our escort I would be very interested in talking to him about our products. He laughed and kindly explained that Malaysia would be such a small market for MedTech that it would be hardly worth our trouble to do business with them. "In 15 years, please come back. We will be ready," he said with that same grand smile he had on our first meeting. What can you say to that? You can't stand there and deny what he had just said and start talking cold hard business to the person that took his time out to show you such a good time and was a true gentleman all of the time.

JAN

I had a wonderful time, interested in everything as we went from place to place. And of course I never lost an opportunity to put in a plug for the environment. In Malaysia I was particularly concerned that the country control growth so that their beautiful island is not overwhelmed by pollution. I had long talks with Wibowo about this. He seemed to appreciate that an American representing the most capitalistic country in the world—at least that's our image—was sensitive to Malaysia's natural beauties more than she might have been interested in filling her pocket. That was my role, I guess. He might have wondered how Matt and I got along so well, one of us ultimately interested in economic growth, market exploitation, and profits and the other in nature's preservation and controlled economic growth.

So we left Kuala Lumpur very culturally enriched and for Matt, maybe in a business sense, educated once again by one of MedTech's potential markets.

We learned later that like any quickly developing country, Malaysia has its problems also. It has a shortage of educated and assembly-line workers. Inflation is rising and imports are beginning to outstrip exports. The government is raising interest rates and encouraging banks to increase their cash reserves to reduce the availability of money. Malaysians are spending too much! But it was also obvious that the Malay government in no way wants to stall development. Unfortunately, Malaysia, like the rest of Asia, has become caught up in the economic crisis of the region. The prime minister, Mahathir Mohamad, has been quoted as saying, "Malaysia wants to develop and I say to the so-called environmentalists: 'Mind your own business.'" Can you imagine the president of the United States saying that? Political correctness hasn't reached most of the world yet and is only an issue in cultures where the general population's opinion counts for something. Now that they are experiencing economic problems from too quick a growth, maybe they will have time to turn their attention to their environment.

Matt and I parted at the airport. I hopped on a 727 on my way to Japan with a stopover in Hong Kong. Matt had a later flight to Vietnam.

MATT

My trip back from Malaysia was rather eventful. As soon as we had taken off, a light perfume vapor came out of the air vents. Later, I was told the perfumed spray is the airline's way of hiding the unattractive smells picked up from some of the passengers' ethnic food they had in Malaysia.

Just as I was settling into a restful position, a monsoon that had been building up let loose. I was ready to go to the pilot and ask for a refund. The flight reminded me of a roller coaster ride with different sized speed bumps in its path. My stomach got really queasy. I questioned whether I was going to make it to Vietnam without dying or throwing up everything. Meanwhile I tried to sit there nonchalantly, looking out the window as if everything was absolutely normal. I was glad Jan wasn't there. I knew she would have made some comment about Mr. Macho having quite a time of it. I didn't need that right then.

QUESTIONS FOR DISCUSSION

1. What commonalties and/or differences do you notice among all of the Asian cultures you have read about so far (Japan, Hong Kong, Singapore, and Malaysia)?
2. Do you think MedTech is going about making contacts with the other Asian groups in the appropriate fashion? Why or why not?

CHAPTER 9

Culture in an Emerging Market: A Look at Vietnam

MATT

The plane circled over the skies of Ho Chi Minh City for a while. A number of passengers, who must be homecoming overseas Vietnamese, or Viet *kieus*, looked very nervous and excited. They looked out the windows of the plane, some even standing up, pointing out to each other certain places they recognized on the land below—maybe a river, a bridge, a street, a pagoda, a building of the former Saigon that they had left behind a long, long time ago.

The Boeing 727 of Malaysia Air Service (MAS) was almost full. Two-thirds of the passengers were Asians, there were a few Australians, and the rest were Westerners. I was unsure about how the Vietnamese people would welcome someone from a former enemy country that still maintains some trade sanctions 16 years after the war ended.

Soon we landed at Tan Son Nhut Airport, which 20 years ago was one of the world's busiest military airports. With fewer than 10 international flights landing daily, the international terminal still looked too small to accommodate some 200 to

300 passengers at the same time. After almost half an hour dealing with the entry and immigration red tape, I finally picked up my suitcase, which had been unloaded by porters from small trucks and placed on the floor of a large lounge. Many passengers had some difficulty finding carts to carry their luggage to customs. Vietnamese and other Asian passengers alike traveled with lots of luggage, including big cardboard boxes containing television sets, video heads, and the like. Obviously, the returning Vietnamese Australians must have gifts for their relatives to evidence their capitalistic living conditions in one of the world's more advanced economies, and these foreign businessmen must also have something small (like cigarettes, bottles of wine) for their business hosts and big (like expensive household electronic goods) for their "girlfriends."

There were still some reminders that I was coming to a country that not so long ago was the fiercest battlefield since the end of the Second World War, where the most expensive lethal weapons from the Soviet Union and the United States were freely tested on a people who I'm not even sure understood what the war was all about. For the people who lived through such sophisticated American and Russian war technologies and the shrewdness of the Vietnamese communists, I felt sincere respect and compassion for all who survived nobly and for all those who died nobly too.

My thoughts were jarred by the hard landing, although I preferred the hard landing nonetheless to continuing to hover above the airport. The view wasn't any more novel after the fifth circling of the airport. John Rosenford, a British fellow who had been doing business in Southeast Asia for about a decade, met me at the airport. Rosenford and one of MedTech's partners had crossed paths several years earlier through a common business deal with some others. They had kept in touch and still had some business dealings in common. He didn't really look the part of president of Dragon Exploration, Inc., the parent company of Pathway Corp. Dressed in khakis and boots, he looked more like he had just come in from a jungle trek. Appearance aside, he was extremely knowledgeable about the local business scene.

"Get to know all the American journalists who are covering this region. You can learn a lot from them," he said. "Meeting them will be much more worthwhile than reading volumes of books," he added. Dragon Exploration is actually a Sydney-based company that had recently given birth to Pathway, the Vietnam affiliate. Dragon's main business is the pharmaceutical industry, and its market is Southeast Asia. Rosenford had just returned from an international business round table conference held in Hanoi, a three-day event jointly sponsored by the privileged *Economist* magazine and rallying some 400 participants, both foreign and Vietnamese. In the capital of the "renovated" (yes, in Vietnam now, *"doi moi,"* or renovation, is the name of the game) Vietnam, some 150 foreign businessmen, journalists, and diplomats, mostly British and American, were honored guests of senior government officials, led by none other than the aging but reform-minded, newly appointed Prime Minister Vo Van Kiet.

Rosenford was greatly impressed by the Vietnamese government's candor and efforts to reform. "They appear willing to open every door for us to explore," Rosenford said. "They tell you that opportunities are ample but not yet identified, that the transition to a more open economy is causing some confusion." Shortcomings were frankly acknowledged, he said, and they were likely to provide cause for bargaining, seeking compromise and concessions from Vietnam. "You can easily complain about poor infrastructure, including inadequate roads, electrical power, water supply and communications," he added. "Telstra, a telecommunications firm from Australia, is winning contracts worth tens of millions of dollars to make Vietnam reachable from the rest of the world. And, to some extent, you can trust the Vietnamese government's pledge to alleviate obstacles to doing business in Vietnam. You definitely get the impression that they are more pragmatic than communist," Rosenford added.

"The whole pharmaceutical industry, from drugs like aspirin, cold medicines, and vitamins of all sorts to medical instruments sells strongly in emerging markets like Vietnam," he said. Rosenford estimated that Vietnam currently has an annual income per capita in the region of $200; if spending for medicines could amount to 3 percent of this income, then the pharmaceutical market would come to more than $400 million!

My concern was less about consumer spending on medicines than it was about how much the government was willing to spend on medical supplies and instruments for their clinics and hospitals. It would be the government that would be our primary client, not individual consumers. Rosenford mentioned that the domestic pharmaceutical industry is small and obsolete. Clearly, any competition for our products would come from outside Vietnam. It was always the same in developing countries. The first company to gain favor with the present government usually has a clear inside edge to gain and keep a monopoly. In developing countries, these things are always so intertwined with politics. And right now, the American government isn't exactly the first country to reach out to Vietnam. Japan has done a better job of that. France has especially maintained a very friendly economic posture toward Vietnam and was very quick to regain a foothold in their economy. The United States, it seems—at least on the surface—is always standing behind principles. Personally, I think the biggest principle it is standing behind for not dropping all trade sanctions is the fact that the United States was embarrassed by the war. The American International Chamber of Commerce in Hong Kong has strongly urged first Bush and then Clinton to lift the trade embargo against Vietnam before it is too late.

Rosenford believed it is a golden opportunity for both foreign pharmaceutical traders and investors in new manufacturing facilities. "How about Pathway and MedTech joining together in a joint venture in Vietnam to import pharmaceutical and medical supplies products into this market and subsequently setting up a manufacturing firm for your surgical instruments?" he suggested. Admittedly, his words sounded convincing. He had an ongoing business in Saigon, something like a trade-related representative office, and it was going quite well apparently. His company was selling medicines and buying "just about anything," including garments and leather shoes, in return, just to have a balance of liquidity.

I shared Rosenford's genuine excitement, but a decision to join him would require negotiations and a more solid basis about the market than just his word.

Rosenford introduced me to Ian Hughes, Rosenford's number one man in Ho Chi Minh. From then on, my time was spent with Hughes. Hughes was an amiable guy in his mid-30s. He had on jeans and a light pink shirt with the sleeves rolled up to his elbows. He greeted me in a warm and friendly manner, and very soon, we were in his Isuzu Trooper on our way to Thu Duc, a suburban district some ten to twelve miles from Saigon, where his office and the Pathway house were located. Even by Asian standards, the roads of Saigon are quite narrow, many with only two main lanes—one up and one down. In fact, there might be more lanes, but unruly motorbike and bicycle riders seem to have effaced all the road lines so there aren't any clear markings. Driving was definitely a thrilling experience. On sidewalks, you could also observe a pervasive invasion of street vendors, newsstands, tobacconists with small carts, refreshment stalls, or even eating places. Lots of people loiter on the sidewalks. Housing construction and public works are almost everywhere. Smoke, dust, and dumps of litter contribute to the high degree of air pollution in this city.

Hughes was quite frank in his talk. I doubted if he was under any instruction by his boss about how he should or could talk to me. If he was, he didn't appear that way. I asked him about the economy, noticing the dense population of the city and the number of people who seemed to be standing around, passing the time smoking and talking. "It is not very well-disguised unemployment," Hughes said. "Agriculture is faring much better than before. Generally Vietnam now can export rice again. But absolute poverty still exists in rural areas, especially in the northern and central provinces. Construction, trade, services, small manufacturing like garment making, food processing are booming—although not very orderly and well directed. But these activities cannot absorb the whole surplus labor force. Meanwhile, more productive manufacturing is still not much. Foreign investors will bring in their machines—but not now. They need more guarantees," Hughes commented. "Vietnamese manufacturers cannot compete with importers and smugglers. And they are more interested in making quick money," he said.

I also raised another question, this time about Vietnam's renovation policies in practice and the reality of the relations between the government and foreign businesspeople. Policies could sound good on paper. But in many developing countries there is a huge gulf between what is said and what is done.

"In past years, Vietnam dealt fraternally with foreigners from communist countries only—with the exception of China, its northern neighbor. At worst, there was traditionally a mutual paranoia between communist Vietnam and the noncommunist world. At best, there was an absence of intercommunication and mutual understanding," Hughes informed me.

The answer from Hughes was thoughtful. The basic message I was culling from our discussion was that we shouldn't have many expectations because doing business in Vietnam as a foreigner will not come overnight. The Vietnamese government is trying to develop suitable policies to accommodate foreign business activity in the country. But before it can succeed in this effort, it has to understand what doing international business means. I figured the learning process in this country could be a painful one, because although they could have foreign advisers, I think some Vietnamese believe they should learn by themselves and accept the cost. In the same way, foreigners are trying to adapt themselves to Vietnam's conditions, wishing they could really understand the institutional framework in which they should operate.

"Their common sense and our common sense are not the same," Hughes piped in while I was lost in my own thoughts. "A lot of time is going to pass before they gain the knowledge and experience to develop a system that is compatible with communist ideals and the capitalistic realities of the outside business world. But I'm sure you didn't anticipate that doing business in Vietnam is like that in the United States or Japan, or even Singapore or Hong Kong."

On this drive, I learned much more about Pathway's business. In fact, Hughes was not the "prime mover" of this business in Vietnam. He had been here for only nine months. It was Sean Connolly, Dragon Exploration's director in Hong Kong, who first had the idea of going to Vietnam and designed the plan and broke the ground before "turning the key" to Hughes. Connolly came to Vietnam as a member of a trade mission from Hong Kong, a front-runner in foreign investment in Vietnam in the early days of this country's campaign to induce foreign capital, and this brief visit triggered in Connolly a reasonable belief that there was a market in Vietnam for pharmaceutical products. At a reception at the Saigon Floating Hotel, Connolly got acquainted with Thu Le, who used to be an interpreter for Saigon's army before 1975 and is now running a "consulting office" of a foreign trade-related company based in Hanoi but with a branch in Ho Chi Minh City. Connolly was very impressed with Le, not only because of his command of English, but also his deliberate offer for help as a "field connection" for any of Dragon's future business plans in Vietnam.

Through Le, Connolly set up contact with Pharmthuco, a state-owned pharmaceutical manufacturing company of Thu Duc district (of Ho Chi Minh City) administered by both the city's Department of Public Health and Thu Duc's local administration. Pharmthuco had a license to import pharmaceuticals and medical supplies of any type. However, it seemed to have some problem with "international liquidity." The foreign exchange reserve of the city was not very generous with a company at the district level such as Pharmthuco. Dragon could have only local currency when it sold pharmaceuticals to Pharmthuco. After signing an "agency" agreement with Pharmthuco to the effect that the Vietnamese company would be Dragon's trading agent in this market, it would help Dragon apply for a representative office license, and both sides would look into the possibility of investing in a manufacturing joint venture in due course, Connolly had returned to Hong Kong with the agreement in hand and quite content about having done so. Rosenford appointed Hughes to carry out this project. Pathway was established for this Vietnam business with Hughes now at the helm.

Our car finally ran on a six-lane highway on the outskirts of Saigon, the only one Vietnam had to date, built more than 30 years ago by Americans during the war years. It had once been called "Bien Hoa Highway" because it links Saigon with Bien Hoa, the capital city of Dong Nai province 20 miles to the northeast of Saigon. Now it is renamed "Hanoi Highway," maybe a reminder that to enter Saigon, the "business capital" of the country, one must go through Hanoi, the "political capital" of Vietnam. At some point, our car turned right, entering a small road in quite poor condition running along a railway. It had much the look of the countryside with a few small fields of rice, but I also noticed quite a few factories lying side by side. The air-conditioned car felt good compared to the hot, sultry sun. It was like night and day getting in and out of the car. The car turned again to a small alley with clusters of bamboo on both sides. "Here we come," Hughes said, pointing to an electric pole, explaining there used to be a big sign there, which read PATHWAY TO VIETNAM, but Pharmthuco had asked him to remove it until Pathway could get a business license. I supposed it was symbolic of the fact that our only meaningful identity in Vietnam was given by our association with a Vietnamese company.

Hughes's residence was located in a large compound that also houses the plant and office of Pharmthuco. It used to be an old villa of a well-to-do family that fled to the United States after the communist takeover in 1975. Pharmthuco was authorized to use this real estate and turned it into a warehouse for its pharmaceutical products, before realizing its sluggish operation was too modest to make use of even a half or a third of the space of this facility. So it was quite happy to let Pathway renovate the house and use it—not only a "gesture of goodwill" but also an attempt to prevent the house from wearing out much further. Hughes had spent more than $50,000 to refurbish the house and make it livable. Painted dark brown, it was a wooden building with two floors elevated from the land surface adjacent to the side of the river. He took me straight to the house, where an attendant was waiting, helping me with the luggage. I was shown to my room, which looked over the bank of the river, where a small canoe was anchored. Very soon, I was back in a large living room, joining Hughes for a few drinks.

Our ensuing conversation helped me learn much more about the medical supply market in Vietnam with its unique characteristics. Although the economy had switched to the market system quite a few years ago, the government still does not allow private or foreign-invested investments in the medical industry on the grounds that "public health" is a matter of highly sensitive importance that private enterprises, "whose only pursuit is profit," should not be involved in.

HUGHES

"Recently, the Vietnamese government has encouraged foreign investors to cooperate with Vietnamese state-owned firms to set up manufacturing joint ventures. No licenses have been issued so far, however. As a result, production has been totally in the hands of state-owned firms and daredevil clandestine producers, many of whom are pharmacists who work in state-owned manufacturing firms or drugstores in daytime, operating mostly in Cholon, which is Saigon's Chinatown. Domestic output has fallen in recent years, and most factories at lower administrative levels, like districts or wards, and even many at province and city levels have had to cease manufacturing. The so-called organized and planned market of the government, which ranges from trading companies at central and city-province levels to pharmaceutical stores at districts and wards, has been shrinking a lot and been taken over by other, officially nonsanctioned means. Because the government has still maintained certain price controls over subsidized products of state-owned firms, state companies can make a profit only by closing their front doors and channeling their goods, including even imported medicines and medical supplies, through the back doors to the government-called 'nonorganized market,' which could hardly be described as a 'black market' because it has been so open and extensive. For the government to say it wasn't going on would be claiming complete blindness.

"Since the early eighties, in order to resolve huge unmet needs for medicines, the government has allowed, even encouraged, its people to receive pharmaceutical gifts from their relatives living overseas. Medicines and related supplies have become one of the hottest items on the ever-present black market, which in fact is a way of life in socialist economies—not really legal but taken for granted. There is no other way. The government can't get any manufacturing going, let alone market and distribute medical products. Foreign medicines and supplies are smuggled into the country from the sea and across the borders with China and Cambodia. These smuggled goods are instantly integrated into the nationwide "unorganized" market system that make the government's own system of distribution look quite ridiculous.

"When we came into Vietnam, we looked at the large market of more than 70 million people, but we did not recognize that the country is still very divided not only between north and south, but north, central, and south, or maybe even among 50 different provinces and cities run by 50 or so local lords. So where do we situate ourselves marketwise, we asked ourselves: in the organized market or the unorganized market? Personally, I prefer having a system of distribution of our own rather than relying on Pharmthuco. Their market doesn't really go beyond this small district, and its salespeople are more interested in getting mixed up with the black market for their own sake."

MATT

I was not surprised at Hughes's account, having occasionally heard stories about trafficking and the black market in China, Russia, and so on. In *Taxi Blues,* a film about Russia in the dying days of the communist regime, while the organized market required unending queues just for prime commodities, everything could be found in the black market, provided you know the rules of the game. But clandestine market activities to this proportion, as described by Hughes, were still shocking to me.

While we were talking, a young man rushed into the room and spoke very quickly to Hughes. From his pidgin English, I understood that Hughes needed to go to see somebody immediately. Something seemed to be wrong with the clearing of a shipment of medicinal drugs from the customs house. So Hughes asked to be excused, saying he would be back to take me downtown.

"Another crisis to solve," he said before rushing out of the house.

From discussions I had at the American Club in Tokyo, I had the impression that a lot of young executives of American companies aspire to be appointed to head branch offices in Asian countries so they can become "lords of the rim." I really doubt many of them could fathom the challenges they would face in an emerging country like Vietnam. "Hughes get five years older since he work here," his assistant My, a local Vietnamese, told me. I had no doubt about that after hearing Hughes recount what had happened that very evening.

Hughes had gone to the customs office to see what the problem was. It didn't take long to figure out he needed to get Pharmthuco involved. He wanted to talk directly to Dr. Tran Van Xuan, director of Pharmthuco, but he could not find Xuan because he was as "elusive as ever."

HUGHES

"He's called a (medical) doctor, but you would be surprised to see quite a lot of people with their name cards carrying their titles as doctors of some kinds! His unwritten life story is that Xuan was a guerrilla fighter during the war. He helped army surgeons carry out certain operations and also worked some time at a dispensary as a medicine auditor in the jungle. After peace was restored in 1975 he was sent to a part-time medical school for three years and made an administrative physician. One of his comrades, Dr. Le Thi Dan, developed her career in the same way but was more fortunate because Ho Chi Minh City needed an "educated" woman in the Party for the position of deputy chairman of the city. The story went that Mrs. Dan, 'the jungle-graduated physician,' once in a position of power, did not forget her old pal Xuan, explaining why Pharmthuco as a district-level firm still could enjoy a few privileges known to only city-level firms and Xuan could be relaxed enough to go to the tennis court every morning or afternoon."

Question 1:   Based on the description of how things work in Vietnam— the market system and position appointments, relation- ships between host and foreign companies—would you like working in that environment? Why or why not?

"I knew Xuan might be with some leaders of the city in some tennis court, so I had to meet Nguyen Van Thanh instead, Xuan's lieutenant, whose official title is 'Director of Planning.' Thanh, a member of the Communist Youth League, is an influential executive, believed to be Xuan's 'heir apparent,' although I could not see why Xuan should disappear in any near future, unless he gets a kick upstairs. Thanh does not speak English well. Communication with him is really difficult, but he prefers not to have an interpreter. He is rather at odds with My, my assistant, because I hired him myself instead of going through him. It's a two-edged sword because Nguyen would have picked some relative of his or a relative of someone he owed a favor. That might have helped my image with him a bit. But I never could have fully trusted any information my assistant would have given me and could certainly never have fully trusted him to keep information about Pathway confidential.

"When I found Thanh, he looked quite upset. He told me that the customs would not clear the shipment over the weekend as expected, insisting that Pharmthuco must show an import license before any action was taken. This was not the first time Pharmthuco has imported a lot of pharmaceutical materials without a license. In previous cases, Xuan has just sent his deputy director, Tran Van Thu, to see the first deputy executive director of the Customs Office of the city with a bottle of Johnny Walker and a carton of 555 cigarettes. The deputy director used to be Thu's boss in the city police department. As fate had it, Thu was purged out of the police following an investigation into a corruption case and designated the 'political commissar' of Pharmthuco. And unfortunately, this first deputy officer had been transferred to the Saigon port authority, and his successor was anxious to serve a reminder that this authority just had a new lord.

"Customs officers at lower levels were taking this opportunity to strengthen their bargaining position. If Pharmthuco did not act promptly to get the right licenses, the customs office would report the case to the People's Committee. Someone might leak this offense to the local press, which is very eager to hunt for 'scandals' involving foreign companies, since the shipment is for Pathway. Either way, there was a strong possibility that the lot [of products] could be impounded. Pharmthuco, as the importer, would be fined.

"So I told him, 'What can I do? You are the importer, you must make sure everything is proper, legal. I never liked this importing without a license. I even warned you people repeatedly that you could not continue this practice forever. I did not feel safe. Neither did you. And it eventually would be you, and you alone, to take responsibility for any risk, loss, or trouble with the government.

"In spite of what I said, I knew quite well that eventually, I might be the one who would have to bear the brunt of all of this. And it could leak to the press. They only write two types of articles: one to praise generously 'well-intentioned foreign companies and businessmen who come here because they love the communists and the Vietnamese people so much,' and another to condemn 'capitalist firms pursuing fast bucks by taking advantage of Vietnam's inadequate preparation for doing business with the rest of the world.'

"In this case, I tried my best to control my temper, because they had already told my boss I was ill tempered. So I told him that I would not agree to another delay, no matter what the situation was. Thanh, Pharmthuco's planning director, called what happened 'regrettable and beyond Pharmthuco's control' but suggested there was still a way. He was going to try to talk to some customs officers at lower levels, but powerful enough, into setting aside the case for at least a week before reopening it. Meanwhile, Dr. Xuan would go see the director of the Department of Public Health seeking a letter affirming this lot was 'in the public interest'; his friend Dr. Dan would be asked to make a phone call to the director of the Customs Office. In order to buy time, Thanh suggested they use one of Pathway 's 'medical gift samples,' some 15 to 20 boxes worth at least $1,000 each. Each box contained an array of medicines. This was not the first time Pharmthuco's staff had poked their noses into these boxes of *échantillons medicales* (medical samples). I knew there were instances in the past when they misappropriated these boxes, but I didn't mind expending one or two or three boxes if the operation of his business needed this kind of lubricant. Even by greasing the palm, though, it would be a week or two before the lot at customs could be cleared.

"In business, I've learned over and over again that time is opportunity, and opportunity is money. One day's delay can be a real disaster. They understand so well that time is valueless to them but extremely valuable to us, so they want to force us to pay for the opportunity cost of time. Basically, it comes down to how much money you have to sink into others' pockets just so you can transact business. It's doable if you're a well-endowed business, but if you're a small start-up, you might be in over your head. Investing for the long term is well and good, but not enough business can wait that long.

"Pathway might have been a good idea, but in a complicated transitional economy like Vietnam, where the people still need much time to learn how to do business, and the legal framework is far from being adequate, to see a 'good idea' through to its fruition takes more than smarts and willpower."

Question 2: *If you were the president of the parent company, Dragon Exploration, Inc., would you continue to invest in Pathway or pull out of Vietnam? Why or why not?*

"It was very unfortunate for Connolly that he first met up with one of Vietnam's many so-called consultants. He's the last man I would trust. In doing business here, you must watch out for those who always try to assure you that 'There is no problem.' Nothing is easy or straightforward in this country, even to get a driver's license. When it was found out later that Connolly's consultant was neither a member of the Communist Party nor a public servant, Connolly was advised to drop the guy immediately. He was a second-rate broker, anyway, and quite a few American businesspeople were just buying his words. Connolly was told to go to another consulting firm run by a government ministry. We were also warned against any directors of state-owned enterprises like Xuan, who is quite fond of bragging about having 'connections with the highest level in Hanoi,' which would help him obtain any investment license for his partner 'with no difficulty,' he'd tell us. Xuan was really eager to work with foreign companies, simply because he believes we are 'cows to milk.'

"Connolly contended that the Vietnamese market would soon become very competitive, so any early comer should take the initiative to strike 'a preemptive coup.' He decided to use Pharmthuco as the bridgehead to Vietnam, agreeing to support this company's activity almost at any price in order to buy its 'heart and mind' and provide the Vietnamese company with foreign 'high-quality' products to sell. The Vietnamese people had developed an aversion to *quoc doanh* (state run), which was synonymous to 'inferior,' 'incompetent,' 'fake,' like *trong tai quoc doanh* (state-run referees), *su quoc doanh* (state-run monks), *phim quoc doanh* (state-run movies), or *giam doc quoc doanh* (state-run managing directors). Connolly also believed he could commit Pharmthuco further to this partnership by setting up a joint venture in manufacturing pharmaceuticals. In the early stage, Pharmthuco did provide Pathway with a shelter and a shield. It had a corner in the office of Pharmthuco. In return, Pathway brought in quite a few valuable machines for Pharmthuco to modernize its plant. The machinery was brought in with the 'temporary' import permit under Pharmthuco's name, but there was an appendix agreement that the equipment belonged to Pathway and was for the future joint venture. My question was what Pharmthuco had in mind for this joint venture. In the first place, Pharmthuco, as a district-level company, was so poorly capitalized that its machinery and equipment became a liability rather than an asset to the firm. In its possession were merely a business permit and an import license, which were deemed 'both necessary and sufficient conditions' for doing business in an economy where permits and licenses were so important.

"Pathway had no permit to open a representative office—for various reasons. No foreign company could have import licenses, simply because they could not open branches in this country. So it had to depend on Pharmthuco for the import trade and even for marketing activity because marketing without a representative office license was an offense according to Vietnam's trading laws. Pathway believed it should be able to open a representative office for the pharmaceutical trade first—before exploring the possibility of investing in a drug-making company. But Pharmthuco showed little interest in helping Pathway have the representative office license. They want us to embark on the investment joint venture plan, even though we're not ready yet for this stage—not until we can measure the market potential by a self-initiated marketing survey.

"Pharmthuco has definitely been less than fully cooperative with us. Xuan, Pharmthuco's director, wanted me to finance a district soccer team, give money to a school in the neighborhood, but I told him I wouldn't fund anything before having the license. I refused to hire people he recommended because I had no need for them; so he was really unhappy, complaining I was not cooperative and did not understand the rule of 'unanimity' in joint venture co-management!

"I've been told that doing business in a country like Vietnam requires a long-term vision, hence patience and tenacity. In the meantime, I feel like a hostage. Without a trading license, we are like a ghost company, and I am a persona non grata in this city. Everything we do can be the cause for trouble any time. We rely totally on Pharmthuco's 'mercy' for survival. The problem is that Pharmthuco is not very merciful, by nature."

MATT

Hughes decided to seek a meeting with the local government in Ho Chi Minh City in order to find out what was going on and assess the possibility of getting their own license. My arranged the event and also served as interpreter for both sides. Hughes kindly suggested that I go with him, so I "could learn something." We went to the office of the People's Committee of Ho Chi Minh City. We scheduled a meeting to talk with officials responsible for reviewing applications by foreign companies opening representative offices and investing in the city. The building where we met is at least a century old and was the office of the French protectorate for at least 50 to 60 years—before the French colonialists withdrew from Vietnam in 1954.

The People's Committee is like a local government, with various directorates operating under its supervision, like ministries working in the government. As a matter of fact, there is a directorate of external economic relations (DEER) dealing with problems of foreign companies. But Hughes was told to come to the office of the vice chairman in charge of DEER because the vice chairman is like the deputy prime minister in the local government of the city, and the head of the directorate is just like a minister. The vice chairman has higher rank in both the local administration and the city's party hierarchy. He is also more well versed with policy-related matters, we were told. This vice chairman has almost a dozen "senior experts," and the first one we met was Sau Tung, who gave us his calling card, printed in English and introducing himself as "Doctor" Tung. Very different from most local businessmen who were dressed in ties and jackets, Sau Tung, in his mid-sixties, was attired in the old fashion of "popular communist cadres": a short-sleeved white shirt hanging loose over his pants and a pair of sandals. On the contrary, we were all dressed up. The suit and ties were seen as a sign of respect and seriousness that foreigners show to Vietnamese hosts. To show he had prepared for a strong case, Hughes also had with him an amply packed Samsonite case. And to win friends, he also brought two cartons of foreign cigarettes, one for Sau Tung and another for Ba Thoi, the other official we were to meet.

Our Vietnamese host took the carton of cigarettes in a casual way. From the tobacco-tainted tips of his fingers and the black decay on his teeth, I figured he must be a heavy smoker. My had briefed us about this northern-born bureaucrat. He had been a senior official of the Ministry of Trade in Hanoi before being sent to Ho Chi Minh City to support the infant administration of the "newly liberated" government in the south. Thousands of bureaucrats from the war-ravaged north moved to the more prosperous south in this way after the war, but after a few years, southern communists were trying to reduce the power of those coming from the north. People like Sau Tung were gradually disarmed, neutralized, isolated—given titular positions like "senior experts." Sau Tung was also known as "Comrade Sung Tau" (which in Vietnamese means Chinese Gun), not only because this is the Vietnamese-style reversal of his name, but also on account of his "background," that is, five years of studying economics in Red China in the fifties and his reputation as a tough boss.

He took from his drawer an iron box of tea and poured a handful of tea into a pot, which was so small I couldn't help wondering how there could be enough tea for all four of us. Then he slowly walked to a table in the corner of the room, took a vacuum flask, and added the hot water into the pot. From where I sat, I could also see he was pouring hot water from the thermos into small cups; then he emptied the water into a bin on the floor. Seeming extremely relaxed now, he returned to us with the teapot and teacups, sat down, poured tea into cups, asked us to have tea. Then he pulled out a Winston cigarette, lit it, and looking up, asked, "What can I do for you, your excellencies?" It was not frustrating, just amusing, for us to be addressed as "excellencies" when My explained to me that several northern party officials and businessmen liked to use the word "excellencies" just to show that they could also afford the luxury of this "bourgeois call."

Hughes briefly explained that he had now been operating for more than six months, believing it would be easy to get a license to open a representative office. It was not, and his business here was more or less illegal. In principle, he could not do anything: sign trading contracts, make payments, receive revenues, buy or sell anything, and he told Sau Tung that he was very nervous, considering he was here legally as a "business guest" of Pharmthuco, not as a licensed expatriate trade representative. But he needed to expand his business, bringing over his clients, like me, for instance (he pointed at me) to explore more business opportunities in this "promised land" (he smiled lightly).

Sau Tung began a lecture on Vietnam's socialist-based market-oriented economic renovation and its open door policy to encourage cooperation with foreign companies. In the course of translating these policies into "concrete" measures, there were certain problems that should be considered, like safeguarding national interest and preventing the abuse of open door policies. "Economic independence is as important as political independence, and we do not want to pay a dear price for economic independence as we did for political independence," he said. Then Sau Tung said that he knew "your excellency" had operated here for six months without a license, but "we do not stop it, because Comrade Xuan has assured me that he is working closely with your excellency, that you have goodwill, and that everything you are doing complies with the law."

In contrast, Tung said, many representative offices were operating independently and without authority. "We have made it clear repeatedly that a representative office cannot engage in profit-making commercial activity, but many foreign companies keep on violating this rule, penetrating into very distant districts in the Mekong Delta or highland provinces to sign contracts and sell motorcycles and color television sets or buy timber, shrimp, coffee, believing we know nothing of it. But we know it all," he said. In this way, "foreign trading companies are competing illegitimately with domestic trading companies and have also triggered market instability. At any time we can stop them from operating by not renewing their licenses or forcing their Vietnamese partner to dissolve the partnership. Foreign companies are here to cooperate, not to compete," he said. He also mentioned the case of an American businessman, Michael Morrow, who "took advantage of Vietnam's open door policy to conduct spying activities."

In the ensuing discussion, we learned that to have a license, a foreign company is required to have an annual turnover of more than $2 million, an amount designed to curb the number of representative offices, check foreign competition against Vietnamese companies, and welcome only "sizable and well-meaning companies" to the country. The application is made to the Ministry of Trade, but prior approval from Ho Chi Minh City, where the office was to be located and registered, is required before the petition is processed. Sau Tung went on to say that each representative office could have one local employee in the early stage. To have more, approval by the ministry was required. To employ local employees, a foreign company could hire directly, with the "ratification of the local directorate of labor, disabled war veterans, and social affairs," or through the government-controlled labor supply service company. A representative office could also employ expatriate managers, provided their skills were not available among local labor.

I was attentive, but Hughes looked quite exasperated, probably because it was not his first time to hear this speech. So he attempted to have some control of the conversation by interrupting Sau Tung: "But sir, how can we reach a record turnover of $2 million if we can't have a license to operate? How can we buy or sell $2 million if we don't have a license to buy and sell? And I would like to differentiate my line of business also. To have a turnover of $2 million in pharmaceuticals is very different from $2 million of garments or oil or shrimp. Vietnam is importing less than $50 million of medicines, and there are more than 100 local importers in this market. Smuggling is rampant in the central provinces. So how could I ever hope to reach $2 million of turnover for you?"

Sau Tung had a gratuitous smile. He assured us, "There will be no problem. It's your experimental period. For the time being, just work with Pharmthuco. After a few years, you will reach that level of revenue. Or the policy may change. I understand you have a joint venture plan with Pharmthuco. It's a very promising plan. As long as you are with Pharmthuco, a trading license is not needed. A license is a measure to make sure your business is under control. But in this case, you don't need it."

"I don't want to be in a position where I can be kicked out anytime Mr. Xuan wants," Hughes responded. I don't want *cong an* (policemen) to visit me in the night and say I have no license so I must pay fines and leave the country."

Sau Tung looked up and said, "We at this city do not mind having a few more representative offices. The more, the better. The problem is with Hanoi [where the central government is seated], with the Ministry of Trade. They want to exert a more effective control. If there were too many foreign companies, they would get lost, could not maintain control. We are filing a report to the prime minister, asking for easing of these kinds of restrictions. The prime minister is a southerner, so he may consider this petition more favorably. We have to wait and be patient," Sau Tung said as he concluded our meeting.

Anticipating Sau Tung would not be of much help, Hughes had also made an appointment with Ba Thoi, an expert on direct foreign investment. At least that's how he introduced himself. He was just next door to Sau Tung, also an odd man out in the hierarchical power system, although he is from the south. My told me in a kidding way that Sau Tung's career had been disrupted because of his "diplomatic smile," which aroused suspicion, and Ba Thoi's career could not go very far either because he lacked just this smile. Anyway, we also had to wait a while as Ba Thoi was repeating the same process of preparing tea.

Hughes began the conversation by expressing his interest in investing in the pharmaceutical industry and admitting he did not know whether the government had a negative or positive attitude toward such plans. Ba Thoi told us in a rather harsh and high voice, "Comrades, your problems are similar to those who did not consult us first before doing business in this country. Not only we can help you learn our policy, but we can also tell you what to do to further your goal. This is a very complicated country because we have the policy of the Central (government), then the policy of the local (government). The license is granted by the Central, but you operate in a local environment, so you must also know local policy. But if you have the local support only, the Central will simply ignore your application," Ba Thoi said with authority. Ba Thoi also suggested that without assistance from his office's experts, investment feasibility studies of foreign companies would not meet the "standard" requirements of the government.

"Suppose we want to have your service and are ready to pay for it. Is there any guarantee we will have the investment license after three or six months, for instance?" Hughes asked.

"We are a government office, not a company to sell any service. We give you information about government policies, measures. For more specific details, you can relate to consulting companies that we can refer you to," he replied. "Oh yeah," Hughes whispered to me. "We know all about the consulting companies."

Then Ba Thoi explained to us why Hughes's investment plan could get nowhere. He said that after nearly five years of working with foreign investors, the government "prepares to soon pronounce a list of priority areas and a list of restricted areas." He continued, "We have more than 100 pharmaceutical factories we have to protect. If you come in and set up 100 percent foreign-owned firms, the whole domestic industry will instantly collapse. That's why in this industry we encourage joint ventures only," he said.

Although I left the meetings greatly enlightened, Hughes was no further than he had been before. Despite the problems in doing business in Vietnam and the lack of a bona fide indigenous industry base in this country, Hughes was persuaded there was a rising expectation running high in most people of all walks of life in this country, a certain sustainable faith because they had the desire, the will, the diligence, and, relatively, the skills and the resources to further their dreams. This conviction of the Vietnamese people was apparently strong because there was a simple belief the current changes were irreversible, and it was highly unlikely they would become passive, inactive, and submissive again if there were any attempts to turn the tide.

I also met Thuan Giao, a well-known Vietnamese newspaper editor, who was probably the most prolific writer in Ho Chi Minh City. From him, I learned the media had launched a vigorous campaign to denounce corruption, incompetence, complacency, and arrogance in both the party-blessed government and its state-owned enterprises. What the media stopped short of saying was that all these wrongdoings, malpractice, and abuse of power were still very pervasive, and the party should take responsibility for this state. Tolerance of such a state was once again irresponsible, which would not make the party more viable, the people less upset, and economic development less troublesome. But Thuan Giao told us the party soon became nervous and finally decided to strangle to death this "Vietnamese-style *glasnost*." From the brief talks I had with quite a few young business executives like My at state-owned firms, private companies, and even government offices, I also learned that their main preoccupation is no longer with a party membership card but scarce opportunities to acquire "real education" so that they could "catch up with the world's knowledge." At many schools, thousands of students of all ages are attending night classes to learn computers, English, accounting, marketing, and so on. I asked Thuan Giao where the teachers come from. He just commented, "It's a good question!"

The more sympathetic I felt about the cause of these nice people, the more convinced I became that they would have a tough time ahead after I heard dismaying stories from some foreign businessmen. Life is outrageously expensive for foreigners in this country. The state still controlls the monopoly of a lot of major services, and it is free to make price. When foreigners fly from Ho Chi Minh City to Hanoi, they have to pay $250, whereas for the same seat, a native Vietnamese pays only $90. Hotel charges, telecommunication charges, house rents are among the highest in Asia, although far from the best. John Bishop was chief representative of a British bank with a strong representation in Asia/the Pacific. He was among the first foreign bankers to have come to a renovated Vietnam. In order to win the hearts and minds of the Vietnamese government in Hanoi as well as the local administration of Ho Chi Minh City, he had done everything he could think of: relief donation, training grants to government servicemen, overseas trips for senior banking officials of the government, courses on finance and banking, research on banking reforms. Bishop had wanted to be one of the first foreign banks to be authorized to open a branch in Ho Chi Minh City, the business hub of this economy.

Unfortunately, he was neither the first nor among the first. The first was a Thai bank, a latecomer, which received the license to operate a branch in Ho Chi Minh City during the visit to Hanoi by Thai prime minister Chuan Leekpai. Among the first were also three French banks, in consideration of France's close political ties to Vietnam and also of France's stubborn fight against the U.S. trade embargo against Vietnam. Bishop's bank could be among the first had he agreed to open the branch in Hanoi, the political capital of the country. "Everything Ho Chi Minh City from the south could have, Hanoi from the north should also have, and should be the first to have it" was a well-understood policy, which Bishop simply did not want to comply with because he didn't believe there were many business opportunities in the north.

Hughes also explained how Vietnam is dismantling its monolithic system of state banks and expanding the banking sector for private participation, since this may affect Pathway's situation. At the time, no private banks are opened yet, but hundreds of "credit cooperatives" all over the country have operated to attract, in the words of a government official, "billions of dollars of redundant savings in the hands of the people still buried under their beds or hidden in the ceiling." Most of the cooperatives, after operating for a few months, are collapsing one over another like a house of cards.

Thanh Huong Perfumeries was not a credit cooperative, it was not even a company, but like many other small "manufacturing units" it was authorized by the local district administration to raise the capital for expanding operation. Anh Muoi Hai (literally meaning Mr. Twelve), 28 years old, in fact had reached only the tenth grade. He had a stall in a small market selling cheap perfumes produced by small local plants. Some of his friends told him that it doesn't take a chemist to manufacture perfumes. You only need to buy some essences and try various blends. So Muoi Hai set up a small "laboratory" at home, located in a slum-like area in Saigon, and started to "produce perfumes." He was given a business license for production, and with his license, he started raising money, first from other fellow vendors in Thai Binh market. It was believed his perfume business was going very well; otherwise, he would not have spent such a huge amount of money for television and radio commercials and newspaper advertisements.

Then Thanh Huong Credit came into being, offering a monthly interest of 12 to 15 percent. The inflation rate was then estimated at 80 to 100 percent per annum, and other credit cooperatives were borrowing at 7 to 8 percent monthly. Thanh Huong did not lend, but was known to be spending all of its money on the real estate trade—buying land, houses, villas, waiting for the D day of the "hotel boom." Not only people in Saigon were entrusting him their savings but also those from all over the country (Hanoi, Hai Phong, Hue, Da Nang, Dalat, Nha Trang, Can Tho, Minh Hai, etc.). The payment of interest went well over several months, coming from the deposits of subsequent clients. People of all strata placed money with him, including several high-ranking officials in the local government and the party organization of Ho Chi Minh City, who were accorded with a "premium" compound rate of interest. A famous American magazine was not reluctant to describe him as "the success story of private business in Vietnam's renovation era." When I was there, Muoi Hai, his wife, and many others of his business realm were standing trial on fraud charges. It was estimated that he had embezzled no less than $20 million from his depositors. His "financial market" already collapsed, because the deposits could not cover even the interest payment—not to mention the reimbursement of principal. It was the first nation-wide credit crash in this country, but no government officials nor government organizations were involved or implicated!

I left on a Wednesday morning, having spent only a little over a week in Ho Chi Minh City. I was very grateful for Hughes's generous effort to make this trip a highly "educational one." I did not believe I could have learned so much had I not met him and benefited from his agonizing experience and invaluable knowledge. His affection for the Vietnamese people was also amazing to me. He told me, "This industrious and intelligent people deserve a better life—at least as good as that of their neighbors. It's too bad the government is having a difficult time running this economy."

Once airborne, I was undecided whether or when I should make another trip to this country. I was only certain of one thing. If we ever did anything in Vietnam, I'd hire Hughes to be our consultant, and with or without him, it would be a tough row to hoe.

QUESTIONS FOR DISCUSSION

1. Do you think MedTech should try to enter the Vietnamese market? What are the pros and cons? If you believe they should, how would you do so?
2. For a foreign company, what appears to be the basis of a successful business in Vietnam?
3. What qualities would an individual need in order to succeed in the kind of position Hughes is in? Do you think Hughes is managing his role well? Why or why not?

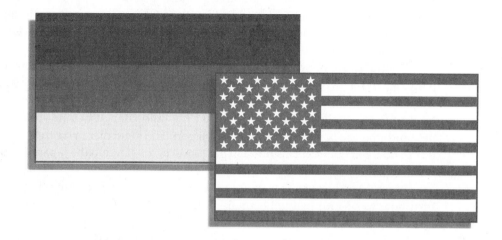

CHAPTER 10

Culture Clash: Do International Buyouts Always Make Sense?

MATT

We were back in Japan about two months and I still hadn't heard from any of my contacts. I had written them all to thank them for their time and to follow up on any potential interest. Having learned by now that Asians in general seem to prefer face-to-face communication, I wasn't totally surprised that I didn't hear from any of them. I didn't take it as a personal affront; rather, I figured it was just a difference in culture—and maybe a little lack of interest too. It might have reflected their preoccupation at the time.

In any case, the Japanese medical supplies market was blossoming fairly well despite problems in other areas of the economy. Sales had been increasing steadily for the last 16 months, averaging about a 10 percent monthly increase. We were clearly a success. I had to hand it to Muhashi. They knew what they were doing. Of course, MedTech wasn't too bad either. The quality rate had increased to about a half percent rejection rate across all the surgical instruments. Although Japan was by far MedTech's largest market to date, business was starting to pick up in the United States and we picked up hints of activity in Europe as well. In the seven months, I had made several trips back to California to help with the marketing strategy. Carl had picked up his responsibilities fairly well, but Jeff and I both thought he needed to show more leadership.

Eventually, we hired a fairly experienced marketing person away from a company one of the investors had helped fund about ten years earlier. Marc Morgan was really sharp and had some good contacts. We initially hired him on a contract basis with the explicit understanding that it would change to a full-time permanent position as soon as I returned from Japan. The logic there was that as long as no "permanent" person was hired in my place, it appeared to the Japanese that the need for me to return was still there.

One of Marc's contacts turned out to be a true gem. He eventually helped us distribute to several of the hospitals in the West owned by American Hospital Corporation.

The best contact in Europe was with a German company, Oberfeldt AG, that distributed pharmaceutical products for most of the largest pharmaceutical firms in Germany and some in Switzerland. Unfortunately for us, though, Oberfeldt AG was beginning to change its overall business strategy to one of acquisitions instead of just distribution. They were seeking to vertically integrate as much as possible. A new management team had come aboard Oberfeldt AG, and as the European Community became more a reality, it began to take a very aggressive stance toward what might help it be more profitable. It was in search of small firms with these four qualifications: they had already shown some success, their products had potential worldwide appeal, there was currently little to no competition in Europe, and the investment price was fairly low.

Of the four criteria, the lack of competition in Europe was an important one. Oberfeldt AG was not ready to invest capital to build a production plant in Europe if that were required. But it was fearful that if there were stiff competition in one of the EC members, particularly France, there would be a lot of pressure to stop imports or make it cost prohibitive to import the products. France, in particular, was very protective over any of its industries and generally unwilling to open itself to the possibility that a foreign firm, outside the EC, might have a clear market advantage.

Oberfeldt AG became very interested in MedTech. And although MedTech was starting to do very well and showed promise, the current investors were not necessarily interested in MedTech's long-term growth potential. As Jeff and I found out, they were more interested in getting a start-up going, attracting the interest of a larger company, selling out and making a lot of money, and then moving on to the next start-up. It seemed like the ultimate business rape to us. But there wasn't much we could do. Jeff's position on the board didn't make any difference. The investors wanted out and Oberfeldt AG was knocking at the door and ready to pay handsomely. So what initially looked like a friendly business relationship—us as the suppliers and Oberfeldt as the distributors—was turning out to be a takeover—a hostile one to several of us at MedTech.

After some short-lived negotiations, the investors sold MedTech for a handsome price. That began the next phase of "development," as I call it. A buyout usually makes life crazy for a while and it did for us too. It did leave Jeff and me in our places, though, guaranteed for at least one year according to the terms of the agreement. The investors did that much at least.

It was harder on Jeff than me, though, in one sense. He had to deal with the Germans directly. I was thousands of miles away on my own and didn't have much direct contact with them except for the visits and a few faxes. When Oberfeldt AG first purchased MedTech, Dr. Bergman became Jeff's overseer. He was senior operations officer, a former senior scientist at Oberfeldt AG before they became primarily a distribution business. After the acquisition for the first several months, Dr. Bergman was in California about half the time and Germany half of the time. He didn't waste a lot of time setting up various policies and procedures to bring what he called "some order and uniformity" to MedTech. A clear organizational chart—the first MedTech employees had seen—was developed and posted.

Part of his concern was standardizing certain procedures to increase the compatibility between MedTech and Oberfeldt AG. I'm not so sure compatibility should have been the goal or at least that their definition of what made us compatible was appropriate. It was obvious that Dr. Bergman felt MedTech was too loosely run. Employees called Jeff by his first name, which wasn't very acceptable. Employees also often walked right into Jeff's office without an appointment, even sometimes when Bergman was with Jeff, which didn't go over very well either.

"How can you plan your time and follow your agenda with unexpected interruptions like that?" he would ask Jeff.

Jeff would tell him, "That's the way we've always operated and it has worked fine. When there's a problem, we do what we need to do to solve it. We go straight to the horse, and doors are always open."

Bergman countered, "But businesses are not farms. People are not horses. Horses are allowed to roam where they want. That is not very efficient for a business. In Germany, we are very efficient at solving problems also. And it is not difficult to talk directly to a manager, but some of the questions your employees ask you, one of your managers should be able to answer. They should not come to you. And if it is important, you might think about setting time aside during the day just for those kinds of calls. In addition, it seems when your employees are not asking you questions, they're often telling you things that could easily be put in a memo, which you could read at a time you have set aside for such communications." And then he added, "Having clear procedures and policies—and following them strictly—is Oberfeldt AG's way of preventing problems from occurring in the first place. It is necessary for the fine-tune functioning of any organization."

Jeff told me he didn't disagree that Oberfeldt AG was probably very efficient. They had two slightly different approaches is all—one method that Jeff liked and was used to and the Oberfeldt AG method.

Oberfeldt AG didn't stop with their tinkering with just the internal workings of the firm. They felt all Oberfeldt AG operations worldwide should be standardized in every way possible. This even included changing the dress and other habits MedTech employees had become accustomed to. Management started having to wear white shirts and ties. Staff had to dress "professionally" also. There were no more Friday "dress-down" days or late afternoon get-togethers with the entire company personnel.

"It is important to look professional at all times, especially when customers visit, and company time can be put to better use than socializing Friday afternoons," Dr. Bergman told Jeff.

Even the parking lot took on a slightly different face. Pre-Oberfeldt AG, parking was a first come, first served situation. Now there were designated spots for Dr. Bergman and an assistant of his, Karl Schmidt, who would often accompany him, for Jeff, and for the rest of upper management. They were the closest parking spots to the building entrance, of course. It really didn't change a whole lot because Jeff and the other management team were usually the first ones to arrive anyway. But this arrangement clarified any ambiguity about hierarchy.

As you can imagine, Jeff didn't accept the changes very well. We knew any buyout regardless of whether it was a foreign or domestic would mean changes, and usually not for the good of the employees. Restructuring the hierarchy, the policies, and sometimes redefining the strategies were all part of the game. That was Oberfeldt AG's choice to make. Our choice was to decide whether we liked the changes or not. The bottom line for us was the changes weren't consistent with us, and we, especially Jeff, felt we were letting our employees down. Despite Jeff's efforts to explain and suggest policy, Oberfeldt AG seemed bent on doing things their way. I can understand that, but the time comes when sometimes the "locals" know best. If MedTech were in Germany with German employees, everything probably would have been okay, but we were in the United States— California no less.

Within six months, the production manager was gone, as was the CFO. Both had been on board since MedTech's beginning. Jeff hung on as long as he could bear it, but he, too, left after another couple of months. We talked quite a while about his leaving and what that would mean for the company. Neither of us felt it was a good move for MedTech, but neither of us felt there was much choice either. When you start a company and employees have sacrificed some home life and personal recreation to put in the extra hours and sweat it takes to start a company, you feel some genuine loyalty there. Now Jeff felt as though he could no longer give something back to the employees. Oberfeldt seemed bound and determined to limit his influence to the point that it almost seemed like it didn't matter who was CEO. Everything was supposed to run according to Oberfeldt guidelines.

Before Jeff left, he asked me whether I would be interested in the position in case he were allowed to make any recommendations. The idea of being CEO was exciting—big leather chair, intercom, personal secretary, big bucks—yeah, those were the perks, just about everything Jeff didn't have! That was the image. The reality would be much different.

Question: *If you were Matt, would you accept the CEO position if offered it? Why or why not?*

I told Jeff that under these circumstances there was no way I wanted to take his job, which is what he expected anyway. It turned out it wouldn't have made much difference, anyway. Bergman put his assistant, Karl Schmidt, in at the helm, which we figured was probably the plan all along. Micromanage the entrepreneurial management team until they decide to leave and then put your own people in. If that was the plan, it was working.

Jeff became CEO of a small start-up firm that one of the investors of MedTech had helped fund. That kind of thing is often done if you maintain a good reputation in the industry. Jeff seemed happy about the new position but had real regrets leaving MedTech before it had really and truly turned the corner and gone public. Going public was the big milestone for a lot of people with start-ups. That's where the real feeling of accomplishment came in (and the real money was made).

As for my situation, the visits to Tokyo became a little more frequent now that Jeff was gone. Bergman and Karl had already come and met all the Japanese connected to the partnership. They had looked over the operation and seemed satisfied in most respects. The last couple of visits were a little more serious, though. I think they both questioned whether I was needed there, and they made some hints about reevaluating the situation. By now it really didn't matter to me because mentally and emotionally I was already somewhat gone. Jan and I had already decided to return to the States as soon as either one of us could find a good job.

QUESTIONS FOR DISCUSSION

1. What are the differences you notice between the Oberfeldt AG "way" and the "MedTech" way? Does MedTech represent the U.S. way?
2. Do you think buying MedTech represents a wise acquisition for Oberfeldt AG? Why or why not? Would there probably be a good fit if Oberfeldt AG were to acquire a typical small firm reflecting your culture (if different from the United States)? In what areas?

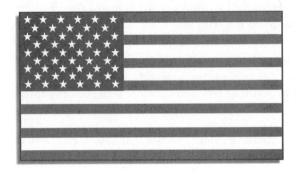

CHAPTER 11

Leveraging the Global Experience

JAN

We arrived in the Bay Area eager to find work that would enable us to buy a piece of the most expensive real estate in America. Before Matt sent out résumés, he contacted Karl Davidson, his former professor at UCLA. Karl suggested Matt visit UCLA in a few weeks to attend an executive development seminar. The seminar lasted a full week, with intensive advanced management classes running each day. Matt particularly enjoyed the session Karl conducted, which focused on the challenges U.S. companies face in the upcoming era of greater international competition. Karl's reputation had grown since Matt had studied with him at UCLA, and he now spearheaded these conferences regularly. Matt invited Karl for a late lunch after the session, hoping to get insight into the current job market. Well, he really needed just a little boost that a proud former mentor might provide to assuage the ego damage incurred doing battle in the field. I'm sure Matt was more productive in his position than MedTech could reasonably have expected anyone to be, but that's hardly ever the way people see their own situation, and Matt is no exception.

In the weeks before the seminar Matt investigated almost a dozen companies that interested him. Karl had suggested he come to UCLA prepared to discuss some of the companies that might employ him. He had contacts at some companies who sent him annual public summaries and mission statements; others he knew of only vaguely, but research materials at the university library enabled him to compile dossiers.

Most importantly, Matt knew I wanted to stay in Northern California. His career had been the priority in the past; we had agreed the next career move would be mine. Staying in Northern California wouldn't necessarily help my career, and certainly wasn't great for family finances, but I felt Matt ought to demonstrate a good faith effort to meet my needs for a while. I wanted Jeff and Michelle to be familiar and comfortable with their extended family, and both sets of grandparents now lived in the greater Bay Area. This part of the country is very appealing even without the incentive of having close family nearby. It's extraordinarily beautiful, well supplied with national parks and recreational opportunities, and peopled with a mixed group of the friendliest citizens in the world. Matt's search for work was confined to the Bay Area—a parameter I continued to monitor. Unemployed people can get rather delusional about the attractions of a solid job offer in, say, Dayton.

While Matt searched for a new job, I worked on my own career. I started by becoming active again in the local Sierra Club. Since I still had friends in the club, I thought it would be a good place to start networking. One of those friends was Heather Irsay, a study buddy from Berkeley who had roomed with me there in my second year. I forget which of us first decided that Law Review was a good idea. Our free time dried up like ski boots on a hot hearth, but we helped each other through.

Heather had remained single, reluctant to lower her standards and unable to find the perfect match. She had already made partner at Brobeck, Phleger and Harrison, one of California's largest law firms, and knew the Bay Area legal scene as well as anyone. She lived in Palo Alto and worked alternately at the firm's San Francisco and Palo Alto offices. After our return from Japan, Heather and I decided to meet for lunch every other Tuesday. I knew the measure of how happy Heather was to see me back in her life—there really is nothing like spending time with an old friend. I trusted Heather's advice, and firmly believed she could help me jump-start my moribund career.

During our first lunch, I expected we would simply catch up on each other's lives. But of course my unemployment was foremost in *my* life, and as I'd hoped, Heather wanted to be of help to me. However, I found her to be awfully pessimistic as she listened to my nascent plans, which featured the big five firms in San Francisco. She suggested I set my sights a little lower.

"Why?" I asked. "What's wrong? Have I been out of law too long? Are most firms only interested in recent graduates?"

"No, that's not the problem as I see it," Heather responded. "Let me just tell you what's going on for most firms. Almost no firm is hiring right now, and top-paying jobs are disappearing. Most firms realize that they only need a few people with big salaries and benefits packages who will work more hours. Because the competition between law firms has become so brutal, most of us have flattened out our work forces in one way or another to cut costs—through early retirement, contract buyouts, or layoffs. Every firm I know of is trying to trim down."

"How do they get by with fewer people?" I asked.

"Part of the problem is solved through computers, fax machines, networks, and so on. It's just easier to get work done by computer using a database like LEXIS than by using a paralegal or junior partner. We got rid of all of our `in-house' support services as well. Now we contract out on a high hourly wage, but because we don't have to come up with any benefits we save almost one-third of the cost we used to pay. Today's buzz word for this is `outsourcing.' Everything that you don't absolutely have to have in-house you contract out."

"How much can a firm outsource?" The term made me uncomfortable—it seemed a little too trendy.

"Well, we used to have an in-house computer support office that took care of all of our computer problems or needs. Now, we 'sublet' from a computer services company for the same help. They pay their own employee benefits and we save a ton of money. We use a lot of temps for secretarial help. We 'sublet' all of our accounting. We've even talked about making all of our staff functions outsourced. 'Rent-a-staff' is what we call it. We even rent paralegals. It's a great time to run a temp agency."

Heather took a sip of coffee and I played with a spoon. "Basically," Heather continued, "it's almost impossible to find a really good job with a good salary and benefits package. I've been with the firm almost seven years, and I still work 60-hour weeks. I have to, since I'm in that 'inner circle' of core employees. We pick up all the extra work left over from all of our trimming down. I can't imagine what kind of hours someone new would have to work in order to get into that circle. Honestly, Jan, I don't see how you could do it with Matt and your kids to worry about. I just don't see a job like mine as a realistic option for you. Have you considered applying to the city or state offices? The workload is reasonable, and in an appeals department you wouldn't have to deal with the public at all."

I was pretty depressed at the prospect of having a job whose salient good point was not having to deal with the public. I changed the subject; we talked of other friends in our graduating class and what they had done since graduation. Soon Heather had to leave and get back to work. We arranged for our next lunch and I returned home feeling irritated and pensive.

That night, I told Matt what I'd heard from Heather. It took some effort—here I'd insisted that the family respect my career move and suddenly it looked as though I had no career to respect. I worried that without a better prospect we would simply follow Matt's lead again. I wondered if I'd already in some way irrevocably committed myself to the mommy track, with the concomitant belief system that biology is destiny. If you weren't the mother of a daughter, perhaps you could consider one life's sacrifice on the altar of family well spent. However, I firmly believe my daughter needs a mommy who is just as human as her daddy. I didn't want Matt's career to once again dominate family choices and considerations, but Heather's assessment of the job market made me wonder what option I had.

Matt, bless his heart, offered to be a house husband. "Should I stay home and take charge of the family so you can work the 60 hours you need to?"

"I might say yes, except that I don't know if I can even find a job, regardless of how many hours I work," I said. "Heather made it sound like no firm is hiring in the Bay Area, and I really don't want to leave here." I threw myself down on the bed next to Matt and thought about my needs and wants. I really wanted to stay close to my parents. And I really wanted to spend time with my children. I really wanted a career, a *real* career with successes and financial rewards and intellectual challenges to be met. I also wanted Matt to be free to pursue his career. And I felt sure that not all of these could happen simultaneously. Things looked bleak.

Question 1: *How would you resolve this dilemma? Your career has been put on hold and now, like Jan, you want to resume it, but you don't want to put your family at risk, financially or emotionally.*

MATT

In the days before the UCLA management development conference, I continued sending out résumés and interviewing with Bay Area companies, in addition to compiling folders on interesting companies. I also arranged to stay with a friend in Brentwood while I attended the seminar. I tried to prepare for the seminar by reading recent business journals and some recently published books regarding international business.

When the day arrived, I made my way to UCLA for the conference with an empty notepad, a few employment options, and a place to stay. The first session covered the "new rules" for a successful career. Under the "old school" (what I had tried at MedTech), a young MBA should join a good company and climb the corporate ladder. At the top of the ladder there awaited a high salary job with great benefits, which led to an early retirement with some stock options. Unfortunately, most of those "old school" jobs had disappeared; the current trend in America is for a very small number of people to earn unconscionably large amounts of money while the rest of us send our children to increasingly dangerous public schools.

Careers in the current fast-moving global economy require new rules. Speed proved the critical competitive advantage. Incredible competition had fostered price slashing, and had reduced everyone's profit margins while increasing the demand for high quality. To compensate, companies learned how to leverage themselves globally: they learned to manipulate their functions in various parts of the world for increased efficiency. For example, in 1993 a company could manufacture a high-quality product, using top labor in Southeast Asia for $4.75 an hour (including legally required benefits) and in the United States, the same product would cost $16.90 an hour. As a result, most companies tried to manufacture as much as possible in Southeast Asia or China and use that to leverage their prices globally.

So what did this mean to a young manager? I discovered the answer in a panel discussion two days later. Young high-potential managers needed to see themselves as one component in the global leveraging process, one panelist suggested. They had to find a way to add value to themselves, to stretch and stay marketable. As always, they needed to "sell themselves," but in a global economic situation that meant upgrading their knowledge and skills at every opportunity.

Young talent, another panelist offered, should not necessarily take the most stable job, but instead work for a company that offers them a great five-year contract. Foremost, they should worry about the specific tasks and projects they need to accomplish during the five years. "Find companies that take learning very seriously," one panelist suggested. "Find a company that wants its employees to attend seminars, retraining programs, and increases their skills—especially companies where, if an employee becomes obsolete, it would pay for the employee to get new training in a more productive area." Most importantly, all the panelists agreed, young talents must be certain to be more valuable either inside or outside the company at the end of the five years.

I reviewed my notes and reflected on my situation. When I finally met up with Karl later that afternoon, Karl reiterated all that I had heard. "Do not get stuck or plateaued in a job that has no learning curve," he said. "Leaving MedTech might have been your best move." He suggested I stay on a strong learning curve, sometimes moving 'laterally' or even taking a pay cut to get into a situation that had a more effective 'developmental stream.' "The key," he concluded, "is to remain mobile and flexible."

Karl continued, "Think of career in terms of chunks that last five to seven years. When you finish that chunk, spiral off into a new chunk. Worry more about 'spiraling' than moving up a career ladder. Think in terms of projects, opportunities, and skills gained, and not career ladders. Always look for new opportunities to grow and improve your value because ultimately, that's your only job security:

your added value to the company. Especially worry about finding skills that guarantee customer satisfaction. Today all companies have become obsessed with customers—we call this the era of the customer. Being involved with key customers is the main source of employee power."

I realized I had unintentionally followed the blueprint Karl suggested. After five years with MedTech I had gained some important skills and experiences that made me more marketable. "Typically, in this country," Karl explained, "an international move means great personal development for an employee, but often ends his career in the corporation. Out of sight, out of mind."

"I know that all too well," I responded.

"But today that doesn't matter very much because not many people can or should stay with the same company indefinitely."

Karl went on to discuss my employment options. Of the four companies that seemed interested in me, Karl focused on Plasmatec. As a new growth company, Plasmatec seemed to fit all the criteria Karl looked for in a job opportunity.

As the week wore on, I heard similar reports from other lecturers and panelists. Every session concluded that, in an ever more global economy, business and business leaders need to be flexible, quick to evolve, and open to new cultures, markets, and ideas. I slowly came to the conclusion that my experience with MedTech might not be a liability and that international business offered the most exciting future.

Question 2: *How could Matt use his experience at MedTech to be more marketable than when he went to Japan—even though he won't still be at MedTech?*

When I returned home, I told Jan all about what I had learned and asked whether anyone had contacted me about a job. Only two companies had called. Johnson & Johnson wanted another interview. The other call came from Plasmatec. The message came from Robert "Doc" Silverman. He wanted me to call him regarding "a position you might be interested in."

I grew excited. I talked with Jan about the position to see what she thought. She agreed the job wouldn't interfere with her career options and seemed pleased it meant we could stay in the Bay Area. So, early Monday morning, I called Doc Silverman, who offered me a position in marketing at Plasmatec. I accepted and agreed to come to the office that afternoon to sign a contract and discuss a few details.

By the end of the day I learned that my new position meant a slight pay cut (starting salary between $70,000 and $75,000) and less prestige compared to what I left at MedTech. But the position had all the advantages I had just heard about at the UCLA seminar. I hoped that my previous international experience and hard work would allow me to advance quickly—once I'd proved my value.

JAN

The next day, I met Heather for lunch. I had continued to network with friends and acquaintances at the Sierra Club and elsewhere and had come upon a few ideas for my career. I decided to run the ideas by Heather and see what she had to say.

"Heather," I said, "do law firms outsource even legal researching?"

"Some do, I'm sure. Why do you ask?"

"Well, I was thinking about what you said last time we were together. If firms are looking for outside people to do their work, maybe I could be one of those people. I'm a good researcher. And we have a computer at home. I could use a modem to hook up to LEXIS and do research on contract. Actually, Matt just got a job that has full benefits for both of us, so I don't really need them myself."

Heather grew excited. "That's a great idea! You can work at home, keep your legal skills current, and you won't have to drive 101. Why didn't I think of that?" Heather paused for a moment to gather her thoughts. "You know, I might have a lead that would be very interesting to you. Let me call you later today or tomorrow to see if I can come up with something."

I agreed. "Do you think most firms would object to me working out of my home?"

"No. Not at all. You need to remember that the whole idea behind this is cost reduction. If they don't have to pay for a place for you to work, they're very happy. Besides, if you work at home you can get some great tax breaks."

"Do you think I could parlay a research job into a full-time job?"

Heather's expression lost some excitement. "I doubt it. In fact, you may feel a little bit like a second-class citizen. The core employees work so long and hard together, everyone else sometimes gets treated like high-paid hired help, which is basically what they are. Really, the only way to get into that inner circle is to work incredibly hard. But who knows?" Heather's expression turned optimistic again. "Anything can happen once you've got your foot in the door."

I felt a pang of anxiety at her description of my position in the company. I did not want to seem less accomplished than other attorneys; I certainly had never been less competent than my fellow students. But Heather continued, "But you know, if you found the right niche, you could make a very interesting career for yourself. Especially since you're in environmental law. That's the one area of law that's really growing right now."

A few days later, Heather called and said, "I have the perfect job for you." She told me about a firm in Los Altos that specialized in out-of-court or alternative dispute resolution between environmental groups and various industries. The law firm needed a part-time researcher to prepare its senior staff members for negotiations between the two interests. Heather insisted that, although relatively new, the mediation area was growing quickly. She arranged an interview for me and said she would call a few people at the firm and give me a glowing recommendation.

I liked both the subject matter and the idea of settling disputes out of court. I did some quick research on the firm, and my interviews went very well. The firm offered me the contract within the week. Since most of my work involved research, they agreed to let me do much of it at home and commute when needed to the office in Los Altos.

Matt and I settled into a routine to accommodate our work schedules. We agreed that Matt would watch the children for three weeknights while a sitter watched them the other two weeknights. I decided to put in four hours in the mornings while Jeffery attended school and Michelle went to preschool, and then three hours after dinner while either Matt or the sitter watched the kids.

EXCERPT FROM MATT'S COMPUTER FILE ON PLASMATEC

Plasmatec is an incorporated private company that produces and markets a highly mobile "noninvasive glucose monitor" (NIGM). The hand-held device reports the glucose level in a person's blood. Nearly all of Plasmatec's customers suffer from diabetes and must regularly monitor their blood glucose level. What sets the NIGM apart from similar devices is that it does not require a blood sample to generate its readings. All other monitors require at least one drop of blood, usually from a pricked finger. To operate the NIGM, however, a person places one finger into one end of the pocket-sized rectangular machine. It diagnoses the blood in a few seconds without breaking the skin (thus the term "noninvasive"). No larger than a small tape recorder, the machine's mobility and simple application make it very popular among diabetics.

The product grew out of research and findings at the University of California Medical School in San Francisco. About ten years earlier, several researchers from UC-San Francisco found a number of investors to form Plasmatec. The NIGM required several years of development before successfully entering the market. Since then, most ongoing product development has originated in Plasmatec's own research division.

The company founders decided to locate Plasmatec in Santa Cruz, California. California appealed to them because it offers a large population eager for "consumer-oriented" health care. Californians buy products designed for private use in the home, possibly because commercial real estate prices are passed on to consumers in the fees charged by doctors, labs, and hospitals.

The founders built their main offices on an acre of land in the middle of a redwood forest north of Santa Cruz and has an amazing view of the Pacific. They chose the spot in an attempt to attract world-class technical and marketing people to the company. Besides the obvious aesthetic qualities of the office environment, the area in and around Santa Cruz offers a wide variety of recreational activities:

sailing, surfing, hiking, mountain biking, fishing, camping, and more. The community provides reliable schools, good youth programs, and seems to remain relatively free from many of the problems of larger urban areas.

Sales at Plasmatec reached the $20 million range two years ago, increased by 5.2 percent last year, and yielded a 9.1 percent increase on earnings and an 11.9 percent increase in earnings per share return on investment. However, the company has just barely tapped the domestic market, let alone markets beyond U.S borders. Most experts estimate that between 2 and 4 percent of the world's population suffer from diabetes. As a result, company executives believe the NIGM could be successfully exported, especially to Asia and Europe where health care plans and individual disposable income make the purchase price affordable.

MEMO

Memo: Plasmatec Internal Files
From: Doc Silverman
To: Ron Clancy, VP International

As per your request to be informed on global progress made by the marketing division:

Recent hire Matt Sumner came on board to join the new marketing team assigned to facilitate the company's international expansion. His former experiences in both Japan and France (as a foreign exchange student) made him the most experienced applicant for the position. As his first assignment on the new team, he's researching potential product niches in the global market. He's been looking into Groupe Techno-Sang in France and the European market.

Matt shows a talent for suggesting good business ideas based on solid technical knowledge of the product and an informed grasp of the market. Seems committed—arrives early at the office and comes in on weekends. Recently offered a formal presentation on the quasi-governmental structure of Groupe Techno-Sang and the likelihood that GTS is vulnerable to a takeover.

I strongly recommend that you attend his repeat presentation to the CEO's Global Strategic Task Force. Attached find summary:

"Only one other company has a technology and orientation similar to Plasmatec: Groupe Techno-Sang (GTS), based in Grenoble, France.

This company's product is based on research done at the Pasteur Institute in Paris, which paralleled that done at UC San Francisco.

"GTS is a division of the large state-owned chemical/ pharmaceutical company Rhône-Poulenc, whose annual sales topped $11 billion last year. With the help of low-interest loans generated by the French government, GTS has created a fantastic research and development capacity, housed in a state-of-the-art plant located in the high-technology center outside of Grenoble. The government assistance has enabled GTS to carry a low level of debt even after their massive construction project; in return, GTS has obligations which private companies in America would find insupportable. By French law, for any company in which the government holds 30 percent ownership the principle of "minority rights" applies. This means that GTS has to ask its parent company Rhône-Poulenc (and, by extension, the French government) to approve:

1. all investment decisions over $1 million
2. any changes in company organization
3. any changes in representation on the board of directors
4. any changes in overall management structure.

"Because of the relatively high levels of unemployment throughout France, the government generally concerns itself more with rapid downsizing and the resulting unemployment in the local region than with debt and capital formation.

"The many strong labor unions in France also limit GTS's flexibility. GTS cannot make any major moves without gaining union acceptance for all lower level workers. As a result, GTS (and French companies in general) has historically been slow to adjust to market conditions, which hampers their short-term financial gains.

"Furthermore, GTS has neither the marketing know-how nor the international interests that characterize our own marketing division, and has no connections in Japan or other major Asian markets—with the exception of Thailand. Plasmatec dominates the North American market by a wide margin, although GTS had made some inroads.

"A recent political shift to the right has encouraged the French government to begin divesting itself of its nationalized companies in order to force them to become more globally competitive.

"Therefore, despite the apparent difficulty and red tape surrounding any major moves, either GTS or its parent, Rhône-Poulenc, might be vulnerable to a takeover by a more nimble company capable of adapting to the European market."

JAN

Matt and I settled into a routine, and I began to feel comfortable with my new job. I worked primarily for six partners at Michaels, Martin and Rowley. They each gave me separate research assignments and deadlines; I learned quickly that it was up to me to coordinate the assignments, since they did not consult with each other. Initially, during some months I had several major projects due at nearly the same time; in other months I had little work.

I also scoped out the differing levels of regard in which the partners held me. The only woman I worked for was considerate of my time, but had clearly fallen prey to the notion that women advance by distancing themselves from other women, and particularly from those on the so-called mommy track. Consequently, although she was very organized and extremely clear in all her tasks, I found the woman's condescension to be a real barrier to my productivity.

Besides this woman, two other partners seemed reluctant to see me as anything more than a paralegal. These men also acted as if their projects took precedence over any other project I might be doing, and they grew irritated when I explained that they had unrealistic expectations in terms of deadlines.

But the other three partners treated me respectfully. Two of the men were far less organized, and thus relied on me to do more than research. Occasionally I was asked to talk with their clients. The oldest partner gave me enormous latitude in formulating my research. He also asked for my advice, often calling me right before or after meeting with clients in order to keep me involved and up to date.

The routine with my job and the children seemed to work except for the sitter. Matt often ended up watching the kids every night because we felt uncomfortable with most of the sitters we found. This proved really taxing for Matt, since he often left very early in the mornings for work. Occasionally I let him rest at night and watched the children myself—especially when I had little work to do. But I tried to resist the impulse to take the kids because I worried about simply drifting back into a situation where Matt's career took precedence. True, his job provided all of our medical benefits and his salary was four times higher than mine; I surely would not have been faulted for throwing in the towel, or perhaps I should say the laundry. But as I saw it, while perseverance might or might not enable me to overcome the mommy handicap, hanging back was a definite no-go, a step down the slippery slope of raising my daughter to marry the first jerk to ask. I owed Michelle as much as I owed Matt—more, if anything.

MATT

I was so relieved when Jan found work she liked doing. I knew Jan held me responsible in some way for her lagging behind the Heathers of the legal world.

This confused me. How did I get named boss in the marriage? Where was the coercion in our agreement to go to Japan? Or in it being up to her to bear the babies? Jan would just throw her hands up when I pushed her on this. I learned not to push, but to rely on the innate generosity of her soul. And she really is generous, as giving with me as she is with the kids. For instance, in the days leading up to my presentation to the Global Strategic Task Force, Jan watched the kids each night. I only left the office to sleep. I checked and rechecked all of my research and honed my delivery in front of Jan's father's camcorder. Doc monitored my progress and let me know who would be at the meeting and what kind of questions they might ask.

The morning of the repeat presentation, Doc entered my office to go over my work one last time. "I don't want to put any pressure on you, Matt," he explained, "but this is the first big presentation the Executive Committee has seen from our team. I'd really like it to go well."

"You're not saying that our committee's survival depends on this presentation, are you?"

"No, no." Doc laughed. "We're not in any trouble. It's just a question of first impressions. I'd like us to give a good first impression. But don't worry. You're very prepared and I think they will really like what you've put together."

Question 3:   *Why are the stakes high in this presentation? Why does Matt sense that this is such a crucial moment in his career at Plasmatec?*

When I finally faced the Global Strategic Task Force, the practice and effort paid off. The group listened attentively, especially Tom McDonald, the CEO of Plasmatec, and Ann Jackson, the representative from the venture capital group. As some kind of proof of his commitment to global expansion, Tom invited me to join the Global Strategic Task Force as a junior staff expert. In this capacity I had the opportunity to talk about my experiences in Japan as well as my knowledge of GTS and the European context. I met often with Tom and the Global Strategic Task Force. They often called on me to do research and offer various strategic options. I also developed a friendship with Doc Silverman; we spent lots of informal time discussing company politics and issues—and my career.

A few weeks later, Doc walked into my office and invited my entire family to a barbecue. I called Jan as soon as he left to run the plans by her. The invitation seemed somehow meaningful to me. One of the sessions I'd attended at UCLA focused on mentoring. I had learned all too well the importance of having someone influential on my side during my unhappy experience with MedTech. The session at UCLA simply reiterated and expanded on lessons I had already learned by experience. The UCLA session demonstrated convincingly that very few people get into important jobs without an influential mentor or sponsor. Many of the really fast-climbing people have two or three mentors, according to the panel.

Doc had already helped me learn about the corporate culture and company politics. He had taught me a great deal about the nature of the organization, what to do and not to do, who the key people were, and what to watch out for—especially in preparation for that presentation to the task force. I realized that Doc might become a very important mentor for me and the barbecue represented a great opportunity to get to know him. I knew from my experience at MedTech that if a mentor liked one of his direct reports, the report found himself invited to all kinds of informal events where the real networking gets done.

I decided to call Jan back, to reiterate how important the barbecue could be. I needed to talk through the plans again, what to bring, what to wear—to make it more concrete in my mind.

DOC

I headed back to my office. I had taken a chance with Matt's presentation to the Global Strategic Task Force and they had eaten up what Matt said. This reflected well on me. I had suggested thinking internationally in the first place and had gotten the investors to hire new employees to work on the international marketing team (one of whom was Matt). Although all the senior executives liked the idea of becoming a global company, I knew this team and my efforts had to produce results. Matt's presentation had been the first real showing from the team.

In some ways, Matt had helped my career as much as his own. I had my hands in far too many aspects of the company to micromanage a new team. I had realized some years earlier that to deliver on big projects I needed energetic, savvy, and competent young talents who stayed loyal. That proved the hardest thing for me to adjust to as I began managing more employees: I depended almost exclusively on the competence of my various juniors. In this case, Matt had "worked his tail off" for this project, and the results made me look as good as Matt.

Lately, I realized my philosophy for a successful company had changed. I worried a little less about market shares and production costs. To be competitive in the future, Plasmatec needed to value and develop at every opportunity young employees who seemed to have great potential. I had recently suggested that the company add a new criteria to their "Senior Executive Performance Appraisals." I argued that the company focus on the progress and development of all its talented junior employees. Because of this new emphasis Plasmatec managed to keep hold of some of their brightest "stars." I felt Plasmatec had the people in place to spearhead some significant expansions over the next few years.

Some of the more senior executives seemed to take an even more paternal approach to their mentoring. Perhaps to compensate for a neglected family life, they tended to treat their favorite direct reports like sons or daughters. I could understand from my own experience how attached a senior executive could become to a report. At a certain point, the senior worried not so much about how the junior fit into the company's future and much more about simply helping that person's future.

"Developing people," I thought to myself. "That's what it's all about. When you're secure about yourself, it's in your own interest to start worrying about others. That's where the real accomplishment lies."

Of course, not everyone worked out. I had learned that unfortunate lesson. Therein lay the risk: failure had a way of sticking, just like success. And just as a junior's success made the senior look better, a junior's failure had an equal and opposite effect.

I put a lot of stock in Matt. I assumed Matt's family would be equal to Matt, but I wanted to make sure his wife and kids would be helpful partners for him. Ideally, they would turn out to be the kind of family Plasmatec could confidently send abroad; the kind of family I could trust with clients, customers, and other seniors. I also wanted to see Matt in a more casual setting. Although we seemed to get along quite well, I wanted to make sure, before I invested more time in Matt, that we could end the day basically liking each other. Fortunately, I already liked Matt, whether we were in the office or out of it. I suspected that Matt's wife and family would prove just as likable.

The Sumners arrived with flowers and a bottle of wine in hand. (Doc's wife) Peggy led the family on a tour of our Santa Cruz home, which has a great view of the Pacific. Nearly ten years different in age, Peggy and Jan struck up a quick rapport. They shared a number of common experiences and concerns. Peggy had recently returned to school to get her Ph.D. in sociology at nearby University of California at Santa Cruz. Jan shared with Peggy the same tension between career and home, and they fell into conversation quickly. Matt and I lagged behind in the tour mixing talk of the office with talk of the home.

The two Sumner children liked Cathy, our 17-year-old daughter, who played games with the children and kept them occupied while the adults talked. After eating, we walked across the street to the beach and continued talking and laughing. By early evening, as the Sumners packed their kids into the car, both families deemed the event a success, and decided to make the get-togethers a more common practice.

MATT

Life moved along smoothly for our family over the next year. We eventually found better child care with Amy Middleton, a woman roughly our age who had a son

Jeff's age. Her husband worked as the first mate on a merchant ship, and so she often spent months alone. To keep herself busy and earn some extra income, she provided child care for working families. She attended to the children's needs, including pickups and deliveries. Our families shared similar values, so we felt comfortable turning the kids over to Amy. They adapted quickly and easily to the slight change in habits at Amy's house, and Jeff really liked her son.

Question 4:   Why is Amy Middleton, the child-care provider, so critical in the Sumners' lives?

Jan's job started consuming more of her time. She complained on a number of occasions about the inconsistencies between partners' expectations. To solve the problem, the firm assigned her to work with only two partners: the woman who was well organized and the older man. As it turned out, the woman partner preferred a highly structured working atmosphere. As long as their relationship remained clearly defined, she had no trouble working with Jan, and as her respect for the quality of Jan's work grew, Jan found it easier to take direction from her. The older man, a very influential partner, had liked Jan's work from the beginning, and had begun to rely more and more on her. He carried an enormous workload, and Jan found herself spending a great deal of time on his projects.

In formal and informal business discussions with the members of the Global Strategic Task Force I focused on several questions regarding the relationship between Plasmatec and GTS: Should they be head-to-head competitors? Or should they pursue some strategic alliances between themselves? And if the latter choice seemed more feasible, what kind of strategic alliance would work best? These questions followed me through most of my second year at Plasmatec and into my new position as global product manager.

By the beginning of my third year with Plasmatec I attended a medical devices convention in New York and, while there, met a GTS representative. We decided to sit down, eat a good meal, and talk about our respective companies. We met at Grenouille, in Manhattan, and hit it off marvelously. Jean-Luc Taillard, international marketing manager at GTS, spoke passable English, and Isabelle Gengembre, a young Frenchwoman with an MBA from ESSEC, joined us at Jean-Luc's request. Typical of her generation, she spoke English very well and occasionally worked as translator for us when communication broke down.

During the three-hour luncheon I learned that GTS might indeed consider a joint venture arrangement with Plasmatec. Jean-Luc suggested an arrangement in which GTS would focus on Europe with Plasmatec's help on business planning and marketing while (conversely) Plasmatec focused on North America with R&D and manufacturing assistance from GTS. He hoped to eventually look for an Asian partner to join them. But if no third company emerged to join them,

Plasmatec and GTS could either collaborate or compete in Asia. I thanked Jean-Luc for the informative lunch and I promised to relay our conversation to my superiors and get back to Jean-Luc very soon.

When I returned to Plasmatec, I met with Tom, Doc, Ron, and the other members of the Global Strategic Task Force to discuss our options. We considered the pros and cons of accepting or rejecting such a joint venture with GTS. Ann, the venture capitalist, pressed another option: that Plasmatec try and acquire Groupe Techno-Sang outright. This plan would require a well-conceived global strategy, for we would actually need to manage the French operation while promoting its rapid expansion into Europe. That meant developing a competent group of international managers who knew Plasmatec culture, and global and, more specifically, *French* management style, in addition to mastering critical aspects of the industry and the local markets.

After discussing the matter for several weeks and through as many meetings, the team decided to explore the less ambitious joint venture option. Tom, Doc, Ron, Brent (the company lawyer), and I decided to go to Grenoble and meet with a GTS team. Arriving at Orly Airport, we traveled by Air France bus to the Hotel Panthéon in Montparnasse to rest and overcome jet lag before going to Grenoble (by TGV, the high-speed train) the next day.

Before leaving for France, I had called Karl at UCLA to find an English-speaking expert on the French economic climate. Karl recommended a man he had taught with during a brief teacher exchange at INSEAD. I arranged dinner with the professor, Paul Jenu, who still worked at nearby INSEAD (in Fontainebleau). According to Karl, Professor Jenu had earned his PhD from Wharton and spoke excellent English.

We met Professor Jenu at a small Parisian restaurant that featured excellent food from the Alsace region. Professor Jenu provided us with a general overview of the French and European business climate and explained that unemployment in Europe continued to increase. The French government had deadlocked in a debate over which direction to take the economy. Some felt unemployment resulted from sluggish corporations hamstrung by government and union regulation. Others argued the opposite: that businesses disregarded too easily their social responsibility to provide the population with work.

The dinner proved informative and helpful. I thanked Professor Jenu for his consultation services and our team returned to the hotel.

The meetings through the next several days offered encouraging results. Our group liked the French business team—they were straightforward in a way I particularly appreciated, having learned not to take this quality for granted. I noticed that the French seemed more preoccupied with technological details, managerial philosophy, and getting to know one another, whereas our team pressed them for financial data and market information. We toured the GTS plant and found it far superior to our own small factory. We were impressed by the GTS research facility and the technical know-how displayed. Most of our hosts spoke some English and came across as both bright and polished.

But we were surprised at the formality of relationships in the head office—very corporate-like and quite different from the loose style common to California high-tech business. The French group, who is formal but often wear sport coats and slacks, seemed surprised that both Tom and Doc dressed in casual clothes and called each other by their nicknames.

We were further surprised by the number of employees GTS carried and their relatively poor productivity ratios. And we were shocked to discover that GTS's business plans and marketing efforts focused mostly on French-speaking Europe. At the end of the second day of meetings we agreed to hire McKinsey, a management consulting firm with offices in Paris and San Francisco, to study both companies and propose a joint venture arrangement. We agreed to meet next at Plasmatec's offices to discuss specific terms, provided all parties saw a solid basis for collaboration and both sides wished to go forward.

Question 5:   *What might these first impressions of GTS tell you about its culture? Where might it conflict with and/or complement the Plasmatec culture?*

QUESTIONS FOR DISCUSSION

1. Matt gets lots of advice from his former UCLA professor and coach, Karl Davidson, and Jan gets advice from her former law school friend, Heather. What parts of this career counseling do you agree with? With what don't you agree?
2. Doc Silverman is acting as Matt's mentor. What are the key dimensions of their mentoring relationship (i.e., why does it seem to work for both Matt and Doc)? Why is this relationship important for Matt? For Doc? What are the possible downsides?
3. What is the best way for a small company like Plasmatec to enter the global marketplace: joint venture (50/50 or majority equity)? Joint licensing agreement? Acquisition? Other? Why?
4. What are the most critical legal-regulatory issues associated with a venture with GTS?

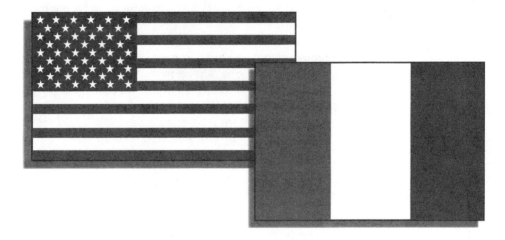

CHAPTER 12

Deciding to Go to France

Memo

Internal Memo: Plasmatec Files
         From: Doc Silverman
            To: CEO Tom McDonald
            Re: Matt Sumner

Have considered your suggestion to pull Matt from the European negotiations to have him explore a joint venture with Mitsusha. Would like to call to your attention to a new hire at Plasmatec, Wes Morito, an MBA from the Thunderbird International Graduate School. Wes lived in Japan for two years and completed an internship there with a Japanese pharmaceutical company. One of Mitsusha's employees is taking executive courses at Stanford University—Mitsusha suggests he be charged with the Japanese staff work.

I strongly recommend that you instead consider Matt for the position of director of European operations. Although it's true that he's done the negotiations once and knows the ropes in Japan, I think his commitment to the GTS project should be recognized and rewarded. Having created the opportunity for us, he's sure to give it his best effort, and his best efforts have been stellar so far. Your decision, of course.

JAN

Matt spent the remainder of his third year at Plasmatec working on the joint venture with Groupe Techno-Sang in France. The new joint venture company, called Transfusions, was to focus on the next generation of the noninvasive hemodiagnostic device, which was just being tested in R&D by the French parent company. Matt was proud of the position he had played in both the inception of the joint venture and its ongoing development. He was particularly proud that his mastery of French made him the key link between the two companies, although, of course, this meant a lot of overseas travel, which was inconvenient and time consuming, but he also got a raise along with his increased responsibility.

As Matt explained it, Transfusions was the result of a compromise between Ann and Tom. Ann had initially wanted Plasmatec to buy GTS outright. She felt a strong need for U.S. ownership in whatever venture they attempted. Tom and several others wanted to make a much smaller commitment and were very concerned about the necessary debt required for a takeover. They settled on a plan in which Plasmatec maintained the majority share of the joint venture but did not attempt a takeover of GTS. As a result they ended up with both majority ownership and a smaller cash commitment. It seemed clear to me that if Plasmatec had taken over GTS Matt would have almost certainly been transferred to France, so I felt a little relieved that the commitment of both the company's resources and my husband's work was less than it otherwise might have been. Or so I thought.

During the same time, I became very involved in my work. Bill Trent, the oldest partner, monopolized my time more and more until I worked almost exclusively on his projects. I also began meeting with clients alone or with a junior staff member. Although I remained a contract employee (albeit with a more lucrative contract each year—a raise I had to jockey and feint for each and every time), my workload had grown so dramatically that I was assigned space at the office where I spent several days each week. Bill had developed a very loyal clientele that provided the firm a significant percentage of its revenue. He groomed me to work with these people on his behalf.

Matt and I slowly became more deeply involved in our careers over the next year. We began to rely more on Amy Middleton to watch our children, since we both spent more time working. The kids seemed to like this arrangement. Amy almost always planned fun activities for them, the kind of things women who read parenting books do—painting their hands to look like the heads of endangered species, making sand-cast candles, letting them use hammers and nails, and the like. I guess there's more to it than baking cookies. I was relieved to have Amy on the job.

Our comfortable routine ended, however, when Tom offered Matt the position of director of European operations. Before discussing the job with me, Matt went to Doc, who persuaded him that the advancement could be critical for his career and, of course, for the joint venture. With Doc's blessing in his pocket, he approached me on the topic. It seemed clear that with the extra income from the promotion, we could pay Amy to do more with the kids and also hire some domestic help to do the laundry and the weekly housecleaning—two chores that had been getting us down. Sometimes it seemed like between the jobs and the vacuuming our family had no time to notice that we were living in the sunny heart of paradise. Nevertheless, I definitely didn't want Matt to take the job if it meant leaving California. My life was busy and fulfilling and, like Matt's, my own career had just blossomed. Busy as we were, having both sets of parents nearby was enormously helpful—they'd take the kids for a weekend every now and again and bring them back chockful of self-appreciation.

So we compromised by deciding that Matt should take the job but commute to and from France. It would have been horrible to disrupt our happy life, tear me away from my wonderful boss, rent out the house, move to France, and discover that Matt's working conditions there were untenable. I didn't want to leave California at all, and I definitely didn't want to leap unknowingly into a nasty situation as we had in Japan. We thought we'd see whether commuting worked, and if it did, we planned to pass the summer holidays together in France. What an opportunity for the kids!

Six months passed according to our arrangement. At first everything seemed to work. Matt accomplished his work by commuting bimonthly to France and by using fax, telephone, and the Internet to communicate while stateside with the office in Grenoble. Sadly, we were unable to spend the summer there because I was in the middle of a very large case involving an oil spill, and I felt uncomfortable taking advantage of the firm after putting so much effort into demonstrating my commitment and competence.

Actually, by this time I was well pleased with my position in the firm, particularly in comparison to the second-class seat I'd occupied for my first year. For over a year I had taken part in actual negotiations, although my most important function was still to prepare the research and do staff work for Bill. The firm valued me; that was clear from the raises I'd accrued, although they had required a yearly pretense that I was on the verge of accepting another job. I was now getting about $65,000 per year as a contract employee ($75,000 for full-time work was considered a good job). After one such charade, which was particularly convincing because I actually had heard about an interesting position at another office, Bill offered to make me part of the firm. The firm sweetened the offer by volunteering to count my time as a contract employee toward my move to make partner, essentially cutting the waiting period in half. I couldn't wait for Matt to return from France to tell him the news!

The day after Bill's offer I had lunch with Heather Irsay. Our biweekly lunches had turned into monthly lunches over the years. Heather was excited to hear about the firm's offer—she has always taken the kind of proprietorial interest in my career that the Chinese are supposed to take in the lives of people they have saved from disaster and death. But she seemed sad, and I was determined to find out why.

"I don't want to be a downer," she explained, "but I'm wondering about the price of success. I'm wondering if maybe I should be more like you."

"What do you mean?"

"I just feel out of balance right now—if you'll pardon the cliché. I'm very happy about the way my career has gone. I couldn't ask for more. But, you know, I always imagined that I'd have at least two kids, and my biological clock is ticking more loudly every day."

Heather finished her glass of wine. "I'm not just depressed because I broke up with Dan," she continued.

"You broke up with Dan? What happened?"

"He wanted to pursue the relationship seriously. I just didn't have the time to devote to it. It's really tough; I still work 60 hours a week."

"I'm sorry," I said.

Heather paused. "Time was only part of the problem, though," she admitted. "It looked like I'd have to reduce my commitment to my career. After years of spending all of my time at the office, it's so much a part of me that I just can't let it go. My prestige and self-esteem are totally wrapped up in my job. And it's hard to walk away from the money, of course. It isn't the money, though. I mean, it buys great vacations, but I don't have the leisure time for a boat or even the desire for a house. But I can't imagine taking a job that would be any less important, less serious, and money is the measure of such things. My salary's mind boggling, even to me."

"It's hard to walk away from good money, that's for sure. Did Dan want you to quit?"

"No. Just cut back—or `diversify' as he said. I was seriously considering what he said until I heard that I might be in line for a federal judgeship. But I'd have to move to Sacramento."

"Heather! What an honor. Especially for a woman. How definite is the offer?"

"There's no offer. Only the possibility. Maybe it's just a rumor. But when I told Dan that I would take the offer if it came, that pretty well ended things."

"I'm so sorry, honey. When did this all happen?"

"About six weeks ago. I was okay with it then, but now I'm having second thoughts. I wonder whether Dan is right. Maybe I do need to diversify. Honestly, Jan, you have the ideal situation. You have children, a career, a husband, your parents and your in-laws nearby. I hate to sound petty, but I'm very jealous of your situation right now."

This statement stunned me for a moment. If anything, I had been unpleasantly, uncomfortably jealous of Heather over the last years. Ironically, when it seemed like I finally, finally might be catching up, Heather had suddenly and simply reversed the direction of jealousy.

"So you'd like to get married and have children? Dan's not the only fish in the sea, surely?"

Heather nodded slowly.

"Yeah, there's always Richard," she said. "Do you remember him?"

"The guy in Chicago? He's been interested in you forever."

"Yeah. Well, lately I've started considering him more seriously. But there's no way he would leave Chicago. And I don't want to leave here. He's suggested a commuter relationship. We could set up home base here or someplace else and spend most weekends together. But if things progress, I just don't want a commuter marriage."

"Well, you don't have to get married right away. You could try a commuter relationship for a while, and see what happens."

"You're probably right," Heather conceded. "But I've seen a commuter marriage. I'd hate to wake up one morning and find myself in one. Did you see that article in *Vanity Fair* last month? It sounded dismal. Not just in terms of divorce statistics, which are significantly higher, I guess. The article suggested that these people just swing into their own worlds. They lose the glue that holds together the relationship. Pretty soon their orbits are so separate they can't really talk to each other. Then the marriage is no marriage at all but some old habit that only kicks in at the convenience of the couple. I have no idea how kids survive something like that. Somehow a fake marriage seems worse to me than no marriage."

I began to worry. This scenario sounded a little too familiar.

"Well, as I said, you have a great setup," Heather continued. "You even have good child care, so you can work without worrying that you're neglecting your primary responsibility. I'm totally jealous. And to tell the truth, I think Dan was probably right. I need to expand, to develop other parts of myself. All work and no slack is as bad for Jill as it is for Jack."

Question 1:   Why does Jan experience anxiety after her discussion on commuter marriages? Why might international travel be hard on a marriage?

That lunch really provided food for thought. I realized that Matt and I spent very short, intense times together and then long times apart. At first, I'd enjoyed how busy our time was together, and frankly, there's a certain freedom in short periods of being the only adult in the house, responsible only to yourself. Now I worried that I'd taken for granted my own personal answer to the universal human question—how do you make love stay? Isn't it proximity that breeds contentment? Certainly in college we'd all noticed that the way to draw a particular man into your life is to spend time with him. Had I become too comfortable with separation from Matt? Were we moving into our own spheres, relying too heavily on our attractiveness to maintain our attraction to each other? And how had the kids been affected? Were the things we could offer them—a strong, happy female role model, expensive lessons and hobbies, a good school system, Amy's loving care—were these enough to make up for our distance from them and maybe from each other?

I was doubly unnerved by Heather's sudden jealousy. Since my return from Japan, I had more or less seen Heather as the standard by which I measured myself. I'd *resented* her for saying I could not become a partner in a law firm, and I'd worked hard to prove her wrong. Now, on the verge of achieving that goal, I was floored by Heather's insistence that I had led the better life all along. At the same time, I felt restless. Now that many things seemed in my grasp, I doubted my desire to follow through. The position on the partner track would lead to a fairly predictable life, which made me a little uncomfortable. I worked on a poem I'd written only a few weeks earlier:

> *My face in the mirror.*
> *It looks different now.*
> *Gaze isn't right,*
> *It shadows the bright that is me.*
> *My face in the mirror*
> *That's blurred by a child.*
> *Sticky fingers*
> *Candied hands*
> *Reach past the glass*
> *Reflecting the face that won't last.*
> *My face in the mirror.*
> *Prepares for the day.*
> *Lipstick the papers,*
> *Briefcase the tasks,*

Smiles at the office,
e-mails some facts that are asked.
My face is too big—
Or too small?—
To look back.
I stare at the mirror
and notice a crack.

Question 2: What does the poem say about what Jan is feeling?

That night I got very little work done. As predictable as I always think Matt is—in a completely mysterious, alien way, I mean—I couldn't begin to imagine what he'd have to say about all this. I wanted him beside me, right away.

MATT

Commuting between France and California was definitely for the birds. Typically, I'd rush off to the airport just a little late, having tried to squeeze in a few last minutes at work or with the family. After 12 hours in the air, I'd arrive in Grenoble with only a few hours of sleep—more if I'd taken a sleeping pill, but the period you spend unconscious under the influence of a sleeping pill doesn't actually promote the REM sleep that your mind requires. It's significantly less boring than reading the onboard magazines, and that's *all* you can say for it. The 9-hour difference in time zones meant that, although I arrived at two or three in the morning, I remained wide awake. Once in my small apartment, I'd toss and turn in my bed, trying hard to sleep for a few hours before the next day. When morning arrived, I'd have to immediately make decisions and act as manager of the office. Staying awake through the necessary meetings was painfully difficult for me. I found myself drinking coffee almost obsessively, even though the sludge Europeans drink irritates me.

After work I'd go straight home and collapse into bed to wake up at one each morning and lie awake until three. On each and every trip, as soon as I adjusted to the new time zone, it was time to return to California, arriving late at night, again exhausted. Because I am a morning person, I usually found the trip to France a little easier than the return trip home.

After three or four trips I came to see my trips as ten-day adventures: five or six days in Europe, two days of travel, two days of recovery after my return. I was sad to see that my family had learned to simply leave me alone for a couple of days after I returned from France. I never want my kids to feel they have to walk on tenterhooks around me—I do try to control my temper, and under normal conditions I think I do okay. I felt terrible about being such a grouch. I wanted to talk to the kids and to Jan, to hear about their week and tell about my own. But I was just too tired.

Despite eating less, I gained ten pounds. When home, the kids and I often went out to eat. I found myself continually starting and then neglecting routines that allowed me time to exercise. And I worried about my growing dependence on over-the-counter soporifics and stimulants to get the old body to adjust more quickly to the time changes. Anyone can see they aren't healthy.

During the next several months, officials at Plasmatec grew more concerned about the commuting arrangement. There was a growing need for a Plasmatec director to take up permanent residence on site in Grenoble. Plasmatec's majority ownership dictated it. Moreover, the Chambéry plant (near Grenoble) was scheduled to manufacture the next generation product within two years, and was currently retooling for the effort. Its location was perfect, since important research was taking place at the Pasteur Institute in France and the key links to prospective new plants in Southeast Asia were in frequent contact with the French. Problems always occur during the manufacturing stage of product development: someone capable and on site could correct such problems, but someone capable but a continent away could not hope to do so as quickly or as effectively. All these factors combined to make the Plasmatec executives feel it was necessary to have one of their own on site.

Tom scheduled a meeting with me on the morning of my return from my fifth and last trip to France. He requested that I accept an on-site directorship of Transfusions in Grenoble, saying I could "write my own ticket" (within reason) as long as I agreed to stay for at least three years and get things started. This came as no surprise to me—it was my information he based his position on, after all. I agreed to talk to Jan and get back to Tom within ten days. I hadn't had a moment with her since my return the night before—not a thinking one, anyway. She'd already informed me that my presence was required at an elegant dinner out that night—the funny gleam in her eyes made me wonder whether she was going to negotiate a third baby or what. Something was definitely in the air.

I thought it rather convenient that we had candles and a fine French Beaujolais before us while I broached the topic of Tom's offer, and since she had made the dinner date, I felt I might be at some kind of advantage in an upcoming negotiation. When she told me of her firm's offer to take her on in the partner track, I was floored. In a moment of silence we realized that the two offers were mutually exclusive. We just looked at each other. Through my Beaujolais-muted irritability and fatigue, I suggested we get away for the weekend, find some quiet time, and talk thoroughly without interruption. We decided to drive to Monterey and leave the kids with my folks.

The conditions seemed straightforward to me as I silently reviewed them on the drive to Monterey. Jan had always resented my position as major breadwinner. If she made partner, I could easily retire and take up consulting, specializing in joint ventures in Japan or in France—the possibilities in the biomedical world are just enormous. We were happy in Los Gatos—Amy was doing a wonderful job, the kids liked school and the Middletons and saw both sets of grandparents often enough that spoiling was definitely a consideration. True, the stress of commuting had proven bad for my state of mind, and consultancies invariably require a lot of travel.

I had called Karl at UCLA from my office to ask him for his input on the Transfusions job. Karl made two suggestions. First, he said, be sure to consult with an expert on international compensation packages. If you don't, you'll get taken advantage of by someone: either our government, or the French government, or Plasmatec, or someone else. Well, the wisdom of that suggestion was obvious, as I reflected on our experience in Japan.

His second comment concerned Jan. "Matt," he said earnestly to me, "most research shows that fully one-third of experiences abroad fail, or end early, because of unhappiness on the part of spouses. If Jan is not fully behind your move to France, you may have to come home early to save your marriage. And that might hurt your career even more than if you'd never gone at all. Be sure that her heart is really into the experience. And if it's not, don't take the position, no matter how good the offer."

I thought about all that in the car. Realizing Karl was right, and that Jan had to really want to go to France, I prepared myself as best I could to help her want to go. The opportunity to "write your own ticket" comes around rarely. I sure didn't want to turn it down.

Although more crowded and a bit more touristy than when we'd last visited the town, Monterey had preserved its charm and romance remarkably well through the years. We rented a small shingled cottage that overlooked the rough ocean beaches and visited the jellyfish at the aquarium, which were eerily back-lit with neon to highlight their nebulous bodies and otherworldly movement through the water. I felt a return of the old spark that initially attracted me to Jan eight years earlier, compounded by the quieter tenderness you feel for someone you know so intimately. Our work-related separation had disrupted that sense of intimacy, and our first night seemed almost like a date.

On Saturday, we broached the subject of our careers. I'd silently rehearsed my pitch in the car and was rather proud of the graphic I'd prepared, demonstrating the economic and pragmatic advantages of moving to Europe, figured in short- and long-term benefits and ratios. The facts all pointed to accepting the job in France over following Jan's career in California; at this point in the negotiations I wasn't about to come forth with the retirement options. It wasn't my best option.

Jan got angry, and we started to fight. I guess I got a little defensive—it's so hard to feel responsible for something as large and indefensible as having been born on the right side of a two-gendered species in a society that recognizes a right and a wrong side. Although for all the hooey about gender roles being acquired and not innate, I certainly have never seen a society where women eat first, although I'll grant you the yin-yang symbol makes a nice set of earrings. After this kind of rambling, useless crap, we lapsed into one of those hopeless silences that beat the heck out of hurting each other. Jan stared out the window. I put my hand (neutrally) on her back and kissed her (neutrally) on the top of her head. Sometimes this helps. Jan hit my shoulder with a knuckle punch as hard as she could—not very hard, that is—and hugged me. Pretty hard. She got a poem out of her purse and made me listen to it. It sounded sad. I was confused: had I wrongly assumed that since the kids were happy and we were living where she had asked to live, she was happy?

Jan went on to talk about her restlessness and her fear of settling on a single, predictable career path, even one that embodied career success. Then she explained how irritating she had found my attempt to sell her on a major life-changing decision. It really brought home to me how one dimensional and—narrow—I had become, I guess, in the course of the past year. So much of my day involved selling and finagling and angling that I couldn't remember how to just talk, apparently. I was ashamed of myself. To demonstrate my good faith, I told her that I'd been considering retiring and starting a consulting business, in order to support her need to work 60-hour weeks and make partner. Initially, of course, it would require a big time commitment and a lot of travel, I felt. But the travel could be timed—as an independent consultant, I'd be free to turn down assignments.

Jan responded by weighing the importance of the family against the importance of our careers. She explained how honored she had felt by the firm's offer, and how hard she had had to work to get to that point. Just as the move to France could not be a quick or easy decision, the move to partner also could not be made very easily. The whole family would have to adjust in either case. And the whole family, including the kids, should have some say. We had found little time over the past few months to really talk. I realized that Jan felt I did not recognize the full significance of her career achievements.

When I understood how important this was to Jan, I apologized to her. "I'm more out of the family than I thought," I said, and I began to worry that, like other business executives I knew, I'd grown further from my wife and children with each career advancement.

Once I opened up, Jan expressed fears of her own that I had never dreamed she'd have. She told me about her conversation with Heather, and how she had become conscious of her jealousy of Heather. Ever since Heather had said she could never become partner, Jan had tried to prove her wrong. But now that she had accomplished her goal, Jan worried that a goal based on resentment—proving Heather wrong—might not be worthy of her.

"While we were in Japan," she continued, "I wondered what would be happening with my career if we had stayed in the States and I had taken a job with some big firm. I thought that I would probably be a lot like Heather: already partner and taking on more responsibility each year. When Heather told me that because of you and the kids, I could never get into a job like that, I felt a lot of resentment toward her. And, honestly, a little toward you and the kids."

I nodded.

"I think that's a lot of the reason why I was so adamant about not leaving for France last year. I saw the same thing happening again."

I began to feel very embarrassed about my attempt to sell Jan on the move to France. I realized how distant I had become from Jan's inner thoughts and feelings—now treating her like a client. I reiterated my intention to turn down the position in France and begin researching how to start up a consultancy.

"Really?" Jan asked.

"On Monday I'll tell Doc that I just can't afford to go to France right now. I'll tell him about you making partner and I'll ask to get reassigned so that someone else can head the joint venture in Grenoble. I'm not sure how it will end up. But even in the worst case scenario—even if I have to take a pay cut—your new job would make up for it. I think it's time to focus on you and your career. You're right; the whole family should be involved in career decisions. And I don't think I've been nearly involved enough in your career."

Jan smiled at me.

"I don't think you get what I'm saying. Listen," she continued, "after I talked with Heather, I took the kids to my parent's house for the weekend. But instead of dropping them off, I stayed and talked. I remember that my father had first discovered his illness when I was about Michelle's age. I remember how the family pulled together and stayed together. Up until the time I went away to Texas, I couldn't imagine life away from them. Over the weekend, I reminisced with my parents about that time, and I realized that most of my happiest memories growing up surrounded the time we all took care of Dad. He can't talk about that time without crying, and neither can I; that period of time holds so many important memories.

"Then I wondered whether Michelle would have any experiences like mine. I worried that our family has become more a function than a family. I realized we had become a commuter family: I go to my place, you go to yours, the kids go to theirs. The only time we spend together involves someone getting picked up or dropped off."

"What you're saying is really true," I agreed. "We're exactly how you describe. I've really lost my focus lately."

"But I'm not just talking about you. It's as much my fault as it is yours," Jan continued. "While I talked with my parents I realized that I had become very different from them—and I wasn't happy about it. That's when I realized that we needed a change. Something to bring the family together. Moving to France might be exactly what we need to recover our unity as a family."

I sat back in astonishment. It was too good to be true. In the spirit of the conversation, I raised a tiny little objection. "What about your dream of making partner? We could change the way our family works without leaving the country—I really don't want you to be unhappy, Jan."

Jan reached over for my hand. "I think I've decided that I wanted the partnership for all the wrong reasons. The offer proves everything I needed to prove. Right now I want something different. I'd like a new kind of challenge. I want us both to focus on a new experience that we can involve the kids in—something like the time I had with my parents and sister when we first moved to Maine."

I felt my eyebrow do the cynical jump, involuntarily.

"*Matt*," Jan said firmly, "you were wrong to try and get me to go to France by making a sales pitch. And we're both wrong to have been so passive about meeting the needs of our family and each other. But France may be the right thing to fix the family—as long as you see our move in terms of the family, and not your career. If we go, you have to spend more time with me and the children than you do now—which might be hard, since you will be very busy. Nevertheless, you have to involve us all in everything you can, and we'll do the same with you. This has to be the family's career move, not just yours."

I thought about this for a minute. I had to abandon the main reason I wanted to go to France (my career) in order to go to France. But I saw a great deal of merit in what Jan had said. It seemed that our family had come to a crossroads where we would either hold together or fall apart.

JAN

For my part, I managed the family's preparation for Grenoble. I checked out several books about French culture and customs and searched for people who had experience working in France. I had Matt check about Plasmatec's method for preparing employees for experiences abroad and asked him to have Karl send any information he had about international moves.

I also sought out the experiences of other families who had spent time in Europe. With a bit of serendipity, I discovered a group of women who had become friends while their husbands worked as expatriates in Europe. The women in this group were older than Matt and me by a decade or two, and they allowed me to join them for lunch one afternoon. I came to the lunch prepared with questions and a pad of paper for notes.

The four women turned out to be very friendly and eager to talk of their experiences abroad. As it turned out, they had met in Belgium. Two of the women had also lived in Germany (since their husbands both served as part of NATO). They all ended up in the Bay Area.

The women suggested a few tricks for success. They thought my French language skills, limited though they were, would definitely help me. Two of the women regretted that they had not immersed themselves right away in an intense language program. One of the military women regretted not involving herself more in the local culture. She attributed a bad experience in Germany to her unwillingness to learn the language and customs of the land.

The women all breathed a sigh of relief when they learned that our kids were both young. One of the women told a lengthy horror story about her two teenage sons' experience in the Belgian school system. Although she loved the experience personally, she acknowledged that for teens the move can be very challenging.

In Europe, another woman noted, children begin tracking in the educational system at age 10. It was her belief that children older than 10 almost never have a good experience in the local schools. The women all agreed that if Grenoble had an international school, we should send the kids there rather than to a French school. I thought I'd look into all the options—sure, cross-cultural experiences can be challenging, but my kids are bright, and I thought the challenge could be good for them. The French system is overly rigid, but their math education is excellent. Immersion is the best way to learn a new language, and I knew my kids could keep up in vocabulary development in English with an organized program of storytime at home.

One woman asked what Plasmatec had done to prepare us for the move. When I said that they had no program to help employees make the transition, the woman seemed shocked and foretold extra struggle because of it. She wrote down several ideas to help me prepare for the move.

The women began discussing the troubles of living abroad: finding reliable places to buy food, clothes, and cosmetics. They began to complain a little about different customs in Europe. But then one woman pointed out that Belgium had been a much easier adjustment for her than when she had lived briefly in Saudi Arabia. Arab cultures were far more challenging, they all agreed.

The women mentioned that I'd need a sense of humor and a lot of patience. They hoped I had reserves of self-esteem to survive the loneliness that often accompanies such a move. These women had moved many times, both nationally and internationally, and they agreed that each land has distinct challenges and rewards. They all said that, despite the challenges, many of their happiest memories came from their times abroad, and they felt certain that our family could succeed in France. They wished us luck, and offered to give me more advice if I needed it. I took their phone numbers, happy to have their goodwill and experience to draw on.

QUESTIONS FOR DISCUSSION

1. What are the most critical aspects of Matt and Jan's dual-career partnership that have been impacted by Matt's international work?
2. How do you react to Heather's jealousy toward Jan? What is your definition of career success?
3. How would you rate the advice Jan received from the four women? What else should the family know before going to France?

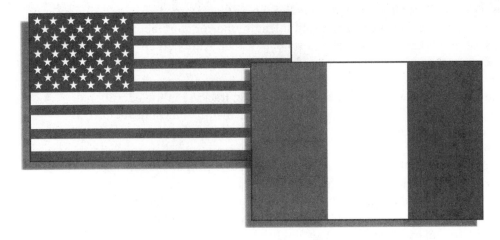

CHAPTER 13

Negotiating the Compensation Package

MATT

Ultimately, we decided to go to France on condition that Karl and Doc could confirm the value of the career move and we stay for no more than three years. We also decided to learn from our experience in Japan and make sure that, before we left, we found good schools for the children. We knew we could negotiate a good compensation package, thanks to Tom's generous offer.

I let Doc and Tom know that we would accept the offer if they agreed to the contract I drew up. Then I called Karl back and let him know of the decision Jan and I had reached. Karl suggested someone who would do a good job at drawing up the international compensation package, and then added a few words of advice.

"Don't forget repatriation in the excitement," he said. "Companies say a lot of nice things to get you out the door, but unless they have a good program for returning expatriates, they may let you drop out of the dynamics of the firm. Most companies work on a day-to-day basis. And whoever is around stays around. It used to be said that an international move is terrific for your development but bad for your career. One way to control against this problem is to get some provisions in your contract that guarantee an option to return at a certain time and at a certain level in the company. Then if the company decides to get rid of you, they can only turn you down at great cost. Make sure your consultant builds a savvy package that has all kinds of safeguards against getting taken advantage of by the company or anyone else. I'm not saying anybody at Plasmatec is trying to take advantage of you. It's just that Plasmatec can change dramatically in three years."

Question 1: ***What do you think of Professor Davidson's advice about seeking professional counseling on international tax/compensation issues?***

I thanked Karl for his advice and promised to keep him informed of future developments. I then made an appointment to see Tom the next week and, prior to that meeting, I met again with Doc, who confirmed that the move would boost my career. I then met the tax consultant and specialist in international compensation Karl recommended, who helped me write the "ticket." I presented the following proposal to Tom the day before our meeting:

1. Stay no more than three years.
2. If Plasmatec fires, transfers, or replaces the Sumners before the three-year contract is complete, the Sumners receive the full amount of the three-year compensation and benefit package.
3. A significant salary increase.
4. Language and culture training in France for Jan and the kids.
5. The various allowances associated with going abroad (see "Conceptual Issues").
6. Continued payments (as at present) into my pension and stock option plans in California and full payment of any additional required French pension and social welfare costs.
7. "Tax protection" or reimbursement for any extra taxes in excess of my U.S./California taxes; but I pocket the difference if a tax advantage ensues.
8. Assurance that if my performance were judged "better than good" or above, I could return to a position in Plasmatec or one of its ventures at a level higher than my current position.

I thought at first that Tom would fall off his chair. All he could say was, "I'll have to check with our personnel people to make sure this is the normal package. Wow! I had no idea it might cost so much. We need you to go, Matt, and we'll do everything within reason to make it happen."

QUESTIONS FOR DISCUSSION

1. Which aspects of Matt's requested expatriate compensation package seem reasonable? Which are unreasonable? What would you add, subtract, and why?
2. If expatriates can ask for and often receive such expensive compensation packages associated with their going abroad, what do you think are the current trends associated with expat management? Are companies sending fewer of them overseas? How are they managing the costs?

CHAPTER 14

Moving to France: The First Six Months

MATT

Jan, Michelle, Jeff, and I finally arrived in the city of Grenoble on a warm day in early August. Exhausted from nearly 18 hours of traveling, we clumsily carried 14 bags of luggage up the stairs of our hotel. Miss Molly, our golden retriever, proved the most difficult "item" to manage. Having spent the entire journey sedated in a large pet container, she would stagger a few feet forward then collapse in a heap on the floor. After much struggle, a bellman helped me carry the dog up the stairs to the hotel room.

Room 207 quickly grew silent as we nodded off one by one. Late that evening I awoke and opened the windows of the room. Feeling a little confused and overwhelmed, I sat by the window and looked out over the quiet city below. The empty cobblestone streets and wrought-iron fences seemed like a scene out of a storybook.

The next morning Jeff (now 11 years old) was the first of the family to wake. He too was drawn to the window, but in the morning the Grenoble market below was teeming with life and activity. Old ladies with gnarled hands sold vegetables. Beautiful fresh fruits were carefully displayed and the cheese vendor sold at least

25 varieties. Rows of colorful flowers sat shaded under awnings. Fish merchants haggled with shoppers and inside the bread shops, men in white coats baked bread in brick ovens. One of Grenoble's specialties is *pogne*, a small cake with red praline nuts. Jeff watched and then hurried to wake Michelle (now 8), less quietly than he might have perhaps.

Soon Jan and I rolled reluctantly out of bed and joined the kids. We dressed quickly and wandered out into the streets. I translated as best I could the meaning of the signs and sounds. I related the topics of the conversations we overheard. Two old men on a bench argued politics. Another group stood around a game of boules whispering strategy about how to get closest to the *cochonnet*, or small wooden ball. Vendors spoke to each other of the weather and complained about market conditions.

After a filling brunch at a small bistro, we decided to go see our new home. Although we'd reserved the hotel room for another week, the house was open and ready to be lived in. The busy streets of the market turned into quiet residential walkways as we made our way through the city. Large regal houses with steel gates and hedges were intermingled alongside the smaller apartment buildings beside us. Michelle became more and more excited as we approached the house. She pointed to homes along the streets asking, "Is that it?" and "Is it this one?" After saying "no" many times, Jan finally nodded her head as we approached an older home with a statue in the garden and a large front door. The owner was a French doctor who lived in northern France, but didn't want to sell the home that had been in his family for more than a century.

The open door revealed a surprisingly cheerful interior. The spiral stairway led to three bedrooms with high ceilings and fireplaces in each room. Another flight of stairs went to the attic and study room. The downstairs consisted of a beautiful living room complete with a baby grand piano and dining table. The kitchen felt small but cozy. And below the main level we found a *cave* (basement) for laundry and storage.

I had three weeks before I was to begin work. Jan and I spent the time moving into the house, becoming acquainted with the area, and getting the kids ready to start school. Each day brought new adventures and discoveries about the surrounding area. Near the home lay a beautiful park with well-ordered flowers and wide gravel paths, nice benches, trees, a *parcours* (exercise course), and places to walk the dog.

Many small shops surrounded our home. The area was once its own town before it became a suburb of Grenoble; this meant it had a small charming commercial district with none of the characteristics common to strip malls in U.S. suburbs. On returning one day from the bakery, Jan ran across a small old church and spent nearly an hour gazing in awe at the beautiful stained glass windows and marble statues. Jeff spent his few French coins in a *patisserie* (pastry shop) that caught his eye with a tempting display of cookies in the window. On an evening walk, Michelle, Molly, and I found a cheerful path in the hillsides outside the city. We returned home anxious to return to the spot with the others. For the first weeks, moving to France seemed perfect. We discussed each day as if reading from an adventure novel.

We soon discovered that many expatriates lived in our neighborhood. They all belonged to Grenoble's growing international high-technology community. The Université de Grenoble was quite renowned in Europe for science and engineering. Due to the influx of internationalists, the local schools had received permission from the Ministry of Education to declare some Grenoble secondary schools *écoles internationales,* as had been done elsewhere in the Paris area, near Geneva, near the Belgian border, and in Strasbourg. At these schools, both French and foreign students could study in another language for part of the day. The Grenoble collège, or middle school, had both English and German sections. In addition, the school provided special tutoring for foreign students. At the elementary level, there were some after-school courses in English. Although French education is free, each second half of the day was devoted to the *anglophone* section at our school, which was run as if it were a private school. All students in the *anglophone* section paid fees, mostly to support a few native-speaking (British) faculty. The Parents Association administered, hired the *anglophone* educators, and paid for field trips and travel. Students prepared homework and exams for both their French-language classes and the classes taught in English.

As the first few weeks of school passed, however, Jan and I grew surprised and then a little disturbed by our children's educational experiences. Michelle often came home with several pages of *cahiers* (notebooks). She explained that she, along with all the other kids in class, had spent much of the day copying as neatly as possible the words written on the chalkboard. Jan wondered if Michelle's classmates had understood the teacher's dictations any more than she had. Even though parents of children from the sixth grade on could register for *permanence* (school care such as study hall in case of teacher absence), classes in the public school were sometimes canceled, and school closed altogether when teachers did not arrive because of a strike or protest. This occurred far too often. One of Jeff's teachers did not come to class once because she needed to study for an exam in her master's program. Later we discovered that some of the notices written in French explained when a teacher would be absent. As a result, Jan was never sure when the kids would be home. On one occasion school was canceled for three days. The *anglophone* section was private and parents could at least count on those classes being held regularly. Jan struggled to maintain a schedule for herself. Many things needed to be done. But when the kids arrived home she felt obligated to stay with them because they had yet to develop friendships and had nothing else to do, not yet being proficient enough in the language to undertake the considerable homework required of French students.

The difficulty of being completely immersed into an unknown language made the first three months of school very difficult for both children. Fortunately, the *anglophone* section gave the children a much needed break. The moody dinners and gloomy faces of our children in the first three months made us wonder whether the move was a good idea after all.

By our fourth week I had become captured by the people and events at the office. My job duties were clearer and my files were under control, and everywhere I looked I saw little solvable problems calling for my attention. Unfortunately, this meant that I had less time to spend on the big unsolvable problems at home. During this time of adjustment, Jan had no car. She complained to me that between her rusty French and her isolation, she and the children felt abandoned. They felt like prisoners in our home.

Jan quickly grasped the importance of speaking French and signed up for lessons five mornings a week at a local language school. She had taken French in high school but (as is typical in American language education) her brief studies taught her how to write some vocabulary words and simple sentences rather than how to speak French. Since French spelling almost never matches pronunciation, she had spent a great deal of time learning the correct spelling of many words. She noted, a little bitterly, that few of the people she met in Grenoble asked her to write anything. It was confusing knowing when to use the formal you (*vous)* and the familiar you (*tu).*

Question 1:   Why does language seem so critical to Jan?

Both of us quickly grew frustrated with French bureaucracy and the endless inefficiency associated with getting settled. To get the utilities connected, we needed to go to an office open only between 8:30 and 11:30 A.M. The local post office was closed between 12:30 and 2:30 P.M. The visas, or cartes de séjour, could be acquired only in person at a large building in downtown Grenoble. The wait in line typically lasted two hours. The paperwork for taxes on our rented home (taxes d'habitation) was approximately one month's rent, and the declaration form was incredibly detailed and time consuming. Many of the French went on holiday for the entire months of July or August. Our local bakery sported a cheery sign indicating that the bakery would be closed the entire month of August. When drivers were on vacation, the buses followed a reduced summer schedule. No buses ran for five full days once because of a labor dispute.

Moreover, Jan felt unsure how to interpret the various behaviors of the people she interacted with. The woman at the bank who was so helpful in opening their new account would not even speak to her when they passed on the street. The maid, who had a boy Jeff's age, refused to bring him to play with Jeff because, it was our impression, she didn't feel comfortable having her child mingle with ours. The neighbors who were very polite when we arrived seemed suddenly very formal and unfriendly. Some shopkeepers acted at times as if they were angry and didn't want our business. Jan had always been very competent in social situations and had handled many diverse relationships well. Now she was confounded and crabby. She saw herself as an educated person, but the locals saw her as unable to speak French with the finesse indicative of educated people.

After several weeks in France, Michelle cut her hand rather deeply on a piece of glass protruding out of the top of a stone wall surrounding the house (part of a security measure to keep intruders out). Because we had not yet established our medical care, Jan took Michelle to a nearby public hospital emergency room and asked them to look at the wound. Fortunately, she found a young English-speaking physician. But the hospital seemed dirty, although the doctor's office and a nearby private clinic seemed very clean and modern. I read an article in the *International Herald Tribune* that the French have the longest life expectancy of any Europeans and also use the most medications. Something must work well.

We were both a bit shocked by the extent to which students as young as Michelle were already smoking and talking about kids only a few years older sleeping around. At the pool we discovered that while discreet, very few women wore swimsuit tops, and all four of us hardly knew where to look when we came across a bare-breasted neighbor sunbathing. The local television stations programmed shows with explicit sex, and children commonly drank wine and beer at restaurants. I thought there was a torrid extramarital love affair going on right in the office that raised my eyebrows. Jan and I debated whether sleepy little Grenoble actually could outdo San Francisco in public vice displays, and we never came to a suitable conclusion. The big difference seemed to be that in San Francisco people are reveling in breaking social mores; in France no one anticipates public attention for behavior that seemed outrageously exhibitionist to us.

Question 2:   What other things strike you as salient family issues? Are these problems or valuable experiences for the Sumner kids?

Despite having spent considerable time at the company already, I soon discovered some cross-cultural difficulties at work as well. My employees seemed reluctant to disagree or even to get issues out on the table where they could be solved. My colleagues found it important to talk at length about philosophy before getting down to task. At every planning session, the managers talked around a topic to find common philosophical ground—a point of agreement. If I tried to find a compromise position, the others rarely agreed. They struggled for some common view that they all shared. Only after discovering such a view could they move on to the topics I considered important. As a result, meetings often dragged on and frequently came to no resolution. I perceived that once the discussion got going, the diagnosis of the problem was excellent, but it was almost impossible to move the group on to solutions and action planning. To compensate, I tried steering discussions more forcefully and attempted to skip over digressions. But this inspired chaos in the meetings—the managers were confused and stubbornly reverted to form, which meant that two discourses occurred simultaneously, neither being successful exchanges.

To make up for the time I perceived as wasted, I started asking my direct reports to take home evening or weekend work. They flatly refused, although even high-level managers and professionals spent excessive time at lunch, sometimes not returning until 4 P.M. I became increasingly resentful of the powerful inertia that prevented our company from becoming more productive.

I started to work longer hours, doing other people's work or sometimes just monitoring their work more closely than I ordinarily would have liked. This continued for several weeks until Jan reminded me of my commitment to the family. I had promised not to let work dominate my time and energy; pushed, I agreed to spend less time at work. But privately I worried that if I couldn't improve Transfusions' efficiency, my career might suffer. I knew that the Executive Committee at Plasmatec would keep close watch on Transfusions, and especially on my ability to run it.

Midway through our fifth month in Grenoble, a package arrived at the office with a UCLA return address. Karl had finally sent off several articles and observations about international moves, the information I'd asked him to send before we left. Karl had been so overwhelmed with other professorial duties, he had not had the time to send us the material.

I opened the package and began skimming the articles. A particular paragraph struck me in an article about culture shock: "When adjusting to a new culture, it helps to have a sense of humor," the article stated. When I thought about it I realized I hadn't really laughed in several weeks. Never a full belly-aching laugh, anyway.

I reread the article more closely. It portrayed our exact situation. Culture shock, I learned, usually occurs three to six weeks after entering a new culture. At that point, the excitement and newness of the situation wears off. The expatriate suddenly finds himself bogged down by strange norms, values, rules, and laws that make little sense (I certainly felt bogged down!). The article then explained that no single factor contributes to the anxiety and apprehension associated with culture shock; instead, many challenges hitting the expatriate simultaneously cause culture shock. The expatriate has to deal with the fear of getting sick, depression, not knowing anyone in the new environment, and living without a support group all at once.

As I read other articles in the packet, I realized my family had fallen into culture shock. I decided to leave work early and share with Jan what I'd read. Back at the house, we sat on the couch and read to each other pieces of articles that seemed to fit.

Jan discovered that culture shock comes not just from the strangeness of a new language, different food, and other environmental changes. Culture shock also involves a sudden change in relationships and values. People meet and become friends in very different ways.

"Culture shock's most permanent symptom reveals itself as a constant inability to figure out what's going on," Jan read. "That is exactly how I feel. People react so oddly to what I do and say. I am always so scared I might accidentally offend someone. I feel so incompetent: I don't know anything. I don't know the laws, the language, or the customs. I sound like a baby with a bad accent every time I speak French. Sometimes I just want to shake people and say, 'I'm smart. I can think. I just can't speak your stupid language.'"

"Jeez," I responded. "I can speak their language just fine, for all the good it does me. Every time I try and suggest something or get something accomplished at work, I get treated like I'm crazy, like I have no idea what I'm talking about."

"Listen to this," Jan continued. "'Difficulties arise when performance breaks down or cannot be initiated in the first place. A person becomes socially inadequate or unskilled. He cannot correctly perform the social conventions of the new society, express emotions, perform rituals, etc.'" She smiled wryly. "That's us, eh?"

As we talked on and dusk fell, Jan admitted how much she longed for her old job and the opportunities she'd had to articulate complex thoughts and ideas. She now had little opportunity to air her feelings and observations, and confessed that she was beginning to feel dull and stupid, as though having third-grade conversations could actually dampen her native intelligence.

I had known that Jan would find staying home dull, but somehow I hadn't realized how meaningless her days would be. Without any support network she spent most of her day avoiding the alien world in which she lived. At least I had the office and the prestige of being in charge there. Jan, instead, spent each day trying to cope with a very different environment—the stores, food ingredients, her French language school, the bus system, the kids' lunches and homework. I worried that the stress might actually harm Jan's health, as had been documented in one of the articles we'd read. She looked a little peaky, off color somehow, or thinner.

Fortunately, over the next six months, we saw the signs of culture shock slowly fade from our lives. We came to realize that in France the people work very hard while at the office. But on weekends and holidays they take full advantage of their time off. The French believe a balance between work and leisure is crucial for their emotional health and also their long-term productivity at work. Except when dealing with officials from Plasmatec or entertaining other visiting Americans, I declared myself more free to be with the family. It seemed normal.

The French consider the dinner hour sacred time, and each evening we spent between one and two hours at the table. This proved to be a wonderful time to check in with each other and relate the day's experiences. In the month of May, every single week contains an official holiday. What a wonderful way to celebrate springtime! Although I found it frustrating to lower my goals at Transfusions, I nevertheless enjoyed the time off.

By our second anniversary in Grenoble, we were really enjoying life abroad. Jan and I were a little surprised at the extra discretionary income we commanded as executive expatriates ("expats"). The IRS offered a $70,000 foreign income tax credit for U.S. citizens, and with the compensation package Karl had helped me negotiate, we were saving more of our income than ever before. Suddenly we not only had the time but also the money to eat out, go to cultural events such as the Grenoble opera and ballet, and travel throughout Europe. In the last two years, we'd toured London, most of Italy, the French Riviera, and Paris. We also went to Gstaad in Switzerland for the children's ski holidays. We planned our next summer holidays for Corsica (having spent the previous summer back in California).

Question 3: *What's happened, finally, to make life so pleasant and enriching for the Sumners?*

JAN

The first six months in Grenoble were painful. It seemed a little like the new-mom blues, although the 24-hour-a-day burden I'd acquired was not a darling little bundle of love but an acutely painful belief that my education and talents were being thrown away, compounded by the guilty fear that Michelle was learning that her needs were to be considered wants and on a lifelong basis at that. Talking about this with Matt is like writing in wind or running water—he's very good at getting plumbers in, and even good at dealing with concrete social problems. But tell Matt you don't have any friends and he finds a church and spreads himself over the donuts and coffee. Tell him you're horribly overeducated for your position in life and he wrinkles up his brow and looks worried. And no matter how many times I remind him that the appropriate response is, "And how does that make you feel?" and that his efforts to solve all my problems demonstrate a lack of faith in my own competence and maturity, he just can't stop the Superman act. He's a dear, and I'm very lucky—I just didn't feel lucky at that particular time of life. I felt like a prisoner, and bitterly reflected that at least in jail a sentence is reduced for good behavior. In a marriage, in any relationship, I guess, rattling the bars of the cage is the best way to get your needs met.

I don't think Matt ever realized just how hard it was for me once the kids started school. He practically salivated over all the "free time" I had, not working, mothering only in the late afternoons and evenings. Sartre says freedom without stability is meaningless; was he a housewife, do you suppose?

This is what my days were like. Initially mornings were not so bad. I'd fix breakfast, check the book bags, send off Matt and the kids, clean the house, plan the dinner. After several weeks, I realized that every single task on my list fit under "maintenance." I stopped keeping lists. I began sleeping after lunch, sometimes all afternoon, or until someone came home.

I remember the day Matt came home to find the breakfast dishes on the table. Molly had pooped on the stairs and I couldn't decide whether to clean up the kitchen first or the stairs. Now, I don't mean 'couldn't decide' the way sometimes a hot dog looks good and sometimes a salad looks good, and sometimes you can't decide. Every time I looked at either the table or the stairs I had an overwhelming surge of what might have been nausea, except that I hadn't eaten in two days, and anyway the sensation was located north of my stomach (but south of my heart).

There was a time when all roads were one,
And my road went up and on so smoothly—
As if it had already been marched by millions.
There was a time when I would stand at the beginning,
Smiling at the bright road
As if my feet would never tire,
And the night were never cold.
But now
So many paths,
and this one so rough.
I stand at the beginning—
Feet frozen, hands cold—
and watch the dark shadows
dance on my road.

Question 4:   Interpret Jan's poem. What is she feeling?

I really, really didn't want to be me. In France. As a housewife.

Matt didn't even notice that I wasn't quite myself, that I'd mysteriously trans-mogrified into a piece of lint in his pocket, leaving my body to fix breakfasts on the days when it wasn't too heavy to lift off the bed in the morning. But one day he brought home a brochure from a nearby school that offered language lessons.

Thank goodness for intellectual tasks. I might have gone stark raving mad without the French course. The language school offered its own cross-cultural challenges, not the challenges that come from having a clearly defined duty to fill an otherwise meaningless housewife's day. Europeans think working is more stressful than being unemployed. I think they're nuts.

I met two women from the French course who became my good friends. Achat, a woman doctor from India, is married to an engineer who works for a French computer software company. He had been assigned to his company's Grenoble research and development center six months earlier, and they planned to stay for two or three years. My other friend was Celia, a Swedish woman and former SAS stewardess, now married to the head of a small technology-based business located in Grenoble. Per, Celia's husband, is Swedish too, and the business is owned by the Swedish ballbearing company, SKF. Achat's son, Ravi, is the same age as Jeff and the boys have similar interests and personalities. Celia has two daughters who liked spending time with Michelle. Matt got along with Ganesh, Achat's husband, but was more at ease with Per, whose education and interests mirrored Matt's. We all lived within a few blocks of each other, and the children attended the same school. Achat was very appreciative of the French system of education, which helped me accept their approach. Surely Indians are the most demanding math teachers in the world, so if the French system met Achat's expectations, I decided it must be okay, even if the *cahiers* worried me initially.

Michelle liked school and did well. She followed most of the French courses successfully and learned quickly in her math class. The French use Cartesian logic and approach math education not through using hands-on materials to solve problems, but through the constant reiteration of abstract rules and memorized facts. It's a system that teaches to the strength of the brightest students, leaving the less able ones to decide early on to become mechanics and models. The philosophy classes were the pride of the school, incorporating history and rhetorical analyses. Michelle developed a close friendship with Caroline, a French girl, and visited her home several times. Kids were not available most evenings because between the dinner hour and homework, little time remained for playing. So Michelle saw Caroline on Wednesday afternoons, when the school had its midweek break, or on Saturday afternoon or Sunday (and whenever teachers went on strike). The French school held Saturday morning sessions.

Michelle also had interesting friends from the *anglophone* section, Sonia and Tamara. Sonia was British and in Grenoble because her mother and father were attached to the university. Her mom lectured as a visiting professor of English and her dad conducted research. Tamara's origins were more international: French and Brazilian. Her father was a French businessman from an upper-class family near Annecy and her mother a Brazilian. But Tamara had been born in the United States while her father was pursuing his MBA.

The school based the *anglophone* section on the British system of education. The curriculum was rather spotty, but the depth of study was excellent, unequaled in any American school I had seen. The children were expected to prepare reports with graphics and a bibliography, and to present information to their classmates aloud.

They took long examinations at the end of each semester and, in general, prepared for the thirteenth grade A-level exams that determine eligibility to attend various British universities. They studied integrated mathematics, not just one subject (e.g., fractions) at a time. Both English literature and written composition were emphasized and the children participated in one major drama event each year.

Jeff picked up French quickly and made several neighborhood friends, all French, with whom he played basketball on the outdoor courts at the elementary school, went swimming at the *piscine* (swimming pool), or played soccer. Jeff's best friend, however, was a German boy named Hans. His father was part of a pan-European (European Union) research team based in Grenoble. The Neubauer family had recently lived in the United States where Hans's father taught at Penn State. Jeff also liked playing with Ravi, the son of Achat and Ganesh. Unlike most American parents, however, the parents of Jeff's friends were very education minded, and as a result his friends spent a great deal of time doing homework with their parents. Playtime occurred mostly on Wednesday and Saturday afternoons and was often scheduled in advance and nowhere near as spontaneous as in America. Jeff found the homework load infringed on his outside interests, and he wasn't as committed to achievement as Michelle. The French school was a little too challenging for Jeff—I worried that he would decide he belonged on the mechanic track. In the States, students aren't tracked until high school, except by the inevitable economic forces that determine the quality of a neighborhood's public school and the commitment to education shared by the neighborhood parents. But French kids are selected out early on, especially on their abilities in mathematics. The objective of most serious and talented French students (and their parents) is to go to the engineering school, Polytechnique, nicknamed "X," even if one wants to pursue a career in business or law. It seemed to me that Jeff was still far too young to be worrying about his academic future as the French kids and my friends' kids did.

Question 5:   What are your impressions of the educational experiences the Sumner kids are receiving? What are the problems?

JAN

Dear Mom and Dad,

Thanks for calling on Michelle's birthday. It really means a lot to her and to Jeff that you two put so much effort into keeping in touch with them. It was so thoughtful of you to include the books for Jeff in Michelle's birthday package. He's at a low point just now. Michelle pointed out on her birthday that Jeff is three years older than she is but he's only one group ahead of her because now she is two threes plus two years old and he is only three threes plus two years old. France has been very good for her math skills!

MICHELLE

Dear Grandma and Grandpa,

Thank you for the Veterinarian Barbie. My friend from school, Caroline, has a dollhouse and we put the veterinarian office in the living room and Caroline's dolls bring their dogs for shots. I like going to Jeannette's house but she doesn't have as many toys as Ashley in California. I miss Ashley, and all my other friends at home. I miss you. It's a good thing I have a brother because if I didn't, I would just be sure that there was something wrong with our family, because we are very different from Caroline's family. They yell at each other when they talk, and her brother hugs and kisses her. Yuck.

School is fun and I like it a lot. Mostly I like recess. We jump rope and share our snacks. There are two sections in school: the English section, which is really, really easy, and the French section, which is way too hard. In the English section we read and do projects and a lot of our work is done in groups. Each group has a smart girl in it and one kid who can't sit still, and we have to work together. This week we learned about the water cycle. Did you know that if you pour yourself a glass of water you could be drinking water that was in a cloud outside my window last year? I said last week, but Miss Rhodes said it would take a long time to get where you are. She has a funny accent because she's from England. I miss you, Grandma. And Grandpa.

If you were here I could take you to school and tell you what they are saying in the French section. I have one teacher who sometimes talks to me in English and I love her—Mlle. Cordonnier. She teaches math and she wants to be sure I understand how to do my drills. Mme. Dupuy, my science teacher, talks to the chalkboard and writes stuff down, and we copy it into our cahiers, and memorize what she writes. Even the kids who speak good French say her classes are stupid. I also have a man teacher, M. Gaillard. His face is red and he yawns a lot and I don't know what he's saying, mostly. Sometimes he doesn't come to school, or he comes really late, and then we are all sent to the cantine, the lunchroom. The boys yell at us and throw things like napkins and spitballs at us. When the lunch ladies are there they make faces but they don't stop the boys, and on Wednesdays there aren't any lunch ladies, so that's the worst.

I like our adventures on Sundays. Mom and Dad sit in the front seat and Jeff and I play I Spy and we drive into the country and go for walks and some- times we go to the movies and I can understand what they are saying, except when they sing. We didn't do this in California, except when you would take me or Jeff and the next week Jeff or me. Can you come and visit us? You would like the bakeries.

Thank you for the sweater, too, I love it. I love you. XOX,

Michelle

JEFF

Dear Grandma and Grandpa,

Thanks for the books. I made the models from the paper airplane book with my friend Hans and we launched them from the roof. If you throw them straight up they have a better shot at finding an updraft. My record is a 9-second flight, and Per only got 7. My friend Blair in California has e-mail, so I wrote him to find that book and launch them from the tower on the hill by the ocean. I bet he can go to 15 from there. I'm lucky he has e-mail, I'd be really in bad shape if I couldn't talk to someone who knows me the way I'm supposed to be. Everyone here except Hans thinks I'm stupid. Hans says if you get good grades teachers give you good grades and intelligence has nothing to do with it, it's all work and reputation. Maybe Hans is stupid. He gets really good grades, though. I don't think Blair even gets grades, we never talked about it. We talked about football, and nobody here has ever heard of it, except for soccer which they call football. I'm in the soccer club which would be fun if I could kick the ball, ever. The coach doesn't have anything to say so we spend a lot of time arguing about the rules. You'd think the one good thing about having every game be scheduled three months in advance is you wouldn't have to argue, like at home when you're playing baseball at the park and some dog takes away home base in his mouth so you can't tell if you're safe. Here, you never just hang out with your buddies, the parents call each other and you can only see your friends, even Hans who isn't even French, on Wednesday and Saturday afternoons, and that's only if they aren't going to equestrian club or swimming club or soccer club. Yeech.

Remember when Plasmatec had season tickets to the Giants and Dad would take me? And I miss the 49ers. It's a good thing I'm on the Net or I wouldn't know what Blair was doing or get any Giant and 49er news.

I miss eating at your house outside on the patio, Grandma. I miss hamburgers and McDonald's, well, they have them here, but Mom won't go there. French people don't drink root beer and their food stinks. Even if you don't like it, they want you to eat everything they put on your plate. There's good bread, though. I like our house, and we see Dad a lot more here than we did in California, but Mom is very crabby. Michelle is good. She's just a kid, but she's a good kid. One day we'll be back in America and I will be so nice to her, I won't ever rattail her while I'm drying the dishes. I sure miss the dishwasher! Well, gotta go. Love, Jeff

MATT

Soon enough we came to believe that we had made a good move. We'd become closer as a couple and as a family, built up our savings, and profited from the invaluable learning experience that occurs through immersion in a new culture.

Pleased with our friendships and the children's education, we often discussed the pros and cons of staying. With a year left on the contract, we began to feel the importance of our decision more intensely.

We saw many pros: a wonderful lifestyle (much better than we could afford in Los Gatos), good schools, more time together, more disposable income, exciting work for me, the cultural abundance of Europe, the good friends we'd found and the pleasure of living an atypical, adventurous life. On the other side of the ledger, however, we feared becoming a part of the "internationalist" set of people who have no roots. We worried that our kids were becoming too European, that they'd wear only black and chain-smoke by 14. Jan's stalled career frustrated her and she missed her family. I worried about my father's health, which recently had taken a turn for the worse.

My work at Transfusions had challenged and often absorbed me altogether. Not many managers in the States have the developmental opportunity of actually running a business, and although Transfusions was small by comparison to GTS and Plasmatec, I was still enormously proud of myself for having somehow gained that opportunity. Europe presented large potential markets, each with unique obstacles and opportunities. New manufacturing technology in Sweden that Per called to my attention could improve operational efficiency. A small company near Munich had captured most of the German and Austrian markets and needed to be considered for possible acquisition. I learned that some scientists in Edinburgh were doing superb research that could advance blood purification mechanisms through a new process that added antibodies to filtered blood via plasma transfusions.

But I often felt frustrated by the many governmental regulations in France and within the EU. Obligated to honor all the prescribed holidays and work hours, one of my salaried employees acted as the leader of the workers association and quickly corrected me whenever he felt the need. I made the mistake once of calling a 1 P.M. meeting on a day when we'd been in conference until noon, after which I was reminded that the staff must have an hour and a half for lunch.

QUESTIONS FOR DISCUSSION

1. What do you like about the Sumners' new life in Grenoble? What seems difficult or problematic?
2. In what ways did the Sumners experience culture shock during the first six months following their move to Grenoble (see the Useful Concepts material in Part II for Chapter 5)?
3. What else might Transfusions have done to accommodate the Sumners' move?
4. Focus on the Sumner children. What do you think Jeff and Michelle are experiencing? What else could their parents do to help them make this cultural transition? Do you see their experience as basically healthy or problematic?

CHAPTER 15

Matt's International Performance Review

MATT

I dealt with a man with some relationship to Rhône Poulenc and Groupe Techno-Sang who seemed very close to the local French government, if not on their payroll. He came around often to monitor accounting practices, employee relations, compliance with environmental and safety regulations, and so on. He lunched often with a man from the Cabinet du Préfet, or local government. I called him "Monsieur Inspecteur," and he ended his visits with a long two-star lunch that my French assistant director and I were expected to pay for. After exchanging conversation about family, food, the weather, the climate for business in Europe, why France leads the world's economic powers and why it needed to remain fiercely independent of American influence, Monsieur Inspecteur would report two or three "irregularities" that he hoped would be "corrected" before his next visit. Then he commonly announced his return in six weeks' time. I later learned that the small red ribbon he wore on his jacket showed discreetly that he had been decorated by France for valiant public service.

Another problem occurred when I tried to carry out the company policy of holding annual performance reviews with my direct reports and asked that they do the same with theirs. In my review of Charles Caussé, the director of sales and marketing, I suggested he spent too much time away from the office and that he needed to shift his focus to include market research and marketing strategy, not just direct sales. I also wanted him to go to Munich and check out the business potential of a German company.

Distinguished and often charming, Charles had been with GTS for 20 years. He typically arrived at the office about 9 A.M. He left for lunch at 12:30 and often returned again very late that afternoon, sometimes the next morning. On those occasions when he did return to the office, he usually appeared near 4 or 4:30 and often a little "under the influence." What's more, his restaurant bill was enormous, and showed him ordering expensive wines and liquors while dining with government officials, other marketing and salespeople in the area, and on occasion some key clients. Occasionally, he traveled to Paris and lunched with GTS colleagues and other buddies from his class at Centrale, one of the prestigious French *grande écoles,* or professional schools. Once I asked him about all this time-consuming and expensive socializing, and he tried to convince me that business in France is conducted via networks and that he was hardworking in the French way. I thought that we Americans network too but in a much more efficient way. Charles seemed to me to be superficially friendly and polite but very aloof; I wondered if I could ever build an authentic relationship with him.

When we held our performance review, for which I had reserved the whole morning, Charles came in at 9:30, even though we were scheduled to meet at 8:30. He had not carefully reviewed his people. He was somewhat uninterested in the marketing data and the sales projections I had generated and wanted instead to talk about philosophy and the theory of sales and marketing in France. He viewed his job as building and maintaining a network of relationships rather than going for more direct results, and he said he was hesitant to go to Munich, maintaining his German was rusty and that he still had bad feelings about the Germans because his uncle's family had been killed by the SS during World War II. He even maintained at one point that performance reviews are essentially an American invention.

Mostly, Charles seemed uncomfortable with me, remaining very formal and unwilling to enter into honest and open dialogue about his role and performance. During the actual evaluation, when I told Charles how he was doing, he became very tense and upset. He told me that this method of direct feedback was "un-French" and that his reputation and honor were at stake.

After all, he was a French reserve army officer and had never been treated like this, even in the military. Critiquing his behavior was, he claimed, incompatible with his academic degree and social background. He pointed out that he belonged to an exclusive golf club.

I observed over time that my colleagues discussed results indirectly and informally in their own performance evaluations with their direct reports. They seemed reluctant to use the formal performance evaluation. None of them had held previous performance reviews with their people as prescribed by Transfusions.

My own performance evaluation was also troubling. I reported to Ron Clancy, VP International, at Plasmatec and had received a very good and helpful evaluation from him during my last visit to California. I also reported to Henri-Claude de Brie at GTS. I had always believed our relationship to be cordial and essentially collaborative. We had held the performance review over a long lunch where Henri-Claude talked at length about his country home near Dijon and more generally about the business environment in Europe. When I received the reviews, however, I noticed I had been ranked "average" in most categories without written comments or rationale. I had tried several times to discuss the ratings with Henri-Claude, but my efforts largely fell on deaf ears. At a meeting for another purpose, Henri-Claude told me I was doing fine and should not bring the matter up again. I wondered if Henri-Claude had different standards of evaluation, just as French teachers reserved their highest marks for the kind of child who at age 10 focused on attending university. I wondered whether he really understood the Plasmatec performance review procedure and the technical English on the forms, or if he just failed to grasp the importance of the performance review for my career. It was painful to me to see that my future could be affected by an unapproachable boss.

I also began wondering whether staying or returning to Santa Cruz would be best for my career. Karl Davidson had told me before going, "this will be a fantastic developmental opportunity but may not be a good career move in terms of Plasmatec. Out of sight, out of mind." During my most recent return to California I'd noticed several new faces. Although my peers were polite, they seemed rather disinterested in the French venture. Most of them seemed to look on the experience as an extended European vacation, and they maintained that the Asian venture seemed the one to watch. Even Doc seemed less interested than he had been.

Transfusions S.A. had done well for a new start-up company, however. Sales had grown 7.4 percent over the past year and although negatively impacted by the strong U.S. dollar, in terms of reporting dollar profits, they accounted for 2.5 percent of total company revenues. I caught some flack for my low productivity ratios. Many Plasmatec people from the operations division had visited the new plant in Chambéry, and all agreed that the state-of-the-art facility beat anything else owned by the parent company. Top management seemed to view the European venture as full of potential and a key part of their overall strategy.

I obsessed over the way my performance looked to Ron and Doc. Although I knew that part of Transfusions' relatively low productivity could be explained as a result of French labor laws, I also knew that low productivity might translate into a bleaker future for Transfusions. So I decided to take action. As best I could figure, I needed to demonstrate in dramatic fashion that I expected everyone to put in longer hours. Transfusions' employees needed to develop more commitment to the company. They were too darn complacent.

I decided that during the next set of performance reviews, I would notify workers that I felt they could be replaced unless they added value to Transfusions. To those who seemed least productive, I would suggest some improved productivity goals that they needed to achieve over the next several months. I thought I'd start by putting Charles Caussé on a two-month probation, with very clear goals to meet and early retirement the consequence of failure. This would certainly signal I meant business.

No sooner did I put this plan into action than I received an unexpected visit from Monsieur Inspecteur. "Shall we share a lunch?" the man inquired. I agreed. During the lunch he lectured me for nearly two hours on the responsibility of business to employees and the social irresponsibility of business practices common in the States. He remained fairly general until, nearing the second hour, he recommended that I back off on Charles and the other executives. I was pretty frustrated at this point, but politely said that while I appreciated the inspecteur's advice, I couldn't see what business it was of his. He became quite angry, and started his lecture from the top. Irritated, I tried to shut the broken record down.

"I heard you the first time," I said. "I simply don't agree. If you have something new to say, then say it. But you have repeated yourself time and again, and each time you say that we have to keep people even when they aren't productive. I want you to recognize that Transfusions is mostly owned by an American company and that we are in global competition with the Asians, who work harder than any of us. And unprofitable companies go bankrupt, leaving us all out of jobs." Suddenly silent, Monsieur Inspecteur slowly turned red and stared at me. Then he stood and stormed out of the restaurant.

The next day, I received notice from the Employees' Committee, explaining that they would strike if any one of them were fired. Perplexed, I approached each of my direct reports with letter in hand. Oddly, they refused to comment and only pointed to the letter I held.

"The letter says it all," they said, and went on with their business.

Charles's behavior changed little over the next few days. I called Doc for advice, and Doc recommended that I pursue my strategy. "I think you need to make clear your expectations. We support you back here." But no one supported me in Grenoble.

Henri-Claude paid me a surprise visit a few days later. He and I talked in my office for several hours, during which Henri-Claude gently prodded me to retract my threats of firing people. "Americans and French do things differently," Henri-Claude said. "In America, you worry less about people. In France we worry much more. And since you are in France, maybe you could worry a little more."

I tried to explain. "The issue isn't just whether I worry about people or not. Whether your company is in France or the United States or Japan or Sri Lanka, the company will eventually fall apart if it isn't productive. Then everyone is out of work."

"But Transfusions is productive. Look around you. You have a wonderful facility. Your employees work hard and are happy. The community respects this company and considers it an important addition to Grenoble. You receive good comments in the local press. It is a very productive facility."

I went on to cite reports of profit margins and productivity while Henri-Claude discussed cultural differences, French unemployment rates, and the status of the company within France. I felt like we were having two entirely separate conversations.

Things quieted down for a week (although nothing changed), until I received a phone call from Ron Clancy. "I'm afraid you can't make any personnel moves, Matt."

"I don't want to make any personnel moves," I responded. "I just want my people to work harder."

"Well, I'm afraid you can't threaten anybody's job."

"Why? What happened?"

"Through Henri-Claude, we've heard from the local French government. They just reminded us of our obligations to the employed community of Grenoble. Apparently, they are worried we're going to start huge layoffs in the American style. There are a mess of penalties that they're threatening if you don't back off. They see your recent threats as a move of bad faith and, I'll quote, 'A misunderstanding on the importance of a safe and humane work environment.' This is especially serious so close to the elections."

"But I didn't threaten anyone—except Caussé—and he's incompetent and lazy. How can I not fire someone like that? Besides, I only talked to maybe a half-dozen top people about being more productive. How can the government see that as 'bad faith?'"

"Well," Ron continued, "that half dozen seems to be the wrong half dozen to upset."

"I guess. What can we do about it?"

"I think the only real option is to drop the matter. You'll have to figure some way to increase productivity without harming the 'safe and humane work environment.' Meanwhile, we'll try and figure out a way to placate the government so you can get rid of Caussé."

"Now I see why GTS let him transfer over. That seems the best method for getting rid of someone—give him to someone else."

I simply let the matter die. Plasmatec got a guarantee from the government that as long as I fired no one, the government would not take any punitive action.

I chose not to apologize; I simply dropped the subject of job security while continuing to encourage my reports to become more productive. Relationships seemed to return to normal.

QUESTIONS FOR DISCUSSION

1. What are the key cultural issues associated with Matt's performance review with Charles Caussé? What should Matt do?
2. How should Matt deal with his own performance review by Henri-Claude de Brie? Should he ignore it? Why or why not?
3. Look at the notes on French labor law for Chapter 10 in Part II. Who is Monsieur Inspecteur? Is he a French government agent? Why, in the end, did his will prevail and Matt had to back off his plan to increase worker productivity and put Charles Caussé on probation?

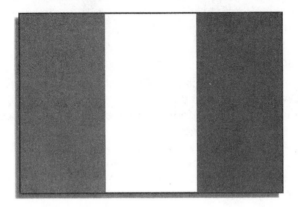

CHAPTER 16

Jennifer Stewart

MEMO

Internal Memo: For Plasmatec Files
From: Tom
To: Doc
Re: People Committee Findings

I recently attended a leadership seminar for senior executives of medium-sized technology-based companies. The seminar focused on the need to develop the talent of company employees. The gist: keep your "knowledge workers" happy (and, as a result, productive) to maintain an advantage over your competitors. It's more cost effective to retrain and develop young employees whenever possible than to lose them to opportunities elsewhere and have to start from scratch.

I'd like to call your attention to Jennifer Stewart, a HIPO (high-potential employee) in marketing. She reminds me of Matt Sumner—another market analyst we hand-picked for the HIPO track—but she's more creative.

Speaking of Matt—still think he'd make an excellent VP International when Ron Clancy retires in two years? Heard he had some labor problems over there—of course, the French like labor disputes. His rise in the company and relatively quick move overseas has not allowed him much visibility here at home. If he's to move further up in the company, particularly to a VP position, he'll need to demonstrate his ability to groom junior HIPOs.

The People Committee is going to formally suggest to the Executive Committee that Jennifer Stewart go to France and work for Matt, which will give him that opportunity. Jennifer is single, which is conveniently cheap in terms of moving, housing, insurance, the works. She'll probably work like a fiend, since she'll be alone among the French. We expect her to master those core competencies of the European operation that differ from ours, and to bring back new ideas. We want her to help Matt look for new business opportunities in Europe. Of course, we really expect her to grow a bit—overseas experiences are very valuable growth opportunities (as Jed is always saying when he harks back to his Peace Corps days—and he's right too; the leadership seminar also made this point). Needless to say, Jennifer's advancement can also help us demonstrate our position as an equal opportunity employer that values bright women in our talent pool—not that she's being given any special consideration.

We'd like to assign her as Matt's special assistant for new ventures, with a stay of 18 to 24 months.

We should make it clear to Matt that he can't just bury her in work—the point is for her to adjust to the French and come home stronger for the experience, in addition to being useful to Matt, and to bring home innovations that have proven their value elsewhere.

> ### *Memo*

Internal Memo: For Plasmatec Files
        From: Doc
          To: Matt
          Re: Jennifer Stewart

We'd like to send you a new manager from the States: Jennifer Stewart. Tom and other members of the Executive Committee and I feel that she possesses the potential to become an important leader in Plasmatec's future—she's a definite HIPO (high-potential employee).

Frankly, this is primarily to provide her with the experience and know-how required to reach the next plateau in the company. Of course, with the product manufacturing process complete, you can use some help with new business development, and that's an area in which she's shone.

Jennifer has become an integral part of her marketing team, but as you know, the work done here has not been sufficiently challenging to truly test her capabilities. The People Committee feels she needs some new experiences that will tax her abilities and push her into a higher learning curve. An international move should develop her understanding of the company and broaden her perspective.

Attached find the relevant policy statement. Please understand that you are to act both as a mentor and as a manager in this case.

We hope you will accept Jennifer and this management development challenge, Matt. We also hope this idea corresponds to one of your organizational needs. The final decision on the matter is yours, of course.

Plasmatec Internal Policy

Developing Future Leaders

The initial selection of a high-potential employee (HIPO) hinges on evaluations analyzed at the annual Executive Committee retreat, where the committee uses annual performance reviews, supervisor recommendations, and submitted educational background, psychological tests, and competency-based profiles to evaluate its future leader employees according to seven general characteristics:

1. All HIPOs should have an MBA or an advanced degree in medical engineering, a relevant medical field, or the equivalent.
2. They should demonstrate an ability to learn from their experience and take initiative.
3. They should have the interpersonal skills necessary for them to work well with customers, colleagues, bosses, and direct reports.
4. They should be able to work effectively in diverse teams across gender, age, cultural, functional, and company boundaries.
5. They should have demonstrated a high level of competence in their specialization, fit into the Plasmatec culture, and be hardworking and willing to make sacrifices for the company.
6. They should be technologically literate and write and speak well—especially when giving presentations and interacting with customers.
7. They should have the leadership potential and competencies to succeed at the next level of management or professional expertise.

If a new employee is found to meet all these criteria, his or her name is submitted to the People Committee. The PC finds mentors (usually more senior executives) to ensure that the HIPO progresses along the correct track, garnering experiences in a wide variety of activities so he or she gains an understanding of the company's structure and goals.

JENNIFER

I came to Plasmatec on a crooked path. Somehow I had always expected of myself that I would become a doctor like my father. I'd worked in the medical lab that he owned which was adjacent to his practice, and I had always identified more with him, his interests and his dreams, than with my mother. Mom manages an art gallery and wears flowing clothes, the whole nine yards in some cases. Once they divorced I spent more time with my father in San Diego than with Mom in St. Louis, and it wasn't entirely the geography of the situation that drew me into my father's sphere.

I graduated from Georgetown in 1988. I'd followed the premed track until the day my girlfriend and I left our organic chemistry notes on a table while we took a break from preparing for the final. Another premed stole our notes. It was then that it occurred to me that if I became a doctor I would have to work with other doctors. I switched to political science.

After a few years in D.C. working on the Hill for different government agencies, I decided to return to school to get an MBA. I was tired of the East Coast, tired of jockeying for position at parties like so many bantam roosters, tired of talking about cars all the time. The University of California at Berkeley accepted me, and I didn't open the other letters.

I was sitting in a Berkeley courtyard café one day, drinking a latte and feeling aimless and shiftless when the perfect career path opened before me like a dream. I realized that I could draw together all the disparate elements of my education and my family past by becoming an advertiser for a health-related business. I began interviewing people who worked for medical supplies companies and realized that my niche was marketing research rather than advertising. Sorry, Mom—but all those premed classes came in handy after all, helping me use the stats program on the PC, and I still love art galleries.

Plasmatec seemed perfect. Plasmatec's recruiter clearly liked me, and stressed the advantages of working for a small informal company set in the hills of Santa Cruz, manufacturing a product that promotes health and human dignity. The company asked me to visit Santa Cruz for a second round of interviews. There on the company grounds was a stand of seven ancient redwoods that had been preserved during the construction of the building, which filtered the light through their branches as though through stained glass in high windows. I loved the people I met, was inspired by their business plans, and thought the whole industry had lots of potential. I accepted their offer that same day, and went to work in the marketing department.

In my first week on the job I received an invitation to lunch from Meg, an MBA in the Finance Department. It came in a basket beautifully wrapped in elf ribbon and iridescent paper that held a hand-thrown ceramic mug labeled *Plasmafem Rules*. On the other side of the cup was the following:

Evolve. Speak out. Innovate.

There was also an assortment of teas and a chocolate bar in the basket.

Plasmafem was an informal club of women who worked for Plasmatec, made up of two physicians, a chemist, a senior plasma technician, and Deborah, the human resources director. They met twice a month for lunch in the cafeteria and sought to support one another and to advise management on women's issues when necessary. Deborah had already alerted the Executive Committee to a number of cases of the glass ceiling, including one egregious example of wage disparity when a woman who had earned a law degree was still being paid an administrative assistant's wage although she was doing the same work as the two male lawyers in the intellectual properties office. This was speedily attended to, with the face-saving concession that as she had only recently passed the bar she could only claim three months' back wages.

The Executive Committee included both Deborah and one of the female physicians. According to Meg, the men on the committee supported Plasmafem and its goals and especially the push to recruit more qualified women into managerial and professional roles so the company might be viewed as "female friendly" and attract the top young women business talent that, in turn, would improve the company's competitive advantage. I was happy to have the support of some older women, and found our lunches highly informative.

Question 1:   Do you think Plasmafem is good or bad for Plasmatec? Should the Executive Committee be supportive?

At one such lunch the female physician from the Executive Committee hinted to me that I was on the junior exec track and could expect a dramatic change of lifestyle shortly. So I wasn't as surprised as Doc expected me to be when he offered me the opportunity to work in France, and I understood that more was at stake than the language training. Grenoble sounded like a lovely town, and I was thrilled to return to Europe for something other than a graduation spree. (I'd had three of those already, characterized by too much alcohol and too little touring—even on the post-high school leg, which was financed by my father, who was attending a conference in Geneva at the time.)

I arrived in Grenoble in mid-March, after Matt Sumner had already been in France more than two years. With an English-speaking real estate agent's help, I found a nice apartment in an established area of the city, near a public park. My building was one of many older well-kept apartment complexes on a busy street near the center of town. I sublet a furnished apartment from a family recently sent to Dallas for two years by their company. I bought a sporty new Renault Clio, went to Paris to see the Louvre and the Musée d'Orsay, and enrolled in intensive French courses.

Although the language barrier was formidable, I managed to situate myself fairly well. I had studied Latin in high school as part of my premed program, and had taken both high school and basic college French. However, I felt foolish mimicking my teacher's accent, which sounded affected, as though she'd watched too many late-night movies. And people spoke so fast I hardly understood a thing.

Matt and Jan met me upon arrival and offered their assistance if I needed it. Matt sent an English-speaking assistant from the office to help me get settled and arrange my various affairs. He also suggested that I not feel rushed to get to work. After hearing of the bureaucratic difficulties I was likely to encounter in arranging all the necessary paperwork for my stay, I agreed to report to the office at the beginning of April.

When I finally arrived, I tried my best to converse with the other employees. I was the only American besides Matt. My fellow employees tried to communicate with me and make me feel welcome, but language barriers made every attempt a little challenging. I also noticed that I met few other women—except the secretaries.

The first few days were terrible, and I longed for a tea basket with a silly mug. Matt explained his expectations, which at this point included only language acquisition and learning the inner workings of the company. He also invited me to his home for dinner with the family. The rest of the time I spent struggling with the language barrier and trying to remember names that sounded like *"toujours jeune seize ans"* being said over and over. All of them, except maybe the saints' first names, Jean, Marc, Luc, and Paul, I lost.

I was able to find the charming house the Sumners occupied without any trouble. I was delighted to find friendly faces and have a night away from the apartment. After several weeks of living in France, I found it immensely refreshing to be in a home where American English filled the air. The children were wonderful—smart enough to be interesting conversationalists already, but not so smart that they seemed otherworldly.

Jan seemed to understand quite clearly how I felt and brought the conversation back to culture shock twice when I had let it fall, not wanting to make a surly first impression. I appreciated her willingness to listen to me gripe about the frustrations that came from spending each day understanding only a fraction of the conversations which surrounded me. While Matt helped the children with homework, Jan and I worked in the kitchen and got to know each other.

During dinner everyone focused on the children, who told us interesting bits from their schoolday. Jeff asked Matt how to handle an aggressive little French kid who was so small he couldn't possibly be aggressive back at him: Matt told him some amusing facts about Napoleon and sent him off to research French insults, giving him the phone number of a Plasmatec employee with four children as a resource. Jan thought it was a good sign that his *problème du jour* was developmental, and not something related to being an American, or inarticulate in French, or unfamiliar with the playground culture or with the rules of soccer.

While we cleared the table, Jan told me about Jeff's difficult first year in France, how he'd gone from being a socially skilled, athletic, self-confident little guy to being a kid who thought of himself as a future mechanic. Jan said she'd been worried sick about him, but then a real turn-around had occurred on a skiing vacation to Gstaad, in Switzerland. First Jeff had his spirits lifted when he noticed that the entire country spoke French with a funny accent. Then it turned out he was a natural skier, all guts and knees, and that reminded him he had plenty of good qualities. When they'd gotten back from vacation the basketball season was under way, and Jeff was nicknamed *l'américain,* and had the double advantage of height and familiarity with the game. After that, the French kids had warmed up to him. "What about Michelle?" I asked, figuring she wouldn't have had the athlete's edge that Jeff had.

"Michelle is really flexible," Jan answered, "I think younger kids probably have an easier time of it, because the world still revolves around their family. And they have an advantage when it comes to learning other languages. After our first month in France, Michelle's French was better than mine."

Michelle came looking for Jan for a goodnight kiss, and I asked her how she liked France.

"France is fine, I guess," she shrugged. "I love horseback riding, and I never did that in California, but here there's a club and I take dressage lessons and I'm learning how to jump. And our vacations are great. We get to stay in hotels with pools and see different countries and the food is really good here."

"But at first you hated French food, remember? You said you couldn't remember what your front teeth were for. You didn't even like dessert," Jan teased her.

"Mom! You let us order French ice cream for the longest time, yuck. We didn't know about *mousse au chocolat* back when we first came. And we thought people were really funny, but now they seem just like us," Michelle said. "Only different." She hugged Jan and ran off.

"We never had any adjustment problems with Michelle. But then, we never had rebellion problems with Jeff," Jan said. I wondered whether expatriating as a family had made Jan's adjustment any easier than mine. However bad I felt, I thought it would be worse to watch my child feeling awkward and unskilled and to not be able to help. There are rough spots in adolescence stateside too. But you don't have to feel as though you personally have pulled the rug out from under your child's feet when the hormonal troubles start, whereas it's clear that moving your entire family to France for three years is optional. Still, the kids were well spoken and comfortable in their skin, and I liked them. Jan and Matt were doing a good job, that seemed clear.

After the kids had gone to bed, Matt and Jan asked me about company scuttlebutt back in Santa Cruz. I learned of the close relationship between the Sumners and Doc's family. Having had the advantage of the Plasmafem doctor's input on the underlying reason I had been sent to France, I understood that among Doc, Matt, and I parallel situations were occurring. I stayed at the Sumners' home until quite late, sharing stories and getting to know Matt and Jan.

As the days passed, I began attending business meetings and conferences. I knew that listening would help me gain fluency more quickly and it's easier to listen to topics which are already both familiar and interesting. Meetings were perfect, with their predictable structure and the French tendency to philosophize. The language of philosophy is almost entirely Latin, and I could merge the French chirps between the long latinate words I understood. Of course, I also wanted to demonstrate from the outset my eagerness to be involved in Transfusions, to demonstrate that I wasn't in France as a tourist. Charles Caussé led most of the meetings I attended. He seemed charming in a slightly smarmy, paternalistic way—is that a contradiction? I'd have hated him in English right away, I'm sure. I often felt like a fly on the wall, watching a foreign language film I barely understood without subtitles and yawning politely in the back of my throat.

After a few weeks, I resolved to say something, anything, to make the men in the office aware of me. I was tired of being ignored. After researching a particular point, I formulated a question I thought important and practiced asking it in French. When the right moment came in the meeting I blurted out the sentence. The four other men turned toward me with surprise. Then Charles said something quickly in French (which I didn't understand), and the other men laughed. Recognizing the confusion on my face, he said in thickly accented English, "Do not worry, *chou-chou*."

I smiled. I didn't know how else to respond. He had just called me "my little darling"—or was it "cabbage head"? I recognized it from Debussy's dedication of the *Mother Goose Suite* to his daughter, but wasn't sure just how it translated outside of a papa-baby relationship. Was it a compliment? As the meeting wore on I became angry, realizing that no interpretation permitted the possibility I had been taken seriously. Charles had been very patronizing, I decided. Moreover, I had acquiesced to his condescension by smiling. I'd given him no reason to take me seriously. Had I become so insecure that now I accepted condescension with a smile? As the meeting continued, I stewed away.

After several weeks, I realized that the only senior women at Transfusions worked either in the lab or as company doctors—with one exception. A woman named Carine Solvay joined the company two weeks after me. Carine was also 28. She had worked previously for GTS before going back to school at the Lyon Business School to get her MBA (CESMA) degree.

Carine also had a high-potential profile for France. She had attended Ecole des Mines (School of Mines) in Paris as an undergraduate. Her father had gone to ENA (Ecole Nationale d'Administration) and was a leader of the central right political party in the Rhône-Alpes region. Her family was considered very established and cultured, one of the bourgeois families of Grenoble, and her grandfather had been one of the top managers at GTS. Through her various networks (family, Ecole des Mines, ESC Lyon, GTS, growing up in Grenoble social circles), Carine knew lots of people and was well positioned to influence outcomes for the good of Transfusions. She was smart, poised, competent, and well connected. If she was politically astute (i.e., did not offend the wrong people, stayed in the right coalitions, used her networks wisely, pleased her bosses) and performed well, she should have a brilliant career. Some even saw Carine as an eventual successor for Matt's job.

I gradually came to believe that most of the men in the office were at least as patronizing as Charles. I'd always gotten a little interest from men who found me attractive and in most offices I'd found one or two men expressing an interest in me. With the EEO guidelines on sexual harassment clear and public, most American men were careful not to risk offending. But these French men made me wary of flirting in the office. Their sense of personal space was entirely too small. When they stepped back their eyes often scanned my breasts before returning to my face. Or my nose. Yeech. I decided these men needed to see me as a human before they could take me seriously as a competent worker and decision maker. I began wearing a vest, cardigan, or jacket every day, and put all my dresses at the back of my closet. To this, they responded by giving me the nickname "Sainte Netouche." I was furious when Matt told me it meant Saint Don't Touch.

I wanted to befriend Carine in the hopes of finding an ally in confronting the chauvinism in the office. Although Carine seemed willing to be friends, I soon concluded that Carine felt differently about flirting in the office. I noticed that Carine generally wore either a miniskirt to the office or a slightly longer skirt with a high slit. And as the weather warmed, I saw that she had abandoned her bra and showed off her perfect tan with blouses that exposed her back and shoulders. She also flirted rather extensively with the other men—even Charles. I started to wonder whether she was actually getting any work done.

Carine displayed the flowers she received from admirers prominently on her desk. For all the attention she got, she rarely mentioned her interests to me (friends, vacation plans, movies and theater, tastes, family, love life), and I didn't feel comfortable asking her about her private life, although it's invariably the quickest path to making friends with another American woman. Despite Carine's seeming friendliness, I sometimes had the impression she was wrapped in plastic. Skin-tight Saran Wrap probably. Anyway, she was definitely not going to be the kind of woman friend I was used to being and having. I wondered if she thought I was competing with her for the attention of the men in the office? It seemed unlikely—they were a short skinny bunch by and large.

Question 2:   *What's your take on Carine? Do you agree with Jennifer's assessment?*

Some time later Matt invited me to join his family for a picnic. The weather had turned warm and Jan wanted to take the children into the country to ride horses. I told Matt I would be glad to go—I got very few offers to do something fun.

The following Saturday the two kids, Matt, Jan, and I drove into the country-side. The sun shone brightly and the fields glistened. They found a spot for a picnic just off the road on a grassy hill. The kids ate quickly and then went to explore the surroundings. The three adults talked. Jan asked me if I still felt frustrated by not understanding the conversations around me.

"In some ways I wish I didn't understand as well as I do," I said, going on to explain the episode with Charles.

Matt and Jan looked at each other as if in recognition of an inside joke. "I'm not surprised," Matt said. He told me of his failed attempt to fire Charles. "I'd get rid of him if I could. But I'm afraid we're both going to have to put up with him."

As the conversation continued, I seized the opportunity to bend a sympathetic ear and complained about isolation. Because I had absolutely no friends I usually spent my evenings at home either reading, writing letters, or watching (but not understanding) the television. French television was mostly a bunch of intellectual talk shows on esoteric subjects anyway. Jan mentioned that, for all the trouble the kids had caused when the Sumners first arrived in France, at least they had provided her company; she thought it must be difficult to be so alone in a foreign country, and said as much in tones sweet to my ear. I pointed out that I'd thought of making friends at work, but the men made me feel uncomfortable, and Carine was like some kind of breathing, talking Barbie doll as far as I could tell. Programmed for friendly responses. Besides the French classes each evening, and the long walks I took for exercise, I had nothing to break the monotony of work and home.

The Sumners sympathized. Jan suggested I join her a couple of times a week at her fitness club, and trade in my lonely walks for an aoerobics class. Many expatriate women met at the club, and Jan said she'd found the French women in the class to be altogether more approachable than the ones in street clothes with scarves jauntily knotted and large earrings.

Matt asked if I thought his presence at the meetings might make it easier for me to follow the discussions. I shrugged. It couldn't hurt at this point, it seemed to me.

"The only way to develop a social life is to keep being friendly to the people you meet," Jan said earnestly, returning to the main point. "It takes time to develop friends. But you will. It took several months for me and Matt to find people we liked to be with. There are so many bright and interesting people here. You're bound to run into someone you like."

"It's true," Matt said. "Actually, of the people we've become friends with, as many are not French as are French. Just wait a while. You'll make friends."

I thanked the Sumners as they dropped me off in Grenoble for "saving my life." Although I was joking, I couldn't deny my desperate need to air out some of my stress, nor downplay the sympathy with which the Sumners had heard my say. I felt genuinely touched by their sympathy, particularly Jan's.

I resolved to make a social life for myself—and I already knew where not to look. The men at work were patronizing, and Carine out of the question. Matt and Jan had the children and each other to keep them busy, so although I looked forward to making use of the support and sympathy they extended, I was quite sure we wouldn't become buddies. I would have to look elsewhere for socializing.

One night after French class, Gisèle, the instructor, invited me and two others from class for coffee. At a nearby café we drank espresso and talked—mixing classroom French with conversational English. Gisèle was in her early 30s. The other two women were both in their mid-40s: one came from Canada, the other from Iowa. The older women both ended up in Grenoble on business—one as a company rep and the other as the spouse of a manager.

Gisèle had lived in the United States several times. Soon after her 18th birthday she worked as an au pair for a family in New Jersey. After some months with this family, a neighborhood family "stole her away" (as she explained it) to work for them as a nanny for their two children. She stayed with this family for a year before returning to France for school.

She decided to perfect her English and become a teacher. During school she went back to the United States for one summer as part of an exchange program. After earning her degree she found a job in Grenoble with the French equivalent of an American high school. She taught English and history. For extra money she taught French in the evening to English speakers. She found that through teaching this evening class she kept a connection with Americans or British, whom she often invited to visit her class, or visited during her trips abroad.

The evening passed pleasantly. The older women shared a taxi to their respective homes, and I offered Gisèle a ride home. On the ride home we continued the conversation from the café. I decided to think up an excuse for doing something with Gisèle. But before I found one, Gisèle invited me to come to a dinner with some of her friends the following Sunday afternoon. I accepted and asked what I could bring to help with the meal. "Flowers," said Gisèle.

Two days later, during a routine marketing meeting, Matt appeared and asked to join the meeting. As the men discussed each point Matt interrupted and asked me if I understood everything or whether I had anything to contribute. This practice made the meeting tediously long, and I found his attention rather embarrassing. Although I was grateful for his help, I didn't enjoy being the odd person out. And on reflection, I thought it best that I prove myself, rather than being promoted by the boss.

At the end of the meeting Matt brought up one final piece of business. In simple ("special") French he explained to Charles and the others that Plasmatec had invested a great amount of confidence and training in me, and that I had a valuable education and a demonstrated ability. "Plasmatec sent her here because she has important expertise to share with us," he explained. "And for no other reason. Jennifer is searching new business opportunities throughout Europe, so we're all likely to be impacted by her work. I know that translating and moving slowly can be irritating. But to have Jennifer sit here and be unable to contribute because of a language barrier is stupid. We need to get her involved."

I felt a little like an ant under a magnifying glass on a sunny day. I wasn't sure whether I should thank Matt for the vote of confidence or pull him aside to tell him to stop singling me out and playing protective, big-brother fellow American. After a small internal debate, I decided to take his statement at face value. After all, I really was a resource of Plasmatec's. For me to sit around unused made as much sense as buying 50 computers and only using 20. I'd always believed I could contribute, and so did Plasmatec. I didn't have to prove myself any more than a computer has to prove its usefulness. If the computer wasn't useful, why was it purchased in the first place? Plasmatec saw me as most useful in Grenoble and Europe, and that's why they moved me. If the others couldn't see this, then they were being wasteful and short-sighted.

The other men in the office, surprisingly, nodded in understanding toward Matt. It was a bit strange seeing Matt act like a formal "boss," but the others had little trouble accepting him in that capacity. Although Charles seemed underwhelmed, he also made gestures of agreement, which made me feel a little more comfortable.

Matt continued to attend some of the meetings and spent more time working with me, taking time to explain the inner workings of Transfusions. Over the next few days several of my co-workers began speaking to me in English. They often surprised me with their ability to articulate their thoughts. But why had they waited to use their English? When I realized that the men could have communicated with me but hadn't, I felt furious at the idea that they had enjoyed watching me struggle. I vowed to be taken seriously in the office regardless of the cost.

Question 3:   Do you see Matt as a help or as a hindrance?

The following Sunday, I arrived promptly for dinner at Gisèle's. The guests included two French men and one French woman (all in their early 30s), a British man in his late 30s, and me. We spent a very pleasant afternoon together, remaining at the table long after we'd finished the food.

From then on Gisèle and I went for coffee or a bite to eat after each class. Gisèle introduced me to French culture, acting as translator, instructor, and friend. Over coffee we often worked through French comic books: Gisele recommended the Astérix books as great materials for learning French idioms and clichés. The great advantage to comic books is the absence of the literary past tense with all the a's in it. They are nearly entirely dialogue, and the Astérix ones are charming and elegant in addition to being clear and simple. Getting the Latin puns helped me feel less intensely stupid—an enormous benefit. Gisèle introduced me to different French foods and the etiquette of eating peculiar entrees. I also slowly became acquainted with Grenoble's night life, a sad blend of flashy discos and imported American films.

By the end of August a rumor grew that Carine had apparently started an affair with the head of her department, Claude Deloux. This apparently led to a small promotion—more in prestige than in pay. I kept an eye on Carine and resentfully wondered how long her career could last if it depended on affairs.

Despite the recent attention I'd received from my colleagues, I recognized a distinct coldness growing in them. On a few occasions I had corrected them when they had spoken out of line. Ever since Charles had called me *chou-chou,* I had been very careful to correct any nickname dealing with my size or appearance. I vowed never to let my guard down. When I corrected the men they seemed to overreact—almost like a child told "no"—by treating me resentfully. Although I didn't regret making distinct boundaries, I was made uncomfortable with my colleagues' coldness. Why did our relationships need to be so extreme? Why either too friendly or too cold?

I felt both grateful and resentful for Matt's help. On the one hand, I felt that without him, Charles would have run me out of the company. On one of the few afternoons he returned to the office from lunch I'd noticed what appeared to be makeup on his collar. It seemed likely that I could expect a come-on from him, the old goat, and I didn't relish the prospect of being constrained to be polite in my turndown.

On the other hand, I definitely didn't like the fact that Matt was behind the improved attitudes of my peers, rather than the slow recognition of demonstrated competence. Although no one else in the office seemed to resent my relationship with Matt (except, perhaps, Charles), I felt that in the back of their heads people treated me well out of fear of retribution from Matt.

When French class finished in June, Gisèle invited me to join her for a July weekend trip to the Riviera. I accepted and took a day off from work. While I packed for the trip I wasn't sure whether to bring my bikini top—I eventually wore it on our first day in the sun, left it unfastened in the afternoon, and forgot it in the tub on our last day. It actually felt pretty good to be half naked on the hot sand, and I fit right in.

As the summer progressed, I found my stress level at work diminishing. As my skills in French improved, my participation in the day-to-day operations also increased. I realized one August evening that my skills had dramatically improved. I discovered some class notes from April and couldn't believe how much more fluent I'd grown since.

I also found an additional social outlet. An old friend from Georgetown, Stephanie Parker, called me. Stephanie had been transferred to the U.S. Embassy in Paris. We had lost contact since graduation because Stephanie's previous foreign service posts had been on Madagascar and then Tahiti. The sudden news of an old friend's arrival brightened my week. Soon I fell into the habit of visiting Stephanie every other weekend. Paris had a large American and British community; and I thoroughly enjoyed the occasional reminders of American culture and companionship.

My visits with Stephanie, however, were disconcerting. I always needed a few hours of English before I felt comfortable with the language again. "It's weird," I explained to Stephanie. "I feel like learning French has made me forget English. But my French is still very bad. Now, instead of knowing two languages, I feel like I don't even know one."

"That's very common when learning a new language," Stephanie explained. "The same thing happened to me. Before you know both languages well your brain has to spend a little time between French and English. For a little while you're unsure of both; you have to forget both languages before you can speak them both."

One evening, after a difficult day in the office, Gisèle and I sat at a café. I had been careful not to speak to Gisèle negatively about any cultural differences between the United States and France; a German student at Georgetown had spent a lot of time alienating us, mostly by focusing on the unusual racial tensions of D.C., a difficult situation to justify. I had learned from him that the knee-jerk and sensible reaction of a host country national whose home is being criticized is "Go home then!" I never wanted to invite this reaction. But on this evening, and after a few glasses of wine, I felt less cautious and expressed some of my frustrations about my co-workers.

As I talked I noticed that Gisèle occasionally smiled. I felt irritated, as if she also didn't take me seriously. As I continued, I became angrier, and the more Gisèle seemed amused at what she heard, the more direct and untoward were my comments. Completely frustrated, I was able to stop myself before I said something really rude.

Gisèle used my pause to respond. "You know, French women don't understand why American women are afraid of being women."

"Oh please," I fumed. "Because we don't sleep with our bosses, does that make us less feminine?"

Gisèle smiled again. She spoke calmly and matter-of-factly. "There is no rule that says French women must sleep with their bosses. In fact, very few women do."

I rolled my eyes. Gisèle spoke a little more harshly.

"What business is it of yours, anyway, what French women do? Why do you Americans always need to help us live our lives? Are we French so ignorant, so uneducated that we don't know what we're doing? Why should you care about the personal affairs of anyone you work with?"

I sensed that we were verging on an unpleasant incident. More reasoned, I said, "I wouldn't care except that I'm in the office too."

"This is what I was saying before about American women. Why do you pretend that there is this one thing you call the 'office' and this other thing called 'home' or 'private life'? Why do you pretend that in the office everyone's business is your business, but at home you can be private? You dressed very sexy in Nice. You flirted with the men there. Why do you change in the office? Why are you a man in the office, but out of it you are a woman? In the office you dress like a man, but at clubs and discos you dress in short skirts and flirt."

"American women don't want to be taken advantage of," I responded. "It's too easy for women to be seen first as sex objects and then, maybe, as competent contributors. We don't want to be appreciated only for our bodies and not for our minds."

"Why must it always be one extreme or the other with you? Why can't you be appreciated for being smart and pretty?"

"Well you should know that it's not that easy," I said. "Men treat us as sex objects too often to think differently."

"Well," Gisèle replied as she lit a cigarette, "if that is how you feel, I think you talk of a problem with your country and your men, not mine. Our work and private life are also separated. But we don't go out of our way to make it an issue. Maybe you Americans are afraid that you cannot separate the two worlds."

I raised a skeptical eyebrow.

"I can show you what I mean," Gisèle continued. "Do women ever bring their children to work in America? No. Because they want to hide that they are mothers. They are ashamed that they can give birth. They are ashamed of their womb."

"Shame has nothing to do with women not bringing their children to the office. Besides, French women don't really bring their children to the office, do they?"

"Of course, not every day. But often, say, when school is out Wednesday afternoons, for example. They bring them to the office cafeteria for lunch. If a woman needs to bring her children with her she can."

I had seen a few children at the Transfusions office. The sight seemed very strange. I assumed that what I saw was a rare event.

Gisèle continued, "French women can be themselves in the office. They can be women. They can be pretty or not. They can flirt or not. They can dress as they please. If someone takes advantage of them, *c'est la vie*. They have learned not to trust that man. But they are free to be themselves. They don't have to hide their womanhood. When a French man flirts with a woman, this does not mean he doesn't take her seriously or wants to sleep with her. It just means he finds her attractive. It is a compliment—a compliment American women should learn to accept. Maybe he likes her only because of her looks. But he also knows if she can work. He can think of her in many ways. He gives her the freedom to be herself."

I puzzled over this for a time. How odd that we both made the same claims—each believing our own way permitted women to be "more free."

"Gisèle, if your way is so free, why are there no French women in charge at my company? There are only two women managers in our office and neither of us is in charge of anything that important. Why aren't more French women in charge at my company?"

"If they wanted to be in charge, they could be in charge. But many French women have other wants and desires."

I rolled my eyes again. "You were doing fine until that statement. I almost bought it. I would think that some women might want to run a company. So where are they? I can't believe that all women would rather not be executives; not all women want to stay at home, raise children, and be fully 'free women.'"

Gisèle wrinkled her nose at my sarcasm. "Of course. But why must it always be one or the other: work or stay at home? Be a woman or be a man? Office or home? In France we don't see things in two. We don't say 'you must choose between this or that.' We see many options, many ways to live."

I paused to think through the credibility of what Gisèle said. I wondered if French women really did have more options open to them. As I was thinking, Gisèle spoke again. "And French women believe that what they do is their own business. A couple can be very passionate in the Paris metro and it bothers none of the passengers. It is a hard thing for Americans to learn—to let other people live how they want to live."

I defused the tension with a comparative anecdote, not wanting to threaten the one friendship I'd managed to achieve. But the next day I found myself rethinking and evaluating what Gisèle had said. I decided to ask Matt about Carine, and found a casual moment when I could talk with him.

Question 4:   How else could Jennifer have had a polite, effective, educational disagreement with Gisele?

"Matt, is Carine a good worker?"

Matt looked a little surprised. "Yes. She is—from everything I've seen. I don't work with her directly, but from what I know she was a great hire. Why?"

I paused before answering his question.

"If you're worried about how you compare to her," Matt said, "you're holding up fine. You have no worries. You're very different from each other, but both of you are very good workers. I'd say you both have great futures in business."

I smiled. "Thanks for saying that, but that's not what's on my mind."

"What is it then?" he asked.

"Well," I said, "you know, she may be having an affair with Claude."

Matt nodded slowly, waiting for a shoe to drop. I'd expected him to be surprised.

"Well," he said after a moment. "I had heard a rumor about that, but I didn't really know for sure." He paused. "Are you concerned about it?"

I raised one hand, palm up.

"When I first got here, I learned about an affair going on between one of my managers and one of his subordinates. Then she got promoted. I assumed the two facts were connected. But no one spoke of it directly—no one seemed to mind, men or women. I worried what would happen—whether I should say something or not. I realized that no one else seemed to care, so I asked myself, 'should I do something about it? Or am I just confronting a different culture?' After a while, he left the company, and she stayed. She turned out to do well in the job. And then she left to go to GTS.

"It's my observation that, with the French, when they come to work they get work done. Whatever personal things are going on between a couple or friends or whatever else in the office, they just don't seem to let it affect their work. I agree that the situation seems ripe for abuse. I don't know how the women deal with it. And I'm glad I've only really seen it on a few occasions. But I'm quite sure Carine didn't get her promotion because of an affair with Claude. In fact, I'd be surprised if she was having an affair with him at all. I believe she just got engaged to a guy from Paris."

I felt unbalanced. Matt paused as though to let me speak, but I really had nothing to say.

"I hope I've helped answer whatever question you had," Matt concluded. "I admit I don't exactly like the way the French handle work and relationships. It's certainly not the American way."

I nodded and went back to my desk to mull this over.

Over the next few weeks I spoke more frequently with Gisèle about gender issues. Although I didn't quite agree with her, I regretted the way I had felt about Carine. I realized Carine was probably quite a remarkable woman. I'd allowed one issue to cloud my judgment so I couldn't see any of Carine's good qualities.

But I still felt great animosity toward Charles. Gisèle often reiterated that the women who encountered such men knew what they were doing. But I still felt that some institutional control and laws should protect women. Gisèle insisted the unions and labor laws protected women against sexual harassment and ensured these women that they could find a job somewhere else, a job they enjoyed more. But I believed this solution was an analgesic directed at the symptom of the disease and not the disease itself.

Sometimes I helped a young woman in my building, Chantal, with her English homework. As a reward, Susanne and Maurice, Chantal's parents, invited me on occasion to Sunday dinner. One Sunday afternoon about this same time Susanne and I found ourselves out for a long Sunday walk and free to talk. I explained to Susanne my observations at the office and what both Gisèle and Matt had said. Because Susanne had worked at Maurice's company until Chantal was born, she seemed quite knowledgeable about both French culture and office relationships.

She had a different perception. According to Susanne, gender politics at the office are based on the French cultural assumption that women are wives and mothers first. This, plus the scarce opportunities for women to balance both work and family (if they drop out for child raising, for example, it is very difficult to reenter the workforce in a professional or managerial role), make for general disregard of French men toward working women. Moreover, according to Susanne, there is a lot of sexual harassment at work and a lot of women respond to their low status by flirting and dressing attractively in order to be noticed.

Susanne believed this was changing with recent court rulings enforcing French laws against sexual harassment and gender discrimination. She agreed with Gisèle, however, that American women seem overly concerned about strict equality, seeming overly businesslike at work and attaching importance to competing against men. She also pointed out that laws in France are more theoretical and are powerful only if actively interpreted and put into practice. So far neither men nor women jurists have actively used the equal opportunity laws; they are only on the books in case of need. In fact, part of the debate in Parliament over harrassment laws was that the "romance" should not be discriminated from the workplace. The French prefer to work out these matters informally.

As the next months passed, I discovered that the feeling of panic with which I'd often begun my day had left me. I discovered that I understood French well enough to miss only a few statements in the day. I still couldn't express myself as well as I wanted, although I could get my ideas across. But understanding what people said around me made work immeasurably easier.

I decided to try and get to know Carine better. Slowly, we became common lunch companions, and occasionally met with others after work. Carine turned out to be extremely well versed in American films, and constantly surprised me with her ability to spout a line (in English) from a movie. I also noticed that Carine had an astonishing ability to do difficult math in her head. She could figure out statistics and ratios in her head that I usually needed a calculator for. And, as it turned out, she had in fact recently gotten engaged to a Parisian businessman. Whether she had ever become involved with Claude or whether the whole thing was just rumor, I never knew. But I certainly felt sheepish about my shabby suspicions!

QUESTIONS FOR DISCUSSION

1. What is a high-potential (HIPO) employee? Do you think medium-sized businesses like Plasmatec have HIPOs? What are some motives behind Plasmatec giving Jennifer Stewart special treatment and labeling her a HIPO?
2. Why is the international move important as a way to train future leaders or HIPOs? From Plasmatec's perspective, why send Jennifer to France? Why not? From Jennifer's point of view why, at this career state, should she go? Not go?
3. Basic assumptions or "core culture" values are based on family, educational, language, ethnic, and religious influences, many of them instilled from early childhood and young adulthood. From this chapter, list three to five basic assumptions or core culture values that are part of Jennifer as a young American professional, growing up in her family and partly molded by Georgetown and Berkeley. List three to five basic assumption or core culture values that are French and are brought out in Jennifer's conversations with Gisèle and Susanne as well as her observations of Carine and the men at the office. Do any universal values about working women and the division between personal and professional life seem to transcend both cultures?
4. What are some problems for a single American professional woman (like Jennifer) adapting to international work that may not be for a single American man? What are some problems for a woman, both partnered and single, with children, working abroad, as compared to a similar man (like Matt)?

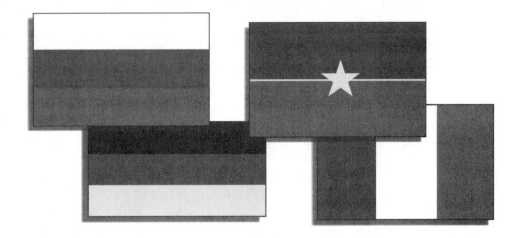

CHAPTER 17

Jennifer's New Business Development

With only a few months left before his scheduled return home, Matt received a call from Doc. Doc and Tom wanted to visit Transfusions.

"I'm looking forward to your visit. But what's bringing you all the way to France?" Matt asked.

"We just want to take a look at the operation. Some things only can be done in person," Tom responded. They talked through the details of their visit. They wanted to stay for two days and look over the facility.

Matt said goodbye to Doc and Tom but did not hang up. He heard the click as they broke off the connection. After a minute of pondering he decided to call Jan.

"I just got a call from Tom and Doc. They're coming to visit us for three days."

"That's nice," Jan responded. "What are they coming for?"

"I don't know. But it's not the reason they said."

"What did they say?"

"They said they wanted to look over the plant, in person. But they could do that in one afternoon. There must be something else they want to do."

"That's strange. But I'm sure they would tell you if they had another reason for visiting."

"Yeah. You're right." Matt started to worry. Was something wrong? He made a mental review of Transfusions. The company had done fairly well over the last year. Their product, a modified noninvasive glucose monitor, had been remarkably easy to market. Like the NIGM, which was useful to diabetics who used it to monitor their blood sugar levels at home, this device could test the blood without breaking skin. But unlike the NIGM, it could be used to detect hepatitis, hemophilia, and other blood disorders. They called the device the "hemodiagnostic device," or HDD.

The first run of the product had revealed several glitches, but most of those had been worked out. The HDD subsequently had proven quite marketable not to home users but to clinics and hospitals, where the HDD's quick, noninvasive application cost less than obtaining blood samples to be sent to a lab.

Matt knew that a substantial profit lay in finding a way to fit the HDD to detect HIV, the virus that leads to AIDS. The nature of AIDS makes quick and private detection very attractive. Research in this area had turned out to be difficult for Transfusions' scientists (just as it was for everyone trying to understand the disease). But because nearly every major breakthrough in research had come from the Pasteur Institute in Paris, Transfusions was uniquely positioned to benefit from each new advance.

Perhaps Doc and Tom felt unsatisfied with the progress Transfusions had made in AIDS research. Matt decided against that possibility. They would hardly fault him for failing to unlock the secrets of a disease as enigmatic as AIDS.

Matt's mind drifted to his conflicts with Charles Caussé. Could Tom and Doc be coming to shake up Transfusions? Perhaps they wanted to come to make some personnel moves Matt couldn't make on his own. But that seemed unlikely.

Were they unhappy with his mentoring of Jennifer Stewart? Matt pondered her development. Certainly her first months in Grenoble had been difficult. But over the last few months she had come into her own. From all Matt saw, she had found an equilibrium with the others in the office. Matt had given her a steady increase in responsibility and had really enjoyed her work ethic. He knew she occasionally stayed late or worked weekends, and Matt admitted to Jan that he found Jennifer's after-hours work refreshingly American.

Matt called a meeting of all the department heads at Transfusions to let them know that Tom and Doc would be coming and to give them all a chance to prepare. He didn't know exactly what parts of the company were open to review, so he decided everything should be prepared.

When Tom and Doc finally arrived ten days later, they spent their first day reviewing various aspects of the operations. That evening, alone in Matt's office, they got down to business.

"Matt, you may know that Ron Clancy is nearing retirement," Tom said.

Matt nodded.

"Well," Doc added, "when he leaves, we want you to think about taking his job as VP international."

Matt was stunned. He hadn't expected the offer. Before he could talk, Doc continued.

"There's one catch. You have to stay at Transfusions for another year."

Tom picked up where Doc left off. "There are two reasons we need you to stay. First, Ron doesn't want to retire for another 14 months. And second—more importantly—we really want to expand our European operations, and we need someone we have confidence in to head the effort."

Matt sat and listened as Tom and Doc explained the Executive Committee's vision for the next several years.

"Transfusions has been a great success, and its future looks bright. Right now, we want more of the same, and frankly, no one from Plasmatec has your expertise in the European market. The ongoing work at the Pasteur Institute is key to new product development, and we want you to explore other innovations in this part of the world that may help us make a quantum leap forward. We need you here for another year to take the next steps in expanding."

Doc continued, "We reviewed our contract with you and we know it only runs for three years. As a way to make your fourth year in Grenoble more enticing we're willing to give you the pay and benefits and stock option package appropriate for a vice president starting next month. When Ron leaves, you'll return to Santa Cruz and assume his position."

After listening for a few more minutes, Matt finally let the news sink in. He asked questions, got details, and grew excited by the plans the Executive Committee had developed. Finally, he paused and said, "I can't do anything without talking to Jan. Ultimately, we'll have to make the decision together."

"We thought as much," Tom said. "Talk about it and let us know what you're thinking. We'll be here until Wednesday to talk things over with you."

Matt went home to talk with Jan.

JENNIFER

Jan called to tell me the good news. She and Matt had been so helpful to me when I arrived in France. Naturally, I was delighted to hear they'd be staying on. Matt became even more enthusiastic around the office as he took on the cause of searching out new products and ideas in Europe, the Middle East, and Africa, his company territory. He formed a task force to research different facilities and interests in Europe with an eye on exploiting new markets through entering joint ventures with other European concerns. Charles Caussé was not on the task force.

Carine and I were both included, and Matt told the team at our first meeting that as the task force leader, I would be doing most of the legwork. Later, Matt pulled me aside to explain that the reason I was being tapped to do the road work for the task force is that Plasmatec wanted me to gain knowledge and expertise in Europe. He hinted that I'll be Plasmatec's European expert abroad after his return to the States, which may be so, but if he was looking to motivate me further, it wasn't necessary. I'm thrilled that people are paying me to pack up a suitcase and go!

MEMO

Internal Memo: For Plasmatec Files
     Subject: European Expansion Task Force Findings
       From: Jennifer Stewart
         To: Matt Sumner

Our task force has arrived at several ideas worth exploring. A possible joint venture with a Johnson & Johnson subsidiary in Heidelberg holds promise for several new adaptations of the HDD. Johnson & Johnson recently purchased a German company that is now part of Orthodiagnostics, and they are interested in sharing research and technology. The Johnson & Johnson subsidiary has already done leading research in bone deterioration consequent to hemoglobinopathies. I visited their facility in Heidelberg and am scheduled to return in two weeks' time.

The second most promising possibility lies with the company RPI in Barcelona. The company functions as a marketer and distributor for medical devices manufactured by smaller entrepreneurs. RPI already sells its products to larger hospitals in Spain, Portugal, and Italy, and wants to sell to smaller clinics as well. Our task force contacted them to see if they might be interested in letting Transfusions finance some of their glucose-monitoring expansion and in return have RPI sell the hemodiagnostic device with a higher return per sale than the standard rate. We believe that since they already have a well-established client list and a leg up in a market where nepotism is a way of life, we have nothing to lose by expanding in that direction under their wing rather than independently.

Our task force also recommends branching out into emerging markets which by definition are not yet saturated with companies like RPI, with an eye on forming connections that could be vastly profitable in the long run. Russia came up as the single largest undeveloped market in Europe, and I have just completed a fact-finding tour researching possible manufacturing sites and joint ventures, and assessing the level of development of Russian medicine.

During my visit to Russia I spent time in Moscow, St. Petersburg, and Vladivostok, which despite being located only 300 miles from Japan is considered our territory because the inhabitants are entirely European, and the social infrastruc—

I was caught mid-memo when my door burst open and Matt flew in. "Breakthrough!" he said. "You know the Pasteur Institute's paper on leukocyte nucleic anomalies in HIV patients that you gave to the researchers in Heidelberg? The Johnson & Johnson subsidiary has identified a protein tracer that your nucleic anomaly takes up which flags our noninvasive diagnostic device! The anomaly is apparently present in 100 percent of HIV positives within one month of seroconversion!"

"So the test should be accurate in seven months after exposure to the virus?" I asked.

"That's r-r-right! And completely without the use of needles, so no risk to the medical technician, no risk of accidental needle reuse. Reusable technology to boot."

"Sounds perfect for Russia," I said, recalling the sterilizing units I'd just seen there.

"Russia's not worrying about AIDS just now. Tell you what I'm thinking, though—Thailand and Macao, brothels to the world, and every last corner of U.N.-funded Africa. In fact, I'd like you to write up the study."

"Right after I write up this file memo about my trips to Heidelberg and Russia," I responded, but he'd already moved on. I sat back in my chair and reflected on the two trips I'd already made as the "legs of the task force," as Carine affectionately termed me.

Germany: The trip to Heidelberg had been very effective, particularly in light of the newest application of our HDD, the diagnosis of HIV infection. Before going to Heidelberg, I'd asked my counterpart at J & J, an American named Hans Steiner, to arrange a tour of the facility and meetings with senior researchers. Heidelberg is an hour south of the Frankfurt airport by train. I traveled with Jean-Luc Lemieux, a researcher from Transfusions who had spent some time in Germany and knew enough German to steer us to the correct platform. When our train pulled in to the Heidelberg *Bahnhof*, I noticed very large white clocks in wrought-iron pillars all over the station, each one set with precision at 1:37. I realized that our train was precisely on time, as our Lufthansa flight had been, and made a mental note to myself to be absolutely timely while in Germany.

"They say a man can set his watch by the trains in Germany," Jean-Luc noted, following my gaze. I appreciated Jean-Luc's willingness to speak English while abroad, for many of the French researchers seemed reluctant to use their English at the office, although English is a required subject for science and technology majors. I guessed Matt had chosen Jean-Luc as the research representative as much for this flexibility as for his technical mastery, and I appreciated Matt's decision.

Hans Steiner picked us up at the station and Jean-Luc indicated that he'd take the back seat, so Hans and I chatted on the road. Hans has an MBA from Michigan and is about my age. He told me he'd worked for J & J for several years in New Brunswick, and then had been sent to Germany where he'd apparently been instrumental in acquiring the Heidelberg firm. His parents were naturalized Americans from Germany, so he spoke both German and English as a native and had studied French and Spanish in school, making international work the obvious choice for him.

Heidelberg was a charming city, with red-tiled roofs and white stuccoed taverns and shops lining narrow, often cobblestone roads.

"This city is beautiful," I commented, thinking that many German cities, although built with a certain precision, lack charm.

"Yeah," Hans agreed. "Unlike a lot of other German cities, Heidelberg didn't get wiped out in the war. But people here worry about the acid rain problem, and the pollution of the Neckar River. Heidelberg's still a manufacturing center, and the river flows right through town."

"Germany has taken strong antipollution measures, hasn't it?" I inquired politely.

"It's the only place in the world where people regularly drop all the excess packaging from their purchases in bins at the store itself!" Hans said. "I guess they figure if you made the mess, you can clean it up."

"That makes good sense," I said, trying to imagine Americans stopping between the store and their car to offload the cardboard from their cereal and cake mix boxes.

"The Germans are nothing if not sensible," Hans said with the distant pride of a descendant.

"Do they perceive you to be German or American?" I asked. He was clearly an American, *à mon avis* (in my opinion), having that faintly rumpled, relaxed air alien to northern Europe.

"Oh, I'm an American. In spades," he laughed. "Every day I hear about the threat of American imperialism or American wastefulness or American educational mediocrity. Not that they're wrong. Ever."

The J & J facility wasn't exactly state of the art, but it looked both functional and productive. Jean-Luc and the German researchers spoke English together without any trouble, sometimes using either German or French to make their point, making me wish yet again that American schools would offer French or Spanish starting in third grade. After the tour we repaired to a conference room, where Jean-Luc posed a number of highly technical questions, most of which were quickly answered by the German team. I found it odd that when Jean-Luc asked a question they had no good answer for, they never said simply "I don't know," but instead stated tersely, "We couldn't possibly know that" or "How could we know that?"

I reflected on my cousin's comment on returning from a year in Germany: "It's a wonder there are any Germans at all—the national character is a terrible combination of complete freedom to criticize and profound hypersensitivity. How do they ever marry?"

Leaving the researchers to their own interests, Hans, an executive of the original Heidelberg firm, and I talked briefly about the logistics of the venture, but soon realized that the real question to be considered before working out the finances was what potential our joint research held. I pulled Hans aside to tell him about Matt's dream of converting the hemodiagnostic device to an HIV test. The Pasteur Institute's recent discovery of a nucleic anomaly common to the polys of HIV victims was most promising, and I wanted to be sure the J & J researchers were pointed in that direction. I left them the paper the Pasteur Institute had published on the polys. We agreed to meet again in six weeks' time to see whether the researchers thought our devices could benefit from their orthodiagnostic expertise, and left open the question of how to accomplish our joint venture.

Jean-Luc and I left the J & J facility feeling energized, confident that our next visit would prove beneficial to both sides. Jean-Luc was eager to return to Transfusions with a hypothesis about bone marrow and blood cell production that could prove useful to the understanding of thalassemia, a blood disorder found in people of Mediterranean descent. I couldn't wait to share my hope with Matt that something big could come of this.

Russia: A week after my return from Heidelberg I left for Russia, with three planned stops on my itinerary. I was to go first to a Russian defense plant in St. Petersburg to consider whether the sensitive laser equipment that detected the level of bilirubin in the blood of a hepatitic patient could be manufactured there. Then I'd arranged a visit to a joint Japanese-Russian private medical clinic in Vladivostok to study which elements of the population were choosing private services over the free governmental care, in order to assess the potential market in Russia for our products. Finally, I wanted to research export restrictions and duties at the Office of Economic Affairs in Moscow to discover whether it would be feasible to manufacture, export, or import in Russia.

Because everyone worried about Russia's infrastructure, I had been collecting documents, tickets, and reservations for my stay more than a month in advance. I invited a Russian emigré to lunch, and had to repack my bags after she told me to leave all but costume jewelry in France and to bring the drabbest luggage I owned on the trip. Her advice came back to me as I stood beside the baggage carrel in Sheremyetovo Dva, one of Moscow's seven airports, for a sorrier collection of bags I never saw. The immigration official scrutinized my papers intensely, and I wondered what it would have felt like to have been a tourist passing behind the Iron Curtain. Far from it, I was met by an expediter who stood in the crowd, waving a sign marked Plasmatec. I had tried to tell my travel agent that I was capable of catching a taxi between two airports and had certainly done the commute from Orly to Charles de Gaulle and from Heathrow to Gatwick on my own before, but he just rolled his eyes.

"The alphabet's different," he pointed out. "There's nothing in Russia that you'll recognize as public transportation, and I wouldn't feel good about letting you take a taxi in Moscow." Instead he'd arranged for the Redcaps, a private expediting company, to give me a ride to the next Moscow airport and to make arrangements for accommodations and translators for me.

As we waited for my bags, I recalled the article I'd read on the plane, which cited the statistic that 70 percent of the money earned by Moscow's workers is paid by foreign concerns, partly because Russian state salaries are even lower than service sector salaries, partly because the private sector is still largely run by foreigners. These provide services that take up the slack between the Russian standard of living and the expectations of the expatriates whose work requires them to live in Moscow. Real estate rentals, restaurants, hotels, clinics, shops—the Russian ones are so poor that expatriates prefer to pay high prices and use those run by foreigners. The Redcaps' service permitted people with money to avoid taking potluck in the taxi, bus, or subway lines outside the airport: an interesting turnaround for a system explicitly designed for egalitarianism. The Redcap accompanied me to Domodyedovo Airport and waited with me there until my flight to St. Petersburg was called, at which time he assured me again that a Redcap in St. Petersburg would bring me to my hotel and provide a translator and transportation to the interviews I'd scheduled for the next day.

I really felt quite spoiled.

At 7:30 the next morning a rap at the hotel door turned out to be the translator, Irina, a middle-aged woman who spoke flawless English with a clipped British accent. We planned to visit Military Installation Number 4, a factory that purportedly had manufactured lasers and missile-guiding devices between 1964 and 1992. The Department of Development had assured me the factory was seeking contracts that would further its goal of conversion to an advanced electrical operation by 1998. The end of the cold war had brought about a reduced demand for laser-based missile guiding systems at the same time that the government of Russia found it necessary to devalue the ruble in a de facto drastic reduction in workers' salaries. Sensibly, defense plants all over Russia were attempting to switch to manufacturing consumer goods such as radios and tape players. Those that produced a line which could be sold abroad stood the best chance of surviving the chaotic economic reconstruction that had swallowed Russia in the late 1980s.

On arrival, we were given a tour of the facility's research and development sector. With my newfound appreciation for language acquisition I marveled at how many technical terms Irina knew in English. Like the European scientists, the Russians all spoke English, and even seemed eager to practice their English with me.

"It's a good sign that everyone here is talking freely to you," said Irina over lunch in the factory's cafeteria. "In 1992 I translated for an American businesswoman who was researching the conversions of defense companies prior to seeking investors in the States, and the executive director of a plant in Yekaterinburg threatened to report her to the KGB for spying. He thought she was being unreasonably curious about military affairs, and of course she wanted precise information on which to base her decision about whether to invest in his plant or not."

"What did she do about the KGB?" I asked.

"Every city has an intercessionary official in charge of foreigners. She contacted him to see if she should take the director's threat seriously, and on his advice, she wrote a memo about her meeting to the consul at the U.S. Embassy in Moscow. Nothing came of it, fortunately. Certainly these days the mafia are more threatening than the KGB, for you and for us as well."

My afternoon appointment was with Dimitri Sakhalev, the director of the defense plant, and with the head accountant. Having faxed ahead a copy of Transfusions' specifications for the lasers, I'd expected to negotiate for the best terms and the fastest output possible. I didn't really think the negotiations would involve the director, who seemingly hadn't read the specs at all, but asserted all the same that we should pay in dollars or francs the going rate for French lasers, depositable in a European bank.

"There is no difference between our lasers and the French lasers," Dimitri Sakhalev grumbled. "Has France a space station? No."

I knew this pretended ignorance of the risks of investing in Russia was just a negotiating ploy, especially since he had made it clear that the profits from the laser sale were to be kept out of the country, with just enough repatriated to pay his workers and his overhead. One reason for this was the 60 percent tax levied by the Russian government on any earned profits; the second was the attractive security of retaining dollars or francs in an account rather than rubles, which lose value daily. I guessed he might also fear a sudden reversion to communism, which is usually followed by the nationalization of all assets. I figured if anything, Dimitri Sakhalev knew more about the risks of doing business in Russia than I did, and that we both knew enough to know risk-benefit analyses were in order. Times of economic chaos can lead to enormous profits, but at any moment, conditions can change.

"You must understand," the accountant interceded. "Our arcs were formerly coming from the electrical products facility in Kiev. But Kiev is now in Ukraine and not in Russia, so we must pay import duties, and their oil supply is no longer reliable. We are seeking an arc manufacturer in the Urals, but this will take some time, developing our contract with them. Yes, of course we can provide your lasers. It will only take some time."

I mulled this over. Was it best to cut my losses here, forget the Russians, commission the lasers from an Irish company for 10 percent less than the market rate for French lasers, or postpone a decision pending final negotiations with the Russian firm? I felt sure I could get the lasers for less than half the cost of manufacturing them in Ireland, for Russian workers earn about 10 percent of a going Irish wage. Even if 20 percent of the lasers were defective, it would still be a very good deal, if all the contingencies worked out—if power supplies, raw materials, and the necessary pretooled parts were available throughout the length of the contract, and if the Russian political situation continued to support overseas deals. I'd expected to finalize the deal, and it was disturbing to learn that the firm had not yet found a source for arcs, a vital component of the lasers. But then, if the firm had cancelled my trip by telephone due to the lack of arcs, I would surely have discarded the option of dealing with them. Having seen the facility in person made me feel more confident that they could pull it off. For all the handicaps their economic system had left them, the Russian scientists impressed me with their knowledge and capabilities; the machines were apparently sound, and I felt sure the company could produce the lasers, given the necessary materials and support.

I arrived in Vladivostok the next day, having spent ten hours in the airport waiting room due to an unscheduled and unannounced delay in departure, and another nine hours in the air. In America airlines are usually straightforward about not being able to locate an airplane. In Russia, you sit on the bench by the gate, snapping to attention every time a stewardess passes, just in case she is heading for your flight. I played cribbage for six hours in the airport with a British reporter who was similarly delayed: her Kafka jokes helped pass the time. Luckily, I'm able to sleep on airplanes and the flight was long enough to feel like a good night's rest. It was odd to arrive a full day after I'd left the hotel, between the wait and the seven-hour time difference between Moscow and Vlad. I checked into the Hotel Vladivostok, a ship-like building perched on the edge of an escarpment overlooking the Amursky Bay. The water in the bathroom was icy cold. The hot water pipes that snaked back and forth along one wall and clearly were intended to heat the towels were likewise absolutely cold. I went out to the *dezhornaya*, the woman in charge of monitoring comings and goings on my floor, and pantomimed a wash. She gave me an electric kettle to fill up and plug in, and a dishpan. There's something very satisfying about communicating with someone whose language you don't speak.

My first appointment in Vlad was with the manager of the Japanese-Russian private medical clinic. Sazaki-san had promised to answer my questions about the makeup of his clientele and his insights into the status of medicine in Russia. In return, we'd promised him a bilirubin detector, since liver damage is rampant in the Far East because of a combination of endemic hepatitis and alcoholism. Transfusion's marketing strategy in this was akin to pump priming. Associating the product with high-tech foreign medicine should glamorize it in the eyes of Russian physicians and hospital managers.

I sat in the Sazakimed waiting area, reflecting on the extra phone line that ran down the hallway and into the Sazakimed office. Ludmila, the translator, had surmised that Sazaki-san rented the phone line from a neighboring office, for the list of businessmen seeking a second line was considered lowest priority at the telephone company. Vladivostok had a telephone directory, but all the copies appeared to be five or ten years old. Russians were accustomed to exchanging business cards and recording telephone numbers carefully in their own address books, so having the numbers officially listed as belonging to a different business confused no one.

A man sitting across from me started a friendly conversation about the history of Vladivostok. He was waiting for his brother, it appeared, and he was eager to practice his English. "I do business—you know, business," he said with an air which confided that being an American, I surely had special insight into the arcaneries of his work. He handed me his business card and then volunteered out of the blue that I would benefit from a trip to a Russian gymnasium and a weight-loss regime. As he rose to hold the door for his limping brother, I filed his odd comment away for further consideration and dropped his card into the ashtray. I'd heard that Russians are quite frank, and I wondered if that might not be related to their economic system. In capitalist countries we engage in a subtle competition with each other, comparing houses and cars and educations. In Russia, where housing and education is state supplied, it appeared to me that personal upkeep took the place of home improvement. Certainly the Russians were the most decorated people I'd seen in Europe, with their large hair bows, bright lipstick, and crisply ironed pleats. Perhaps the willingness to make personal remarks was related.

I called Ludmila's attention to the man's comment. "Does it strike you as unusual?" I asked.

Ludmila snorted, but in a ladylike way. "He is just a Russian man. Russian men—well, they are not polite."

"No," I thought. It's possible that living in France has raised my standards for a truly intentional put-down, but he just did not seem like he was sneering. Impolite, maybe, but not rude—something else.

Sazaki-san invited us into his office, where a large brunch was laid. Like most workplaces in Russia, the clinic had a kitchen and a cook who prepared meals for the staff. He explained that while his salaried workers earned more than their counterparts working in the state clinics, until enough Russians had disposable incomes, restaurants would continue to serve only people who had little choice in where to eat, for restaurant food was considered unhealthy. Under the Soviet system, amenities such as lunch and transportation were typically provided to workers, although salaries remained too low for workers to afford cars, and good fast meals were difficult to obtain.

"Sazakimed was probably prohibitively expensive for people who did not eat in restaurants," I thought.

"What kind of clients use Sazakimed?" I asked. Sazaki-san waved to a full Rolodex on his desk. "All kinds. The American and Indian consuls. The Peace Corps, the Asian merchants . . ."

"And Russians?" I asked, wondering whether my trip was a bust.

"Certainly. I have just seen a gunshot wound in a man who is probably with the mafia. He told me he went to two state hospitals last night. In the first one they removed the bullet, but they had no penicillin for him. In the second one, there was no penicillin, and no electricity either. He went home to bed and came here first thing. You understand that an ordinary Russian would not be able to afford our fees, and would go to a third and a fourth hospital, or perhaps to a friend who works in a pharmacy to obtain this penicillin. Our service is very good, and our clinic is clean, but most Russians will not come here."

This was not good news from my point of view. "How long do you think it will take before ordinary Russians can afford your clinic?" I asked.

Sazaki-san frowned. "You are asking a very big question," he sighed. "I myself would not be here if I didn't believe that Russia will improve quickly and dramatically. The clients we have today are sufficient to maintain operating expenses, but my dream is to have an international HMO in 20 years, with clinics here and in Magadan, Khabarovsk, and possibly China. We do expect to serve the local population."

"And you are willing to wait for that to happen?" I inquired. "Not knowing how long it may take?"

"Well, life here is good," Sazaki-san replied. "I like Russians. They are philosophers. My staff has been very good to me. When the dairy broke down and butter was unavailable, two different nurses brought me gifts of butter. They knew that I had not yet learned the custom of buying extra food in case the stores are empty tomorrow."

Sazaki-san volunteered to take me on a tour of a nearby Russian hospital so I could witness Russian medicine firsthand. I was quite sure hospitals don't permit unscheduled field trips, but Sazaki-san waved away my objections.

"I have a friend," he explained. "We share opinions on cases sometimes, and I help him when I can. Every other Wednesday I show medical training videos at my house, and several Russian doctors come."

"I'm beginning to understand how important friends are in Russia," I remarked. "I guess I would like to take that tour."

As it happened, an emergency forced Sazaki-san to remain at the clinic. However, he insisted that Ludmila and I go to the Russian state hospital without him, saying his friend would be happy to see us alone.

The walls at the State Hospital Number 2 were painted a dingy gray-green color supposed to age without exciting complaint. Ludmila translated for Dr. Yevgenny Nikolai, Sazaki-san's friend, who wanted to know how often the walls are washed in American hospitals.

I couldn't imagine the point of washing the walls. "I don't think hospital walls are washed in America," I answered. "The floors are probably washed every day."

"Hah," Dr. Nikolai said with obvious satisfaction.

"He wants you to know that in Russia the walls are washed once weekly," Ludmila translated.

"Hmm," I said noncommittally. I'd never seen a dirtier veterinarian clinic, I thought to myself, much less hospital. It was possible that the walls were wiped with disinfectant every week, but it was unlikely that the floors had ever seen the working end of a scrubbing machine, and the little old janitors were just not doing it for these floors. In some places the tiles were gone, and windows were boarded across, giving the hospital the sad air of an inner-city public school fallen on hard times.

The doctor indicated that we were not to enter the sick wards, but took us to view the ultrasound. It was an enormous machine, a dinosaur in age and size. A sterilizing unit in an adjacent office reminded me that needles were reused in this hospital. I felt sure that Russia would really benefit from Transfusions' product, and wondered whether I could think of a mutually beneficial barter, for clearly hospitals did not have cash for new machines, even traditional ones.

Once on the street I asked Ludmila about the status of Russian women, for despite the preponderance of Russian men in our meetings, all the people I'd seen actually working were women.

"In Russian the word for gender, *pol,* is the same as the word for floor. So we have a saying—'a woman's floor is her ceiling.' Do you follow me? But women are often middle-level managers. Women here work very hard and are less prone to alcoholism. Of course, women who have families do not rise in the office unless there is a grandmother in good health who will do the shopping. It's a 20-minute wait for bread, and separate lines for milk, meats, vegetables, and cheeses. The bread and milk must be bought fresh every two days, for they spoil quickly. Truly, you can understand why most women have only one child."

"So women work all day and then spend a lot of time shopping and cooking?" I asked. "Don't the men help?"

"Well," Ludmila considered. "There are some men who are very useful. And there are some women who can get work out of even a useless man. But the work is never finished, you know; we all must grow potatoes in the country to be sure that we'll eat in winter. Men are helping, yes." She said it without much enthusiasm.

We were traveling on foot, since she had assured me that everything worth seeing in Vladivostok was two steps away, but she had neglected to mention that both steps were uphill, and I wished I'd worn more comfortable shoes. I appreciated the experience of cramming into a *tramvye* with a hundred others for our unexpected field trip to the hospital. Authentic, *quoi*. While I was on the tram (which is what we call a trolley) I worried about whether we would ever be able to get off, as boarding passengers squeezed us toward the back of the car. But Ludmila had an elbow move the Bears could have studied, and I was carried along in her wake.

I decided to pump Ludmila for as much information as I could, since she seemed forthcoming. "Can we go for a cup of coffee?" I asked.

"Maybe," she responded. "Anyway, there will be tea. We have a saying—when there is nothing, there is tea."

The saying clearly applied to the café we entered a few moments later. The selection included 15 buns and a couple of the egg white and sugar pastries I'd learned to eat in France, but no coffee, cream, sugar, or lemon. There was black tea, a strong, bitter brew with an iridescent slick across the top that might have been tea oils but was more likely someone's lipstick. Bright lipstick, no doubt. I checked the cup for stains.

"Why do you suppose men are more at risk for alcoholism in your country than women?" I asked, figuring it was okay to risk offending a translator I'd probably never see again.

"Isn't that also the case in your country?" Ludmila countered.

"Yes, but even in New York we don't use a quart of vodka per person per day, as I've read they do in Moscow."

Ludmila seemed to accept this. "It's hard to be a man," she replied. "Russia has always been a patriarchy. The priests were the fathers of the parish, the landowners were the fathers of the serfs. The tsar was called "dear little father." Men are very powerful here, in principle."

"So you think individual men expect to have more power than they actually get?" I asked.

"Yes, they like to think that they are lords, and women serfs," Ludmila responded. "But consider: a month's wages buys a kilo of fish. The work that really matters in a household where man and wife both have Russian jobs is the work of shopping and cooking, a woman's work."

I suddenly saw a connection between the businessman's overly personal remark and the pride Dr. Yevgenny took in having walls washed more often than our walls. Chalking the man's rudeness up to a cultural need to feel pride in the absence of real power made it that much easier to shake it off.

"I don't want to make our men sound like lunatics," Ludmila quickly added. "I think psychologically Russians are very similar to Americans. We want to do our best, to have pride in our work. We want our children to live better lives than we live. But two generations have sacrificed so much for communism, and now we are told it doesn't work. And we see it for ourselves." She rotated her empty teacup, staring into it. "For decades we were told that no one knew how long it would take to build the world's first communist society. Now we say no one knows how long it will take to tear down the world's first communist society."

"Come on," I said to her. "You have a tremendously well-educated population. And I can see that people here really know what it is to work hard. Your country is huge, and rich in natural resources. How long could it take?"

The question returned to me on the airplane back to France. My third stop, researching export restrictions in Moscow, had been a nightmare of bureaucratic entanglements. I'd been sent from the Office of Economic Affairs to the Regional Office of Economic Development to the Department of Defense to the brand-new Consumer Affairs Commission. In despair, I finally called Dimitri Sakhalev at the Defense Plant Number 4 in St. Petersburg.

"Don't worry," he said authoritatively. "No one is taking responsibility for such decisions now. I have a friend who works at the port and I can get the lasers out of the country."

"No, no," I remonstrated. "It must be legal. Transfusions does not participate in smuggling operations."

"Relax," he reassured me. "It is simply a matter of forming a joint venture with a Finnish company. It will be a paper venture, you know, with a Russian emigré who now lives in Helsinki. My friend will research Finnish export procedures and call you in a week."

I pulled my chair back up to my desk and focused on my memo. I had already decided to be circumspect with VP Ron Clancy until hearing from Dimitri Sakhalev's friend in Helsinki, to leave myself an out if the deal soured. As I saw it, buying the lasers in Russia, despite the risks caused by the current economic and political chaos, could build bridges for Transfusions that would be important ten years down the road. It was a personally risky decision for me, since I was at the stage in my career when most managers are conservative, leaving the risk taking to more established executives. Nevertheless, if Sakhalev sounded competent and informed, I already planned to try ordering a small batch of lasers as a test of the facility's capabilities. I'd use my hesitancy to get a rock-bottom price on the lasers, of course, and I'd make it clear that the price could be renegotiated only after the third successful delivery. If the Russians really believed their lasers were competitive with Irish or French lasers, they'd jump at the chance to prove their product worked well enough to justify the risks involved. Now all I had to do was put together a plan that Matt would support—a plan that, together, we could sell to Plasmatec.

Our task force contacted the UNICEF medical office in Lausanne, Switzerland. They were interested in outfitting the United Nations' UNDP-funded clinics with the hemodiagnostic device, but were concerned that the sickling trait, highly prevalent in the African population, might skew the test results. Thus the studies Transfusions had already completed in France would need to be repeated in Africa, where the concentration of sickle-cell trait was greatest in the world. So three months after my return from Russia I was scheduled to go to Burkina Faso, a tiny landlocked country south of the Sahara in West Africa. It was no accident that Burkina was chosen, for a good friend of mine was director of the Catholic Relief Services office in the capital city, Ouagadougou, and she was instrumental in locating doctors who were willing to supervise the testing.

Burkina Faso: A few weeks later I stepped off the plane into a blast of hot, heavy, smoky air. We picked our suitcases off the tarmac and carried them in to the customs line. My friend, Mary Gorman, elbowed her way past a line of guards and grabbed one of my bags.

"Bonsoir," she smiled brightly at the soldier, who didn't seem to have checked my bags. "Come on," she said to me, turning and making her way toward the door. I shrugged at the soldier, who scowled, but made no effort to stop Mary.

"I didn't think he was done," I said, catching up to her outside the terminal.

"No, he probably wasn't, was he," Mary agreed. "But what could you possibly smuggle into Africa? They are just silly, these kids with guns."

"All the same, they're big guns," I pointed out.

"No-o-o. Well. They don't have bullets, see. Mostly. Think of the guns as police badges. They probably cost the Burkinans less than badges would have, what with Russia and the United States falling all over themselves to give guns away for the past 20 years. Now China."

Despite her words, I was nonplussed by the number of soldiers with semi-automatics standing on busy street corners all the way into town. The road we drove on was paved but the edges of it were rough, and mopeds and antique bicycles often swerved into the path of the car in an effort to avoid dropping down onto the dusty shoulder. Along the road were tables full of piles of fruits or eggs, and brightly dressed women wearing babies tied on their backs stood at every table.

"Look there," Mary remarked. "See the kids playing bocce ball? They make the balls themselves out of old Nescafé tins."

The car turned down a narrow dusty path with walled compounds on either side, and a smiling man sitting under a shade hangar of sticks and banana leaves leaped up to open the gate as he caught sight of the car.

"The guard," Mary explained. "There isn't any violent crime in Ouagadougou so far, but bad things begin in the coastal countries and move inland. The drug-resistant strain of malaria, for instance. Are you taking Mefloquine or Chloroquine with Paludrine?"

"Choice B, I think. One pill a day and two on Sundays?"

"Your best bet is not to get bitten by mosquitoes. I notice you're wearing pants—that's sensible."

"Really? This is my airplane outfit—but I brought a lot of skirts. I thought women are always supposed to wear skirts and blouses with long sleeves in Muslim countries?"

"That's so in North Africa, where the Muslim influence is strong, but in sub-Saharan Africa you're an honored guest first and a white alien second and a woman third, so be comfortable. I wouldn't wear shorts, of course," Mary responded, "but then I wouldn't wear shorts in Chicago either."

"Aren't most Burkinans Muslim?" I asked, sure I was right.

"Oh yes, mostly Muslims and some Christians too. A few are seriously religious, but most celebrate feast days with beer, if you know what I mean. It isn't at all like Morocco, where you can't get a beer in a hotel and the women travel in pairs on the street even by day. Burkina is an easy place to live. West Africans are the friendliest of Africans, and Burkinans are the most honorable people of West Africa. The name of the country means 'Land of Upright Citizens.'"

"Get a little enthusiasm, Mary," I laughed. "I'm glad you're happy here." Mary led me to a guest room dominated by a four-poster with a square mosquito net tent. A lizard clicked at us from the wall.

"Towels on the bed, dinner on the terrace," Mary said. "Wash up."

I always feel a little remote after a long airplane ride, as though my mind isn't able to move at 500 miles an hour and hasn't yet gotten to where my body and bags are. It's not that I can't think—but I certainly can't think well, sometimes for a couple of days. Luckily, this trip was eight hours straight south, so the time didn't change. But the troubling magic carpet nature of jet travel remained. I'd gotten on in an airport that resembled every airport I knew, with clean running water and people standing about in orderly lines, and I'd gotten out in the 1940s, in the bush, no less. Something about the speed and the huge distances involved in transcontinental flights is really disturbing to me.

Not to mention transocean trips, with time changes. I know Matt drinks coffee and takes No-Doz to deal with jet lag, but shoot, I can't even handle laughing gas at the dentist's office. Anyway, Jan has told me how it is for Matt when he comes home after a business trip that he's taken stimulants to handle. He collapses into bed for two days, then he's expected back at the office in working order and she doesn't find out for a week how his trip went. She calls it the transcontinental drift, because she gets so angry with him. He falls asleep in front of the television for another week.

I felt a little better after I showered. Night had fallen, but the air was still just as hot and heavy, scented with cook fire smoke and a night-flowering jasmine that twined up Mary's porch post.

"It's funny how your perceptions of what makes a situation good or bad change as you age," Mary said, and I settled in for the kind of retrospective gab you can only have with old friends. "In college all I needed was a job I enjoyed, a clean place to live, and a circle of like-minded friends. Now I envision two old ladies sharing a spot in the sun on a porch somewhere, and I wonder what the widowed one with children had to give up. Of course, I also wonder if I can be happy as the unmarried one."

"Opportunity costs?" I queried.

"Exactly. Look, I've done a canoe safari in Zimbabwe, climbed Kilimanjaro, flown in a hot air balloon over herds of elephants and zebras, been protected by warriors with spears from lions who left paw marks outside my tent, raced in a Land Rover with a pair of cheetahs—how many people from Oak Park can say that? Theodore Roosevelt aside, of course."

"Roosevelt had kids too," I pointed out.

"Roosevelt had a wife," Mary replied. "Life would be a lot easier if we were all assigned a human being who understood from birth that they were to be happy with less. I want more. I'd rather have a wife than be one, especially the "dependent spouse" of an employed expatriate.

"How so? They get to see all kinds of exotic places—you just said that was key to you."

"Women who don't work have a hard time finding an entrée into the culture, wherever they are. And at the same time, their whole day is spent abroad, in a way that is not the case for most Americans working abroad. At CRS, for instance, we all use Apples, the office structure is the same as it is in Baltimore, the work I do is very similar to the work done by my counterparts in Peru and Djibouti. But housewives here typically share their space with African servants, which is not exactly offered as a Girl Scout badge, and every time their spouses switch posts, their environment changes radically—the language, shopping, food ingredients, everything. Not to even mention friends. And friends are even more important to people who don't work because they have all this time to fill."

"So working is the key to being happy abroad, you think?" I asked.

"The missionary wives do great, though, and they don't have office jobs. Maybe you need a spiritual commitment to make it past the cross-cultural differences when they are as big as they are here. Or maybe it's just that missionaries have so many friends in the African community. They get to stay in one country for years and years too," Mary reflected.

"Businesses aren't supposed to permit that," I pointed out. "Business thinks humans acclimate too quickly to alien norms, and companies don't want to pay to keep Americans in positions abroad if they're going to expect three-hour lunches and five-hour workdays. Have you 'gone native'? Do you have African friends?"

"Sort of," Mary answered. "I mean, yeah, sure. There's a really interesting Ghanaian businessman who comes by and plays Scrabble with me a few times a month. His name is Business, and he's a bit of a wheeler-dealer. He wins every single time, always with two-letter words like 'xi' on triple-score spaces. I think he just memorized all the two-letter combinations in his dictionary. It isn't the way Scrabble was played in college, but it's a winning strategy. That's a good metaphor for having African friends, in fact. They aren't friends like you make in college, somehow, yet wherever you go you need friends, so you figure out your best chance at commonalities and you pursue them."

I wondered if Carine played Scrabble.

"Take the Brits, for instance, who've had centuries of experience in overseas administration and expatriate life. They've evolved this tradition called the hash. Every Friday someone lays out a race path and anyone who wants to join comes and 'runs' the path. It's an activity with built-in topics of conversation. It's the perfect way to interact with people you in no way resemble. That's probably the key to feeling good overseas—finding activities that don't require a lot of conversation. And studying the language. Of course."

"Of course," I agreed, grateful that French is spoken in Burkina.

The next morning I rode off to Dano to meet Hille Joerger, the doctor supervising our tests. Mary had arranged a ride in a CRS Land Rover, and as we passed pickup trucks chock full of passengers, roofs piled high with baggage, I appreciated yet again the air conditioning that meant my HDDs weren't going to arrive coated in dust. Dano is a sleepy little town with a dug-out water reservoir, a bakery, and a PTT (post office) at its center. I commented that the marketplace was nearly empty, and the driver explained that only every eighth day did the villagers gather there.

"Why not once a week? Wouldn't that make keeping track of the market day a little easier?" I asked.

The driver laughed. "You think there are calendars here?" he responded, gesturing at mud brick and thatch huts lining the street. "It has always been eight days, no problem." It was only after I'd lived in Dano for a couple of weeks that I began to distinguish some French words in the streams of the native language I heard on the street. When I realized that most of the French words I heard were calendar words—*demain, mercredi*—I gained some insight into his response.

Hille greeted me with the hearty handshake used uniformly in Africa, between women as well as men, and we examined the HDDs together. I was to train the lab technicians in their use. The room Hille offered me was considerably less finished than Mary's villa in Ouagadougou, but it was wired for electricity and Hille ran the generator between 6 and 10 P.M. to provide light, cool the small freezer, and run a single ceiling fan. Like everyone else I quickly learned to rise at 5 A.M. to take advantage of the cool weather.

Hille's generosity in permitting me to live with her for the course of the study really impressed me, and her hospitality under troubled conditions was also remarkable. Dano was experiencing a water shortage, which meant we washed our hair only once a week, and our clothes took on a reddish tinge from being rinsed in muddy water. The only vegetables in the market were tomatoes and onions, but Hille had a larder full of canned foods. I recognized the level of organization required in hardship conditions to maintain a home life that supports a productive work life.

After training the lab technicians, I went to the *Mairie* (city hall) to present my project to the town administration, as Hille had requested. The secretary listened intelligently while I explained that I needed to see the health and education officer, and told me to take a seat on the wooden bench. I sat for three hours, then left, disappointed the man was unavailable but determined to see him as soon as I could. The next day I repeated the travail, but brought study materials to pass the time. On the third morning I came before the doors opened, eager to catch the officer before his day began. That morning another woman who also waited outside the Mairie struck up a conversation with me.

"Where are you from?" she inquired. "Ah, I have a friend in Quebec. It is not far."

I understood that was enough of a connection, and spoke to her about my project and my plans for the day.

"But you want to see M. Ouedraogo? He has gone to Côte d'Ivoire and will not return until after the weekend."

Stunned, I sped in to confront the secretary. She confirmed that the officer had been gone for the two days I'd waited in her office, and asked me to return on Monday. When my anger took away my French and I began scolding her in English for wasting so much of my time so needlessly, she took on the frozen expression of a New Yorker on a subway and began examining her nails. My friend from outside also turned away, startled and seemingly embarrassed that I cared so much for my time and so little for the delicate feelings of the secretary.

The following Monday I returned and spoke to the *fonctionnaire* (clerk). He required some documents from the Health Department in Ouagadougou, he explained. I stopped myself from informing him that I planned to begin testing immediately, but I passed by the PTT to telegraph Mary to ask for help in obtaining the papers from Ouaga. After a quick lunch, I went to the clinic to begin testing.

"Where's Jean-Pierre?" I asked Hille, not seeing the lab technician who had seemed to grasp the use of the machine best.

"He's ill," she responded. "Infectious hepatitis."

Thus Jean-Pierre provided the first blood to be tested—we monitored his bilirubin levels for the next three weeks. But we couldn't draw his blood as part of the AIDS-HDD study, which required Elisa tests to be done as controls in Ouagadougou, because his system was too weak. Our targeted patients were pregnant women, a hospital population whose health typically mirrors the population at large and who by definition are at risk for HIV. However, in the course of the next two weeks the number of meningitis patients in the clinic grew by a factor of two, then four, then eight. Hille grew increasingly worried about meningitis vectors in the outlying villages. She conferred with M. Ouedraogo at the Mairie, and they announced over the radio and at the mosque that the Dano market would not be held until further notice, in order to prevent the spread of the airborne killer.

I retreated to Ouagadougou to consider my options, and spent the next three days vomiting and hallucinating with a breakthrough case of malaria and a fever of 104 degrees. The morning I first ate breakfast, I broke down and cried. The work I'd done hadn't gone anywhere. It was less than useless. Since I hadn't been productive upon arrival, when I was fresh and healthy, how could I possibly finish my task in my current state of despair? Mary was not properly sympathetic. "You've been *wawa*'ed," she said. "'West Africa Wins Again.' Well, if there were easy solutions, we wouldn't be here."

That was when I realized 'going native' could mean something other than taking long lunches. Mary was accustomed to having nothing work out as planned. I suppose if you met delay at every turn, you'd either learn to lower your expectations or be shipped home in a basket with bars. Business can't afford to have the edge taken off a worker's productivity—but Mary wasn't in business.

As I saw it, I could reschedule my visit in two months, since meningitis is seasonal, or I could try to form a relationship with a clinic here in Ouagadougou, or I could call Matt and ask if there wasn't a more organized country where the population was equally given to sickling disease, or, heck, I could fake my data—just kidding.

I began to see why business likes to move people around and work primarily in the developed world.

QUESTIONS FOR DISCUSSION

1. How would you apply the cultural frameworks to this chapter? Do this for Germany, Russia, and Burkina Faso.
2. Of the three projects outlined in Jennifer's memos to Matt (one in each country), which show the most promise and why? Where are the weak points?
3. Maybe because she's sick, Jennifer is discouraged about Africa. What would you do to salvage and make productive the African project?

CHAPTER 18

Coming Home:
The Challenges of Reentry

JAN

"Bonjour, mesdames et messieurs, nous vous accueillons à bord vol . . . ." The sound of the stewardess's voice faded as I began thinking about returning to the States and all that meant. I don't know if I was beginning to be nostalgic about leaving France, but I began to realize more than before that our life here in France had come to an end. Matt was already in California at the Santa Cruz facility to ease the transition for when he came on full time. I was coming to join him to look for a home and to meet some of the people I had contacted about a part-time law practice. I had decided that I didn't want to go back full time. It's funny how you change over time. In my case, it seems so long ago that I had this dream of righting all the "wrongs" being done to the environment. Then the move to Japan . . . that was the start of my moving along a different path. I'm not sure I knew at the time what deciding to go to Japan meant in terms of my future. At the time, I thought it would be just a black hole in my professional life, just a temporary blip in my career pursuit.

Yes, something in me has died along the path I've followed, but other things have come alive. Do I have regrets? Sure, I would be lying if I said categorically "no." Something that's so much a part of you, that you have so much energy for doesn't go away without regrets. In fact, I'm not sure it really ever goes away . . . more like buried. All my life I have been involved in nature in some form or another. It is a part of me, part of who I think I am. And no matter how much I might like to deny it, the status of being a professional is also hard to surrender. When others find out you're an attorney, there's automatic respect that comes with it—maybe not for the profession—but for the intellectual capacity to become one and the perception of power attorneys have.

Would I make the same choices now about my life that I have made? Probably. I never became an attorney for the prestige. It was only a by-product, and I don't think I would have become addicted to that. And no matter how much passion I had—and still have—for the environment, my relationship to my family is more important to me. I think that's part of my heritage from my own family as a child. I can't imagine having been raised in a family where my parents were largely absent from the home, where professional success was more important than being an integral part of our lives. I know others would say you can have both, a full-time career and a great family life, but I'm not so sure. There has to be compromise. No matter how good you are, there are still only 24 hours in a day.

I guess I had become too accustomed to being home with the kids, being a significant part of their lives. Priorities change with experience, and I decided I could have a great impact on the physical and social environment by rearing our children well. Maybe I wouldn't be able to claim success in keeping the so-called civilized world at bay, that same world that would destroy the natural and replace it with the artificial for the sake of an extra dollar or two. If I help my own children develop a love and respect for our environment, I can claim some measure of success.

Question 1: *Do you think Jan's perspective is really true or is it a perspective that simply justifies what has happened because it would be too painful to admit a serious error in her judgment about her career?*

"Mom, can we rent the headsets to watch the movie?" Jeff asked, interrupting my thoughts.

The flight was long and I had a lot of time to read and think. The last few weeks in Grenoble seemed to have blurred by me. Making calls to EDF-GDF (the nationalized French electricity and gas company), arranging for the movers, selling the cars—each day seemed to just fade into the next. Finally, when the day arrived to leave, I must admit I experienced a lot of melancholy. I think the kids did too.

It was hard to give up experiencing the kind of personal growth that was only possible as expatriates in France—or any foreign country for that matter.

Both Jeff and Michelle had become fluent in French. Learning a foreign language is not just a useful item to put on your résumé later on. Language also reflects how you see the world, and I think that even at their ages they will use this experience to help them appreciate the diversity that exists in peoples. We've had a lot of discussions about differences in cultures and perspectives. Despite some of the problems the kids had integrating into French schools, they also witnessed true acts of kindness. I will never forget the French truck driver who stopped along the highway to ask if we needed help. Our car had finally sputtered to a stop and Matt had a hard time figuring out how to lift the hood, let alone fix the problem. After a few questions and tinkering with the carburetor for a few minutes, the truck driver figured out the problem. It was in the fuel pump, I gathered. He went back to the truck, used his knife to cut out a kind of seal out of some thin cardboard from a cereal box he had, and replaced the leaky seal in the fuel pump. It worked.

In Grenoble we had a lot of discussions about "right" and "wrong" versus "their" way and "our" way, but we've also talked a lot about basic human sameness also. I think the truck driver's example, and others, will always be a part of our family's memories of living in a foreign culture.

The whole experience was challenging for all of us, each in a different way. The fact that we felt successful in the end meant a lot. I think for all of us it built our confidence, our belief in ourselves and our abilities to take on the challenges and make it all work.

Question 2:   Given the discussion about the Sumners' experiences living abroad, would you accept a position in a foreign country? And if you were a nonworking spouse?

As we neared Kennedy Airport in New York, it was great to see the Statue of Liberty in New York Harbor. Some of the passengers even clapped to celebrate their arrival in the United States, which made me realize how much I had missed home. The hot humid July air in New York reminded me of those hot, sultry July days in Grenoble, though. That part I didn't miss!

The flight from New York to San Francisco was uneventful apart from a rough spot over Wyoming and the constant snores of the man in front of me. The kids would nudge his chair a little and he would stop for about 7 seconds. I told myself I had survived in Japan, lived through the oppressive humid summer heat of Grenoble, tolerated haughty French schoolteachers, and on and on. Surely, I could last through a few hours of snoring. Somehow, in a trivial way, this seemed like the last trial I was to face before coming home.

The plane finally touched down over the Bay and Matt was waiting for us at the gate. We picked up a second rental car and went immediately to my parents' home in Napa for the weekend. Mom and Dad were their usual teary-eyed selves.

Hugging them reminded me of how much I had missed them too. It's amazing how many memories can be bundled up into feelings that pass through in a hug only lasting a few seconds. Mom and Dad both looked the same, but I think Dad was suffering physically more than he was letting on. We all spent the weekend catching up on family news and our experiences in Grenoble and getting over our jet lag. The kids and I spent some time weeding in the garden to help Dad out. His back was bothering him more and more. Leaning over to grab the weeds left him in what seemed like a permanently curved position.

Matt had business meetings Monday morning, so I went to see Heather. We talked about everything—law, the job market, French men, friends. Also, she had heard there was a new small law firm that was interested in growing its environmental law area. It was located in Los Gatos, a small city at the base of the Santa Cruz mountains. I was so excited. It made me also realize how much I had missed the professional and intellectual environment I had been away from for so long. Working there would be perfect. We could live in the Santa Cruz mountains and both of us would have a short commute. Of course, I had no idea whether they were hiring or whether I would be attractive to them. I had kept up as well as I could with the environmental law statutes and some of the more prominent cases. Heather had sent me case updates, and I was a member of several environmental associations from general ones, like Wilderness Society, to a more specialized one in the legal area. When you're a few thousand miles away, even with the Internet, you don't realize how dependent you become on others to keep you somewhat informed. You can really feel out of it.

Matt had taken time in his busy schedule to look for a home while we were still in France. We both thought it would be important to get settled as quickly as possible. The kids were great troopers, but too many transitions can be stressful on everyone, especially children, I think. Matt found a beautiful rustic home near Scotts Valley in the Santa Cruz mountains. He had sent pictures and described as much as he could about the location. I felt a little uneasy making a decision without ever seeing it, but I had a good feeling about this one and gave my okay. I knew the kids would love it—at least they had better love it. It had large rustic wood beams throughout, a beautiful rock fireplace in the center of the family room, and a large redwood deck that looked out over the mountain valleys. There was even a work room with all the tools that Matt has never used and probably never will. He never was the fix-it type, and I didn't have any delusions he would become so. He was too wrapped up in his work. We had two acres so our neighbors weren't stacked up on top of us, and I actually felt like I could breathe. This was more like the kind of home I had longed for ever since I had left Maine.

Handling all the paperwork for the house from France by mail was cumbersome but doable. Thank goodness for Federal Express, not to mention e-mail so Matt and I could communicate rapidly but without the huge costs of a telephone bill. Over the next few days, the small things—seeing all the familiar billboards, hearing everyone around us speak English, going to the grocery store, filling a "normal"-sized fridge with gallon-size milk containers—all this reminded us of how comfortable it is to be in familiar surroundings despite the fact that our way of life in France had become very natural.

One day as I was driving into Scotts Valley to do some shopping, it really struck me as I passed one of those upscale tract developments off 17. I would have felt totally depersonalized being in one of those large stucco tile-roofed homes with my neighbors eight feet away on both sides. How can people live like that, I asked myself. It would seem like a sellout in some way to me, like I had moved not only physically but valuewise also so far from my Maine roots. Growing up, we had lived in a rural part of Maine where most everyone was either a craftsman, store owner, or part-time farmer of some sort. It seemed like such an easy life as I look back on it. The seasons came and went. Friendships were stable. We all shared in a simple life. Material differences were negligible or else I hadn't noticed. But in these tract neighborhoods it seems everyone is an engineer or executive of some sort; Mercedeses, BMWs, and Lexuses commonly line the driveways. The more I thought about it, the more thoughts of that lifestyle repulsed me, and the more I clung to whatever I had that kept me in touch with myself.

Kick-starting my career was tougher than I had anticipated. The job interview went well with the Los Gatos firm and they hired me right away. I was supposed to be in the law office a few times a week, but it didn't quite work out that way at first. With Matt starting a new job and the kids experiencing a mixture of frustration and excitement at school, I slipped back into the position of "taking care of things." Actually, I didn't really slip back into it; I had never gotten completely out of it since going to Japan. I convinced myself that my career had been put on hold this long; it could wait a little while longer until life settled down for us. I negotiated coming into work once a week for the first three months and expected that by that time, everyone would be well settled in. I hated to do it because I wondered if I was once more in the syndrome of having my boss question my commitment to work.

Matt's difficult transition was clearly job related. With his promotion, he had more responsibilities and new ones that were quite different from those in France. Instead of sharing oversight of one operation—in Grenoble—he now had corporatewide responsibility for all international operations. This included coordinating a lot of the activities among the foreign facilities themselves, and sometimes between the U.S. operation in Santa Cruz and the rest of the world. Dealing with Europe now meant dealing with the European Community (EC) as a whole instead of individual countries. Many of the EC regulations were designed to protect Europe's economy from "intruders." Given the heavily government-subsidized medical industry in Europe, the paperwork and time waiting for approval—if given—for "imported" medical products was sometimes so long and arduous that it gave European firms time to develop equally good or better products.

What complicated things for Matt personally was his nature to become involved in company operations. Although he had learned in Japan to play a less active role and then in France to "leave certain things alone," his interest in what was going on still pushed him to become more involved than he probably needed to be. This was perhaps compounded by the fact that he had a lot of latitude to do his job. No one was really around to watch over his shoulder.

In Africa, pushing ahead with a market opportunity required skills that Matt hadn't fully developed in Japan or France. He wasn't used to meeting with people at the ministry level and didn't know all the rules of the game. But promotions were often just that, he told himself—a step up to something new, requiring a quick learning curve and development of new skills. "I'm not afraid of that," he told me.

He had taken on challenges before that had stretched him. Now there was the new work environment at the office he had to get used to—new faces, new politics, new responsibilities, new office procedures, and so it went.

"The workday is really different from the one I'd finally gotten used to in France," he told me after his first week at the office. "Having the secretaries call me by my first name seems really strange. The extended coffee breaks to "connect" in the morning aren't typical here. Lunches are fairly quick affairs usually in the company cafeteria. Politics and economics are referred to only if there is some direct connection to our business. Like a conversation I had with John, the VP of manufacturing, and some others yesterday. He mentioned that the slight rise in interest rates by the Fed was probably going to mean he wouldn't refinance their house this year. In France, there would have been at least a half hour debate first on whether the rise in interest rates was good or bad. And it wouldn't have focused on refinancing someone's home. They would have discussed its probable effects on the French economy and its relationship to the rest of Europe and their economies and currencies.

"Here most of the debates seem to center around the sport in season—baseball right now. If you aren't up on the Giants or A's, and all the other teams for that matter, you're left out of the conversation." Matt shook his head. "There was a time when I knew all of that stuff, but that was 10 years ago. George Wilcox knows the batting averages of everyone on the Giants team. Even Cheryl Taylor gets into the conversation. I just kind of stand there with a blank stare and smile at the right times. Hell, I've been out of circulation so long, I don't know that kind of detail anymore. In France I was lucky to follow the teams' win-loss records in the *International Herald Tribune*. I've got enough on my mind without having to start memorizing the sports page," he complained.

When Matt said that, it almost startled me. I hadn't realized just how "far" we had come since our early days in the Bay Area. Matt had been a sports fiend. He knew all that stuff back then—who had just been traded to which team, whose salary contract was holding up the final team roster, and on and on. Now, nearly a decade later, having been in Japan and France for most of that, Matt's breadth of interest and experience seemed so far removed from what it had been. I wondered whether he appreciated it or regretted it.

"All that's not even everything that makes it tough to readjust," he complained, interrupting my thoughts. "The other day, Susan, the gal over in finance responsible for coordinating our major Asian accounts, made a major error in a sale to one of our Taiwanese accounts. This wasn't the first time, either. Instead of going to her directly, as I would have before I worked in France, I discussed the issue with one of my colleagues, George Howell , the assistant VP I inherited from Ron. A few days later, in a casual conversation with Deborah Newell, the VP of human resources, she mentioned she had heard rumors that George Howell was going around wondering out loud why I had mentioned the problem to him instead of going directly to Susan. It made me wonder what else I'm doing that isn't appropriate here," Matt muttered. "It took me long enough to learn how things are done in France, but I keep thinking I should be able to just slip back into my own culture without a problem," he added.

Having to relearn and adjust to these norms annoyed him at first. They were one more obstacle in performing what was already a new and challenging job. Sometimes he even had language problems. In presentations to Doc and some of the other executives, words—English words—wouldn't come to his mind but the French word would. This bothered Matt, since he never had any problem expressing himself before. "I wonder how long it's going to take to get the French out of my head," he complained.

Unfortunately, he also had to endure looks of "Who are you?" those first few weeks. "Sometimes I think the others wonder what planet I dropped in from," Matt told me one day. "I get the feeling when I request something a little out of the ordinary that it's taken half-heartedly, or if I make a recommendation to the other executives on my level, they automatically discount it a little as something coming from someone who hasn't 'been around.' It isn't anything they say. I just feel it. Like sometimes there's this slight pause or their response doesn't directly relate to my comment. It's almost like I'm back in France without being in France. I feel like I've paid my dues and these jerks, most of whom have never stepped foot outside the United States, are in their own little world," Matt said one night as he pulled back the bed sheet to get into bed. "I even brought it up to Doc last week because I had just gotten tired of it," Matt added as he turned onto his side.

Matt continued, "Doc listened carefully and in the end reassured me that I had nothing to worry about that time wouldn't cure, but I'm not convinced."

Matt really needed a lot of encouragement from me those first few months just to get adjusted; unfortunately, so did I and the kids. Everyone needed those great virtues of understanding, patience, and a listening ear, but none of us always had the energy to do it. There was a fair amount of stress during that time and a few more arguments than we usually had. It was really tough and I wouldn't want to repeat it.

Matt confided in me one day that he wondered whether he was climbing the ladder faster than his experience warranted. I assured him that if that were true, Doc and the others would not have recommended him for the job and they wouldn't have sent him to France in the first place. If they had confidence in him and had been grooming him for a top job, I told him he should just apply the same work ethic and skills to this new job as he had to past positions. Still, some things are easier said than done.

With much more responsibility than he had before, he felt more was expected. That translated into longer hours at the office and more meetings. He often didn't come home until 9 or 10 o'clock those first weeks. He had reached the corporate level now and felt a combination of inadequacy and excitement about the new job. He was so preoccupied that he didn't have a lot of time to help with all of the things we had to do to settle in. He felt guilty about it but that didn't change the reality all that much.

Weekends, when Matt didn't go into the office, he and I worked together, though, planning out the next week, deciding what had to get done and how we wanted to approach it. The first few weeks our planning, and my doing(!), was mostly around buying cars, going to the DMV, getting insurance, opening bank accounts—all of the mundane things you usually don't think about that had to be done.

Jeff was in ninth grade now and was having his own difficulties adjusting. He felt somewhat as though he had been in a time warp. Although life had changed drastically for him, everyone else had continued on a much slower track or on just a different track. He felt out of place at first but was eager to fit in. His math teacher found it particularly challenging to teach him geometry. Although Jeff had gone to an international school in France, they taught math using a mixture of the American system and the French system. In France the elementary school math curriculum mixes algebraic and geometry concepts. This continues on into the upper grades where algebra and geometry are taught. In the United States, basic algebra is taught as an entirely separate course from geometry. The other kids in Jeff's class hadn't been exposed to as much geometry as Jeff had. But he didn't know as much algebra as his classmates did.

For the first several weeks, a tutor and I taught Jeff algebra to bring him up to the same level as the other students. I was intrigued by Jeff's insecurity about the whole situation. It was as if he had only been half dressed and was sent off to school that way. He was embarrassed by his math skills compared to the other students even though probably none of the other students knew he was behind. He had also missed the day when lockers were assigned because we hadn't gotten the announcement through the mail. We were still in France at the time. So he had to take one of the leftover lockers, which in his case meant he had a locker with those one grade below him. I know this seems like a small thing, but to a kid who is desperately trying to fit in, to Jeff it seemed almost insurmountable at first.

The two obvious factions at school didn't help either. Jeff learned very quickly there were the local, indigenous kids—the "rednecks" the others called them— and the "techie snobs" that had all moved into those stucco cities I mentioned earlier. There certainly weren't gang wars, but it was obvious neither side felt any kinship for the other. Jeff told me both groups walked differently, talked differently, and had obviously different interests.

"The 'rednecks' walk like they own the place," Jeff commented. "And they have these country accents," he added. I would sit him down periodically and try to get him to view this group as another culture, just like the French represented another culture. I explained to him that even in the States there are subcultures that have different values and customs because they are raised differently. Neither one is better or worse, I reminded Jeff. And besides, I let him know it was the "techie kids," like him, who had invaded the others' territory and not the other way around. I could tell he wasn't internalizing everything I was telling him, but I knew he knew eventually it would all work out, just like it had in France.

Jeff's emotional reaction sometimes superseded his intellectual thought, though. "This sucks, Mom," he would tell me in his own vernacular. I wasn't sure sometimes whether he wished we were still in France or if he wished we had never gone—probably the latter at his age.

In his French class, he knew more vocabulary than the professor did, especially street language. Students started asking Jeff how to say things that weren't in the textbook—the kind of things that are sometimes purposely left out of textbooks! I think he sensed the teacher's frustration with this. She was better in grammar than Jeff, but her accent wasn't as good. Nothing was said between Jeff and the teacher, but Jeff sensed he was walking a tightrope.

"Elle ne sait pas de quoi elle parle" (She doesn't know what she's talking about) he would tell me sometimes those first few weeks. I told him even if she didn't know what she was talking about, he needed to let the teacher be the teacher. And he needed to learn more grammar.

Michelle seemed to adjust a little more easily. She made friends right away and a few boys took an immediate interest in her. Maybe she was the "new girl on the block," so to speak. She had a few problems adjusting at school, but she seemed to fit in more easily than Jeff. She had friends over at the house within a few days of moving in.

After several weeks, life got easier for me, mostly because it got easier for everyone else. Matt had begun to settle into his new routine, although it was still difficult and even busier than before. He was out of the country sometimes for a week and then back for a couple of weeks and then gone somewhere else for a day or two, then back, and so on. Jeff had finally accepted his "mislocated" locker and he and the French teacher figured out a way to work together. Either that or they tolerated each other. Jeff didn't mention her much anymore so I assumed the cold war was over.

Some of the U.S. norms weren't difficult to get reaccustomed to at all. Having stores opened during lunch was a gold mine. I had almost gotten used to the fact that everything closed down between noon to 2 and sometimes to 3 o'clock. I can't tell you the number of times I had forgotten about the sacred lunch hour in France and had to make two trips into the downtown because I couldn't finish everything by noon. Having 24-hour convenience stores was helpful too, even though it wasn't always convenient (!) to go into Scotts Valley from our home just to pick up something small. Paying a reasonable price for gasoline instead of $5 a gallon as we had in France was a real delight. Not having to put a coin in the slot on the shopping cart to get one was nice. And not being charged for grocery bags and having someone else bag my groceries were little bennies I really appreciated. And of course, being able to turn right on a red light seemed reasonable to me. I never could figure out why the French didn't adopt this practice.

Still, each of us felt like something was missing. Whether it was the walks in our neighborhood in France, the visits to the open *marchés*, or smelling the side-walk *crêperies* in the fall, it was hard to pin down. And we were all disappointed that the only Yoplait yogurt in stores in the United States was all low fat. It just wasn't the same. We couldn't get the variety of cheeses we had in France. After asking around and visiting several stores in the Bay Area, I finally found Caprice des Dieux, one of our favorites, at a specialty import-export store, although they weren't always able to stock it. Gone, too, were the *pains au chocolat* (light rolls with a piece of chocolate inside) we all had gotten used to as an afternoon snack. I don't know if it was a combination of all these little things or what, but there was just something missing, a void in our lives that seemed hard to shake during the first months.

And I must admit, it was challenging to be with other people sometimes. Most of our neighbors had never been outside the country. Their world seemed so narrow. It was difficult sometimes relating to them. Fortunately, there was an Indian family on the block who had just moved from India. The husband had accepted a job with Seegate. They were going through many of the same problems we had experienced in Japan and France. We had a lot in common, more than with other Americans it seemed at times.

Practicing environmental law helped me a great deal through some of the challenges. I had to use a lot of that energy that could have gone toward nostalgia for a more positive purpose.

Question 3: Should companies have a responsibility to help their expatriates and families readjust to repatriation? What could they do?

I got into a couple of cases that had to do with local developments, one in the Scotts Valley area and the other in Portola Valley. There was real animosity between the developers and the locals (i.e., the "redneck" population, as Jeff put it). Town meetings were yelling matches sometimes. In the Scotts Valley case, I represented the city, which I wasn't used to doing, since most of my cases had involved representing an association of landowners with strong vested interests in keeping the area undeveloped or in developing it. The basic issue in this case was whether the development was going to overtax the sewage capability in that area of Scotts Valley. Many of the individual owners in the area were on septic tanks, but the developments were typically on sewer lines.

The Portola Valley case was much more interesting. It was about whether the development would disrupt the natural ecosystem. I didn't think from the start the neighbors—the ones banding together to bring the suit against the developer—had much of a chance. The development was to be five 3-acre parcels, each with a home on it. There wasn't much record of any endangered animals or anything else in the area, so it was an obvious uphill battle all the way from the start. I advised them and my managing partner of the potential high cost and probable eventual loss of the case, but the neighbors were willing to push on.

So over the course of several months, between the difficulties of getting adjusted to work, helping Jeff with his problems at school, getting settled in and starting gardening projects and the like around the house, we all seemed to limp through that somewhat difficult process of coming "home."

But we got there. It was just another challenge, another road to cross.

QUESTIONS FOR DISCUSSION

1. What were the different kinds of adjustment the Sumner family had to get used to (i.e., work, interaction, general)?
2. What seemed to be Matt's principal challenges in adjusting to his work? What differences between the French and U.S. way are evident from the challenges Matt faces in adapting?
3. For Jan, what were the most basic challenges she faced those first few months after returning to the United States? And for Jeff and Michelle?

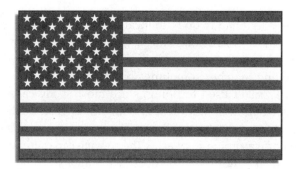

CHAPTER 19

Matt's Perspective from Top Management

"Vice president of international operations, hey?" I'd say to the mirror in the morning. Most of the time I thought it was a brilliant stroke of personnel management on the part of Tom McDonald and Doc and anyone else who'd had the foresight to identify me as a HIPO. I was the best choice for the job. I am flexible, well educated, experienced in cross-cultural and management issues, and very, very smart. Then I'd nick my chin or drop my tie clip in the inaccessible space between the cabinet and the tub and think, "Ouch! When will they realize I'm faking it?"

My strategy for dealing with these minor but complete breakdowns in self-concept has always been to ignore them. There was no real reason for me to feel insecure, the solid sound of my new title notwithstanding. My duties dovetailed closely with those I'd had overseas, where my supervision was minimal, so I was well prepared to handle the increased responsibility as I stepped into Ron Clancy's shoes—or, more accurately, his desk, his role in the office, and his spot at the top management team's table in the upstairs conference room.

Tom McDonald was clear about my role in the office. I was to represent the company on any international matters to stakeholders external and internal, including customers, suppliers, shareholders, the media, government representatives at home and abroad, and, of course, our employees and their labor unions. I was charged with coordinating all international operations with an eye to maximizing their ROI (Return on Investment) by hedging on exchange rates, minimizing manufacturing and labor costs, and setting up offices to maximize overseas tax advantages. On the way to mastering all the possible effects that local conditions (government, labor, supplies) might have on our production and marketing capacity, I was to identify international HIPO managers in my office and abroad who might be groomed for positions such as mine. Furthermore, as a member of the top management team, I was to actively pursue the future of Plasmatec by being tuned in to changes in the global business climate that might dictate a corresponding internal adjustment. As the international expert, I would be expected to influence the top management group on the global implications and opportunities involved in general business decisions.

Of course, there were unstated elements to my new role too, which could hardly help but influence my standing in the company. I knew it would be foolhardy to discard immediately everything Ron Clancy had left me—his policies, his methods of organizing his staff, his staff itself—but at the same time, I'd had an effect on the French, and Transfusions, cultural differences notwithstanding, and I was determined to make my mark on Plasmatec. As I saw it, the first step was mastering the politics and the unwritten social contract between my staff and management that embodied Plasmatec culture. Understanding the deep culture of Plasmatec would enable me to model an appropriate executive style, and it would make me a more effective team player. I knew the importance of being a team player.

Clancy himself had a solid reputation as a team player: he was perceived as reliable and level-headed, better at implementing strategies than inventing them, perhaps, but by no means the last one off the block. I already had a good feel for Clancy's modus operandi from my time in France. He had done an excellent job starting up our joint venture operations in France and Japan, giving free rein to hand-selected leaders he had had reason to trust. The country leadership in those two companies was sound. They could be relied on to continue to turn profits.

However, I thought I could probably improve on Clancy's performance, which lacked the foundation of overseas experience and the entrepreneurial orientation I brought to the job. I felt fairly sure that barring uncontrollable fluctuations in the global economy, I could make the overseas operations more profitable. It seemed clear our production was limited by management constraints and that rationalizing our management would enable us to expand our ventures overseas. I wanted a system designed to allow general managers with different national territories to work together, and I envisioned a central warehousing plan, a computer for tracking and filling regional orders, a Net presence, the works.

But first I had to dope out the Plasmatec culture, to make sure I was shaping our future from the inside, as it were. I met with some unexpected resistance from some of the VPs, including Deborah Newell, the VP for human resources who had helped Jennifer adjust to life at Plasmatec. I'd arranged to meet Deborah for lunch at the cafeteria one day to discuss extending the internship program for overseas HIPO employees—a low-level intervention, I felt. But I got the distinct impression that she thought I didn't understand what Ron Clancy had done. She seemed to assume that once I got the Clancy logic, I'd get with his program. I had a similar encounter with the VP for sales, Ramon Valdez. Ramon and Deborah just didn't think I had the stature, the silvering solidity of a Ron Clancy, it appeared. Even the operations VP, who was familiar with the work I'd done at Transfusions, was a little too quick to point out that Transfusions was foreign and unique. He actually asserted that the experience of leading a French staff might not "transfer" to California, as though it were a driver's license or something.

Anyway, Tom was securely in my corner, in part because he'd proposed me for the job, so my failure would reflect right back on him. It never hurts to be supported by the CEO! Doc, of course, was my staunchest ally. Doc was now a senior assistant to Tom but still on the Executive Committee, and he fed me inside lines and told me whose opinions to seek, whose friendship to cultivate. I always came away from meetings with Doc newly grateful for his intelligence and accessibility and his interest in me. It renewed my faith in myself, and I periodically reminded myself that since I could never repay Doc for his attention, I could only pass it on.

The likeliest HIPO among my own staff was Maria Borges, a Brazilian from Rio who had the fierce ambition of a high-status person from a developing country. I liked her charm and her wit, but I really admired her ability to shut down an opposing argument at a meeting. She had sound instincts for which plans would fly, and when she committed to a project it was as though hanging in the balance was her last chance to live in a country where the pursuit of happiness is considered an inalienable right. In her enthusiasm she reminded me a little of Jennifer Stewart.

Jennifer had returned from France to head up a marketing task force for a new product launch, a position I considered a sad waste of her skills and experience. It seemed top management wasn't sure how to best use her French experience, and the task force was a stop-gap measure. Naturally, she was running it with her usual efficiency.

Truth be told, I'd looked into Jennifer's situation not simply because I was trying to pass on Doc's gift to me, but because I felt thwarted in my efforts to master my new job by the assistant vice president international, George Hale, who had been a protégé of Ron Clancy. George wanted me to sit back and enjoy meetings and meals with clients while he ran the whole show à la Clancy. He had a really irritating habit of grabbing face time at meetings. Not that he was a bad speaker. I just resented feeling upstaged by an assistant with a better grasp of my new territory than I had, as yet, and my instinct was to set him down like an avocado with a worm in it. I really needed loyal people around me during this active period of fact finding, people who could help me figure out all the new stuff, and who would cover me until I could do the job on my own.

In addition to George and Maria, my staff at headquarters included an administrative assistant and a young intern from the Monterey Institute of International Studies, an Asian American named Yoshi who spoke fluent Japanese and solid Mandarin. I felt sure that Jennifer would work well with Maria and Yoshi, and George put my back up. So after a couple of months I "sold" George as an assistant VP to R&D—not terribly difficult, since I had no complaints with his work or character, and he had stellar recommendations from Ron, but a slightly touchy situation anyway, as horizontal intraoffice transfers often are. Ten minutes later I'd named Jennifer director of new business and Maria, director of global operations.

Soon I felt secure enough with the new staff arrangements to make visits to the field, where I familiarized myself with the staff, the daily operations, the peculiarities required by host country governments and local customs, and above all, the market opportunities previously missed. I already knew all about Transfusions, of course, and went to France just to check up on my successor, who was clearly doing a fine job. I also wanted to be sure Carine Solvay was being groomed for future leadership. The Japanese joint venture was also running smoothly, and I got reacquainted with the unusual work habits of the Japanese in addition to visiting my favorite sushi chain, the one where the chefs place the entrees on a conveyor belt and the clients help themselves as the food goes by. The waitresses keep track of your plates, which are color coded for price, and tea flows freely from a spigot at each place. Further evidence that the Japanese are the world's most organized society.

We now had competent nationals heading our plants in France and Japan, but there were only four persons at headquarters who held passports that were not American—and one was Canadian. We had few foreign nationals who knew the Plasmatec culture or who were being adequately prepared for future leadership positions within Plasmatec. This struck me as a serious oversight but one that could be easily remedied.

Meanwhile, Maria and Jennifer were working on industry analysis with a global stance. The Internet was an invaluable research tool, permitting them to obtain data on foreign hospitals and clinics, tax structures, import/export regulations, labor conditions, you name it. I'd always thought of Jennifer as a big-picture thinker, and I came to appreciate her visionary capacity, which was well paired with Maria's skepticism and penchant for detail. They both had a healthy dose of political acumen and the good judgment to know when to intervene and when to let things ride. It felt good to know I had intelligent and loyal support back home, and they kept me clued in on office doings while I was away.

When I returned, I felt it was time to take inventory of where I'd been and where I planned to go next. I'd created a team I really trusted, I'd experienced the nuts and bolts operation of joint ventures, I'd developed a feel for the dynamics of the Executive Committee, and I thought it was time for me to start pitching some ideas at them. I copied the following outline so I could practice delivering the speech to my biased but powerless critics first:

I. Manufacturing
   a. run current process by efficiency engineers
   b. develop robotic assembly lines to reduce labor costs
II. Management
   a. select and develop non-American HIPO managers
   b. develop a global coordinating mechanism
   c. foster local initiative within universal guidelines
III. Money
   a. find regional tax shelters
   b. research exchange-rate hedging
   c. seek further joint venture governmental support
   d. bring more foreign nationals to head office for acculturation and training
IV. Marketing
   a. push for higher share of existing markets
   b. seek growth-oriented markets in the developing world

Jan, my first biased critic, just looked at me. She was a little crabby about my recent absences, which makes her prone to minimize any concrete evidence I bring home to prove I do work for the paycheck I receive, but like any brilliant and sensitive lawyer, she's willing to put her feelings on hold if I totally debase myself before asking for her honest opinion.

"I'd need more information before I could respond to this," she said, waving the outline in the air. "Robotics, for instance. Do they really cut costs? Wouldn't the capital investment required for machine tooling and repair overcome the labor savings, and in the long run, wouldn't those unemployed ex-laborers be unable to participate in the economy, thus lessening demand for your high-tech product?"

"Actually, both the French and the Japanese plants are already more modern than our American and Mexican plants. And the labor costs are higher in France, at $21 per hour, and in Japan, at $19 per hour, than they are in America, where we count $16 per hour, and in Mexico, of course, where it's $7.50 per hour. The added costs in France and Japan include better benefits and vacations, which are required by law. In America, our priciest benefit is medical insurance. But that at least supports our market, hey?"

"So what you're saying is that robotics replace workers in France and Japan because labor costs are higher there?"

"Exactly. So I'm going to propose that France and Japan produce more of the high-end sophisticated products while Mexico gets modernized with an eye to doing the labor-intensive parts of the products, like the cloth work on the surgical supply kits. Robots don't do hand sewing."

Jan groaned. "Let me guess—you're closing the American plant, right? We can't even compete with the French?"

I sidestepped that one. "We also need a plant in China or Vietnam for labor-intensive, low-technology products. Labor costs there are only a couple of dollars an hour, and the work ethic is high. Plus, it'll give us a bird's-eye view of a truly lucrative future market."

Jan didn't want to hear about tax shelters, so I skipped that part. But really, it's incredible how well just a little attention to detail pays off. A friend of mine who worked for a large multinational corporation in France told me their accountants had discovered that by setting up a European Logistics Center (ELC) in Belgium, they could avoid taxes on 15 percent of their pretax income. The Belgian government would treat income that flowed through this ELC to the States as tax free because Belgian taxes are limited to the operational costs of the office. The loophole permitted them to reduce the average figure of 40 percent paid in taxes.

Similarly, I learned that by declaring a European corporate headquarters in one of the low-tax Swiss cantons like Zug or Neuchâtel, we could pay lower taxes than anywhere else in the European Union. The office would require only a couple of staff members, including one specialist in European finances, and an assistant. Learning these startling financial tricks made me determined to find similar situations in Asia. Savings like that could really shape the future organization of regional operations. It seemed to me that if Singapore was going to turn out to be the Belgium of the East, I'd better learn about it before we established offices in Bangkok or Kuala Lumpur.

"What about this last part?" Jan asked.

"The U.S. Department of Commerce estimates that by 2010 exports to 12 big emerging markets (BEMs) will exceed those to both Europe and Japan. Among these are the Chinese economic area, which includes Taiwan and Hong Kong, South Korea, Indonesia, Vietnam, India, South Africa, Turkey, Poland, Mexico, Argentina, Chile, and Brazil," I read from the notes I'd prepared. "I think Jennifer will jump at the chance to explore joint venture opportunities and market expansion in half those places. First we'll send her to eastern Europe for Poland, the Czech Republic, and Hungary, then to Argentina, Chile, and Brazil, and last to China, Southeast Asia, Malaysia, and Indonesia. Maybe Maria can go with her to South America and Yoshi can accompany her to Asia." I reclaimed my outline, folded up my notes, and sat down on the couch.

"Did you skip a section besides finance?" Jan asked.

I pulled my notes back out. Leave it to a lawyer. "Yeah. We need a new breed of manager, people born elsewhere, or married to foreigners, or educated overseas, as Michelle and Jeff have been. We need more sophisticated thinkers, people who won't buy the idea that there is something wrong with our company closing plants in the States."

Jan raised her eyebrow.

"Come on, you know that putting production and some finance overseas is rational. And so is the idea that a French guy, well, umm," I backpedaled hastily—"it's conceivable that a foreigner could do a better job as VP international than I am doing. So part of my job is to select HIPO managers from our overseas operations and groom them to fit into Plasmatec's California culture. Global companies need global leadership. So we form personnel committees for each region and ask them to identify high-potential employees. The HIPOs will take part in an International Exchange Program (IEP) designed to bring young foreign HIPOs to the United States and to various regional headquarters to serve one-year special assignments, and American HIPOs serve overseas. The focus of the IEP is to help future leaders learn a global perspective and better understand Plasmatec culture.

"Meanwhile, longer expatriate assignments for more seasoned managers will be designed to respond to work needs, but certainly Plasmatec in Santa Cruz will benefit from the global perspective other nationals will add. And, of course, having Americans manage companies overseas promotes the American and Plasmatec cultural ethic."

"Can you track the Plasmatec stats to check whether they support that assertion?" Jan asked.

"That'll be built in too. Once a year, two global task forces will be formed to help the company solve international problems and to explore global opportunities. I'll supervise the teams, but their reports will go to the Executive Committee, to be sure they get attention at the top. Incidentally, this will increase the visibility of the HIPOs on the team. I'm thinking that will be essential for the development and high profile of the stars we recruit from our overseas offices. We can't promote people we don't know."

In addition to recruiting Jan's competent and intelligent advice, I took the opportunity to hire UCLA Professor Karl Davidson, the man who had helped me negotiate both my contract and my return ticket stateside, as a consultant. I needed his opinion on personnel organization and global expansion. My gut instinct was that management was the main bottleneck; our research, design, production, and marketing talent was good. How could I maximize management?

While lunching at Robert's, a Middle Eastern deli in LA, Karl and I talked about the fine line between decentralizing just enough and decentralizing to the point of missing out on global synergies. Certainly the trouncing our machine-tooling industry took at the hands of the Japanese in the seventies led us all to adopt the motto, decentralize or die. Overcontrolling from headquarters constrains competitive advantage; that much is clear. An ideal company is fast in production, logistics, research and development, and customer service. Speed requires excellent local management and decentralized team-based decision making.

"Still, to overlook the advantage of economies of scale and cross-boundary but within-company collaboration is foolhardy," Karl reminded me. "It's possible, at least regionally, to share research and development, manufacturing, distribution, even some marketing research and advertising, as well as common administrative services, financial and tax programs, information technology, and personnel services. Just as important, it's possible to benefit from the different know-how of diverse businesses and functions."

"And your point about regional sharing . . ."

". . . would include the necessity of leaving space for local innovation that takes culture and taste into account. You probably wouldn't use a coed beach volleyball game in an athletic shoe commercial in Jordan."

"Plenty of sand there," I cracked. "And, more to the point, if we plan to sell surgical instruments in the developing world, we'll start with reusable, sturdy versions of the ones we're touting as practically disposable in France."

"Exactly." Karl reached for a lemon slice. "And if you discover that yellow is bad feng shui, you might not want to use your normal cheery American packaging on the outside. In general, Asians like things wrapped and rewrapped anyway, so hiring an Asian marketing consultant is unavoidable."

"Asia," I said, my mind on great vistas of people willing to work for the price of the ice in my soda.

"The next great marketing frontier," Karl agreed, misunderstanding my intent.

"One day, yes, of course," I said. "I was just thinking how lucky we are to be in a position to hire workers in China for $1.50 per hour to make products we plan to sell in Europe where the marketplace pays $20 per hour. How long before China's wages normalize?"

"Frankly," Karl said, "We can only take advantage of this situation because tools like modern transportation, e-mail, fax, telephone, and video conferencing make it possible to coordinate a complex global operation. Meanwhile, the ready availability of these tools makes it likely the Asian wage will catch up far faster in the next century than it has in the last one. It isn't just a matter of doping out the right place to manufacture and the right market to sell in, and then resting on your laurels. The key to competing in a global economy is always going to be cultural adaptability, quality, good price, and service."

"Which means, decentralize enough to maximize speed, and synchronize operations enough to maximize global synergies. *Got* it."

I took these ideas of Karl's back to the office to kick around with my brilliant team. It felt just great to finally be able to pay Karl for his input—I'd owed him big time just about long enough. And, of course, it was the company that paid him; I had had the good fortune to count him in my network and he had benefited from my advancement in the company.

Jennifer had too. She was thrilled to be out of the new-product marketing task force and back on international issues. She and Maria hit it off very well, and we spent long hours over pizza and take-out Thai debating how the principles of international management applied to Plasmatec. We told stories from the field and picked apart the well-known global strategies of big companies like Johnson & Johnson. The man who had shared with me the secrets of the Belgian tax shelter his company used had also told me about a form of organization they called "business management." His company was a *Fortune* 500 firm with a reputation for global competitiveness that he felt was well deserved, and due in great part to their good planning.

This company's strategy pivoted on the assumption that the best way to balance decentralization and economies of scale was to locate each of the main businesses in that place in the world where the biggest market or the most complex operations existed. My friend's own office was located in Brussels because the European market yielded the most profit, and the two key production facilities were in Germany and France. So the global business manager and his two assistants (who were all Europeans) spent time traveling to headquarters in the States, but key managers in the United States, Brazil, Japan, and elsewhere also trekked over to Belgium to consult the European operations.

My friend maintained that synergies could be maximized at a regional organizational level: in his company that meant there were VPs for North and South America, Asia, and Europe (which included the Middle East, Africa, and eastern Europe). The European VP was responsible for coordinating the office in Brussels, a finance office in Switzerland, and the plants in France and Germany, in addition to key distribution centers located in Scandinavia, the UK, Holland, Dubai, and Pretoria. A task force of European marketing managers directed common market research and advertising campaigns, and hardware and software technologies were coordinated by a separate task force. The company shared some administrative services (financial, accounting, personnel, government relations) with other parts of the parent corporation, permitting economies of scale.

However, local managers were empowered to interact with customers, to propose innovations in product application, and, of course, to motivate and manage their people in competition with other local employers. The local managers were very influential and could attract significant financial resources from the company if they had sound ideas and a good track record.

I laid out all these ideas to Jennifer, Maria, and Yoshi, and they shared theirs with me. Maria had trained in Brazil with a Brit who ran the Latin American office of a medium-sized computer software company whose parent corporation was

American. Their organization was appealingly simple and hinged on the idea that financial targets were the bottom line, and the home culture was the language on the accounts sheet, as it were. In other words, the manager was given corporate support as needed and was expected to meet clearly defined financial targets while maintaining the corporate culture of the parent company. To that end, her boss had spent three years in the U.S. headquarters in Boston, learning the American way. His company even had a culture statement outlining how they worked: the values, the limits, the taboos.

"Sounds like a control trip," I observed.

"No-no-no-no," Maria corrected me. "His input was valued. He was invited to key manager meetings in Boston designed to update the finer points of their corporate culture. And the only assessment method was a pair of critical report forms, not too complicated, which he filled out and submitted monthly, detailing productivity, quality control results, and reported customer satisfaction. He felt part of the strategy-making process and was committed to the direction the company was taking. And apart from that—the cultural indoctrination, the report forms, and the bottom line—he ran his own business."

The more I thought about that, the more it appealed to me. Since we were a medium-sized firm, it seemed best to go with a simple and decentralized form of organization, with an emphasis on clear strategy, clear cultural guidelines, a financial target, and a straightforward reporting system. If I could combine that vision with my earlier plan to use a common computer tracking system for filling orders and obtaining supplies, I would benefit both from the synergy of sharing common needs and the flexibility of giving local leaders plenty of autonomy.

As we hammered out a strategy to submit to Tom and Doc, I reflected again on how lucky I'd been to be able to lose George and pick up Jennifer. We were leaning toward partnering between our office (International Operations) and Human Resources for the purpose of training managers and HIPOs from at home and abroad in Plasmatec culture. Jennifer and Maria were good friends with Deborah Newell at HR, and Deborah had finally fully accepted me within a couple of weeks of Jennifer's installation in my office. I knew off the record that she'd be delighted to undertake a more active role in teaching Plasmatec culture. "Isn't teaching inevitably the best way to modify it?" she asked, and while in principle the culture, or at least the culture statement, would be hammered out with a lot of input from everyone, I could certainly see her point.

Our management plan included an emphasis on global task forces. We planned to invite key managers from abroad to spend time in Santa Cruz, taking in our distinctive corporate culture and getting face time with the people responsible for developing and promoting them. We defined new performance appraisal and selection criteria to emphasize global competencies, including language ability, familiarity with other cultures, flexibility, and creativity, as well as the more traditional qualities of entrepreneurship and personal initiative. The exchange program I'd discussed with Jan would permit us to develop future global leaders, people who could work well on cross-country task forces and utilize the already existing informal networks within our little company. We were not about to let local leaders hoard their best people!

Lastly, we were committed to using global leveraging to increase profits via more efficient manufacturing, shared research and development, market research, and advertising (which would be shared at the regional level), and the currency exchange hedging and tax shelters I'd outlined earlier. I liked the way the ideas I'd garnered on management dovetailed with the dreams I had for Plasmatec.

I called Karl again, this time as the best qualified critic of my team's efforts. I arranged to have him join Jennifer, Maria, Yoshi, and me in San Francisco to review the draft of our plan. We hoped to come out of this meeting with a proposal for Tom and Doc, a proposal we ultimately hoped to put before the Executive Committee.

The morning before our lunch with Karl in San Francisco was a hectic one. I had charts to prepare, a glitch on the laptop's program to iron out, and two meetings. But because my secretary understands that Doc comes first, she connected him. "Matt," said Doc, "I've got a brilliant young Pakistani engineer in production who, if I'm any judge of character, looks to me like a future Plasmatec manager. He's lived in Pakistan, India, Singapore, Germany, and the States, and his wife is German. He was trained at the Indian Institute of Management and has all the right moves. Tom and I would like him to work in your section, but under the supervision of Jennifer, who will be responsible for grooming him. If you could just keep your eye on the work she does with him, we'd be pleased. I'll send Tariq Hussein up to see you and Jennifer. Appreciate your help, Matt." As Doc hung up, I dropped my anxious consideration of all the details necessary to make the morning meetings come off flawlessly. For an instant I could really see the unending circle of people, managing and being managed. Maybe I was about to meet the *future* vice president international of Plasmatec.

QUESTIONS FOR DISCUSSION

1. What else should Matt be doing in his role as VP international at Plasmatec? What responsibilities would you eliminate? What would you emphasize? What would you keep the same?
2. How would you organize and staff the international office at Plasmatec? What would you do differently? Which of Matt's ideas seem particularly worthwhile?
3. What are the key issues underlying the broad global strategy Matt has outlined for Plasmatec?
4. Matt has begun to outline a strategy for Plasmatec. How would your proposals differ from Matt's?

PART

II

Conceptual Lessons

USEFUL CONCEPTS

The following management topics are related to Chapter 1 and discussed here:

- Individual values
- Cultural values
- Comparative values
- Dual-career couple issues

Knowing Your Values: Their Relationship to Management

This first chapter introduces the main characters and their views on various issues. The purpose is not just to familiarize you with the characters. It is also to get you to think about some issues that Matt and Jan have already confronted and will continue to deal with throughout the book. Although the issues you will cope with in your own personal and professional life may differ in kind or degree, the challenges Matt and Jan face here are typical of those most couples confront when trying to manage their careers individually and collectively.

Individual Values

Values are one of the central drives in our lives. In any setting, our choices are driven by a number of factors—our goals, the contextual factors influencing us, and certainly our values (out of which grow our goals and that determine largely to what extent contextual factors do influence us and how). In international business, a number of situations may put us (and our values—individual and cultural) in contact with others of differing individual and cultural values: as an expatriate living in a foreign country; working with an inpatriate in a firm within our own country; as a salesperson, purchasing agent, or technician, in contact with a foreigner via e-mail, telephone, and so on.

Regardless of the form of contact, how each of us analyzes a situation, argues a position, and communicates is influenced significantly by our personal values. In short, our effectiveness as an individual within a multicultural context will be determined largely by our values and our awareness of those values.

In the space provided, name two or three values that you believe are central to who you are, how you conduct your life, why you make the decisions you make, and so on.

_____

_____

_____

_____

_____

_____

_____

_____

In addition to the previous ways of understanding our personal values, the following may be helpful.

Family Origins. Our values are determined to a great extent by our family origins. In this case, Jan's upbringing in rural Maine has obviously influenced her individual values. She loves and appreciates the outdoors and participated extensively in outdoor activities as she grew up, especially with her father. Her love and respect for the environment has spilled over into her choice of professions—environmental law—as it did her university extracurricular activities at UT-Austin. In addition, her closeness to her family is clear, which probably stems from her very close relationship with her family, particularly with her father.

These two factors—love for the environment and her concept of family and its importance—can be seen as constant values in her life as she makes choices throughout the book.

Name the one, two, or three values you think you have acquired or had reinforced as a result of having been reared in your family environment:

_____

_____

_____

_____

_____

_____

Our individual values are also related to gender and generational issues. Matt's fairly clear view on traditional roles is probably related to the fact that he is male and grew up in a family where the father was the primary "breadwinner"; although Jan has a strong passion for her work and obvious intellectual capability, her view on marriage and its importance seems to override her personal ambition (unlike Matt). Is this attitude related to gender? That is debatable.

In terms of generational issues that help form our values, both Matt and Jan are products of the late sixties. Typical values that initially came out of that era include a freedom from traditional thinking and values, and a rethinking of the purpose of one's life or at least a refocusing on that purpose. Love, peace, and fraternity were the bywords of the hippie generation. These values seem to have been lost as that generation entered the reality of professionalism and the work force.

How have your gender and the generation in which you were born influenced your values and perspective?

_____

_____

_____

_____

_____

_____

_____

Birth-Order Effects. Some evidence indicates that individuals differ based partly on their order in the birth line. First-born children can be obsessed with feelings of responsibility and expectations of perfection; middle-born children often sense fewer "parental" responsibilities than first born, but because they're sandwiched between other children, they learn values of compromise and negotiation skills; last-born children are often said to be the most relaxed and care-free. Because of a more relaxed parenting, perhaps, they learn that work and responsibility should be balanced with fun and relaxation.

In addition, different cultures place different obligations or expectations on individuals according to their different birth order. In U.S. Caucasian culture, the oldest child in the family typically is expected to provide an example to the others, and some supervision. In Hispanic and Asian cultures, generally the eldest has more formal responsibilities toward younger siblings. The behavior of younger brothers and sisters is clearly a reflection of the older children in the family as well as the parents and extended family.

Of course, the rewards can be greater also for the eldest in the family of non-Caucasian cultures. Often the principal or entire inheritance goes to the eldest male child.

Explain how you think your birth order has influenced your values and personal beliefs:

_____

_____

_____

_____

_____

_____

_____

_____

Career Orientations. We can also examine our values by evaluating our career interests. When we make choices about jobs, switching companies, returning to school for another degree, for example, those choices are typically driven by our orientation (see Chapter 12). However, it could be useful even at this early stage to begin thinking about how Matt's and Jan's personalities and values focused around their professions have encouraged certain choices they have made. Certainly, Jan is driven by passion for her work. Matt must also have a certain amount of passion. He appears to want to make a difference in what he does, but not for social reasons.

As time passes, it will become clear whether these values are stable ones and whether others surface.

Integrate Your Personal Values. Reflect on your primary values in light of the discussion here. These might include attaining professional success, developing a good character, acquiring material wealth, having a family-centered life, and so on.

In the space provided, as you review your answers to the previous questions about values, beliefs, and perspectives, note the underlying commonalities and explain them here:

_____

_____

_____

_____

_____

_____

A discussion of our individual values, however, would be incomplete without discussing them within the context of larger cultural values we are exposed to every day.

Cultural Values

What larger cultural values do Jan and Matt represent? What about your own cultural values? In other words, what is U.S. culture as Matt and Jan might reflect it? What are the cultural values of other members of your class as reflected in their personal values? What are those values and philosophies that bind those that live in the United States (or any other country), despite regional, ethnic, and urban-rural differences?

Describe what you believe is the essence of U.S. culture in terms of the *most fundamental values:*

_____

_____

_____

_____

_____

_____

_____

_____

In discussing mainstream U.S. culture and major regional differences, do Matt and Jan exemplify these regional values and philosophies? Can you support your answers with evidence from the text?

Assessing Your Own Cultural Orientation

Use the following two instruments to help you understand your own cultural orientation.

Low- and High-Context Assessment

Directions: Read each statement and determine to what degree you agree with the statement on a scale of 1 to 5. Put your number in the blank to the left of the statement:

    1 = You strongly disagree
    2 = You generally disagree
    3 = You are somewhat neutral
    4 = You generally agree
    5 = You strongly agree

____ 1. I typically find myself much more preoccupied with making short-term plans (i.e., what I'm going to do this weekend) than long-term ones (i.e., what I'm planning on doing or being in several years). (reverse)

____ 2. In my spare time, I am more likely to be found doing something by myself than with others. (reverse)

____ 3. I probably feel more comfortable having a clearly defined place that is mine where I can control whom I interact with.

___ 4. When someone is correcting me, I would rather the person just tell me what he or she doesn't like and not make "suggestions." (reverse)

___ 5. My natural work style is to finish one thing before moving on to the next. (reverse)

___ 6. A commitment I have made to others is more likely to supersede one I've made to myself. (reverse)

___ 7. I feel comfortable talking about subjects like my future, my family, and so on, with most people, even if I have only known them a short while. (reverse)

___ 8. I prefer having things completely spelled out from the beginning than to start operating without an overview of the situation. (reverse)

___ 9. I dislike it when things don't go according to plans.

___ 10. I have several really close friends who are friends for life rather than a lot of friends who come and go in my life.

___ 11. Beyond knowing my first name, I consider my age, my family status, my profession (or my parents' professions) as private matters reserved for only a few close friends.

___ 12. I would feel more uncomfortable having a contract that *doesn't* list every detail pertaining to the agreement than to have some "gray" areas which would require negotiating later on. (reverse)

___ 13. Changing plans—even at the last minute—is no problem for me.

___ 14. A fair amount of my spare time is spent phoning or writing friends I don't see often.

___ 15. Having a hedge or wall around my house would seem too confining to me. (reverse)

___ 16. It is usually better to call "a spade a spade" (be direct) than to hide a situation's "true colors" (be indirect). (reverse)

___ 17. It bothers me when I am late to appointments. (reverse)

___ 18. If I had some significant problems I needed help solving, I have any number of individuals I could easily turn to for help.

___ 19. Those I term my "best friends" know just about everything about me and I would never have a problem telling them things that are very very personal.

___ 20. If my boss or teacher were wrong, I would be more likely to tell her or him than to simply suggest there might be another answer. (reverse)

Scoring directions: Add up your points according to the categories listed (Time Dimension, Relationships Dimension, etc.). If it indicates to reverse—to score the item, do the following:

If you put 1 for that question, score it 5.
If you put 2 for that question, score it 4.
If you put 3 for that question, do not change the score.
If you put 4 for that question, score it 2.
If you put 5 for that question, score it 1.

Time Dimension: 1, 5, 9, 13, 17 (25 points possible)
Relationships Dimension: 2, 6, 10, 14, 18 (25 points possible)
Space Dimension: 3, 7, 11, 15, 19 (25 points possible)
Communication Dimension: 4, 8, 12, 16, 20 (25 points possible)

Add up the points for each dimension individually. Then total the subtotal scores you developed from the individual dimensions to arrive at a total score to indicate your overall cultural tendency.

Interpretation of Score

1. For each subdimension, the total number of points possible is 25. Although it is difficult to develop absolute cut-off values and interpret those values with complete confidence, the following provides a guide:

20–25: high
15–19: medium
10–14: low

Time Dimension—the lower the score, the more you tend to be preoccupied with time, sequential in your process, and generally shorter-term in perspective. The higher the score, the less you are preoccupied with time, the more parallel processing you do, and the longer-term perspective you have.

Relationships Dimension—the higher the score, the more relationships hold a central place in your life. You spend more time developing them and maintaining them than others do. The lower the score, the more tasks usually claim a central role and the development and maintenance of relationships are somewhat peripheral. This does not mean you do not value relationships; it simply means relative to other people, you value task accomplishment more than they and therefore your time and energy is not oriented toward relationships as much.

Space Dimension—the lower the score, the more open you are emotionally/psychologically, and therefore the more open with physical boundaries as well. Information about you that others might consider private, you can divulge fairly comfortably. You also are physically more accessible to strangers in that you might allow them into your home or give them a lift if hitch-hiking more easily than others. In essence your "personal" space is more open; you are more approachable by more people with varying ranges of familiarity.

Communication Dimension—the lower the score, the more explicit (direct and specific) you are and you like others to be toward you. You dislike having to wonder what people mean by their indirect statements and you would likely push them to be more specific.

2. For a total score and its interpretation, add up the scores for each dimension.

If you scored: 80–100: You are a high-context person
60–79: You are a medium-context person
40–59: You are a low-context person

Simply put, a low-context person is mostly driven by tasks and their accomplishment, generally views the development and maintenance of relationships as more of a hindrance, or at least more of a means than an end, and because the "task" is so important, appreciates directness and explicitness. This individual also dislikes hierarchy and sees it as a barrier to communication and knowledge, both of which are necessary to "get things done."

A high-context person, in contrast, places high value on relationships and sees them more as ends than means, although they might indeed be valued as part of a network that allows task accomplishments. As a result, much of this individual's time is spent cultivating and maintaining those relationships. Because relationships are so central, maintaining harmony among them is critical; therefore, avoiding direct and explicit statements that might offend someone is typical. When these relationships are developed, a clearer boundary develops between who is "in" your circle and who is not. As a result, those who are not part of your circle are not trusted as much and are excluded from "accessing" you or those in your circle. Hierarchy or other ways of defining and differentiating groups (we-they) are typical with high-context cultures. (See Hall, 1976, for a more detailed discussion of this theory.)

Hofstede's Dimensions

Directions: Read each statement and determine to what degree you agree with the statement on a scale of 1 to 5:

> 1 = You strongly disagree
> 2 = You generally disagree
> 3 = You are somewhat neutral
> 4 = You generally agree
> 5 = You strongly agree

___ 1. Careful planning is necessary to maximize life's potential.
___ 2. Competition is probably the essential component for progress.
___ 3. One's individuality should be prized and protected. (reverse)
___ 4. Equal rights for everyone is fundamental to a society. (reverse)
___ 5. Traditions are critical to any group and help give it identity.
___ 6. Taking risks is just "part of the game" and a necessary part of gaining advantage. (reverse)
___ 7. Quality of life is determined more by good relationships than by personal achievement and success. (reverse)
___ 8. Security is found in numbers more than in any individual's capabilities.
___ 9. It would be perfectly acceptable to disagree with your manager/professor.
___ 10. I would rather take a long time to plan something and to ensure a good result even if I am not as fast as someone else.

___ 11. Stability and security are more important to me than change and potential opportunity.
___ 12. Life without personal ambition would be unfulfilling.
___ 13. Your identification as a member of a group is essential to your well-being.
___ 14. It is important to know your place in society in order to know how to behave.
___ 15. Usually what is right depends on the situation more than on any absolute truths.
___ 16. Revolutions should always be considered as a potentially desirable way to change things.
___ 17. In all honesty, I would have to say that my behavior reflects that I live to work more than I work to live.
___ 18. Achievement is largely a result of individual accomplishment. (reverse)
___ 19. Those in higher positions are entitled to more rights than those below them.
___ 20. It is better to act quickly to hopefully take advantage of apparent opportunities than to take more time to analyze things to make sure it's really going to work out.
___ 21. Rules and regulations are absolutely necessary.
___ 22. Survival of the fittest is better than creating a society where dependence reigns.
___ 23. I get more pleasure out of achieving something on my own than accomplishing something in a group. (reverse)
___ 24. A boss and her or his employee are more peers than they are superior-subordinate. (reverse)
___ 25. Knowing history really doesn't help one avoid repeating mistakes. (reverse)

Scoring directions: Add up your points according to the categories (under "Questions Related to Each Dimension"). If the question indicates to reverse score the item (reverse), do the following:

If you put 1, score it 5.
If you put 2, score it 4.
If you put 3, score it 3.
If you put 4, score it 2.
If you put 5, score it 1.

Questions Related to Each Dimension

Uncertainty Avoidance: 1, 6, 11, 16, 21 (25 points possible)
Masculinity-Femininity: 2, 7, 12, 17, 22 (25 points possible)
Individualism-Collectivism: 3, 8, 13, 18, 23 (25 points possible)
Power Distance: 4, 9, 14, 19, 24 (25 points)
Short-term/Long-term: 5, 10, 15, 20, 25 (25 points possible)

Interpretation of Score

For each dimension you scored 20–25 points, you are high on that dimension.
For each dimension you scored 15–19 points, you are medium on that dimension.
For each dimension you scored below 15 points, you are low on that dimension.

Uncertainty Avoidance—Scoring high on this dimension means that you strive to avoid uncertainty. Ambiguity, lack of clarity, and so on, bothers you a great deal; you push for clarification.

Masculinity-Femininity—Scoring high on this dimension means you are more "masculine," that is, the more you work to live, place importance on professional success, believe competition is good, and so on.

Individualism/Collectivism—Scoring high on this dimension means you view an individual more as part of a group or groups than as an individual. People's roles are defined more by their group membership than by individual desires or ambitions. A higher value is placed on developing and maintaining harmony in your relationships.

Power Distance—Scoring high on this dimension means you see individuals as part of groups that are differentiated by their power, as in a hierarchy. Rights, privileges, and opportunities are not equal among people, and perhaps should not be.

Short-term/Long-term (Confucian Dynamism)—Scoring high on this dimension means you ascribe to the belief that truths can be relative, that what is right or wrong can easily be situation-dependent. You view life in the long term and your efforts reflect that. You are more willing to invest time now for the future than looking for a quick return. For you, stability is essential either to maintain time-tested traditions or in order to set goals, plan, and act to accomplish those goals.

(See Hofstede, 1991, for a more detailed discussion of this model.)

Comparative Values

Understanding your individual and your culture's values are important to understanding underlying influences on your behavior. It is also very helpful in understanding other cultures as well. Research and experience have clearly shown that cultures differ in their values. The following highlights some aspects of African and Russian culture. A number of aspects of both cultures are clearly different from that of Western cultures. The challenge for a Westerner would be to understand the differences in cultures and then be able to manage those differences. (This does not assume all Western cultures are alike; they're not.)

a. African cultural values relevant to management:

Attitude toward authority: African societies tend to be very paternalistic and hierarchical. They are egalitarian within the same age group but hierarchical from one group to another with clear subordination for those younger members within each group.

Attitude toward commitment: Often for Africans to commit themselves to someone requires several witnesses. These witnesses may well be asked to remember the facts of the situation at the time the commitment was made. Particularly in Saharan societies, personal commitment can be counted on. One's honor is one's word.

Attitude toward decision making: Reaching a consensus is critical in most African societies. They tend to seek unanimity and prolong discussions for hours or days in order to reach consensus. Judgments made by authorities tend to reflect the consensus reached.

Attitude toward labor: Given that African societies are very communal, and that "who" you know is often more important than "what" you know, social bonds are paramount. As a result, what is often regarded as laziness is actual constructive relationship-building activities, serving to reinforce the social bonds that exist. Farmers, for example, tend to adopt innovations only when the expected increase in economic terms does not destroy or change existing social bonds.

Conclusions about management given the preceding attitudes: Managing an African could obviously be very different from managing an American who has learned the attitudes typical in the United States: questioning of authority, commitment based on individual values, decision making that can easily be shared with those lower in the hierarchy, and a high emphasis on "what" you know as based on degrees and/or performance.

(For an interesting reference to African (Malawian) management tendencies, see Jones, 1986.)

b. Russian cultural values relevant to management:

Leadership and power: In traditional Russian society (until the revolution in 1917), power was in a few autocrats. The vestiges of that in modern Russian society are still reflected in a very centralized leadership style. This is contrary to a Western, Anglo style of shared power.

Responsibility: Because power was centralized, responsibility has traditionally been considered to rest with those in power. This has resulted in micro-management and macro-puppets. Workers were rewarded for following rules meticulously. Although those in this former system are trying to grow away from this mentality, it is not easy given the generations of workers so trained and rewarded. In Western societies, delegation of authority and, in part, the responsibility is more typical.

Motivation: Russians have been raised to not sense personal responsibility in the workplace and therefore lack the accompanying motivation. The economy has traditionally planned centrally. The workers' responsibility has been to carry out what was already planned. There have been no incentives for producing more or a better quality, and there has been no real punishment for doing less than is "required." The absence of a market environment in Russia has created a wide gap between Western management and Russian management styles. This difference is evident in the difficulty Russians are having today in trying to change to a market environment management mentality.

(For more information on these topics about Russians, see Puffer, 1994 A and B.)

Comparing Values and Behaviors: Cross-Cultural Incidents Exercise

Directions: For each of the following incidents, explain how you would react.

1. You have met with two French representatives three times now to discuss a business deal. Apart from the talk of the business venture, you have also discussed politics, sports, and even family vacations. They seem to enjoy their time with you, sometimes discussing things very intensely and other times joking appropriately. They continue to call you by your last name (Mr. Johnson; Mrs. Luong, Miss Connelly, etc.). How would you react and how would you refer to them? Why?

_____

_____

_____

_____

_____

2. You have made a business trip to South America, visiting company representatives in Venezuela, Chile, and Argentina. Each time you have arrived on time to the appointment but your host has either returned from other business very late or let another meeting with someone run as much as 45 minutes into your time. What is your reaction?

_____

_____

_____

_____

_____

3. Your firm imports and mills exotic wood from various Asian suppliers. One of them is a Malaysian forest company. You have received trees that are

slightly under the quality you have contracted for. This means you must either sell them to clients requesting lower grade lumber or refuse them. To try to correct the problem for the future, how would you go about it?

_____

_____

_____

_____

_____

4. You are a construction supervisor in Botswana in charge of building a tunnel through a small mountain. This will cut the transportation time in half from the capital to a series of outlying cities. You are under a tight deadline to finish the project. Already there have been several unforeseen delays. One of your Botswanian workers comes to you and says he needs time off to help take care of his sister who is ill. How would you react?

_____

_____

_____

_____

_____

Dual-Career Couple Issues

Understanding your own and other cultures is important to good self-management. As you come in contact with other cultures, you need to make decisions that reflect a balance in your needs, others' needs, and the requirements of the task. One of those "others' needs" increasingly in most societies means your spouse or "partner." Because increasing numbers of dual-career families characterize the work force, it also affects decisions related to managing a career in an international environment. We will see this through Matt's and Jan's career decisions in later chapters.

In the first chapter, however, Matt and Jan have the difficult decision of determining whether they will remain separated while he is going to school at UCLA. At this point in their careers, typical of people their age, their focus is on their own career development. Matt decides it would be best for him to get his MBA.

Although he could get the degree in the Bay Area, he doesn't apply to all the possible schools in that area. Instead, his choice of program reflects his career objectives of moving into marketing and thus he selects programs with the best marketing programs.

Similarly, Jan has just begun her career and in a firm where she could apply her energy and efforts to the environmental causes she so believes in. With any career, there is an initial investment of getting to know co-workers, understanding the various available resources, having others connect with you, and so on. Jan feels she has begun an important investment in a cause she believes and she does not want to surrender her progress. In any professional environment, the norm of working hard the first few years to "pay your dues" and demonstrate competence is typical. As a result, Matt and Jan make the difficult decision to live somewhat separate lives during the "MBA" years.

As with all experiences, however, they both learn something important about themselves relative to the importance of their careers. They decide that if there is a next time, they will not put their careers first; instead, they will put their marriage first.

Dual-Career Decision Issues. Issues related to dual-career family decision-making are complex. Trying to balance career and family needs results in internal and external strains. The inner strain refers to the balancing of career and family and the external comes from comparing one's chosen lifestyle against what one considers the "normal" lifestyle along with societal pressures for valuing achievement and career mobility.

The decision-making process that dual-career couples use to determine career moves, including long-distance commuting, has not been thoroughly studied yet. Models have been developed but not adequately researched. Nonetheless, questions a dual-career couple should ask themselves about the decision-making process include the following (Anderson & Spruill, 1993):

1. What was the initial issue that raised the question whether to commute or not?
2. What alternatives were considered as options in this decision process?
3. What information was collected and from whom prior to making a decision?
4. How was the information evaluated?
5. What was the reaction to the decision and to the implementation of the decision?
6. What re-evaluation process was used to reclarify the appropriateness of the decision?

Examining Matt and Jan's decision process should be instructive and for those of you who are married or have a "significant other," think about these questions in the context of one of your major decisions.

The common denominator to what drove Matt and Jan's decision was each individual's career commitment. This limited the information gathered and probably would have been used to selectively ignore information collected had they done a thorough search, including talking to other long-distance commuter married couples.

One study (Anderson, 1992) showed that commuter life is desirable for couples that are characterized by the following:

- less family financial burden
- greater perceived family well-being
- being at the later stages of the family life cycle

Other suggestions based on research from this study for dual-career couples considering a commuter marriage include (1) strength of the independent nature of each partner, (2) the degree to which couples are systematic in their decision making (the more systematic the better), (3) the time frame set to reevaluate the commuter marriage decision.

Other variables that can affect such decisions include the following:

1. Stage of your family life cycle.
2. Division of labor between spouses/partners.
3. Length of commute.
4. Time separated.
5. Stage of career development.
6. Commitment to career and marriage.
7. Available support networks.
8. Individual personalities and values.
9. Extent of company support.

One research study (Anderson & Spruill, 1993) found the following when couples evaluated whether to accept a long-distance commuter relationship:

1. 49% of the couples considered one spouse changing his or her career or taking a lower status job.
2. 38% seriously considered leaving things as they were rather than changing.
3. 28% considered one spouse quitting his or her career altogether.
4. 10% considered both spouses' changing jobs and moving to a third location.
5. 10% considered commuting only because there was a time limit on the commute.
6. 5% considered termination of their marriage.

The same study found the following interesting statistics:

1. 62% of the couples said each spouse was in total agreement with the commute.
2. 26% said there wasn't total agreement and the next phase of their career was in negotiation.
3. 12% were in complete disagreement over the commute issue.
4. 40% reported being satisfied with the decision.
5. 46% were resigned to the decision.
6. 4% expressed resentment.
7. 58% reported they had considerable difficulty making the decision and 42% said they had relatively little difficulty making it.

8. 66% said they had not set up any reevaluation time when they would reconsider their decision.
9. 51% felt the commute was beneficial to their career and 46% felt it was positive for the well-being of their family.

Of those who end their commute, the following was found:

1. 46% of the wives move to the husbands' location.
2. 38% of the husbands move to live with their wife.
3. 8% of the couples move to a third location.
4. 9% of the couples end up divorcing.

CONCLUSION

This chapter has focused on introducing: (1) the main characters in the book, (2) the difficulty of managing a dual-career family, (3) the importance of self- and cultural-awareness, and (4) the reality that being an effective cross-cultural manager also means good self-management and (if married) marriage-management.

References

Anderson, E. (1992). Decision-making style: Impact on satisfaction of the commuter couples' lifestyle. *Journal of Family and Economic Issues,* 13 (1): 5–21.

Anderson, E., & Spruill, J. (1993). The dual-career commuter family: A lifestyle on the move. *Marriage and Family Review,* 19(1/2):131–147.

Hall, E. (1976). Beyond culture. Garden City, NY.: Doubleday.

Hofstede, G. (1991). *Cultures and organizations: Software of the mind.* London: McGraw-Hill.

Jones, M. (1986). Management development: An African focus. *Journal of the Association for Management Education and Development,* 17 (3):202–216.

Puffer, S. (1994a). Understanding the bear: A portrait of Russian business leaders. *Academy of Management Executive,* 8 (1):18–29.

Puffer, S. (1994b). A riddle wrapped in an enigma: Demystifying Russian managerial motivation. *European Management Journal,* 11(4):473–480.

CHAPTER 2

USEFUL CONCEPTS

For nearly all of the developed countries, most of their economic growth is outside their own domestic markets. Although some firms remain focused on domestic markets, most divide their attention between domestic and foreign markets. This evolution has changed how organizations approach their own growth and organizational structures. When to go international and how to organize to target international markets are essential identity questions a firm must address.

This chapter explores whether MedTech is ready to enter the international business arena (or even if they're not really ready, do they have a choice?). The two areas of focus in this chapter are these:

- MedTech and its product and organizational life cycles and where MedTech is in that process.
- MedTech's human resource experience relative to the international marketplace, particularly as reflected in their negotiation style.

MedTech and Its Product and Organizational Life Cycle

A common model of product and organizational life cycle describes the following product life cycle stages:

Stage 1: A domestic firm with domestic production and domestic markets.

Product implications: a product to fit the taste of a domestic client.

Organization implications: a domestic structure only.

Stage 2: An exporting firm when domestic markets become saturated or when there is simply international demand; production is still usually domestic.

Product implications: a product that might or might not be adapted slightly to the foreign client(s). The adaptation might be required by the foreign country to conform to its regulations or the adaptation can be purely discretionary—to better suit the client's tastes.

Organization implications: the organization might develop an international division as the exports become increasingly important. The international division is the direct interface with the foreign markets and handles all the documentation and product distribution. Many firms do not develop a separate international division, however, and work through international brokers and agents.

Stage 3: An exporting firm with international production sites as foreign competition develops and pricing becomes a key focus.

Product implications: the product itself might remain the same but the production costs are less because labor is typically cheaper and the total product costs can be less if transportation from producer to consumer is lessened sharply. The product can become more cost competitive as a result.

Organization implications: the organization becomes a direct investor in a foreign country(ies) and now has foreign manufacturing sites. Foreign employees are hired. Knowledge of host laws becomes important.

Stage 4:   A firm with sales and production operations in its foreign markets to reduce manufacturing costs and to become closer to the clients.

Product implications: the product might reflect changes due to an increased focus on sales being closer to the foreign markets and trying to address foreign market requirements—required or discretionary.

Organization implications: structurally, the firm has foreign sales offices; firm-client response time might be much better to offer more effective service and better adapted products as a result of having physical sales presence in the foreign country.

Stage 5:   A firm with complete operations (production, sales, human resources, accounting, etc.) in one or more of its foreign markets where the structure could be a national, regional, or worldwide structure, or some combination of those.

Product implications: the focus at this point becomes acknowledging foreign markets as meriting complete attention; therefore, products might be adapted to a great extent if there is a national or regional focus, or, where the focus is at the world market level, products will be produced where supplies and manufacturing costs are the lowest in order to compete more by cost than by product adaptation. With some products, world-wide standardization of products and processes might occur.

Organization implications: in the product adaptation context, production and sales are closely tied and physically in the same country. The firm will have a corporate headquarters but might be quite decentralized in its market focus. In the product cost-reduction context, production and sales can be in separate countries. Having suppliers, producers, and sales in different locations requires a great deal of coordination effort that is not necessary when there is a national or regional focus. This operation is typically called a world-wide integration strategy and requires a centralized structure in order to administer the coordination.

Organizational Life Cycle Stages and MedTech. In which stage is MedTech? Because MedTech's product line could appeal to doctors anywhere in the world, MedTech is trying to break into the domestic and foreign markets somewhat simultaneously. MedTech might ask itself also if it should produce locally or in a foreign country with lower labor costs. During this time, MedTech has been approached by a Japanese firm. As a result, MedTech is thinking of jumping into stage 2 without having the experience of stage 1. Is this a wise move? A necessary but potentially dangerous move? What are the opportunities and risks of doing so? Your answer to the first question at the end of Chapter 2 should respond to these questions.

MedTech's Human Resource Experience in the International Marketplace: Negotiation Style

On the surface, MedTech lacks the product experience in the marketplace and it also lacks the experience in personnel to understand a completely new market, especially a foreign market. Matt is a novice and Jeff doesn't seem to know any more about the Japanese or doing business internationally than Matt. For example, even though Matt knows exchanging cards is an important ritual, he doesn't realize how or why that is the case. He seems ignorant that the Japanese take business cards with both hands and examine it out of respect to the giver and to determine that person's relative importance in the firm based on his title. Further, the fact that MedTech seemed to expect an answer from the Japanese at the end of their visit in Japan shows that MedTech is unaware of how Japanese make decisions and the time they take to make them.

From the lack of information given about the investors, and the lack of advice given to Jeff, we can conclude that none of them has any experience worth sharing with MedTech's top management. The question is to what degree this inexperience will play a negative role in their partnership should they join with the Japanese firm. Respond to these issues also in your answer to the third question at the end of Chapter 2.

Negotiations. The tendency in negotiations is for American businesspeople to lay everything out on the table and expect the other "team" to make a counteroffer. When no counter offer is immediately forthcoming, the silence typical of Japanese negotiators becomes too much for the Americans. They begin to add more information, repeat the offer, or even indirectly make suggestions of a counteroffer, themselves. As the Japanese maintain more silence, the Americans continue to talk, revealing more and more about their position. The Japanese listen until the other side has apparently explained most everything. Then they ask questions that can seemingly go on forever. They ask questions so they can understand as fully as possible the other side's position.

No decision is made by the Japanese after the initial negotiation session. Instead, those who were in the negotiations report the information and their impressions to others in the firm. In fact, often those in the negotiations do not have the decision-making power to fully represent the Japanese firm. After reporting to others in the Japanese firm, others' reactions, impressions, and questions are gathered for the second round of negotiations. This habit can have several iterations, so weeks or even months may go by before a decision is made. Slowly but surely, consensus in the Japanese firm is achieved. This time line might not fit the expectation of the other team. American businesspeople typically schedule a set number of days to visit the Japanese. Because the Japanese are not in as much of a hurry, it gives them a decided advantage. The American team, for example, feels compelled to arrive at a decision much earlier than the Japanese. As a result, when the time comes near to depart and the negotiations seem to have stalled (because the Japanese are still in their decision-making process), the Americans are likely to give more and more concessions in order to reach closure.

The Japanese firm very often has a third party in the negotiations, which might be invisible to the foreign negotiators. This third party might be the firm's bank or the government. A representative of the bank or the government might be present at some of the negotiations and might not.

Pierre Casse (1982), an intercultural communications expert, suggests the successful American negotiator do the following:

1. Know when to compromise.
2. Take a firm stand at the beginning of the negotiation.
3. Refuse to make concessions beforehand.
4. Avoid revealing more information than absolutely necessary.
5. Accept compromises only when negotiations are deadlocked.
6. Keep a maximum of options open before negotiations.

Casse also compares the negotiation styles of the Japanese and North Americans:

Japanese Style	North American Style
Values emotional sensitivity	Values logic
Hides emotions	Direct and fairly open
Uses power plays and conciliation	Uses arguments and litigation
Loyal to employer	Loyal to self, often above employer
Saving face is critical	Saving money is critical
Influenced by special interests openly	Hides influential special interests
Uses silence when troubled or when right	Fills up silence typically
Written information must be accurate	Written information should be accurate
Written contracts are flexible	Written contracts are in cement
Group's good is of most importance	Group is not considered as critical
Gets to know the other decision makers	Remains informal but impersonal also
Cultivates a good emotional social setting	Avoids mixing business and pleasure
Looks toward the long term	Oriented toward quick results

As you can see, the Japanese and North Americans characterize opposing styles that can seriously affect negotiations. We see much of this in the negotiations and posturing done by MedTech and Muhashi. MedTech is interested in sharing the facts, and tends to be direct and expect straightforward answers. They want to conclude a deal without getting to know their potential partners on a more personal level. The Japanese take their time, cull a great deal of information, mix social and business a lot, are indirect in many of their responses to protect the "group" (i.e., to not commit to something before all those who should be involved are consulted), and so on. (For an excellent discussion on decision making in Japanese firms, see Keeley, 1998.)

However, compare Casse's recommendations with those of Griffin and Daggatt (1990):

1. Build relationships; don't do deals.
2. Focus on interests, not positions.
3. Create and claim value.
4. Know yourself and the other negotiator.
5. Learn to communicate.
6. Listen.
7. Maintain contact.

Griffin and Daggatt's suggestions are much less strategic in a win-lose sense than Casse's. Instead, they are oriented more toward a win-win strategy.

Which approach would you suggest for MedTech? Which approach is Muhashi using?

Finally, Varner and Beamer (1995) combine several sources to explain a number of important issues that must be considered when negotiating between cultures:

1. Expectation for outcomes
   - Does each side have the same goal(s)?
   - Does one side have a relative advantage?
   - What are each culture's views on winning, losing, and compromising?
2. Members of the negotiating team
   - What is the relative status of members of the negotiating team? Is it important to have high-status members?
   - Are there members with special expertise? Should there be?
   - Is a translator necessary? What are the advantages and disadvantages of having a translator for a team?
   - How much decision-making power does the other team have?
3. Physical context of the negotiation
   - Is the site and space used for negotiations conducive to a comfortable discussion?
   - Is the schedule and agenda appropriate for the outcomes desired? Is there adequate time to discuss issues thoroughly?

4. Communication and style of negotiating
   - Are the styles of communicating the same in both cultures? How are silence, emotion, and honor used to communicate and interpret? (See Casse's previous list of differences between the Japanese and U.S. styles.)
   - Is the relative importance of style and substance the same in both cultures? (U.S. style tends to be task oriented, moving quickly from introductions to the central reason for meeting; most Asian, Arab, and Latin cultures tend to be less direct and very conscious of appropriate protocol before addressing the central issue(s).)

Analysis of the preceding issues is particularly applicable to understanding the negotiation process and outcome between Muhashi and MedTech.

References

Casse, P. (1982). *Training for the multicultural manager: A practical and cross-cultural approach to the management of people.* Washington, D.C.: SIETAR.

Griffin, T. & Daggatt, R. (1990). *The global negotiator: Building strong business relationships anywhere in the world.* New York: Harper Business.

Keeley, T. (1998). *Host country national managers in Japanese subsidiaries in Southeast Asian countries and Australia: Communication, flow of information and decision-making processes.* Ph.D. dissertation, Queensland University of Technology Brisbane, Australia.

Varner, I. and Beamer, L. (1995). *Intercultural communication in the global workplace.* Boston: Irwin.

Related Readings

1. Janger, A. R. (1980). *Organization of international joint ventures.* Conference Board, N.Y., N.Y., 787.
   Excellent overview of the different issues facing international joint venture partnerships.
2. Dreifus, S. (Ed.). (1992). *Business international's global management desk reference.* New York: Business International Corporation, McGraw-Hill.
   Excellent reference book for different topics and can be used throughout this text. Several articles are relevant to this chapter and to stimulating thinking about the issue of globalization. A few examples include the following:
   a. "Seven organizational alternatives for MNCs in the 1990s" (p. 1).
      Describes the seven major options for corporate organization, mentioning mixed structure and matrix overlay as the prevalent forms in the 1990s.
   b. "What is a global company?" (p. 71).
      Describes the differences between multinational companies and global companies, terms that are often misused as synonyms.
   c. "The international side of mergers and acquisitions" (p. 93).
      Topics include implications of operating internationally, organizational design, integration, host country regulations, and so on.

   d. "JVs in Korea: Points to consider" (p. 121).
Considers the pros and cons of forming joint ventures in Korea. Some of these considerations can be applied to the Japanese environment.
   e. "The down side of competitive alliances and how to cut your risk," (pp.100–102).
Describes some of the risks companies face when entering joint ventures, especially with the Japanese, and provides options to reduce the risks. Provides concrete examples of real company problems and solutions.

3. Takada, Y. (1996). *"Ten important points to make a successful business in Japan."* International Business Collaboration Council Japan.
Taken off the Internet. To contact the author: yoshi@venture-web.or.jp.
Copyright IBCC Japan c/o NABA Corp. 2-1-14 Meguro, Meguro-ku, Tokyo 153 Japan.
Short paper that outlines basic but important points to doing business in Japan. It is a very good introduction and complement to this chapter.

4. Befu, H. (1993). The gift-giving in a modernizing Japan. In S. Durlabhji & N. Marks (Eds.), *Japanese business: Cultural perspectives* (pp. 109-122). Albany, NY: SUNY Press.
Gives the cultural foundation for the strong, institutionalized custom of gift giving in Japan, an important but symbolic relationship-building/maintenance block for the Japanese.

5. Chow, J., & Wang, C. (Producers). (1990). *Doing business in Japan* (video). Seattle, WA: KCTS.
PBS Adult Learning: one. videocassette, 28 minutes. Topics: quality, society consensus, time factors, 4 Ps (patience, presence, preparation, product), protocol, Coca-Cola, Estée Lauder, and other successful businesses in Japan. Phone number: 1-800-443-1999.

6. Hall, E. (1976, July). How cultures collide. *Psychology Today,* pp. 62–68.
Superb introduction to culture as a context—low or high—and the basic differences between the two types. Because this framework is used throughout this book, it is extremely helpful to have this background.

7. De Mente, B. (1987). Profile of Japan's business world. In *How to do business with the Japanese.* pp. 55–72). Lincolnwood, IL: Passport Books.
Discusses the history and development of Japanese trading firms *(zaibatsu),* and the importance of these firms in the Japanese economy; advantages and disadvantages of the Japanese organizational system; and the mental health of the Japanese workers.

8. Reeves-Ellington, R. (1993). Using cultural skills for cooperative advantage in Japan. *Human Organization, 52*(2), 203–205.
Written from the perspective of an anthropologist who created a program to educate business people in intercultural issues and avoid miscommunication between Americans and, in this case, their Japanese counterparts.

CHAPTER 3

USEFUL CONCEPTS

In this chapter, we focus on some of the contrasts between the stereotypical American and Japanese business cultures and on the types of joint ventures open to MedTech and Muhashi. The specific topics of focus are these:

- Key differences in Japanese and American business culture
- Partnership options between MedTech and Muhashi

Key Differences in Japanese and American Business Culture

The Keiretsu Organization and Short-Term versus Long-Term Perspective

MedTech, the American firm, is generally oriented toward the short term, wanting to press on quickly, whereas the Japanese take their time, research MedTech thoroughly, and present their case to the parent company for approval. MedTech doesn't even understand that Muhashi is one company in a large conglomerate of firms which plays out much like a family. This structure, developed from the feudal days of Japan and pre-World War II, was called the *Zaibatsu*. The Americans disbanded much of the Zaibatsu, although some of it re-formed and took much of the structure it had previously. This same structure in Japanese business today is referred to as the *Keiretsu*. The corporate office is the parent and it has multiple levels of firms within its structure and multiple industries represented as well. The relationship between corporate and affiliates resembles a family. The corporate office is the parent and the family of firms it heads are its "children," from those firms at the top of the value chain to those at the very bottom (i.e., the most basic suppliers).

Many Japanese firms that foreigners perceive as independent entities are actually part of a Keiretsu (see Keeley, 1998). As noted earlier, the Keiretsu was often started by a large family clan that headed a feudal system. The feudal system served as a blueprint for the industry relationships that are created: a head firm (feudal lord) with its major manufacturing branches (the elder feudal family members) and these firms' suppliers (the serfs). Feudal systems were enforced by the feudal lord's military structure. Keiretsu groups have been enforced by many years of developed "loyalty" (initially through force or constraint, later by tradition and fear of being blackballed).

A firm must respect its network and adhere to all the unstated rules that regulate their relationships. Muhashi is in this network and must behave respectfully as any child should to his or her parent. Showing respect involves doing one's homework thoroughly and talking to the necessary individuals in the parent firm, essentially having informal approval of the venture even before the formal presentation. All of this takes a great deal of time. Decision making is notoriously slow in Japanese firms, especially those that are part of a Keiretsu family.

MedTech, in contrast, only has its investors to answer to. The investors have little to no major impact on operational authority in MedTech, but they are directly or indirectly pressuring MedTech to show some promise quickly.

Communication Differences

We often think of communication as oral. Certainly Japanese and English are two very different languages, and the only way MedTech and Muhashi officials can discuss a deal is because of the ability of the Japanese to speak English. However, as this chapter clearly illustrates, speaking the same language doesn't mean real communication is going on. Language is only a surface element of deeper cultural roots. Language reflects values, beliefs, and assumptions, but these aspects of communication often are not obvious.

In this chapter, the Japanese are communicating the importance of trust and credibility within the context of collectivism. The Americans communicate the importance of product, pricing, and distribution—the surface elements of a business relationship—within the context of individualism.

These differences are obvious in the concerns and statements of each firm's representatives. The Japanese say it might take 50 years to reach a large market in China, Muhashi has been operating this way for 75 years and its customers know and trust Muhashi, a business relationship is like an arranged marriage, MedTech and Muhashi might consider exchanging personnel, and so on—all statements indicating the importance of trust and developing credibility within a relationship.

The Americans, conversely, want someone in Japan to "oversee" the operation, to represent MedTech's interests, thereby communicating a lack of trust in the partnership. As Jeff put it, "No one's going to look out for MedTech's interests but MedTech." Further, from the Japanese perspective, the Americans communicate a lack of interest in developing a closer relationship: "Only once did they arrange for an after-hours get-together," commented one of the Japanese delegates. In another instance, Matt communicated to the Japanese that he lacks the judgment to distinguish between what is appropriate in public versus private when he impulsively blurted out that his wife was pregnant.

To the Japanese, the Americans seem impatient, lacking in judgment, and self-interested. To the Americans, the Japanese seem unnecessarily slow and conservative, perhaps only semi-interested in a business deal.

Oyama (1994) found several major themes in the communication problems between Japanese multinational corporations (MNCs) and U.S. host country nationals:

1. *Formality.* Americans speak easily about personal matters and prefer an informal atmosphere.
2. *Social hierarchy.* Japanese method and style of interacting depends on an individual's relative status and age and on the job relationship and the gender of each person. Although this is true to an extent among Americans, an egalitarian culture is much more characteristic of U.S. companies.

3. *Ambiguous communication strategies.* Because Japanese are individuals within an interdependent network in which mutual obligations are incurred, they tend to be tentative, indirect, and ambiguous in their language and commitments. Options need to be kept; maneuverability needs to be possible. Hence, "Yes" in Japanese can mean "Yes, I agree," as in low-context cultures (Australian, British, American, etc.) to "Yes, I understand your point," to "Maybe, we'll see," to "No, I don't think so."

4. *Cultural identity.* For Americans and most English-speaking cultures, the English language becomes the common lingua franca because of the high degree of monolingualism among Anglo cultures. Thus no clear line is drawn between hosts and foreigners through use of language. The Japanese, conversely, although they sometimes speak English quite well, often use their own language to maintain cultural stability and identity and distinguish Japanese from foreigners.

Thus words are only a small part of communicating. What is behind (or underneath) those words is much more important in actually reflecting the essence of a culture. We can summarize some of the major differences between the Japanese and the Americans in this chapter by listing these three fundamental cultural differences:

American culture	Japanese Culture
Short term	Long term
Individualism	Collectivism
Openness	Closedness (partially related to collectivism)

Such differences, to a large extent, are why the context of communications is so important and why Hall (1973) describes high- and low-context cultures. The kind of communications, implicit or explicit, is necessary to understand if both cultures are to work together effectively.

The following table shows some of the critical differences in the communication styles of Japanese and Americans (Goldman, 1994):

Japanese Style of Communication	American Style of Communication
Indirect verbal and nonverbal	Direct verbal and nonverbal
Relationships oriented	Task oriented
Confrontations discouraged	Confrontations acceptable
Often purposely ambiguous	Prefers clarity and specificity
Delayed feedback	Immediate feedback
Group considerate	Individual focused
Intermediaries used extensively	Intermediaries considered obstacles
More reserved	More assertive

Probably one of the most cited illustrations of miscommunication is offered by Harry Triandis (1977; with some adaptation):

Oral Communication	**Conclusion Drawn**
American: "How long will it take you to finish this project?"	American: I'm getting his buy-in.
	Greek: His behavior makes no sense. He is the boss. Why doesn't he just tell me?
Greek: "I don't know. How long should it take?"	American: He doesn't want to take responsibility. Greek: I want him to tell me what he expects.
American: "You are in the best position to analyze the requirements.	American: I'm pressing him to take responsibility. Greek: What nonsense: I'd better give him an answer.
Greek: "10 days."	American: He lacks the ability to estimate time; this is clearly inadequate for this project.
American: "Take 15. Is it agreed? You will do it in 15?"	American: I'm offering a verbal contract. Greek: If he thought it would take 15 days, why didn't he say so in the first place? These are my orders: 15 days.

In fact, the report needed 30 days of regular work. So the Greek worked day and night but at the end of the 15th day, he still needed one more day's work.

American: "Where is the report?"	American: It's important that I hold him responsible for what we agreed on.
Greek: "It will be ready tomorrow."	
American: "But we agreed it would be ready today."	American: I must teach him to fulfill his obligations. Greek: He's stupid and incompetent. Not only did he give me the wrong orders, but he doesn't appreciate the 30-day job I did in 16 days.
The Greek hands in his resignation.	The American is surprised. Greek: I can't work for such a man.

This example clearly illustrates the importance of understanding cultural assumptions and beliefs rather than language only. Similar miscommunications, but of lesser magnitude, are occurring between Muhashi and MedTech officials.

Partnership Options Between Medtech and Muhashi

In this chapter, MedTech and Muhashi are in the process of forming a partnership. As the discussion on communications reveals, both firms are getting to know each other, making some false attributions in the process about the motives, or "personality," of the other firm. As they explore their potential business partnership, they eventually must decide the kind of partnership they want.

Partnering with a domestic or foreign firm involves basically the same options: contract manufacturing, management contracting, joint ventures, licensing, or some other form or hybrid. The most likely forms for Muhashi and MedTech are joint venturing or licensing. MedTech isn't searching for a manufacturer but a distributor, so contract manufacturing (MedTech would pay Muhashi to manufacture its products) isn't the solution to MedTech's problem. Further, it is doubtful the instruments could be manufactured for less money in Japan than in the United States given Japan's higher wages. Contract manufacturing is normally done in countries where the wage is very low in order to save on manufacturing costs. Hence many U.S. firms (and others) contract with manufacturing firms in Southeast Asia and Mexico (*maquiladoras*).

Management contracting doesn't make sense either because Muhashi doesn't need to hire management experience from MedTech. It needs a product it can sell.

In short, licensing Muhashi to manufacture and distribute MedTech's products or partnering in the form of a joint venture are the two most viable forms of partnership for the two firms. In a nutshell, licensing involves one firm authorizing another to duplicate something the licensing firm does itself (e.g., use a manufacturing process, produce a product or service, etc.). The licensee might not want to incur the financial cost of exporting or marketing to a foreign market. Or it might not have the expertise to do so. Instead, it gives these responsibilities to an interested firm that pays the licensee for the product or service it can now distribute. At that point, the licensee has little authority over the licensor, which means less control over the promotion, distribution, and pricing of its products being sold in the foreign country. For firms that might want more control, but are also willing to incur more investment, a joint venture (JV) might be a good alternative: two firms join to complement each other's distinctive competence (i.e., one firm has a superior technology and the other has a superior marketing approach, etc.). Both firms have a financial investment, the organizational structure combines both firms, although typically it is predominantly one, and authority for decision making is shared, even though some countries' laws require the host firm to have majority ownership.

MedTech clearly does not want to surrender its control over the distribution of its products, even though in essence it has a weak bargaining position, which is exploited by Muhashi. With any form of partnership that deals with two firms from different countries, like MedTech and Muhashi, the complications are tremendous. Two different cultures and two different legal systems make it very difficult to enforce a contractual agreement if necessary. These complications form major challenges to foreign firms that want to do business together.

Even though international licensing and joint ventures both face the common challenge of managing differences between two cultures, there are differences between the two that should be noted. (Some of the pros and cons, however, are in relation to whether the choice to license or do a JV was the best choice in the first place.)

a. Licensing

   Basic advantages: low initial investment, quick entry, control over partnership

   Basic disadvantages: potentially less commitment from the licensee and potentially less direct exposure to and influence on the foreign market(s)

b. Joint ventures

   Basic advantages: more equal commitment and investment on both sides, usually creating a longer-term commitment

   Basic disadvantages: usually less control over the operation, more investment in money and time, usually takes longer for market entry because of more complex agreement

When to Enter Into a JV
- at host government insistence
- to reduce costs of building a plant
- to increase economies of scale
- to gain local knowledge
- to spread the risks of the investment
- to more easily enter the market
- to improve competitive advantage

Why JVs Typically Fail
- partners don't get along
- partners renege on their promises
- managers working in foreign operations don't adapt
- the markets disappear

For a good discussion of international joint venture issues, see Frayne and Geringer (1995), and Schuler, Jackson, Dowling, and Welch (1991).

As the story of MedTech and Muhashi progresses, it will become clear how a number of these points become real issues for their successful partnership. Of the four major reasons why joint ventures fail, two of them are directly related to the management of a firm's human resources: partners that don't get along and managers who don't adapt to the foreign environment. In addition, partners that renege on their promises is also indirectly related to the overall management of an enterprise, its ability to follow through on commitments, and its initial strategy development.

References

Frayne, C., & Geringer, M. (1995). Challenges facing general managers of international joint ventures. In *Readings and Cases in International Human Resource Management* (pp. 85–97). Editors: Mark Mendenhall and Gary Oddou. Cincinnati: Southwestern.

Goldman, A. (1994). The centrality of 'ningensei' to Japanese negotiating and interpersonal relationships: Implications for U.S. Japanese communication. *International Journal of Intercultural Relations, 18* (1) (pp. 29–54).

Hall, E. (1973). *The silent language.* New York: Anchor.

Keeley, T. (1998). *Host country national managers in Japanese subsidiaries in Southeast Asian countries and Australia.* Unpublished dissertation, Queensland University of Technology; Brisbane, Australia.

Oyama, N. (1994). *Japanese intercultural communicative strategies in multinational companies.* Unpublished dissertation, Arizona State University.

Schuler, R., Jackson, S., Dowling, P., & Welch, D. (1991). The formation of an international joint venture: Davidson Instrument Panel. In *Readings and Cases in International Human Resource Management* (pp. 70–84). Editors: Mark Mendenhall and Gary Oddou. Cincinnati: Southwestern.

Triandis, H. (1977). *Interpersonal behavior.* Monterey, CA: Brooks/Cole.

Related Readings

1. Working in an Eastern culture. (19). *Japan.* pp. 292–305.
   Despite its age, one of the best, most succinct articles on multi-facets of Japan and still extremely accurate about contemporary Japan. Topics covered in this ten-page article include language and communication, dress and appearance, food and eating habits, time and age consciousness, reward and recognition, relationships, attitudes and beliefs, business attitudes, and values and standards.

2. Hall, E. & Hall, M. (1987). The vocabulary of human relationships in Japan. In S. Durlabhji & N. Marks (Eds.), *Japanese business: Cultural perspectives* (pp. 109–121). Albany, NY: SUNY Press.
   Extends material in "How cultures collide," suggested reading for Chapter 2, and recommends reading essential for understanding interpersonal relationships in Japan.

3. Befu, H. (1974). An ethnography of dinner entertainment in Japan. In S. Durlabhji & N. Marks (Eds.), *Japanese business: Cultural perspectives* (pp. 123–140). Albany, NY: SUNY Press.
   Contrasts the style and depth of meaning of dinner entertainment between the United States and Japan. Although the focus is very specific (dinner entertainment), it highlights the significance of such a custom and reinforces the notions raised in readings 1 and 2 here.

4. Janger, A. (1980). Organization of international joint ventures. New York: The Conference Board Report no. 787.
   Excellent overview of the different issues facing international joint venture partnerships including the problems companies face when planning in the new environment, control of the joint venture, the basic structure of joint ventures, and so on.

Culturgram™ '98

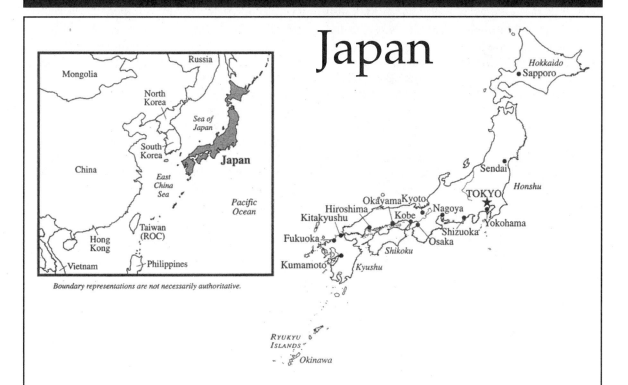

Japan

Boundary representations are not necessarily authoritative.

Japan consists of four main islands, Honshu, Hokkaido, Shikoku, and Kyushu. Covering 145,882 square miles (377,835 square kilometers), it is just smaller than Montana. Japan experiences all four seasons. On Hokkaido and in northern Honshu, winters can be bitterly cold. To the south, a more tropical climate prevails. Otherwise the climate is temperate with warm, humid summers and mild winters. The western side of the island is usually colder than the eastern (Pacific) side. The islands are subject to typhoons in September. Japan also has many dormant and a few active volcanoes. Mild earthquakes are fairly common, and more destructive ones hit every few years. The January 1995 quake in and around Kobe killed more than five thousand people and was the worst of several quakes since a 1923 Tokyo quake that killed 140,000.

History

Japan is known historically as the Land of the Rising Sun, as symbolized in its flag. Beginning with Emperor Jimmu in 600 B.C. (according to legend), Japan has had a line of

continued

emperors that continues to the present. From the 12th century until the late 19th century, however, feudal lords or *Shoguns* held political control. These *Shoguns* expelled all foreigners in the 17th century on the suspicion they were spies for European armies. Not until 1853, when Matthew Perry (U.S. Navy) sailed into port, did the Japanese again have contact with the West. The Shoguns lost power in the 1860s and the emperor again took control. The current emperor, Akihito, took the throne in 1989. Akihito's father, Hirohito, was emperor from 1926 to 1989. Hirohito's reign was called *Showa* which means "enlightened peace." The deceased Hirohito is now properly referred to as "Emperor Showa." Akihito's reign is called Heisei, meaning "achievement of universal peace."

Japan established itself as a regional power through military victories against China (1895) and Russia (1905). Involvement in World War I brought Japan enhanced global influence, and the Treaty of Versailles expanded its land holdings. The postwar years brought prosperity to the rapidly changing nation. It soon began to exercise considerable influence in Asia and subsequently invaded Manchuria and much of China. On 7 December 1941, Japan launched a successful air attack on U.S. naval forces at Pearl Harbor. Its military machine swiftly encircled most of Southeast Asia. But in 1943, the tide of the war turned against Japan. The United States dropped atomic bombs on Hiroshima and Nagasaki in the summer of 1945. Complete collapse of the empire and surrender ensued. A military occupation, chiefly by U.S. forces, lasted from 1945 to 1952. In 1947, Japan adopted a new constitution under American direction, renouncing war, granting basic human rights, and declaring Japan a democracy,. The United States and Japan have since maintained close political and military ties despite periodic trade tensions.

Japan's postwar focus was on economic development and the country experienced rapid change and modernization. The Liberal Democratic Party (LDP) generally controlled politics after World War II, but scandals in the 1980s and early 1990s led to high-level resignations, splinter parties, and a weaker LDP. In 1993, it lost its majority and served as a coalition partner to the rival Socialist Party under Prime Minister Tomiichi Murayama. Newly appointed LDP leader Ryutaro Hashimoto restored his party to power when Murayama resigned in January 1996. Hashimoto was named prime minister and led the LDP to victory in the October 1996 parliamentary elections.

THE PEOPLE

Population

Japan's population of 125.4 million is growing at 0.2 percent annually. Although Japan's population is half that of the United States, it resides on less than 5 percent of the total territory of the United States. Japan is therefore one of the most densely populated countries in the world. Nearly 80 percent of all people live in urban areas. About 45 percent are concentrated in three major metropolitan areas: Tokyo, Osaka, and Nagoya. Tokyo is the world's most populous city. Japan is 99 percent ethnic Japanese, with a small number of Koreans (about 680,000) and Chinese. Native Ainu live mostly on Hokkaido. All non-Japanese must register annually with the police and do not have full citizenship rights.

Japan's Human Development Index value (0.940) ranks it seventh out of 175 countries. Adjusted for women, the index value (0.901) ranks Japan 12th out of 146 nations. This gap

continued

reflects Japanese women's inferior social status and limited access to resources that allow them to pursue personal goals as freely as men. Overall, Japan's impressive level of economic and social organization is diminished by a high cost of living and the stress inherent in an emphasis on work, a lack of affordable urban housing, high urban population levels, and inflexible social institutions.

Language

Japanese is the official language. Although spoken Japanese is not closely related to spoken Chinese, the written language (*kanji*) is related to Chinese ideographs (characters), which were adopted in ancient times. The Japanese also use two phonetic alphabets (*hiragana and katakana*) simplified from these characters. A third phonetic alphabet (*romaji*) uses Roman letters. People are losing their ability to write the complex *kanji* as they rely more on computers. English is taught in all secondary schools and is often used in business. The Japanese place great worth on nonverbal language or communication. For example, much can be said with a proper bow. In fact, one is often expected to sense another person's feelings on a subject without verbal communication. Some Westerners misinterpret this as a desire to be vague or incomplete. The Japanese may consider a person's inability to interpret feelings as insensitivity.

Religion

Traditionally, most Japanese practiced a combination of Buddhism and Shinto. Shinto has no recognized founder or central scripture but is based on ancient mythology. It stresses man's relationship to nature and its many gods. All Japanese emperors are considered literal descendants of the sun goddess,

Amaterasu. Shinto was important historically in ordering Japanese social values, as illustrated by the Code of the Warrior (Bushido), which stresses honor, courage, politeness, and reserve.

Shinto principles of ancestor veneration, ritual purity, and a respect for nature's beauty are all obvious in Japanese culture. Many households observe some ceremonies of both Shinto and Buddhism, such as Shinto marriages and Buddhist funerals, and most have small shrines in their homes. For most, however, this is done more out of respect for social tradition than out of religious conviction. About 1 percent of the population is Christian.

General Attitudes

Japanese society is group oriented. Loyalty to the group (business, club, etc.) and to ones superiors is essential and takes precedence over personal feelings. In business, loyalty, devotion, and cooperation are valued over aggressiveness. Companies traditionally provide lifetime employment to the "salaryman" (full-time male professional), and the salaryman devotes long hours of work to the company. This tradition was undermined by the recession of the early 1990s but is still a pillar of society. Devotion to the group reaches all ages; even members of a youth baseball team will place the team's interests over their own.

Politeness is extremely important; a direct "no" is seldom given, but a phrase like "I will think about it" can mean "no." Also out of politeness, a "yes" may be given quickly, even though it only means the person is listening or understands the speaker's request. The Japanese feel a deep obligation to return favors and gifts. They honor age and tradition. Losing face or being shamed in public is very undesirable. *Gamam* (enduring patience) is a respected trait that carries one through

continued

personal hardship, but it has also been used to dismiss the need for social change.

Nevertheless, even as many traditions remain strong, Japan's rising generation is beginning to revise society's view of economic security, family relations, politics, and male and female roles.

Personal Appearance

Conformity, even in appearance, is a characteristic of the Japanese. The general rule is to act similar to, or in harmony with, the crowd. Businessmen wear suits and ties in public. Proper dress is necessary for certain occasions. Conformity takes on a different meaning for the youth, however. They will wear the latest fashions (American and European) and colors, as long as these fashions are popular. Traditional clothing, called a *kimono* or *wafuku*, is a long robe with long sleeves, wrapped with a special sash (*obi*). The designs in the fabric can be simple or elaborate. The *kimono* is worn for social events or special occasions.

CHAPTER 4

USEFUL CONCEPTS

The international management topics embedded in this chapter are the following:
• Expatriate selection
• Dual-career couple issues

Expatriate Selection

Expatriates fall into different classifications. Those identified as high potentials are given international assignments because of their high potential status. An international assignment is usually seen as a necessary step in the high potentials' sequence of developmental assignments. Other expatriates are highly skilled technicians or engineers who are sent to a foreign country as problem-solvers or trainers. Often those in the host country subsidiary or client's firm, for example, need expertise in trouble-shooting problems with products sent to them. Part of that expertise might include training of the host nationals so they become less dependent on the parent company or supplier. The third and largest category of professionals who become international assignees are those in the right spot at the right time with the right qualifications and interest. These might be marketeers, financiers, accountants, manufacturing personnel, or others.

Currently, these individuals are selected primarily because of their technical expertise and their willingness to go. However, given the challenges of a foreign assignment, it is best to broaden the criteria to include those more related to an expatriate's ability to adapt to the foreign environment.

Although paper-and-pencil tests or more expensive experiential exercises can be used to determine an employee's likelihood of adapting, there are also several straightforward questions that can be asked of an employee with a history in the firm (Oddou, 1991):

1. How easily and how quickly has the employee adapted to changes in the workplace—expected and unexpected changes?
2. How open-minded and diplomatic is the employee about opinions, attitudes, and behaviors that differ from his or her own?
3. Does the employee enjoy meeting new people and learning about them?
4. How self-confident and self-reliant is the employee?
5. How cohesive are the family members and how supportive are they?
6. Does the employee deal effectively with stress?

Most of these questions are related to more fundamental issues that Mendenhall and Oddou (1985) have found to be linked to adaptation. Through conceptualizing various research findings, they found three orientations that describe one's likelihood to acculturate successfully: a self-orientation, an others-orientation, and a perceptual orientation. We discuss each of these generally and then apply them to Jan and Matt to determine the wisdom in selecting Matt to go overseas.

Self-orientation refers to overall feelings of self-efficacy and ability to manage stress. Two of the most important aspects of this orientation include past experience and stress management. The more confident an individual has become because of success in achieving results in various situations under various conditions, the more likely the person is to adapt well to a new setting. Conversely, a self-perception that one has largely failed in important past experiences will impede successful adaptation.

Similarly and simultaneously, feeling stress in a new culture is inevitable, so having a method for dealing with that stress is essential. Stress management is very personal. Research has shown that some find healthy retreat and regeneration through meditation, prayer, or indulgence in a favorite sport or other rewarding activity in the new environment that had a positive effect in one's own culture (i.e., attending concerts, plays; walking on the beach, etc.).

Looking at Jan, for example, we can assume she has high self-efficacy. In all her outdoor experience in Maine, she has undoubtedly confronted difficult situations—even survival situations—in hiking the tallest peaks in Maine. Winter treks are especially dangerous if participants are not properly prepared and trained. Jan surely developed a sense of "can do" more than the average person her age. Moving away from a small town rural atmosphere to Austin, Texas, also probably tested her skills to survive and succeed in a different environment. Her success there took her to Berkeley's Haas School of Law, where again, she was successful in a very competitive, survival-of-the-fittest environment.

In terms of Jan's orientation toward physical exercise, we know she has been much less active in her outdoor endeavors, such as skiing and backpacking than when she was younger. To provide some relief, however, we know a common stress reduction method she was looking forward to was attending the Tokyo ballet and concerts, and that she has a strong American support system through the American Club, which includes social events. Plus, she and Matt tend to bounce impressions and information off each other, which is a healthy sign of communication rather than repressing their thoughts and feelings.

The second aspect of acculturation, *others orientation,* refers to the desire to cultivate associations and ability to get along with others. It is an interpersonal, interaction dimension. The more an individual expresses a need to develop friendships or associations and demonstrates the ability to maintain the relationships, the more likely he or she is to acculturate well to the host culture. This dimension, then, includes linguistic ability as well. Connection to the foreign environment is best done through the indigenous people. There are several real benefits to such connections: the nurturing of our social being, as sources of information for understanding and functioning, and so on.

In this respect, Jan (and Matt) will always be limited in their depth of integration into Japanese society—assuming they would be allowed in! Although Jan seems friendly enough (there's not a lot of information given about her "need" to develop associations), much of what seems to drive her is her loyalty to causes.

We could probably assume that most of her meaningful associations are centered around those who share her causes. Based on the text, not a lot of Japanese seem cued in to the environment, or else she hasn't found these groups. Further, she speaks no Japanese really and so does not have and will not have access to many relationships or to deep relationships. Finally, because having relations with the host nationals is not only social but also becomes an information source to help the foreigner reach the "deep" culture, Jan is missing an important source of information. Certainly, many of her American women friends at the American Club do not seem to demonstrate an intimate understanding of the Japanese.

The third orientation, the *perceptual orientation,* refers to an individual's mental mapping of a new situation. To the degree that one keeps an open mind, maintains an objectivity, and withholds judgment about the hosts until a reasonable amount of diverse evidence is in, the individual will likely be successful in adapting to the new culture. An open mind, of course, allows an individual to entertain the possibility that others see differently, do differently, and expect differently. Objectivity and the withholding of judgment until more information is in increases the probability of drawing accurate conclusions. Accurate conclusions are important for both general understanding of the hosts and for improved functioning in their culture.

With regard to the perceptual orientation, Jan seems to be at least moderately effective if not more. The fact that she does not share the opinions of the American women who criticize the Japanese culture leads us to believe she is more objective than they are. In addition, she prefers to associate with those who "shared her enthusiasm for new experiences and seem open to changes and trying to understand the foreign culture."

In summary, Jan seems to have the necessary inclinations and abilities to adapt fairly well.

Preparation for Japan. Research (Oddou, 1991) has shown that the firms with the best success rates and reputations for successful human resource management share certain characteristics with respect to their expatriate programs:

- some cultural and language instruction
- technical advice
- a site visit to the host country
- career support for accompanying spouse

The preparation usually involves cultural and language instruction over a period of about a month or longer before departure. It also involves technical advice concerning the compensation package, retirement benefits, and so on. Part of the preparation includes a visit to the host country to locate housing and schooling if necessary. Finally, for dual-career couple situations, the best firms also provide support for the spouse to find work. This sometimes comes in a guarantee from the employee's firm to employ the spouse. Many companies also work with consortia to find a job; for example IBM works with an HP or Sun Micro Systems office to find a comparable employment for its employee's spouse (and vice versa).

In Matt and Jan's situation, what occurred is very typical of small organizations—even mid-sized organizations much larger and more experienced than MedTech. The move to Japan was fairly spontaneous, not allowing a lot of planning. Even if it were forecasted six months in advance, it is unlikely a firm as small as MedTech would have had the resources or the foresight to have made some of the preparations just mentioned. In this case, there was no time for seminars or language instruction. And there was no in-house expertise on compensation packages for expatriates. Nor did Matt or Jan have the experience to know better.

The only real preparation that occurred was the visit to Tokyo by both Jan and Matt to look for housing. It also gave them an idea of the cost of living, leading to Matt's request for a salary increase. In general, though, they were quite naive on this first expatriate experience.

Dual-Career Couple Issues

Some material about this topic was introduced in Chapter 1 regarding Matt and Jan's decision to have a long-distance commuter marriage while he attended MBA school at UCLA. Here again, Matt and Jan confront an important decision: whether to go to Japan or not. This decision has obvious effects on their careers. If they don't go, Matt's career will be less enriched and he won't become the contributor to MedTech he would like to. Being a contributor is an important career anchor for Matt; it reflects an important value to him. In fact, it is the most fundamental reason why he left Hewlett Packard and took a job with a start-up firm, MedTech.

But if they go, it is Jan's career that suffers significantly—much more than Matt's would if they didn't go. In fact, it is likely Jan's career will suffer to the degree that Matt's will develop. At this point, Matt is essentially asking Jan to surrender her career prospects to his; that is, her career would—at least for the time being—become subordinate, Matt's the primary. Of course, it is doubtful Matt really understands that. He seems to be caught up in his enthusiasm about the opportunity to go to Japan and make the difference in MedTech's success.

How Matt and Jan manage this and similar issues will determine how well they manage their professional and personal lives. Regardless of whether MedTech has an outstanding opportunity and is on the verge of success, if the individual who might represent MedTech (Matt) is on the verge of personal failure because he can't manage his marriage well, MedTech's opportunities are of little consequence. Matt's personal life will spill over into his professional life and impact his effectiveness in his job.

Decisions within a dual-career couple context often relate to issues about *perceived control* (Malden, 1987). Studies have shown that wives perceive control when they feel confident in their conflict resolution skills and are happily married. In other words, in the context of a possible commute situation, if the wife believes she has good conflict resolution skills and her husband is not purely self-interested (being happily married presumes both partners are interested in the other's happiness), the decision will be more acceptable—whatever the decision.

The self-perception of good conflict management skills is important to the belief that one will not fall victim to a strong personality or too persuasive a speaker (glib tongue). Being happily married means love and concern for each partner, wanting to maintain a certain level of harmony and stability, and so on. It is clear why both of these elements (conflict management skills and happiness in marriage) are important elements in arriving at a mutually satisfying decision. Studies also point out, however, that perceived control can relate to how the decision is made and not just what decision is made.

In Matt and Jan's situation, although Matt's position was clear and rather self-centered, he attempted to give Jan her "space" to think it over. How Jan reacted to this was critical. Had she perceived Matt as manipulating her, she probably would have reacted differently (the self-interest issue). Although it was obvious Matt wanted to go to Japan and he made that known to Jan, he was also honest about it, thereby giving the impression the self-interest wasn't calculating. The fact that Jan was probably confident in her conflict resolution skills given her experience in college and her work as an attorney also helped her view the situation as nonmanipulating.

Other research shows that three variables in particular are critical to couples' successful consensus decision making (Godwin & Scanzoni, 1989):

- a perceived loving/caring partner
- commitment to one's partner and marriage
- cooperation in past conflict situations.

In Matt and Jan's case, it appears as though each partner loves and cares for the other. It also appears as though each is committed to the other, particularly because they vowed they would never have a commuter marriage again. It could be argued, however, that it is Jan who has given more than Matt at this point and so we know more about her love and commitment to Matt than vice versa. We also know that Jan has been the one who has been somewhat more cooperative with Matt than Matt with Jan.

In conclusion, many women might not have made the same decision as Jan. Each couple is different, and priorities and values differ by partner and partnership. Jan came from a stable, traditional family. It is possible that this background, coupled with her own values, has encouraged her to make a decision that will satisfy the marriage requirements given the apparent conditions (i.e., put marriage above individual interests).

References

Black, J. S., Mendenhall, M., & Oddou, G. (1991). Toward a comprehensive model of international adjustment: An integration of multiple theoretical perspectives. *Academy of Management Review, 16,* 291–317.

Godwin, D. & Scanzoni, J. (1989). Couple consensus during marital joint decision-making: A context, process outcome model. *Journal of Marriage and Family, 51,* 943–956.

Malden, M. (1987). Perceived control and power in marriage: A study of marital decision making and task performance. *Personality and Social Psychology Bulletin, 13* (1), 73–82.

Mendenhall, M. & Oddou, G. (1985). The dimensions of expatriate acculturation: A review. *Academy of Management Review, 10,* 39–48.

Oddou, G. (1991). Managing your expatriates: What the successful firms do. *The Human Resources Planning Journal, 14,* 301–308.

Related Readings

1. Selecting: Finding the right people. (1982). In S. Black, H. Gregersen, & M. Mendenhall (Eds.), *Global Assignments: Successfully expatriating and repatriating international managers* (Chapter 5, pp. 53–89). San Francisco: Jossey-Bass.
   This chapter discusses mistakes made by American companies when selecting employees for overseas assignments. It compares the selection process used in America with the ones used in Japan and Europe. Finally, the chapter discusses different methods of selection, and selection factors that predict the expatriate's spouse and family success.

2. Human resource selection. (1995). In M. Mendenhall, B. J. Punnett, & D. Ricks (Eds.), *Global Management* (Chapters 12–14, pp. 401–431). Blackwell.
   Focuses on a company's different options when selecting employees for overseas assignments. It also studies the impact of culture shock and the dimensions of international adjustment. The chapter provides useful tools in the employee selection process. Also see "Training for international assignments," pp. 437–461.
   Emphasizes the need for cross-cultural training. Discusses why some American companies do not use it and why they should. The chapter provides different approaches to cross-cultural training.

3. The road to success: What does it take to be a winner. (1985). In L. Copeland & L. Griggs (Eds.), *Going international: How to make friends and deal effectively in the global marketplace.* New York: Random House.
   Lists and explains briefly seven traits that should be used to select expatriates: "hard like water," "resourceful independence through people," "curiosity," "positive regard for others," "emotional stability," "technical competence," and "motivation." Based on what is known about Matt, he can be evaluated against most or all of these to determine whether he seems like a good choice.

4. Solomon, C. (1994). "Success depends on more than job skills." *Personnel Journal, 73* (4), pp. 51–60.
   Excellent overview of the major issues facing expatriates. Also treats topics that continue into Chapters 5 and 6 here and should be used as a reference there also. See the discussion of the typical adjustment curve for expatriates and compare it to Matt and Jan's experience in Japan.

5. Mendenhall, M, & Wiley, C. (1994). "Strangers in a strange land: The relationship between expatriate adjustment and impression management. *American Behavioral Scientist, 37* (5), pp. 605–620.
   Explores the effectiveness of impression management in the expatriate adjustment process. Impression management is defined as the tendency to present oneself in a socially desirable way to others. Its effectiveness is analyzed within the contexts of the individual, the position, the organization, and the culture novelty. The article also presents a case study of an American expatriate in Japan, and cites examples pertinent to the Japanese environment.

CHAPTER 5

USEFUL CONCEPTS

The following topics are covered in this chapter:

- Japanese culture
- The function of religion in Japan
- Expatriation acculturation
- An expatriate adjustment model

Japanese Culture

Culture can be analyzed in several different ways. Two of the ways in this text include Hofstede's framework and Hall's high and low context. A third way is simple yet very useful. We have alluded to it already when referring to oral communications and the underlying beliefs, values, and assumptions they represent. It introduces you to the idea of culture manifesting a surface element and a deeper element. The surface aspect is everything we take in through our senses: sight, sound, touch, feel, and smell. It is the buildings we see, the expressions on faces, the architecture used, the size and type of cars, the loudness of voices, and so on. The deeper element is that which lies under the surface aspects, that which gives rise to those buildings, expressions, and so on. It is the values, assumptions, and philosophies of the culture.

For example, a flamboyant architecture can reflect the value of aesthetics or the importance of "presentation." Employees who do not work overtime might reflect a value of balance or an assumption that one's personal time is of as much value as one's professional role. A society that usually dresses very similarly (e.g., businesspeople in conservative suits) might believe that uniformity, and not individuality, is important.

In summary, we can infer values, assumptions, and philosophies about a culture from the surface elements we experience through our senses. This process of inference, although faulty because it is done through our own cultural "lenses," is important to our understanding and predicting appropriate behavior in a foreign culture.

In this chapter, some of the surface elements in Japanese culture that reflect deeper-level values are organization of physical office space, the educational system, and the work ethic.

Organization of Office Space

The desks are all congregated together with the boss's desk facing all the others. The employees' desks are side by side with space to mingle and converse with others. Generally, the employees with more seniority sit closer to the manager. There are no cubicles. Everyone can see everyone else and overhear conversations.

The deeper values reflected in this arrangement might include the following:

- encouragement of open communication
- peer pressure and competition (i.e., the importance of maintaining an enviable workload)
- hierarchy (i.e., although there are no offices, the hierarchy is obvious with the senior members sitting closer to the manager and the manager's desk facing all the others).

Educational System

The highly competitive entrance requirements discussed in this chapter, the emphasis on national testing, and a clear hierarchy in ranking of institutions all characterize the Japanese system. These traits reflect obvious values on competition, achievement, hard work, and also on hierarchy or status.

Work Ethic—Long Hours

Traditionally, the Japanese have been hard workers, particularly in modern times since World War II. They have often worked ten- to twelve-hour days, six days a week, especially the management levels. This surface characteristic of long hours demonstrates the Japanese value on hard work, their competitive spirit, and their loyalty to their employer, or, viewed from what some is more realistic, their reluctance to change employers because of the social stigma.

One large, international research study (MOW, 1985) shows clearly the importance of work in the lives of the Japanese (see the following exhibit).

The Relative Importance of Work in Eight Countries

(The higher the mean score, the more central and important in life to the people of that country)

Country	Score
Japan (7)	7.78
Yugoslavia (former) (5)	7.30
Israel (4)	7.10
United States (3)	6.94
Belgium (1)	6.81
Netherlands (1)	6.69
Germany (1)	6.67
Britain (0)	6.36

(The number in parentheses indicates the number of countries statistically significantly lower in reported importance of work to their lives.)

This trend appears to be changing slowly in Japan, particularly with the new generation of white-collar workers. In the long-term future, a greater balance between work and play might be expected. In addition, plenty of research evidence shows the Japanese commitment to their work and firm might be more from a sense of obligation and financial need than because of intrinsic interest in their work, particularly among nonprofessionals.

The Function of Religion in Japan

Religion plays a more or less important role in a society depending on that society's historical roots and beliefs. When doing international business, it can be very helpful to understand something about the host culture's religious roots and, in some cases, practices today that reflect those roots. It is said that much of the U.S. work ethic comes from Protestantism, a religion that encouraged the hard-working individuals who first came to America over 200 years ago. In Muslim countries, it is helpful to understand that prayer is done five times a day; that modesty in women is not just a social view but a fundamental belief in their religion, that normally a woman and a man would never be left alone if they are not married—including business meetings. In Hindu countries, it is important to understand that although the caste system is not as rigid as before, there is still a very strong social caste system that reinforces the idea of a social hierarchy. It is essential to recognize this hierarchy in terms of the power within the society—whom to give what responsibilities, how much to expect from certain people, whom to go to for permission for specific decisions, and so on.

In addition to actual functional reasons for understanding a culture's religious heritage, there is also the simple issue of communicating an appreciation for a country's culture. Knowing something about the religion(s) of a country can be very helpful in social conversation with businesspeople from the host country. It reflects an appreciation, an interest; it reflects the fact that time was taken to know something about the host people's country. In most countries of the world, particularly those reflecting high-context cultures, this kind of appreciation helps build a good foundation for trust in a business context.

In Japan, the people are very tolerant of religious beliefs because they have taken a very eclectic approach to worship. Most Japanese include multiple religions in their daily life. Their indigenous religion (Shinto) and first adopted religion (Buddhism) allow for the belief in other philosophies or gods. However, in general, religion plays a very superficial role in the daily life of the Japanese.

The principal religions/philosophies in Japan are Shinto, Buddhism, and Christianity, although there is some influence of Confucianism also. Only about one-fifth or less of the Japanese proclaim themselves religious believers. Most of these are Buddhists, then Shintoists, with a relatively small minority of Christians. Because of the separation of church and state, no religious instruction is allowed in public schools.

Shintoism. Shinto is a "naturalistic" religion because it grew out of the everyday life of the Japanese centuries ago. Shinto gods, or Kaman, are worshipped through shrines *(jingo)*. There were innumerable gods in Shinto religion as it was practiced in the beginning because every natural thing had its Kaman. However, it has evolved to be mostly a worship of ancestors. Still, the Shinto priest is the one who is invited to the openings of new restaurants, buildings, and so on—and even for the acceptance of new machinery in a Japanese business—to dedicate it by purification so it will serve its purpose without evil effects (i.e., someone getting hurt, a machine producing defects, etc.).

From the nineteenth century, Shinto became regarded as the national religion and the emperor became deified. After World War II, however, religion became separated from the state and has been limited to worshipping shrines. Japanese go to their public shrines at the Shinto temples when a child is born or for marriage ceremonies. Before going on long trips, some Japanese visit shrines to pray for safety; students pray to pass entrance exams. Each shrine has its own religious festivals each year where the Japanese set up booths and sell various merchandise, including small shrines they place in their homes for daily "worship."

Buddhism. Siddartha Gautama (c. 563–483 B.C.), from India, is said to be the originator of the Buddhist religion. Having been protected within his father's castle, Gautama had not been exposed to the reality of pain and suffering that those who were less fortunate experienced. After having slipped out of the castle and experienced this, he was shocked and decided to seek an explanation for life as he now understood it. In his wanderings, he often meditated to reflect on what he saw and to seek an answer. One day, the story goes, sitting under a tree, he became enlightened about the causes of pain and suffering and also about the way to live one's life to avoid these things. Suffering was not the "right" way, but neither was a life of luxury. The right way, Gautama understood from his enlightenment, was what he would call "the middle way." The middle way is expressed through the "four noble truths" and the "noble eightfold path."

The four noble truths are these:

1. All existence is suffering.
2. Suffering is caused by desire because no desire can ever be completely fulfilled forever.
3. Suffering ceases when desire ceases.
4. Following the noble eightfold path relieves suffering.

The Eightfold Path:

1. Right view is understanding and accepting the four noble truths.
2. Right thought is freedom from lust, ill will, cruelty, and untruthfulness.
3. Right speech is abstaining from lying, tale bearing, harsh language, and vain talk.
4. Right conduct is abstaining from killing, stealing, and sexual misconduct.
5. Right livelihood is the avoidance of violence to any living thing and freedom from luxury.

6. Right effort is avoiding and overcoming what is evil and promoting and maintaining what is good.
7. Right awareness is contemplating the fact that the body is transitory and loathsome, of contemplating the feelings of oneself and of others, and of contemplating the mind and other phenomena.
8. Right meditation is complete concentration on a single object to achieve purity of thought, thought free from all desires, hindrances, and distractions, and, eventually, free from all sensation.

You can see that most Christian and Islamic beliefs parallel those of the Buddhist in the eightfold path. This is a fairly common ground for most world religions.

Buddhism also believes in the concepts of karma and nibbana. Karma is a Hindu concept that Gautama interpreted in an ethical context: bad begets evil; good begets good. Karma applies to the physical, mental, and moral worlds.

Nibbana, similar to the concept of Nirvana in Hinduism, is the escape from suffering, having reached that state of complete implementation of the eightfold path and having joined a completely differing state from the one experienced in this life. That is enlightenment.

Buddhism came to Japan via China and Korea. Prince Shotoku of Japan in the seventh century A.D. became fascinated by this new thought and adopted it as his own. It wasn't until the twelfth century, however, that Buddhism went beyond the aristocracy of Japan to the common people. About this time, Zen became a common practice among the Samurai class.

In everyday life in Japan, it is possible to see the effects of Buddhism in its art, literature, and architecture. Carefully manicured gardens, flower arrangements, and other artifacts reflect the influence of Buddhism. Buddhists believe in the complete interdependence of life—humans on nature and nature on humans. They are intertwined, and taking care of nature, being in nature, can lift our sense of being. Buddhism preaches tolerance and equality, although it is hard to see these in Japanese society regarding their attitudes toward non-Japanese.

There are different sects within the Buddhist religion or philosophy: Theravada, Mahayana, and Zen, each one with different characteristics. The Mahayana Buddhists have added to and modified somewhat the original teachings of Buddha (Gautama), which the Theravada Buddhists adhere to strictly. They inhabit the northern countries in Asia: China, Taiwan, Japan, Korea, Tibet, Mongolia, and Nepal.

Zen Buddhists are known for their emphasis on meditation. Peace of mind, serenity, can be achieved only through the practice of deep meditation (*zazen*). This has become a popular practice in Japan even though all those who practice are not declared Zen Buddhists.

Christianity. The Christian religion first reached Japan in the mid-1500s via the Catholic church. Although Christianity was embraced by the ruling class without much difficulty (not that Buddhism or Shintoism were set aside to embrace Christianity—they were seen as compatible), later feudal lords came to see it as a threat to their order and banned it. Christianity preached that God was the head and only he should be worshipped and ultimately obeyed. This did not encourage loyalty to the lords. In the later half of the nineteenth century, after Japan sought relations with Europe and the United States, it again opened its doors to Christianity.

Expatriate Acculturation

A discussion on expatriation can be approached in different ways. Chapter 4 in Part 1 focused on selection criteria. The preparation and overseas support of expatriates are also important factors to understand and compare with Matt and Jan's far too typical experience.

Preparation

Expatriate preparation may consist of the following areas:

- language preparation
- cultural preparation
- career management (i.e., explanation of how expatriation fits into the overall career of the expat and the assigning of a domestic manager as a domestic mentor for the expat)
- retirement and benefits preparation (i.e., explanation of how this move will affect the person's retirement and benefits)
- logistical preparation in home country (i.e., help in selling or renting of home, etc.)

In fact, even the firms considered to have the best practices do very little to prepare their expatriates. Among the issues just listed, management of the expat's career is probably the most significant. The domestic manager assigned to mentor the expatriate is usually the expat's current (pre-expatriation) domestic manager. This person maintains regular contact with the expat and begins searching for a position several months before the expat is scheduled to return.

Overseas Support

- continued language support
- continued cultural support
- logistical preparation in host country (i.e., help in locating new housing, schooling for children if necessary, etc.)
- career management (the assigning of a host manager as a host mentor for the expat)

Here again, the assignment of a mentor to the expat. is extremely helpful. The mentor takes charge of the person's socialization, including giving cultural information, helping the expat to understand the organization, becoming an intermediary when necessary, and so on.

When we speak of helping the expat (and his or her family if that applies), it is mostly in terms of adapting to the culture and overall management of the expat's career. Research has shown that expatriates follow a typical sequence of acculturation. Part of the sequence includes experiencing culture shock, a normal human response to the stress of moving to a new environment where formerly successful social strategies are no longer appropriate or useful. Although the response of an individual may vary in terms of the length of time spent in each stage and the level of bicultural comfort eventually attained, the adjustment pattern is common enough to be considered a syndrome of the human psyche.

Lysgaard (1955) described the pattern of adjustment as a U curve experience, ranging from an apparent high-functioning initial stage (mostly because of a lack of integration with the culture) to a low-functioning stage as a result of repeated failures when attempting to use one's typical strategies in the new culture. Finally, as the individual becomes more proficient (which does not always occur), satisfaction and a higher degree of functioning return (hence, the U curve).

Others, including Pedersen (1988) and Furnham and Bochner (1989), believe that within the larger U curve there are actually many smaller U curve experiences. In addition, those who never do become fully functioning in the new culture experience a J curve. These researchers have identified several predictor variables that affect the course of culture shock in an individual:

1. The control of the degree of contact with the host culture. The greater the contact, the more the potential shock.
2. The individual's intrapersonal variables (age, experience, language skills, resourcefulness, independence, fortitude, ambiguity tolerance, health, and appearance). Generally, the younger the individual, the more experience one has, the more probable the successful adjustment.
3. The individual's interpersonal support system.
4. The "cultural distance" of the new culture from one's own (i.e., the more different, the more difficult to adjust to—although other research shows this is not always the case, depending on one's expectations).
5. The geopolitical conditions in the host culture, including the availability of goods, the prevalence of disease, crime, war, and so on.

Stages of Adaptation

The typical stages of adaptation an individual experiences in a foreign country are these:

1. The *honeymoon* stage is characterized by an abandonment of one's normal responsibilities—a freedom usually only experienced on vacations. At the same

time, however, the individual's identity is still stable. In the new culture, everything is neat, cute, interesting, and so on. The individual is enamored with the beautiful architecture, the different fashion, the wonderful museums. In other words, the individual is attending to all the surface elements of the culture that stand out because they are different from one's own native surroundings. Basically, it is a romanticized vision of the situation.

In the text, there is some sense that Jan is experiencing this aspect of "acculturation." This is natural and occurs to everyone who doesn't have a sole focus on work. With Matt, it appears as though his primary interest is his work and the recreational side of his life suffers from this focus. As a result, Matt doesn't appear to experience this stage of adaptation.

2. The *disintegration* stage, where as one begins to have to function at more than a tourist level in the country, one realizes the differences one is experiencing can be difficult, incomprehensible, and frustrating to overcome in order to achieve an even basic sense of competency. Likely, the individual has little or no social support system, feels responsible for his or her inability to perform, and so on. Some people never move out of this stage and lose their sense of self-efficacy. Eventually, the individual returns home early or becomes psychologically impaired, works less effectively, and sometimes retreats from the culture physically, emotionally, and mentally while still remaining in the country.

   Jan's experience with this is more related to her sense of isolation than it is a direct confrontation with cultural differences. Because she isn't working at first, she has no place to direct her energies and intelligence. Such a predicament tends to keep her in a less mature stage of adaptation because she isn't confronting differences that impede her ability to accomplish things as much as Matt is. She is isolated from confronting cultural differences except as they relate to issues like shopping and transportation.

   Matt, in contrast, is trying to determine his role in the joint venture and trying to influence the Japanese in Muhashi. In doing so, he confronts clear differences in how things operate in Muhashi from his experience in the United States. The result is some level of culture shock. Matt becomes frustrated with his inability to "get things done."

3. Those who survive and move successfully through the culture shock reach a new level of understanding of the culture, called *reintegration*. They begin to understand why things work the way they do. They begin to understand the deep level of the culture also to some degree—the values, assumptions, and beliefs of the host nationals. This may result in some stereotypes about the culture, but they reflect an observed pattern, indicating the newcomer has had enough experience to begin to see those patterns. Reaching this stage usually takes several months for a beginning understanding and can be several years before integrating the "pieces" to see the culture holistically. Training can speed the process immensely. Training can take the form of self-instruction, organizational training, being mentored formally or informally, and simply wanting to understand the host culture and reflecting on one's experiences to make sense of them instead of using that energy to become emotionally distraught.

4. If the expatriate continues to adapt, he or she moves into the *autonomy* stage. In this stage, the individual becomes increasingly independent and objective. The independence reflects increasing success based on a better understanding of the host culture.

Later, Matt is invited by some Japanese co-workers to come to their bar with them after work. It is here that he learns how things operate in Muhashi and why. Matt reaches a higher level of adaptation as a result and begins to know how to operate in Muhashi (and Japanese) culture. However, it is questionable whether he actually reaches the *autonomy* stage because he seems to require information from his Japanese peers in order to understand better.

5. Finally, the last stage is that of *interdependence*. This represents the ideal situation, where foreigners have become so proficient in the host culture that they can function as a host. They experience the range of activities and emotions that any other host member experiences. At the same time, they maintain a healthy perspective on the differences between cultures, can express the differences well, and understand the basis for those differences.

In this chapter, Jan didn't realize until near the end that she had been experiencing a shallow level of depression, reflecting a lack of acculturation. Such depression occurs because one is not integrated into society. One has no clear objective or structure, feeling as though one is not contributing any real value to anything. The individual has moved from a state of confidence and competency to a state of low self-efficacy and feelings of ineptness.

Jan had the advantage, however, of being open-minded. This chapter talks about some of the other American spouses who complained about the educational system and other things that seemed rather inconsequential to Jan—the smells of the fish market.

More than anything, then, this chapter introduces you to the mentality Jan brings to her foreign experience—an open-mindedness and curiosity. These are essential ingredients to eventual successful adaptation.

An Expatriate Adjustment Model

For a complete framework of international acculturation, probably the most comprehensive model in the management literature to date is one based on research and developed by Black, Mendenhall, and Oddou (1991) (see Figure 1 at end of chapter). It proposes there are anticipatory and in-country adjustments to be made and that each one can be broken down into several components.

Anticipatory Adjustment

Anticipatory adjustment is composed of individual and organizational components:

Individual components: Training and one's previous foreign experience. These two largely determine how accurate one's expectations are before going to the foreign country.

Organization components: Expatriate selection methods and the criteria used to select the expatriate. The more thorough the methods and comprehensive the criteria, the greater the likelihood the expatriate will be capable of adjusting to the foreign country. The criteria that should be used in selecting the expatriate were discussed in the last chapter. Thorough methods include careful interviewing of the potential expatriate and careful analysis of the person's work record and personal characteristics. Further, having the potential expatriate interview with former expatriates and their families is critical for an accurate perception of what lies ahead. Including the potential expatriate's family in the selection process is also very important.

In-Country Adjustment

There are individual, job, organization culture, organization socialization, and nonwork components to the in-country adjustment process.

Individual. These have already been named (self-efficacy—or self-orientation; relational skills—or others orientation; and perception skills).

Job Characteristics. These include role clarity (how clear one's role is to oneself—what am I supposed to accomplish?), role discretion (how much autonomy do I have in accomplishing my job?), role novelty (how much of my job is new to me?), and role conflict (does accomplishing my job put me in conflict with others doing their jobs?). Research seems to show that the clearer one's role, the more discretion one has, the less novel it is and the less conflict one experiences, the more likely one is to adapt to the foreign work environment.

Organization Culture. Another important variable in determining one's tendency to adjust to the new culture is the organizational culture of the firm abroad. This is composed of three facets: organization culture novelty (how new the culture of the organization is—the policies, procedures, management style, decision-making methods, etc.); social support (are there others of one's own culture available to help encourage, empathize, explain, or otherwise help the expat?), and logistical help (is there logistical help available for finding housing, locating suitable schooling for children, etc.?). As would seem logical, the more similar the foreign organization is, and the more social and logistical support one receives, the more likely one is to adjust.

Organization Socialization and Nonwork Variables. Organization socialization refers to the methods the organization uses to socialize its members and the content of the socialization. For the expatriate, the issue is whether the organization attempts to socialize the expat and how compatible the method and content are with what the expat is used to. Previously, we spoke of the importance of a host mentor, someone who takes charge of socializing the expatriate to the new organization and its members. In addition, nonwork variables include how well the spouse and family (if applicable) adjust and how new the culture in general is to the expatriate. Generally, the greater the difference in norms and language, the more difficult it is to adjust.

Three Types of Adjustment

Thus far we have talked about adjustment as though it were unidimensional. Research, however, has shown it to be multidimensional: adjustment to work, to interactions with the host nationals, and adjustment to the life in general in the foreign country.

Although each of the previously named variables has not been shown to be related to each of the three types of adjustments, there is probably insufficient research to say categorically which variables are related to which adjustments. For purposes of instruction, we simply list the three kinds of adjustments with the proviso that not all the variables are all related to each adjustment.

Application of the Black, Mendenhall & Oddou Model

Take each component of their model and briefly apply it to Matt, and where possible, to Jan's experience. Use it to show how well you would expect them to adjust to the Japanese culture. Be prepared to discuss your assessment in class.

1. *Anticipatory adjustment variables*
   a. Training (language and cultural training)

   _____
   _____
   _____
   _____

   b. Previous foreign experience

   _____
   _____
   _____
   _____

   c. Organization selection method and criteria (the process used to select Matt and the criteria used to select him)

   _____
   _____
   _____
   _____

2. *In-country adjustment variables*
   a. Individual variables (self-efficacy, relationship-building skills, perceptual skills that Matt—and Jan—have.)

   _____
   _____
   _____
   _____

   b. Organization socialization tactics, explicit or implicit, and content. (How did Muhashi attempt to help Matt learn "the ropes" at Muhashi; was it explicit (e.g., formal orientation and training) or implicit (learn by watching, inquiring, etc.)?

   _____
   _____
   _____
   _____

   c. Job characteristics (role clarity and discretion allowed Matt; novelty of his position/professional experience, and conflict inherent in the position he holds)

   _____
   _____
   _____
   _____

   d. Organization culture (novelty of Muhashi culture, support system— socially and logistically that Muhashi affords Matt)

   _____
   _____
   _____
   _____

   e. Nonwork variables (culture novelty of Japan and family-spouse adjustment of Matt, Jan, and the children)

   _____
   _____
   _____
   _____

3. *Expected adaptation to Japanese culture and Muhashi*
   Based on your preceding analysis, how well would you expect Matt and Jan to adapt to their new environment? Predict their adaptation in each of the following areas:
   a. Work adjustment (Matt):

   _____
   _____
   _____
   _____

b. Interaction adjustment (both Matt and Jan):

_____

_____

_____

_____

c. General adjustment (both Matt and Jan):

_____

_____

_____

_____

References

Black, S., Mendenhall, M., & Oddou, G. (1991). Toward a comprehensive model of international adjustment: An integration of multiple theoretical perspectives. *Academy of Management Review, 16*(2), 291–317.

Furnham, A., & Bochner, S. (1989). *Culture shock.* London: Routledge Press.

Lysgaard, S. (1955). Adjustment in a foreign society: Norwegian Fulbright grantees visiting the United States. *International Social Science Bulletin, 7,* 45–51.

MOW International Research Team. (1985). *The meaning of working: An international perspective.* London: Academic Press.

Pedersen, P. (1988). *A handbook for developing multicultural awareness.* Alexandria, VA: American Association for Counseling and Development.

Related Readings

Religion

1. Seward, J. (1972). "Their religions." In *The Japanese* (pp. 187–210). New York: William Morrow.
   This chapter provides a detailed historical background of the major religions in Japan (Shintoism, Buddhism, Zen Buddhism, and Confucianism), and discusses their effects in Japanese culture and social organization. It also shows the contrasts between Christianity and the other religions adopted in Japan.
2. Durlabhi, S. (1990). The influence of Confucianism and Zen on the Japanese organization. In S. Durlabhji & N. Marks (Eds.), *Japanese business: Cultural perspectives* (pp. 57–75). Albany, NY: SUNY Press.
   Explores the success of the Japanese organization as a social system in relation to Confucianism and Zen. Provides an explanation for the strong needs seen in Japanese organizations for lifetime employment, community orientation, collective conscience, as well as a brief historical background of Confucianism and Zen in Japan.

Nonreligion Resources

1. De Mente, B. (1987). Gakubatsu (rule by cliques). *Japanese Etiquette and Ethics in Business* (pp. 30–33). Lincolnwood, IL: Passport Books.
   Discusses the university system in Japan, its focal point as a place where important relationships are developed and one's career can be set. It can add insight to Satoh's career description in the chapter.
2. Mariko, S. (1994). Five fatal symptoms of the Japanese disease. *Japan Echo 21*(2), 68–74.
   Exceptional article on Japan because it contrasts the old Japan (which is still very much alive in large part) with the new Japan. In the context of this contrast, it also discusses discrimination as an artifact of homogeneity, women in the work force, the Japanese work ethic, creativity, and civic morality (in *Japan Echo* by S. Mariko, *21*(2), 34–58).
   This article could certainly be useful for Chapters 4 through 7. The discussion goes well beyond discrimination against other ethnic groups to discrimination against anything foreign.
3. Takahashi, N. (1992). Engineering education in Japan. *IEEE Communications Magazine, 30*(11), pp. 28–36.
   Technical article about re-engineering education in Japan. Offers a good comparison of the Japanese versus the American system in the first few pages, but gets very detailed afterward in dealing more with educational reform.
4. Concar, D. (1993). Examination hell. *New Scientist, 140*(1993), 51–53.
   Focuses on the battle Japanese students wage in order to enter Japan's best universities. Provides a description of the *juku* (cram schools), and the expenses of education in Japan. Also questions the effectiveness of this system and how it affects the development of creativity in Japanese students.
5. Black, S., Gregersen, H. & Mendenhall, M. Adjusting: Developing new mental road maps and behaviors. In *Global assignments: Successfully expatriating and repatriating international managers* (pp. 115–136). San Francisco: Jossey-Bass
   Focuses on the process of adjustment during global assignments. Among the issues discussed are the factors that influence cross-cultural adjustment, the different areas of adjustment, and anticipatory and in-country adjustment.

Expatriate Adjustment Model

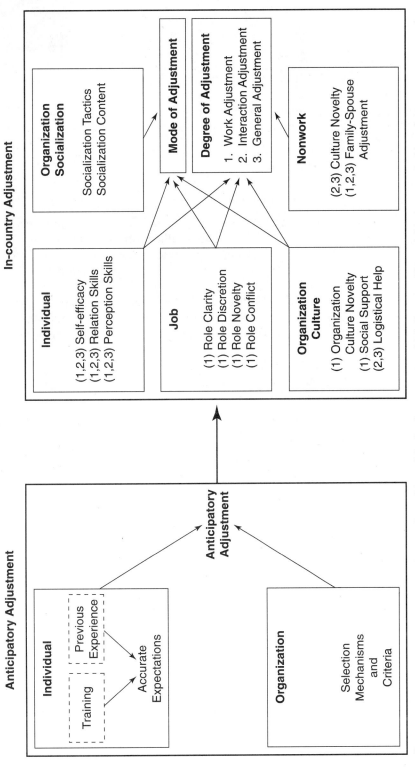

Anticipatory Adjustment

In-country Adjustment

Framework of International Adjustment[a]

Anticipatory Adjustment

Individual

Training
Previous Experience
Accurate Expectations

Organization

Selection Mechanisms and Criteria

Individual

(1,2,3) Self-efficacy
(1,2,3) Relation Skills
(1,2,3) Perception Skills

Job

(1) Role Clarity
(1) Role Discretion
(1) Role Novelty
(1) Role Conflict

Organization Culture

(1) Organization Culture Novelty
(1) Social Support
(2,3) Logistical Help

Organization Socialization

Socialization Tactics
Socialization Content

Mode of Adjustment

Degree of Adjustment

1. Work Adjustment
2. Interaction Adjustment
3. General Adjustment

Nonwork

(2,3) Culture Novelty
(1,2,3) Family-Spouse Adjustment

[a] Numbers in parentheses indicate the numbered facet(s) of adjustment to which the specific variable is expected to relate.

CHAPTER 6

USEFUL CONCEPTS

This chapter also covers a variety of topics very relevant to understanding management in its international context:

- Career systems
- Ethnic prejudices
- Managing cultural diversity
- Joint venture relationships

In looking at career systems, we focus on the Japanese, and to a lesser extent, the U.S., and French. Because all countries suffer to some degree from ethnic prejudices, which can have profound influences on doing business with these countries and on managing different ethnic groups domestically, these issues are very important topics.

Now that Muhashi and MedTech's business partnership is well underway, it is important to examine their joint venture relationship again as it reflects a more entrenched partnership and more sophisticated management questions.

Career Systems

The Japanese Cohort Career System

As explained in describing Satoh's experience, the Japanese career system in large companies starts most obviously at college graduation. The largest Japanese firms hire cohort groups from the best universities in Japan (Tokyo University, Keio University, etc.). A cohort group might consist of 50 to 100 or more graduates from the same university. Most of them are engineers, reflecting Japan's largely manufacturing-based economy. These cohorts are hired at the same nonsupervisory level in different areas of the firm: manufacturing, marketing, finance, and so on. They remain there for approximately six years before moving to a supervisory position. However, during these training years they are usually moved around within their functional area at least two times to gain a broader perspective of the firm's operations. For example, they might move from product development to marketing research to marketing strategy.

What qualifies them to take a supervisory position is not their performance per se but traditionally is the time they have spent in their first positions. Typically, all cohorts move at about the same rate in the first part of their career.

They then act as supervisors for another three to five years depending on their performance and the attrition rate above them. At this level, however, performance is only one important criterion determining their ability to move to a low middle management position (usually a section chief). Again, time is probably the most important element, but as the Japanese economy continues to suffer, more emphasis is being put on performance. After another five years, if there are open-ings and if the individual's performance has been adequate, the Japanese likely move to a solid middle management position.

After a number of years here, typically around the age of 50, the individual might move to a director-level position, the first level of upper management. Some individuals never reach the director level in the parent firm they are hired into and stay at a middle management position until retirement. Others are "retired into" a director-level position in a subsidiary or joint venture firm before retiring.

Implications of the Japanese System. The implications of the Japanese career system are several.

a. *Motivation.* Although things are changing in Japan, for most young Japanese the grand objective is still to be hired by one of the giant Japanese firms that maintains lifetime employment. In order to get into one of these firms and enjoy lifetime employment, one must graduate from the best universities, which means graduating from the best high schools, the best junior high schools and so on. Everything is pointed toward gaining employment with one of the large, powerful Japanese firms (Honda, Sanyo, Matsushita, Sony, etc.) by passing the national university entrance exam at a high level in order to get admitted to one of the best universities. In short, Japanese youth learn a *keen work ethic, focus, and dedication* at an early age. They learn to *sacrifice*. While others might be enjoying themselves on the weekend or after school, those destined to work in the best companies are studying extra hours and forgoing pleasure.

After achieving employment with one of these firms, long hours (often 10- to 12-hour days) and long weeks (usually six days) are still the norm (although the slow economy has curtailed the necessity for some of that). Why do the Japanese continue to work so hard for so long? Partly because it is part of the unwritten reciprocal agreement. In the conglomerates, the firm gives lifetime employment, assuring the individual and his family of the security and status so important to the Japanese. The company will take care of the employee and his family. In exchange, to *fulfill the debt* then created by the firm's generosity, the *employee gives his "life"* to ensure the continuation of the firm. To not work hard and not be a strong team player would mean an unwillingness to acknowledge this debt. This would bring dishonor to the indi-vidual and his family. To "lose face" in Japan is to lose your place in society. Losing your place in society is tantamount to death for a Japanese. After all, life in Japan is still learning where you fit into the "group" (your family; your com-pany). Your very identity is inseparable from the "group."

In smaller firms, employees work hard because it is simply a matter of sur-vival. Competition at the small-firm level, especially among the small manu-facturing firms the large ones subcontract to, is fierce. And particularly during economic downturns, the larger firms "squeeze" their smaller "associates" to reduce costs while maintaining the same quality. It is these smaller firms that suffer first and perhaps the most during economically bad times.

Certainly, this notion of reciprocation between employees and employers is basically unknown in the United States. The mentality is generally totally different: the individual in the United States, as in other strongly individualistic cultures, looks out for himself and the firm does what is in its best interest. Hence there is a clear need for attention to motivation.

Japanese firms, small and large, have traditionally not had to entice their employees with motivational schemes as is the case in the United States, and in some other countries. Instead, the motivation comes from within as a reflection of sensing one's place within a collectivist society.

The ancient origin of this relationship between firm and employee comes from feudal days. The lord of the land required serfs to produce for him in order to maintain his power base. In turn, the lord offered protection from warring lords and a small plot of land for the serf's and his family's existence. Over time, this relationship evolved into the modern practice of lifetime employment. It was in the feudal days and it is today in the best interest of the employer and the employed to "protect" each other.

In modern times, it has been the post–World War II need that has driven the Japanese to once again create this symbiotic relationship. Economically devastated, Japan had to pull together to build a strong manufacturing base. Economic survival meant "tying the knot" again between employee and employer within the large family Japanese organizations that were still held in place by their strong networks.

Now that the Japanese economy has began to suffer from extreme debt and a slowing demand, the need for such a reciprocating relationship between employee and employer is questionable. Some Japanese are beginning to consider their options. Consider the following:

In a survey by Sumitomo Bank of 500 men in their 40s and 50s, about 4.5% said they would choose their present job again if given the choice. There was clear dissatisfaction with low pay, limited holidays, and considerable overtime. Further, Frankel and Takayama (1993) report that in a study of 10,000 men in Tokyo between 20 and 39, nearly 40% were thinking of changing jobs.

In addition to theses trends, the Asahi Bank conducted a study in 1994 ("Crumbling Japanese-style," 1995), and found that 27% of all enterprises queried felt the lifetime employment system was breaking down and 64% felt it would have to be modified. A large majority of the firms reported they did not care if their employees had worked in another firm before being hired.

Clearly, there is a trend toward job mobility in the Japanese culture despite the fact that traditions still prevail in many companies.

This mobility is even more clear in other select studies. Tachibanaki (1984) presents data that show most Japanese change jobs at least once in their lifetime. In his study, only a third to a half, depending on their age (participants ranged from early 40s to early 50s), had worked for only one company. Still, this is an extremely high figure compared to what would be true in most American firms. In Silicon Valley, for example, most employees, especially marketers and engineers, typically switch firms every three to four years (in good economic times).

A figure often given is that 30% of Japanese firms practice lifetime employment (Shimada, 1986). Of course, those who are employed for their professional life at these firms include primarily male university graduates.

b. *Communications and coordination.* Effective communications occur when the channels are clear, information is "untainted," reflective of genuine desire on the part of the communicators and when the information is timely. Japanese corporations tend to have slower but overall probably more effective communications than U.S. firms. Channels are clear when individuals have a structure of communications to follow. Such a structure is given by clear position relationships. However, having such a structure by which information flows can impede speedy resolution of problems. Communications in Japanese corporations tends to be horizontal and vertical but not diagonal. Thus to move diagonally in Japanese communications requires more time and involves more people. The employee must respect the hierarchy and always communicate through his or her direct manager when communicating outside the peer group.

The information, however, tends to be unpoliticized relative to communications in most other countries. This is in part true because of the lifetime employment practice. The Japanese cadre in these large organizations tend to stay with the same firm for life, and their loyalty to it is significant. Having such loyalty means their interests are much more aligned with the interests of the organization. The fact that promotions are also much more structured in process means there is less politicking, or selective information filtering and disseminating, than in firms in cultures where promotions are based mostly on one or two managers' viewpoints.

With a lot of communication occurring in the Japanese organization, many people share similar information. Sharing such information and also with their consensus decision-making style, coordinating efforts becomes much easier.

c. *Deep-level cultural values.* At the deep level, the Japanese career system still relates to the fundamental Japanese values of collectivism (i.e., the importance of relationships): cohort group recruitment and promotion rate; sacrificing individual time for company; network development and maintenance; communication channels and sharing of information.

U.S. Career System

Obviously, the differences between the Japanese and American systems are stark. Large U.S. firms do not hire cohort groups from one or two universities; in fact many of them like to hire from several universities in order to specifically create diversity. From the very start in U.S. firms, it is performance that counts rather than primarily connections. As openings arise or are created to make room for a "rising star," those individuals with the best performance are theoretically quickly slotted into them. Traditionally, the faster one moves up, the better it is viewed and the more promise the individual has in the firm. As a generalization, if four or more years pass after being hired and the employee is not moved into a more important role—often a supervisory one—the individual either moves to another firm or realizes he or she is not destined for upper management in the firm.

Increasingly, however, careers are not spent in one firm. At the risk of generalizing, there is a 3- to 5- year growth track by many employees followed by a similar stint in another firm. The individual seeks a career track that matches his or her needs for job interest, personal growth, and promotional opportunity.

In short, whereas the emphasis in the Japanese system is to learn patience, learn the company and its culture well, establish solid horizontal connections in the company, and develop a strong team ethic, the U.S. system typically encourages impatience (move up as quickly as you can—don't get left behind or else move to another firm), learning just what you need to know to perform your job well (emphasis is on specialization), and working well with others yet realizing that promotions are based on individual performance. Increasingly, the *emphasis is on self* as the center of one's career track, quite the opposite of the typical Japanese careerist.

French Elite Career System

France still has somewhat of a class society, albeit a modern and somewhat flexible class society. Traditionally, and still very true today, generally those individuals who attend the *grandes écoles* are destined for top management positions in middle to large French manufacturing or utility companies. In the distribution sector, this is much less true. The *grandes écoles* are the technical universities (the polytechnic schools), the engineering schools, although the top business schools are also very highly regarded. Within the polytechnic and top business schools, there is a clear hierarchical order, with the Paris schools typically on top. For top-level administrative positions in French government, one must have graduated from the equivalent university, ENA (national administrative school). Entrance into these *grandes écoles* is by performance on national entrance tests, emphasizing math and sciences to a large degree.

Being a graduate of these top schools, unless one's performance is obviously poor to average, it can be assumed the graduate will reach some level of upper management. In other words, performance is important but pedigree is at least as important. (The French career system is covered in more detail within the French section of Part I.)

Ethnic Prejudices

As previously alluded to in other chapters, every culturally diverse society typically has a hierarchy in terms of a "majority" ethnic group and the "minority" ones (quotes are used because the "majority" refers to the amount of power or influence rather than absolute numbers). Very often, different segments of the society are associated with different aspects of markets or different power positions in the society. For example, certainly in the United States, whites hold most of the power positions in government and business, yet there are segments of government and business that reflect significant numbers of other ethnic groups, often as a result of affirmative action and equal employment opportunity policies. As a result, public institutions and private institutions, closely allied to the government in terms of markets, often reflect significantly greater numbers of Asians, Hispanics, and blacks.

Other cultures, as we see in Chapter 8, also reflect this power structure relative to ethnic groups. Because market entry into a society is essential to market growth, businesses must be conscious of the importance of the power structure of the country as it relates to ethnic groups.

This chapter discusses the traditionally strong ethnic prejudices within Japan. At least partly due to historical relationships, many Japanese, particularly the city-bred Japanese, have reportedly thought of themselves as superior to other ethnic groups and to rural Japanese. This sense of superiority is not reflected in verbiage as much as in actual behavior—similar to the somewhat exclusionary behavior the Japanese exhibit toward foreigners in general in the marketplace.

Having conquered Korea during one of their wars, the Japanese brought back Korean women and men as mistresses and slaves, respectively. As Koreans have gained more status within Japan, they have still remained so-called second-class citizens. Rural Japanese have likewise maintained a somewhat lower-level status from the educated, city-dwelling Japanese. In addition, other ethnic groups, whatever they be, are excluded from the same privileges most Japanese have available to them. How much of this prejudice is from historical relationships, that is, based on experience, versus prejudice based on innate feelings of superiority, is not clear. Some Japanese sociologists claim that because Japanese experience with foreigners, historically, has been more as enemies than friends, this has bred an innate mistrust of foreigners. We see this relationship economically with foreign businesses trying to do business in Japan. They are often excluded from many insider privileges because they have not been part of the "network" for many, many years. They have not been part of the "family."

Every culture has its ethnic prejudices and challenges. Japan is not alone. In the United States there are sometimes strong feelings toward other groups among the Asians, blacks, whites, and Latinos/Mexican Americans/Hispanics. In France, there are ethnic issues between the "indigenous" French and the North African French-speaking Arabs who live in France. In Singapore, there are underlying feelings among the Chinese, Malays, and Indians, and the list could go on and on.

What are the sources of these relationships? Are they historical? Has the present generation in each of these societies inherited misdoings by its forebears? What is being done to try and resolve the differences? And very importantly, what does this have to do with international business and managing others from different cultures and subcultures?

These questions lead to the issue of how to better manage increasing work force diversity, which we discuss in the next section.

Managing Cultural Diversity

In every country there is diversity, whether it be from ethnicity, gender, age, or religion. The challenge is to manage that diversity for the benefit of everyone. In countries such as Singapore, as we discussed in more detail in Chapter 8, martial law, government policies, and moral education seem to be the primary forces behind managing their society, including their ethnic groups. In other countries, such as the United States, policies such as affirmative action and equal opportunity are government-leveled methods for trying to manage certain aspects of the diversity in that country.

Nevertheless, beyond governmental intervention, organizations certainly can and do play a powerful role in determining how diversity is managed.

Cox (1991) has developed a model which shows three major types of organizations and their *degree of minority-majority employee integration:*

Monolithic Organizations
1. Minority group must assimilate into the majority culture (i.e., minority must adopt their behaviors).
2. Little to no structural integration of minority members occurs (i.e., no diversity policies or structures are developed regarding hiring, job placement, or job status profiles for minority members).
3. Little to no informal integration of minority members into networks and activities outside of work occurs.
4. Outright discrimination is evident against minority members.
5. A large gap in commitment to the organization characterizes the minority-majority orientation.
6. The degree of conflict between minority and majority groups is virtually nonexistent because of the impotence or passiveness of the minority group.

Plural Organizations
1. Minority group must assimilate into the majority culture (as monolithics).
2. Some structural integration of minority members occurs (i.e., some diversity policies or structures are developed regarding hiring, job placement, or job status profiles for minority members).
3. Limited informal integration of minority members into networks and activities outside of work occurs.
4. Discrimination is evident mostly institutionally; less so among employees.
5. A medium to large gap in commitment to the organization characterizes the minority-majority orientation.
6. The degree of conflict between minority and majority groups can be quite high because of the more egalitarian culture between both groups.

Multicultural Organizations
1. There is clear cultural pluralism within the organization.
2. Full structural integration of minority members occurs (i.e., some diversity policies or structures are developed regarding hiring, job placement, or job status profiles for minority members).
3. Full informal integration of minority members into networks and activities outside of work occurs.
4. No substantive discrimination or prejudice exists.
5. No gap in commitment to the organization characterizes the minority-majority orientation. Both groups feel equally a part of the organization.
6. The degree of conflict between minority and majority groups is low because no real distinction is made between the two groups.

Of course, to a large extent, organizations are only reflections of their larger society. For example, in Japan, virtually no non-Japanese hold important positions in government or business. Furthermore, almost no female Japanese hold important, substantive positions in government or business. In Sweden, although men hold most of the higher-level positions in government and business, there appears to be little discrimination against women. It is apparently more a matter of individual choice.

In the United States, organizations have been trying to deal more effectively with the diversity issue than in the past. Unfortunate events such as the Los Angeles riots and Rodney King beating have raised to the surface some of the latent conflict existing between ethnic groups. Firms have begun to institute policies to create more equality in response to socially driven motives. They have also begun to be more strategic in managing the diversity in order to use it as a strategic advantage.

Oddou found in his research (1987) that many companies in the Silicon Valley area viewed ethnic and other diversity as a potential asset, particularly given the large numbers of highly qualified Asian and Indian professionals and the high numbers of Asian and Latino population in nonprofessional positions. In order to integrate these groups into the larger work force, high-tech companies have employed a number of strategies:

1. Giving English as a Second Language (ESL) instruction, paid for by the company.
2. Adopting some aspects of the multiple cultures represented (e.g., cafeteria dishes from various countries, celebrating their holidays, etc.).
3. Using bilingual assistants to help in their recruiting and hiring practices.
4. Initiating cross-cultural mentoring, wherein managers "adopt" foreign-born employees to aid in their professional development.
5. Making cultural information available to managers of foreign born.
6. Increasing the number of seminars to teach diversity management.
7. Giving bonuses to employees for increasing their language skills based on standardized testing.

Of course, many other things can and are being done to manage diversity in all of its manifestations including being aware of and better managing the acculturation of those less familiar with the host culture.

Two researchers (Cox & Finley-Nickelson, 1991) have developed a model that includes factors affecting acculturation and levels of acculturation:

Individual Factors	**Intergroup Factors**	**Organizational Factors**
Culture group identity structures of minority culture members	Degree of similarity of norm systems	Degree to which cultural diversity is valued
	Degree of complementarity of norm systems	Organizational culture identity structure
	Knowledge of specific cultural differences	

Modes of Acculturation
Assimilation
Separation
Deculturation
Pluralism

Basically, this model states that these factors determine to what degree acculturation occurs:

- the strength of one's identity with one's own culture
- the degree of differences between minority and majority cultures and the knowledge of those differences
- the value of diversity seen and cultivated by organizations

The mode of acculturation ranges from assimilation to pluralism. Assimilation means minority members must surrender their differences in order to function effectively in the majority culture. Separation refers to those minority individuals who refuse to give up their own cultural identity in order to be assimilated; as a result, two separate cultures exist. Deculturation occurs when individuals have lost their own former cultural identity but have not completely adopted or been adopted into the majority culture. Finally, pluralism refers to the highest degree of acculturation—true integration of both cultures, giving rise to a third kind of culture.

All of these states of acculturation can be permanent, depending on the situation. Obviously, there are benefits and costs to each type of adaptation, although most would probably agree that pluralism is the goal.

Joint Venture Relationships: Muhashi and MedTech

Joint ventures are an excellent example of an organizational structure that can become a pluralistic type depending on the owners and managers of the two companies.

JVs of any type between a Japanese firm and a foreign one usually reflect a mutually benefiting relationship. The Japanese firm typically serves as distributor with all the necessary relationships, and the foreign firm supplies the product. Of the two elements, providing access to the market undoubtedly serves to put the Japanese firm in the "dominant" position. In addition, for those "protected" industries, Japanese law disallows majority ownership of a joint venture by a foreign firm.

We see this superior-subordinate relationship between Muhashi and Medtech as reflected in Muhashi's relationship with Matt. Muhashi is clearly running the show when it comes to marketing decisions. Matt sometimes gives input, most of the time he feels ignored, and often only when asked does Muhashi explain its reasons for what it is doing. This does not mean the relationship is a poor one. If products sell well, both firms benefit. Muhashi certainly knows the local market and has been successful. Active intervention by MedTech in the marketing aspects is probably unnecessary and undesirable. *What needs to be managed is their mutual expectations.* At this point, MedTech, via Matt, is still wondering what its role is and is in the process of determining that. Their relationship was essentially fixed from the beginning, but MedTech's understanding of their relationship is evolving.

A discussion about this relationship is not unrelated to the ethnic prejudice issue previously discussed. The Japanese are, for all intents and purposes, economically unfriendly to outsiders. They have dealt with each other in an interconnected and hierarchical fashion for so long that their system has been essentially complete within itself.

References

Cox, T. (1991). Multicultural organization. *Academy of Management Executive,* pp. 34–47.

Cox T. & Finley-Nickelson, J. (1991). Models of acculturation for intra-organizational cultural diversity. *Canadian Journal of Administrative Sciences,* 8(2), 1–15.

Crumbling Japanese-style personnel management system. (1995, April). *Japan 21st,* p. 67.

Frankel, M. & Takayama, H. (1993). The freedom to choose. *Newsweek,* p. 51.

Oddou, G. (1987). Unlocking a hidden resource: Integrating the foreign-born? *Northern California Executive Review,* 1, 1–5.

Shimada, H. (1986). The perceptions and the reality of Japanese industrial relations. In L. C. Thurow (Ed.), *The management challenge: Japanese views.* Cambridge, MA: MIT Press.

Tachibanaki, T. (1984). Labour mobility and job tenure. In M. Aoki, (Ed.), *The economic analysis of the Japanese Firm.* New York: North-Holland.

Related Readings

1. Shakai, T. Gakubatsu. *Japanese Etiquette and Ethics in Business.*
   This short article is about the university system in Japan, its focal point as a place where important relationships are developed and one's career can be set. It can add insight to Satoh's career description found in the text.

2. Johnson, C. (1993). The institutional foundations of Japanese industrial policy. In S. Durlabhji & N. Marks (Eds.), *Japanese business: Cultural perspectives* (pp. 141–154). Albany, NY: SUNY Press.
   Excellent article that adds depth to the explanation of the LDP party's traditional influence on Japan and the linkages in general between government and business.
3. Mariko, S. (1994). Five fatal symptoms of the Japanese disease, *Japan Echo, 21,* (2), 68–74.
   Exceptional article on Japan because it contrasts the "old" Japan (which is still very much alive in large part) with the "new" Japan. In the context of this contrast, it also discusses discrimination as an artifact of homogeneity, women in the work force, the Japanese work ethic, creativity, and civic morality.
4. De Mente, B. (1987). Finding, hiring, and keeping employees. In *How to do business with the Japanese: A complete guide to Japanese customs and business practices.* (pp. 127–150), (1987). Lincolnwood, IL: Passport Books.
   Describes Japanese hiring practices, discrimination, attitudes toward the foreign born/educated, and the problems that American companies may encounter when trying to hire in Japan. It also touches on the issue of lifelong employment and mobility in the Japanese business world.
5. Black, S., Gregersen, H., & Mendenhall, M. (1992). Adjusting: Developing new mental road maps and behaviors. In *Global Assignments: Successfully expatriating and repatriating international managers* (pp. 115–136). San Francisco, CA: Jossey-Bass.
   Focuses on the process of adjustment during global assignments. Among the issues discussed are the factors that influence cross-cultural adjustment, the different areas of adjustment, and anticipatory and in-country adjustment.

CHAPTER 7

USEFUL CONCEPTS

The following topics are the focus of this chapter:

- Power structure and hierarchy in Japan
- The importance of building and maintaining relationships in Japan

Power Structure and Hierarchy in Japan

As discussed in Chapter 6, it is essential in international business to recognize and work within the power structure of a given society. There are several manifestations of the importance of hierarchy in Japan that are mentioned in the chapter: first, the incident in the restaurant-bar where Matt addresses the waitress as if she were a child or a pet without realizing he was using the wrong word for "you"; second, the description of the *keiretsu* organizations as hierarchical structures with the most important parts of the organization at the top and the least at the bottom; third, the different treatment given men and women in Japanese society, as reflected in hiring and firing policies, where women are hired generally on a "part-time" basis (even if the part time is full time in hours) so they can be easily let go in economic downturns and are still not regularly hired as lifetime employees.

In addition, in companies, uniforms are worn for identification (and classification) purposes, and it is mostly women who are at the lower level in the companies and who are therefore required to wear the uniforms; tea bearers in firms and other establishments are women, even though these women might have a college degree; finally, women's thoughts on their husbands' professional decisions are still not as sought out or as welcomed in Japan as in much of the rest of the world. This is evident in the advice Matt's Japanese friends give him on how to approach Mr. Satoh to mention that he cannot remain in Japan much longer. They tell him to not mention how his wife feels because they know Mr. Satoh will not give it any credence and it will undermine his confidence in Matt.

There are two essential pedagogical points about the discussion on hierarchy, both of them fairly obvious: (1) hierarchy is based on and reflects the power structure in Japanese society. Japanese society is not one of egalitarianism, although it is becoming more so with the economic downturn pressuring the Japanese to develop a more flexible and responsive society. Instead, it is still more a society of power relationships that have tended to remain stable over generations of time; (2) Japan is a country of interconnecting relationships, the topic of the next section.

The Importance of Building and Maintaining Relationships in Japan

The importance of relationships is reflected in at least two parts of this chapter: First, the description of unions, how they are organized, their membership composition, and their relationship to the firm; second, Satoh's clear reluctance to endorse the exchange between Matt and Carl, Matt's replacement at MedTech.

Unions are typically organized within only the large companies, the ones that offer lifetime employment and other such benefits. They consist of all nonmanagerial ranks plus the first level of management in the company. This kind of composition with overlapping union membership only serves to strengthen shared perspectives between nonmanagement and management. The result is typically more effective communication, more common values, and a sense of greater interdependence. This is reflected in the incident stated in the chapter with Sony's president Akio Morita, who, it is said, asked his union to strike. The underlying statement was to remind Sony management how indispensable its nonmanagement workers were, creating a stronger bond between the two.

The second situation that specifically indicates the importance of developing and maintaining relationships in Japan pertains to the Matt-Carl exchange. Satoh explains to Matt that he is already familiar with all the contacts within Muhashi and they with him, that he had already invested three years in Japan and someone new would have to start all over, and finally, that Muhashi was getting ready to introduce him to others within their distribution network. This was as direct a message as Satoh could deliver without coming out and saying, "No, this is a terrible idea."

For the Japanese, this practice reflects the importance of relationships developing over time and the trust that ensues. Matt views his role in Japan as principally symbolic. Therefore, what makes good sense is for him to let someone else be the symbol so he can make a substantive difference back at MedTech.

Related Readings

1. Ohta, T. (1988). Work rules in Japan. In S. Durlabhji & N. Marks (Eds.), *Japanese business: Cultural perspectives* (pp. 153–167). Albany, NY: SUNY Press.
   Provides a description of Japanese labor standards and laws. Important issues include termination of contracts, working conditions, wages, accident compensation, and occupational safety and health.
2. Masataka, I. (1994). People as databases: An analysis of Japanese-style management. *Japan Echo, 21* (4), 55–61.
   Much of Chapter 7 is about organizational life in Japan. This article looks at the sources and uses of order in Japanese organizations and related issues such as motivation and obligation. Like the article on five fatal symptoms cited in the last chapter, this article sets the discussion in light of changes occurring in Japan.
3. De Mente, B. (1987). Peculiarities of Japanese unions. In *How to Do Business with the Japanese* (pp. 151–156). Lincolnwood, IL: Passport Books.
   Brief description of unions in Japan and their functioning. The author also gives some warnings regarding unions to foreign firms wishing to establish operations in Japan.
4. Kopp, R. (1994). How the Japanese approach to personnel management is changing. In *The Rice-Paper Ceiling* (pp. 221–232). Berkeley, CA: Stone Bridge Press.
   Discusses different factors that threaten the Japanese system of lifetime employment,

and eventually will force a drastic change in personnel management. Among the issues covered are the problems with efficiency, lack of specialization, the effect of the current system on motivation, the values of the younger generation of Japanese, and changes companies will have to make to maintain competitiveness.

5. Kopp, R. (1994). Participating in Japanese-style decision-making. In *The Rice-Paper Ceiling* (pp. 141–151). Berkeley, CA: Stone Bridge Press.

 Discusses the style of Japanese decision making. It explains the importance of *nemawashi,* the discussion of ideas with key decision makers, and the *ringisho* process of decision making. Finally, the chapter provides some advice to Americans conducting business in Japan to help them adapt to this new process.

CHAPTER 8

USEFUL CONCEPTS

The topics covered in Chapter 8 serve to reinforce several very important concepts. In addition, this chapter broadens the topic of relationships, reinforces the importance of ethnic group understanding, and relates an important Chinese belief that guides many modern, educated Chinese businesspersons today.

The Importance of Building and Maintaining Relationships In Asia

This chapter, as those about Japan only, also extols the importance of developing relationships before proceeding on to business matters. This is a characteristic of all high-context cultures: Arabic, Latin, African, and Asian societies. In all three locales in this chapter, an obvious attempt was made to take time to show Matt and Jan around their cities and/or islands and to give personalized attention—even when there was no real intent on developing a business relationship—and even though the two parties had only a small amount of time together. This reflects the importance of developing a relationship—no matter how abbreviated—before entering into specific business discussions.

The Hierarchy of Ethnic Groups

In Chapter 7 we discussed discrimination as it relates to ethnic and other differences. Ethnicity is not just an important issue in Japan. In most Asian countries, particularly those that are not homogeneous, it continues to play an important role. In Hong Kong, there is not much ethnic diversity beyond Chinese because of very strict immigration laws, among other reasons. There are, however, the powerful, rich Chinese and those that are much less well off materially. This difference manifests itself in the type and location of housing as it does in all countries. (Many of the less endowed Chinese live closer to the airport in large apartment complexes, for example; most of the rich live in luxurious apartments or homes closer to or on the sides of the mountains surrounding the harbors—where many expatriates live.)

However, in Singapore and Malaysia, there are multiple ethnic groupings with a clear hierarchy or division among ethnic groups. In Singapore, although it is commonly believed there are underlying animosities between the Indians, Malays, and Chinese, the extreme tight government control on all groups in the former British colony has given the impression of peaceful coexistence. Plus, there is some attempt to encourage harmony by requiring children in schools to sing a song about living in peace and harmony.

In Malaysia, although the Malays and the immigrant Chinese have tended to get along, with the modernization of Malaysia, there is growing tension among the groups. The Malays have apparently become more interested in gaining control in the business sector.

These ethnic differences and challenges can be compared and contrasted to the Japanese-Korean issues that still tend to characterize Japan. One of the most obvious differences is the reason why the ethnic groups are mixed. In Japan, Koreans were brought back as slaves from the war with Japan. Their role from the start was subservient. In Singapore, as with Malays, the Chinese emigrated from China. Because of their strong network and work ethic, they were able to surpass the indigenous people. The Indians in Singapore came as poor, uneducated people and did not have the same work ethic or connections to wealth as the Chinese.

These differences have obviously created interesting implications for management in these countries. In Malaysia, the power dynamic is principally between the government (Malays) and business (Chinese). Each side cooperates because it helps the country as a whole. Most often in business, it is the Chinese who own and run the enterprise and the Malays or other economically less endowed groups who work on the factory floor.

In Singapore, the Chinese have been high achievers (as they are seemingly everywhere in the world—Africa, North America, etc.), allowed to flourish under the British and reach high positions in government and industry. There is a more pervasive Chinese influence as a result. They have not had to share their power base as in Malay, and by and large, they seem to not want to do so. The management dynamic here is between management (largely Chinese) and nonmanagement (largely Malays, Indians, and less educated Chinese).

Indigenous Belief Systems

A society's behavior is shaped by many beliefs. Some of those beliefs reflect recent knowledge and modern practices; others reflect age-old traditions and belief systems. Although some of the age-old beliefs might seem strange and antiquated to more modern societies, it is important not to dismiss such beliefs. Such ways of thinking still influence people's thinking and should be respected.

Although only briefly mentioned in the section on Hong Kong, the feng shui belief of the Chinese still does have an important effect on Chinese thought and decisions. Because the Chinese are an important influence in a number of Asian countries, it is worth mentioning here. The Chinese believe life is composed of energy and energy systems. *Chi*, for example, is one's central energy force that can be directed and used to influence people and events. It can also be used to heal oneself physically. A follower of feng shui believes, for example, that sickness and disease is usually the result of the natural system of energy flow being blocked. Reopening those blockages so energy can flow where it should releases the healing forces in the body or releases the natural energy flow in the environment. "Deblocking" such flow could include acupuncture, moving furniture to different places, lowering stairway railing, redesigning a straight front sidewalk, and so on. Everything has an energy source and the field of energy is dynamic. Energy that is positively directed flows from mountains and rivers in a certain direction. Therefore, when building a home or building, it must be positioned so it is in harmony with the energy flow in that particular area. If it isn't, the building might be in direct confrontation with the energy flow, which would cause those in the building to suffer from negative energy or the lack of positive energy. The result, for example, could lead to employees who get sick more often and to poor business dealings.

Similarly, the Chinese believe that harsh angles (e.g., square windows) block energy flow and create a negative tension at that angle. Stairways that open to the door are bad because they allow a potentially unhealthy flow of energy in relationship to the outside.

For a Westerner, these beliefs can seem superstitious and appear nonsensical. Whether they are true or not, however, is not the issue. Many of the Chinese—including well-educated, successful businesspeople—believe in feng shui and act on it. The challenge for the Western businessperson is to acknowledge that others believe in it and to respect it. It is no different from the custom or Western belief that people can make of their lives what they want. This can be difficult for some fundamental Muslims to accept because of the belief that God is in charge of our destinies. Yet this Western notion (perhaps especially American) of manifest destiny must be understood if foreigners are to understand Westerners' behavior.

Related Readings

1. Chow, J. (Producer) & Wang, C. (Co-Producer). (1990). *Doing Business in Hong-Kong* [video]. Made for KCTS, Seattle, WA; PBS Adult Learning Satellite Service, 1991. KCTS phone number: 1-800-443-1999.
   Presents informative case studies including individuals from Citibank and Regent International Hotels and entrepreneurs who have succeeded in Hong Kong. Illustrates the customs of the business community and the culture of the people.
2. Kao, J. (1993). The worldwide web of Chinese business. *Harvard Business Review, 71,* (2), 24–34.
   Describes the style of Chinese business that takes place not only in China, but in any country with a Chinese-based economy (Taiwan, Singapore) or a significant Chinese population. The article highlights the influence of Confucian values in the way Chinese conduct business, the importance of the family over so-called strangers, and trends in Chinese business operations.
3. *Malaysia,* a culturgram produced by the Publications Division of the David M. Kennedy Center for International Studies, Brigham Young University, P.O. Box 24538; Provo, UT 84602-4538.
   This culturgram gives a brief background on most of the country's facets: its history, the people, their languages and religions, general attitudes, customs and courtesies, lifestyle, and level of development.

CHAPTER 9

USEFUL CONCEPTS

The topics covered in Chapter 9 relate to emerging markets in developing countries where a low-context culture operates in a high-context culture. The topics are about three principal areas: (1) the importance of relationships, (2) ethical and social responsibility issues within the context of those relationships, and (3) business development issues in emerging markets. In this chapter, we will focus only on issue #2: ethics and social responsibility.

We have already treated the topic of relationships in Asian countries (high-context cultures) in some depth in previous chapters. And although the issues surrounding business development are of interest and provide a context for studying cultural issues, it is not the focus of this text. Nonetheless, some of the related readings at the end of this chapter relate to this topic for those who wish to pursue it.

Ethics and Social Responsibility

This chapter includes a number of situations that raise the question of the appropriateness of the particular action by Pathway or Pharmthuco and their relationship to each other and with various individuals representing different business or government offices. In fact, at least 12 situations involve ethical dilemmas.

Francesco and Gold (1998) have enumerated a number of ethical issues that increasingly affect the relationship between organizations (and individuals within) in international contexts:

1. Theft of intellectual property
2. Bribery and corruption
3. Intentional selling of dangerous products
4. Environmental pollution
5. Intentional misrepresentation in negotiations.

The issues that Pathway has experienced in Vietnam include bribery and perhaps intentional misrepresentation in negotiations. Pathway, Pharmthuco, and government offices have attempted to facilitate their own objectives through gift-giving and favor-granting activities. However, much of the relationship between Pathway and the government and Pathway and Pharmthuco has been dictated or advised by Pharmthuco. In fact, it could be construed that Pharmthuco has intentionally misrepresented itself to Pathway. However, Pathway has its own interests at heart. It could be said that it is using Pharmthuco to gain market entry initially with the hope of becoming independent of them later.

If MedTech were to enter Vietnam, it would clearly be subjected to many of the same situations as Pathway. Pathway might be a more understanding partner to MedTech than Pharmthuco has been to Pathway. However, MedTech would still have to concern itself with licenses and such as well. Undoubtedly, licenses would be no more easily obtained from the government than they have been for Pathway.

When an individual or firm faces an ethical situation, it can respond in a variety of ways. Kohlberg (1969) says responses to ethical situations reflect any one of the following six stages of moral development:

Stage 1: The "obedience and punishment" stage. What is right and wrong depends on what those in power want.

Stage 2: The "individualism and reciprocity" stage. Right is determined by what produces the greatest good for the individual responding to the situation. This often means entering into agreements with others to form reciprocal relationships. The motive is always self-interest.

Stage 3: The "interpersonal conformity" stage. Right is determined by what is expected of the individual from others, especially those close to the individual.

Stage 4: The "social system" stage. What is right is determined by one's duty within a social system.

Stage 5: The "social contract" stage. Right is more determined by what the individual values or thinks is right than what society says is right. What is best for the majority of the people is the criterion often used to make decisions.

Stage 6: The "universal ethical principle" stage. Right and wrong are determined by the principles that are freely chosen by the individual. The individual is also willing to have everyone live by the same principles.

For Kohlberg, this list represents a hierarchy of moral principles. Stage 1 is the least "mature" and stage 6, the most. The stages move from self-centered definitions of actions and those dependent on others' opinions to those that are more independent and less self-interested. This assumes, however, that individuals in societies are equally free to choose actions; that is, an individual can realistically be independent of his or her social milieu. It also perhaps assumes a universal set of principles of right and wrong. For example, in collectivist societies, or high-context societies, stages 3 and 4 are default positions. The emphasis on relationships and their importance in these societies emphasizes one's obligations to others. The African who is fortunate enough to find work in a government post has obligations to his kin, who may easily number close to 100. These obligations include financial ones because he is in a position to earn more money than others, particularly those who are unemployed. Because government posts often do not pay adequately to cover these obligations, the individual is "forced" by social obligations to his family (kin) to increase his income. This is most easily and naturally done through accepting money or gifts from individuals who need his approval for something. Is this wrong? Perhaps it is in a society that values individualism, where one does not "owe" anything to others as an inherent part of being a member of an identifiable group (i.e., family, tribe, etc.).

In Pathway, Connolly understands the importance of gift giving and reciprocation. Pathway "donated" machines to Pharmthuco and gave medical supply samples to customs officers without too much difficulty in order to form agreements or get action. Connolly, however, is obviously becoming impatient with the kind of reciprocating system in Vietnam that sometimes has no short-term results. It is because of this interdependent system that Connolly feels Pathway is held captive, unable to maneuver freely. Pathway is dependent on Pharmthuco to be able to operate at all. Pharmthuco is dependent on local authorities to authorize business dealings because Pharmthuco doesn't even have all the licenses it needs to operate free of the "system."

Of course, Connolly should realize that Pathway will probably never be totally independent of the interdependent system in Vietnam. There will always be someone's hand to grease. That is simply the nature of a collectivist society, particularly a developing one. The experiences Pathway has in Vietnam point clearly to differences between collectivist, developing countries, such as those in Southeast Asia, and individualistic societies, such as the United States.

Vogel (1992) discusses the basis of differences between U.S. business practices and those of other cultures in determining what is "ethical":

1. The United States is a highly individualistic country. In that environment, more responsibility is given to the individual to determine what is right. Little social obligation is involved.
2. In European countries, although most still value individualism, the individual is more influenced by his sense of the company's responsibility than in the United States. The company's responsibility is often shaped by its relationship to its community, that is, how connected it is to its community and the community's values.
3. In the United States, because social obligations are not a primary motivator, the individual often looks to rules that have been established. These rules, laws, or codes are usually accepted as the decision rule.
4. In the United States, laws are often given a moralistic basis. The law is "right." Therefore, the same laws that govern U.S. citizens should govern those of other countries also. Other countries do not view their laws as universal.

The argument for cultural relativism or absolutism is both complex and simple. In previous chapters we learned the *relative* importance of relationships according to one's culture. In high-context cultures (Asian, African, Arabic, and to a lesser degree, Latin), relationships are extremely important. This high value on relationships creates a complex web of power structures, both formal and informal. These power structures are not always synchronized, but often act independently of one another. The commonality among these power structures, however, is that there are those in need of more power and those who can grant it. This reality creates, in turn, the necessity of gift giving and favor granting for mutually benefiting relationships.

Is "right" and "wrong" universal? Or are they relative to the culture's fundamental beliefs? Blanchard and Peale's (1988) proposed "ethic check" for decision makers suggests asking these three questions:

1. Is it legal?
2. Is it balanced? (Is it fair to all those affected and in the short term and long term? Does it promote a win-win situation?)
3. How will it make me feel about myself? (Will I be satisfied? And when others learn of my decision, will I be proud?)

In collectivist societies, it is unlikely that these would be the questions that would guide most people's actions. Probably the most fundamental questions would be these: Will this action maintain existing relationships? Will it respect the hierarchy? Will anyone I am identified with be ashamed because of my decision?

In Chapter 9, the decision to give medical samples to government officials, which they most likely sold for profit, might have been legal (i.e., no law forbade it). It might have been fair to all parties given the context, but how did Connolly feel about it? How would you feel about it?

In conclusion, the chapter on Vietnam illustrates the inherent complexity of doing business in a developing country; a high-context culture; and where a low-context, individualistic culture tries to operate in a high-context collectivist culture. What is appropriate behavior in one culture may not be in another. Ethical connotations may be levied or not. The difficulty of shedding personal notions of right and wrong is obvious. Eventually it can lead to a crisis of identity if taken to the extreme and if one is not able to integrate the new system of beliefs with one's own.

References

Blanchard, K., & Peale, N. V. (1988). *The power of ethical management.* New York: Fawcett Crest.

Francesco, A., & Gold, B. (1998). *International Organizational Behavior: Text, readings, cases, and skills.* New Jersey: Prentice-Hall, (pp. 47–48).

Kohlberg, L. (1969). Stage and sequence: The cognitive developmental approach to socialization. In D. A. Goslin (Ed.), *Handbook of socialization theory and research* (pp. 347–480). Chicago: Rand McNally.

Vogel, D. (1992). The globalization of business ethics: Why Americans remain distinctive. *California Management Review,* 35 (1) (pp. 30–49).

Related Readings

1. Drinkall, J. (1995, July/August/September). Decision strategies with international issues Vietnam business alert. San Francisco: Decision Strategies International. (415) 576-1122 or jdrinkall@igc.apc.org.

This publication gives a succinct overview of the economic situation in Vietnam for Westerners trying to enter. It mentions that Childress, a Southeast Asian expert and key White House National Security Council adviser, estimates as much as 40% of Vietnam's economy is conducted under the table and over half the imported goods are smuggled through Cambodia and China.

2. Barr, C. (1997, September 19). Vietnam's glow fades for US investors. *Christian Science Monitor (International)* (p. 7).

This article is similar to Drinkall's (see no. 1). It uses the example of an American former military pilot in Vietnam who tries to operate a helicopter operation in Vietnam (for business only). The difficulties he faces are discussed as they reflect the current business environment for foreigners in Vietnam.

3. *Business planning and resources: Vietnam business travel.* (1997). International Strategies, Inc., 11 Beacon St., Suite 1100, Boston, MA 02108. www.aexp.com/smallbusiness/resources/expanding/global/reports/11176090.shtml.

Excellent publication for those preparing to go to Vietnam for business dealings. A very practical guide that covers everything from visa requirements, to customs and business etiquette, to packing for the trip, to banking and business hours, to dining and entertainment.

4. Vietnam law on foreign investment. (1996, November). www.vietnamaccess.com/law/6law-il/htm.

Technical document that gives the legal regulations and conditions regarding foreign investment in Vietnam, including joint ventures. It includes six short chapters.

Culturgram™ '98

Socialist Republic of
Vietnam

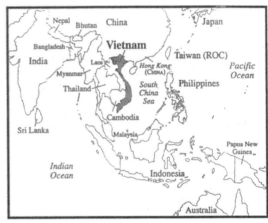

Boundary representations are not necessarily authoritative.

BACKGROUND

Land and Climate

Covering 127,243 square miles (329,560 square kilometers), Vietnam is just larger than New Mexico and extends from north to south for nearly 1,000 miles (1,600 kilometers). Flat deltas in the north and south are separated by central highlands. Hills and mountains are found in the far north. Summer rainfall is heavy in the deltas and highlands. While the south experiences a mostly tropical climate, the north has four seasons (two are short); winter months are chilly, but temperatures do not reach freezing. In the south, May to September is hot and rainy, while October to March is warm, humid, and dry. Temperatures are often above 84°F (29°C). Approximately 22 percent of the land is arable; 40 percent is covered by tropical and highland forests.

History

Vietnam's recorded history began in the first century B.C. Centuries of Chinese domination ended in 939, when Ngo Quyen defeated invading Chinese troops to establish the Ngo Dynasty. A succession of Vietnamese dynasties followed until the French imposed colonial rule in the latter 1800s.

The Japanese occupied Vietnam during World War II, installing a pro-Japan government while retaining Vietnam's monarch. After defeating Japan, the Allies divided Vietnam into two zones for the purpose of disarming Japanese troops. In the south, the British completed the task and restored French rule. In the north, China also completed the task, but Vietnam's emperor, Bao Dai, abdicated after an uprising (called the Autumn Revolution) in Hanoi and other major cities. The *Viet Minh* government was a communist-initiated organization that included other anti-French parties. It took over rule when Bao Dai abdicated, and on 2 September 1945, communist leader Ho Chi Minh proclaimed the nation's independence. Negotiations with France broke down in 1946, and the first Indochina war ensued. It culminated in France's defeat in 1954 at Dien Bien Phu.

The 1954 Geneva Accord called for national elections in 1956. The southern regime led by President Ngo Dinh Diem refused to recognize the accord. This gave communists in the south pretext for an uprising. Northern Communists first aided and then joined their southern comrades. Collectively called the *Viet Cong,* these troops fought under North Vietnam's leadership. The Soviet Union and China backed North Vietnam. Supporting its containment policy, the United States sent supplies and troops to help the south against the Viet Cong. The war spread to Laos and Cambodia. After years of fighting, support for the war in the south and in America diminished. U.S. troops withdrew in 1972, and the Saigon regime fell to the north in April 1975. Saigon's name was officially changed to Ho Chi Minh City, but most Vietnamese still call it Saigon. Thousands of families fled; those remaining faced difficult years of poverty, repression, and international isolation.

In 1976, Vietnam's north and south were officially reunited as the Socialist Republic of Vietnam. The United States refused to recognize the government and imposed a crippling economic embargo that it did not lift until 1994. After the "American War" (as the Vietnam War is known in Vietnam), troops under Cambodia's Pol Pot repeatedly attacked southern Vietnam. In December 1978, Vietnam invaded Cambodia, deposing the genocidal Pol Pot regime and installing a government (led by Hun Sen) loyal to Hanoi. In 1979, China invaded northern Vietnam for a short time. Vietnam, exhausted by war and occupation, withdrew from Cambodia in 1989.

Vietnam turned its attention to internal development. In 1986, *doi moi* (renovation) became the guiding economic policy. *Doi moi* is characterized by economic restructuring, more private enterprise and other market-oriented policies, and more open international trade.

The withdrawal from Cambodia allowed Vietnam to seek renewed relations with the United States. Washington opened an office in Hanoi in 1991 to coordinate the search for American soldiers missing in action and to pave the way to better relations. The United States lifted its trade embargo in 1994, which the Vietnamese welcomed as the final end of the American War. American companies quickly began to invest in Vietnam, joining firms from other countries that had already been there for several years. In 1995, the United States and Vietnam normalized relations and

continued

opened embassies in each other's capitals, but the "normalization" process continues.

Rapid economic growth began to slow in 1997, as Vietnam struggled with rampant corruption and crime. The country's leadership triumvirate (President Le Duc Anh, Premier Vo Van Kiet, and Communist Party Secretary Do Muoi) did not run in the 1997 National Assembly elections due to their advanced ages. Since the president and prime minister must be legislators, those men resigned from office and will be replaced when the newly elected Assembly meets in September 1997.

THE PEOPLE

Population

Vietnam's population of 73.9 million is growing at 1.6 percent annually. More than 35 percent are younger than age 15. The majority of people live in rural regions, mainly in the Red and Mekong River Deltas and along the coastal plain. The largest cities are Saigon (five million) and Hanoi (three million). About 88 percent of the population is ethnic *Kinh* (Vietnamese). The Chinese (2 percent) form an important merchant class. The rest of the population consists of Khmer, Hao, and Cham peoples in addition to more than 50 highland minority groups, each with its own language and culture.

Over the years, many Vietnamese fled their country, often in difficult circumstances, in search of better conditions. There are large immigrant and refugee communities in the United States and elsewhere. Many refugees are being repatriated from other Asian nations; others would return voluntarily if the political system in Vietnam were to change.

Language

Vietnamese is the official language, although ethnic minorities still speak their own languages at home. Vietnamese is monosyllabic; each syllable is a word, but up to four syllables can be joined together to form a new word. For instance, *thanh* (fresh) joins with *nien* (years) as *thanh nien* (youth). Each word has six tones and therefore six possible meanings. The word's tone is indicated by a symbol usually located above the word's main vowel. English is the most popular foreign language to study. Older people may speak some French. Some adults speak Russian or another foreign language because Vietnamese would often work in other communist countries prior to 1991.

Religion

Vietnam's constitution has always guaranteed freedom of religion, but only now are people able and willing to take advantage of it. Buddhism is practiced by 55 percent of the population. Temples and pagodas are busy with people offering prayers for success and health to various gods and goddesses. About 12 percent of the population is Taoist and 7 percent is Roman Catholic. Christianity is becoming more popular in cities. Some ethnic minorities remain animists, practicing a reverence for all living things.

Regardless of religion, nearly all Vietnamese venerate their ancestors. The Vietnamese believe the deceased are accessible to help or hinder the living. Almost every Vietnamese family has an altar for ancestor worship. Family members place fruit and/or flowers on the altar on the first and middle days of each lunar month. They also burn incense and offer prayers to ancestors for support in overcoming misfortune and obtaining good luck.

General Attitudes

Vietnamese respect those who respect others. Children must respect teachers and parents. Vietnamese value marital fidelity, generosity, gentleness, and hard work. The lazy, selfish, and disloyal are despised. Neighbors help each other and families support one another. Vietnamese hope for a future of wealth and security but worry that traditional family and cultural values will be lost in a modern economy.

The Vietnamese lived under Chinese domination for one thousand years, followed by almost one hundred years of French colonialism (1858–1954). Then came 30 years of civil war that included the war against the United States. This long struggle for independence has given the Vietnamese a deep sense of national pride. People focus on the future rather than the past. They often are baffled by the fixation many Americans still have with the American War, which they see as past history. In fact, rather than being anti-American, most people have an interest in all things American.

As Vietnam faces the future, people are both happy and unhappy. Urban areas are enjoying better basic services, a more open cultural atmosphere, and a growing economy. Unfortunately, the countryside—where three-fourths of the population live—continues to be neglected. Peasants are still dominated by party officials, still lack access to cultural opportunities and basic services (health care and education), and still live in grinding poverty. Such inequality encourages urban migration and strains urban infrastructure.

Personal Appearance

Everyday dress for both men and women generally consists of slacks worn with a casual cotton or knit blouse or sport shirt. For special occasions, women wear the graceful, traditional *ao dai,* a long dress with front and back panels worn over satin trousers. Men might wear shorts at the beach or work site but not otherwise in public.

CHAPTER 10

USEFUL CONCEPTS

The two remaining topics covered in this last chapter in the Japanese section are very important issues in international management:

- Organizational culture and its role in acquisitions
- Managing foreign acquisitions

Organizational Culture and Its Role in Acquisitions

Culture has been defined as the combined assumptions, beliefs, and values that become manifest in common behaviors relative to similar stimuli. Organizational culture, of course, is similar but delimits the culture to an organizational context. It is commonly thought that rites, rituals, heroes, symbols, language and stories reflect an organization's culture.

Rites

Rites are typically organized ceremonies that indicate a "vertical" movement within the organization (i.e., a lesser important position to a more important one; an increase in salary; a parking space with your name on it; etc.).

Rituals

Rituals are also organized ceremonies but not always formally organized. They might have no meaning in terms of "vertical" movement. Doughnut breaks, going out to eat with the salesperson, company parties, and listening to voice mail messages when first arriving at the office are all examples of rituals.

Heroes

Heroes are individuals in company history (sometimes current "history") who are extolled for significant accomplishments. Celebrating, talking about, referring to these individuals results in extolling certain values also. A company whose personnel continually refer to the 80-hour weeks so-and-so put in to get the prototype up and running are essentially saying the most valued people in the company work long hours and do whatever else is necessary to make the company a success. The manager who told the VP "where to get off" because the VP had incorrectly blamed one of the manager's employees for something might become a hero within the manager's department. Thereafter—even if the manager leaves the firm—when employees refer to the manager who stood up for his employees, they are extolling the values of strength under adversity, of team mentality, and so on.

In a high-context culture, where relationships—and power structures—must be strictly reinforced, the manager in this example would not normally be viewed as a hero. Instead, he would lose face and be considered a "loose cannon" who couldn't be trusted. Clearly, we define our heroes by what our culture's values are.

Symbols

Symbols are usually physical things that represent abstract values or norms. In the United States, the Heisman trophy symbolizes great accomplishments in college football—discipline, talent, and achievement to the highest degree. Company 20-year pins represent the value of longevity and fidelity to the firm. Because longevity is not the norm in many U.S. industries, it is rewarded with such symbols. In a country like Japan, loyalty can usually be expected and therefore is not rewarded with such visible signs. A trip to Hawaii for a high-performing salesperson symbolizes the value the firm places on high achievement. Names on parking spaces symbolize hierarchy or if it is an "employee of the month" space, it can represent the value the firm places on high-performing employees.

Language

Firms often have their own language to describe certain events, people, or processes. Someone who is "hardcore" is totally dedicated to whatever he or she is doing. It can represent a lack of flexibility also. A "temporary" employee might in fact describe someone who has worked in the same company for years but who has never been offered a "permanent" position. Such practices as reflected in the language can be construed to reflect a value on budgeting and cutting costs because "temporary" employees are not normally entitled to all the privileges and benefits of "permanent" employees.

Stories

Recounting stories about heroes are not the only ones told in companies. Stories can be told about the employee who got fired for stealing from the company, about the engineer who purposely faked data in order to present a good product, or about the company Christmas/holiday party that cost $500,000. Each of these stories reflects someone's perception of a value. The story about the engineer could represent the value on honesty (for the individual) or the value on expediency and scapegoats (for the company) or the value on "rewarding 'A' while hoping for 'B.' " The Christmas/holiday party could represent waste from one person's point of view or lavish rewards for people's hard work from another's perspective.

Each organization has its own culture, then, as reflected in its values. Different organizations have different values.

From what you know about MedTech and Oberfeldt AG, list descriptors that you think accurately depict the culture of each.

For example, a descriptor might be "open," "loose," or "political."

Oberfeldt AG   **MedTech**

_____   _____

_____   _____

_____   _____

_____   _____

_____   _____

The implications of an organization's culture in an acquisition situation should be obvious: the acquiring firm must ask itself if the culture of the to-be-acquired firm is different from its own and if that will hinder the development of a healthy relationship.

Managing Foreign Acquisitions

There are a number of similarities between managing a foreign acquisition and the issues facing joint venture partnerships. Some of these concepts should be a review of material in Chapter 3. We highlight the most relevant material here from Chapter 3.

Why Purchase Another Firm?
- at host government insistence
- to increase economies of scale
- to gain local knowledge
- to more easily enter a market
- to reduce costs of building a plant
- to spread the risks of the investment
- to improve competitive advantage

1. Reviewing the reasons just listed for purchasing another firm, explain what the principal business reasons are that make sense for the MedTech acquisition:

_____

_____

_____

_____

_____

_____

_____

_____

Why Buyouts Typically Fail
- the firms don't get along—different styles, cultures, and/or objectives
- too much debt encumbered by the buying firm that renders it unable to remain competitive in its own markets
- the markets disappear

2. Reviewing the reasons why most buyouts fail, which ones most closely describe the situation with MedTech and Oberfeldt?

_____

_____

_____

_____

_____

Potential issues to be resolved by the purchasing firm include (1) the assignment of managers to the acquired firm, (2) the ease of transferring human resources and their competencies, and (3) the loyalty of management in the purchasing firm. Relevant questions to ask about each of these three areas include the following:

The Assignment of Managers to the Acquired Firm
- Who will be selected? What criteria will be used to make the connection? Will the "leftovers" be chosen (i.e., those much less qualified)? Generally, studies show that expatriation has a negligible or negative effect on the transferred manager's career. In addition, often it is difficult to continue the manager's retirement and tax benefits. How might this affect who is willing to transfer to the JV?

The Ease of Transferring Human Resources and Their Competencies
- Are there legal considerations imposed by the countries involved?
- Do both firms have ample capable managers available?
- The loyalty of management in the purchasing firm: Will they play sides?

• Will transferred managers be more committed to the acquired or the parent firm? How will this affect the management of the acquired firm?

3. How are the issues just listed related to the Oberfeldt-MedTech relationship?

_____

_____

_____

_____

_____

_____

According to Hoecklin (1995), a multinational firm has four options in trying to manage the differences between parent company culture and the foreign company culture:

1. Build a strong corporate culture internationally.
2. Develop a common technical or professional culture worldwide.
3. Rely on strong financial or planning systems that will bring coherence to the differences.
4. Allow each different corporate culture to exist without intervention.

McDonald's and IBM are examples of firms with strong corporate cultures that are largely imposed on the foreign culture. Both companies have been successful. IKEA, the Swedish furniture maker and distributor, allows each foreign site to determine some local adaptation while keeping the basic corporate values intact. IKEA has also been successful. Oberfeldt A.G. does not seem to be as successful in transferring its corporate culture to MedTech. The differences are perhaps too stark, so the new organizational culture imposed by Oberfeldt is not well accepted. Perhaps if Oberfeldt had tried to develop a common culture around technical and professional expertise, the relationship would have been more successful.

Companies like Elf-Aquitaine, the French chemical/pharmaceutical firm, focuses its culture worldwide on the strong technical expertise related to its products. Technical knowledge, competence, and skills are the glue that holds the firm together internationally. "Unity through professionalism" is its slogan.

Emerson Electric, a U.S. leader in manufacturing electrical-related products, emphasizes strong planning procedures. Individual cultures are allowed to exist, but each company or division must execute a very thorough, fairly standardized planning process.

A fifth method of managing the diversity, although it is not mutually exclusive of those just named, is through cultural integration in one or more of the following forms:

- Making boards of directors more international
- Holding international meetings where people share information
- Forming multicultural teams
- Increasing the numbers of foreign-born in company headquarters
- Having an ongoing expatriate and inpatriate program
- Sharing "best practices" around the world
- Increasing the numbers of personnel attending seminars with international attendees within the firm (and also outside the firm)

References

Hoecklin, L. (1995). *Managing cultural differences: Strategies for competitive advantage.* Reading, MA: Addison-Wesley.

Related Readings

1. Schein, E. (1990). Organizational culture. *American Psychologist, 45* (2), 109–119.
   Excellent article for an overview of ways to understand organizational culture. Schein describes organizational culture and provides some excellent examples of each component.
2. Florida, R., & Kenney, M. (1991). Transplanted organizations: The transfer of Japanese industrial organizations to the United States. *American Sociological Review, 56,* 381–398.
   Discusses the impact of one culture's work style on another culture that doesn't share the same deep-level cultural values. It discusses the success of the Japanese automobile industry in transplanting to the United States. Compare with reference 3 here.
3. Ellegard, K., Jonsson, D., Enstrom, T., Johansson, M., Medbo, L., & Johansson, B. (1992). Reflective production in the final assembly of motor vehicles—an emerging Swedish challenge. *International Journal of Operations & Production Management, 12,* 117–133.
   Discusses the difficulties of transplanting humanistic work designs in the Swedish automobile industry to other cultures that do not share the same humanism or egalitarianism.

CHAPTER 11

USEFUL CONCEPTS

In this chapter Matt is searching for a new job and Jan is trying to reestablish herself in her career. After attending an executive education seminar at UCLA, Matt eventually lands a position at Plasmatec, a company specializing in medical devices. They are in part attracted to Matt because of his international experience. Matt then helps Plasmatec analyze a possible global strategic alliance with Groupe Techno-Sang (GTS) in France, and a mentoring relationship between Matt and Doc Silverman evolves.

This chapter focuses on two main concerns: entering a new market via a global alliance and the mentoring relationship. The nature of careers in the new world of work (UCLA seminar), transitioning careers for both Matt and Jan after Japan, and French labor laws and social benefits are interesting subtopics as they relate to the GTS alliance.

Global Strategic Alliances

Chapter 3 discusses the pros and cons of various forms of global alliances and it might be useful to refer to that material. In this case, Plasmatec has decided on a joint venture with GTS.

Contractor and Lorange (1988) pointed out years ago that alliance forms of international investment are outnumbering wholly owned subsidiaries by a ratio of 4 to 1 and this trend has been rapidly increasing since then. Contractor and Lorange list a variety of alliance type arrangements:

Type of Cooperative Arrangement
- technical training/start-up assistant agreements
- production/assembly/buy-back agreements
- patent licensing
- franchising
- know-how licensing
- management/marketing service agreements
- partnerships in exploration, research, development, production
- equity joint ventures

The further down the list, the more the arrangement requires extensive managerial attention and integration. Thus equity joint ventures require the most attention.

Dr. Stephen Tallman (1994), associate professor of International Strategy at the David Eccles School of Business, University of Utah, points out the pros and cons of a joint venture:

Pros of a Joint Venture

Increases the loyalty of managers and workers

Encourages the transfer of organizationally embedded, implicit knowledge and group skills

Provides all the synergistic effect

Allows the freedom to access information, monitor performance, and control operations that would be subject to intense negotiation in a contractual mode

Cons of a Joint Venture

Increases the risk of partners stealing your ideas

Increases bureaucratic costs that are included with cultural differences

Requires early reduction of the deal to small numbers bargaining without an established ownership relationship

Requires a lot of managerial time in negotiation.

Mentoring

Matt forms a mentoring relationship in Chapter 11 with Doc Silverman. Effective developmental relationships that involve mentors and mentees, according to Clawson (1980, pp. 154–161), have these components:

Role complementarity:	seniors or superiors feel they should be teachers, and juniors or subordinates feel they should be learners
Respect:	the parties are mutually respectful and positive about one another
Trust:	a high level of trust exists between them
Consistency:	the superior or senior responds consistently to the subordinate or junior, thus reducing the feeling of vulnerability of the junior
Being informal:	effective developers play down their difference in status and make the subordinate feel empowered
Openness with information:	as trust develops, the best mentors openly share useful and scarce information with their mentees
Appropriate level of intimacy:	the relationship is close, even extending beyond the office, but not pathologically intimate or too close
Frequent interactions:	most mentees meet rather frequently with their mentors, about once per day or once every two days

Setting high standards: effective mentors or developers set high standards for their mentees and work hard to help the junior acquire a larger perspective

A Note on French Labor Law

French labor unions are attached to political parties and represent broad constituencies. In France, industrial relations are usually determined by government policy and the dialogue between employees' associations and trade unions. They often seek political reform and broad social reorganization and operate along social class lines, trying to protect the less powerful from those with higher status and more wealth.

But actual union membership is not as critical as the role of employees in managing the enterprise. The Employee Participation Act requires that employees coexist with or co-manage companies. Owners of French firms must contact staff representatives and inform them of any managerial changes being considered that could impact employees. The Comité d'Entreprise (Works Council) must consult with the staff, via its representatives, on all matters pertaining to working conditions, health, and safety. The staff representatives also participate on all governing boards, including the board of directors.

If owners and managers disagree with the staff, they are not obligated to follow staff input. Among the items that must be discussed but not followed are working conditions, so-called layoffs, the company's annual social report, collective reductions in the work force, mergers, structural changes in the company, social activities, and information on the general state of the business. The government frowns on management that ignores worker recommendations. The last power play open to workers is collective bargaining and a possible strike.

The right to strike in France is sacred. French strikes are often emotional displays of power, aimed as much at the government as at the company. French strikes tend to hit hard, even cripple the country, but are generally short-lived and designed to require social legislation that regulates certain industrial practices. A large number of people participate in French strikes, but on average, only 2.7 days per year are lost in productivity as a result of worker strikes (Bean, 1994, p. 136) as compared to 16.6 for union workers on strike in the United States. This is because American strikes tend to last much longer.

Matt's Résumé

RESUME

NAME: MATTHEW H. SUMNER

EDUCATIONAL BACKGROUND:

- Renssaeler Polytechnical College, BS in mechanical engineering, 1980

- University of California at Los Angeles, MBA, 1986

WORK HISTORY:

- Six months travel (1980-81)

- Hewlett-Packard Co., design engineering, 1981-84

- MedTech Corp., engineering, manufacturing and director of operations (Japan), 1986-91

INTERESTS:

- Travel and Culture

  - spent senior year in high school in France, speak French

  - lived 2 years in Japan with MedTech, speak limited Japanese

- Hiking and outdoors

- Rebuilding classic cars (own 1957 Chevrolet Bel-Air)

FAMILY:

- Married to "Jan"

- two children: Jeff (6) and Michelle (3)

Jan's Résumé

RESUME

NAME: JAN BROCKTON SUMNER

EDUCATIONAL BACKGROUND:

- University of Texas at Austin, BA in American literature, 1980

- University of California at Berkeley, JD environmental law, 1983

WORK HISTORY:

- Jones, Mortimer and Clark, San Francisco, 1983-87

- patent work and legal research in Japan, 1989-90

- Michaels, Martin and Rowley, Los Altos, 1991 - present

INTERESTS:

- outdoors, hiking, backpacking, cross-country skiing

- environmental issues (Sierra Club)

- travel and culture (lived in Japan 1988-91)

FAMILY:

- Married to "Matt"

- two children: Jeffery (6) and Michelle (3)

A Note on Employee Social Benefits in France

Matt and Plasmatec are concerned not only about labor laws but also about benefits and social security costs. Table 11.1 (Deloitte, Touche, & Tohmatsu, 1997, p. 133) gives these rates for France according to percentage of salary.

TABLE 11.1
Employer Social Security Rates

Type of Contribution	Basis of Calculation	Rate (%)
Sickness insurance, including death insurance	Total salary and wages	12.8
Old-age pension	Salary and wages up to FF 13,720 per month	8.2
	Total salary and wages	1.6
Family allowance	Total salary and wages	5.4
Lodging assistance: All employers	Salary and wages up to FF 13,720 per month	0.1
Employers with more than 9 employees	Total salary and wages	0.4
Work-related accident and Disease insurance	Total salary and wages	Varies according to risk in each firm
Supplementary pensions: Nonexecutives	Salary and wages up to FF 41,160 per month	3.75
Executives	Salary and wages up to FF 13,720 per month	5.25
	Salary and wages between FF 13,720 & FF 54,880 per month	11.25 a

a. A complementary contribution is also due at a rate of 0.036%.
b. The total rate of 17.50% is spread between the employer and employee as agreed upon by those parties.

In the United States, for example, a basic social security tax (for old age, survivors, and disability) is levied at a rate of 6.2% on wages to a threshold amount (for 1997 of $4,055). The hospital insurance tax is levied at 1.45%. These amounts are matched by employer contributions

Deloitte, Touche, and Tohmatsu, 1997, p. 481.

continued

TABLE 11.1
Employer Social Security Rates—cont'd

Type of Contribution	Basis of Calculation	Rate (%)
Supplementary pensions: Executives—cont'd	Salary and wages between FF 54,880 & FF 109,760 per month	Up to 17.50 b
Unemployment insurance	Salary and wages up to FF 13,720 Per month	5.13
	Salary and wages between FF 13,720 and FF 54,880 per month	5.26
Salary payment insurance	Salary and wages up to FF 54,880 per month	0.25

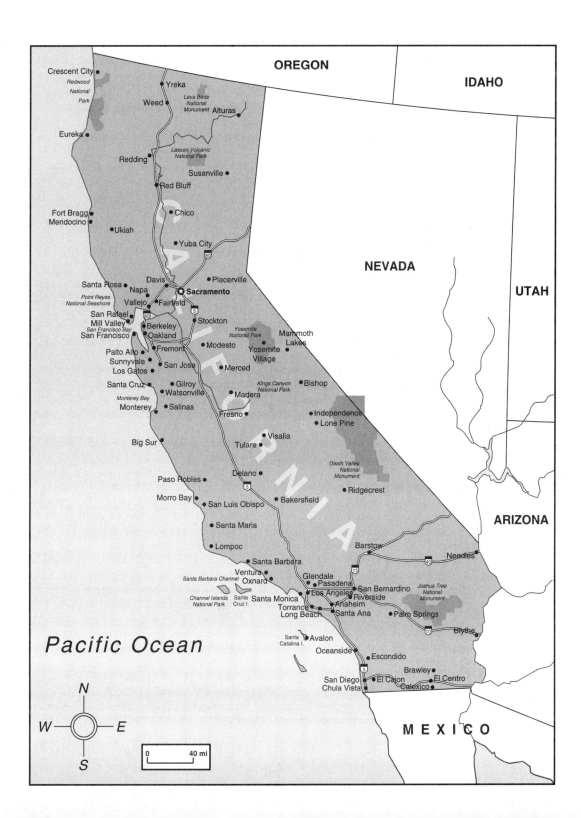

OREGON

IDAHO

NEVADA

UTAH

ARIZONA

MEXICO

Pacific Ocean

CALIFORNIA

Crescent City

Redwood National Park

Yreka

Lava Beds National Monument

Weed

Alturas

Eureka

Lassen Volcanic National Park

Redding

Susanville

Red Bluff

Fort Bragg
Mendocino

Chico

Ukiah

Yuba City

Davis

Placerville

Santa Rosa

Napa

★ **Sacramento**

Point Reyes National Seashore

Vallejo

Fairfield

San Rafael

Stockton

Mill Valley

Berkeley

San Francisco Bay

Oakland

San Francisco

Yosemite National Park

Mammoth Lakes

Palto Alto

Fremont

Modesto

Yosemite Village

Sunnyvale

San Jose

Los Gatos

Merced

Santa Cruz

Gilroy

Watsonville

Kings Canyon National Park

Bishop

Monterey Bay

Madera

Monterey

Salinas

Fresno

Independence

Lone Pine

Big Sur

Visalia

Tulare

Death Valley National Monument

Paso Robles

Delano

Ridgecrest

Morro Bay

San Luis Obispo

Bakersfield

Santa Maria

Lompoc

Barstow

Needles

Santa Barbara

Ventura

Glendale

Santa Barbara Channel

Oxnard

Pasadena

San Bernardino

Joshua Tree National Monument

Channel Islands National Park

Santa Cruz I.

Santa Monica

Los Angeles

Riverside

Torrance

Anaheim

Long Beach

Santa Ana

Palm Springs

Blythe

Santa Catalina I.

Avalon

Oceanside

Escondido

Brawley

El Centro

San Diego

El Cajon

Chula Vista

Calexico

N
W — E
S

0   40 mi

References

Allen, T. D., Russell, J. E. A., & Maetzkel, S. B. (1997). Formal peer mentoring: Factors related to proteges' satisfaction and willingness to mentor others. *Group and Organization Management, 22* (4), 488–507.

Arnold, J., & Johnson, K. (1997). Mentoring in the early career. *Human Resource Management Journal, 7* (4), 61–70.

Bamber, J., & Landsbury, R. (1993). *International and Comparative Industrial Relations.* London: Routledge.

Bean, R. (1994). *Comparative industrial relations: An introduction to cross-cultural perspectives.* London: Routledge.

Bridges, W. (1994, September 19). The end of the job. *Fortune*, pp. 62–74. CBI. (1994, January). U.S. Department of Labor, UNICE.

Clawson, J. G. (1980). Mentoring in managerial careers. In C. Brooklyn Derr (Ed.), *Work, family and the career* (pp. 144–165). New York: Praeger.

Contractor, F. J., & Lorange, P. (1988). Why should firms cooperate. In F. J. Contractor & P. Lorange (Eds.), *Cooperative strategies in international business* (pp. 3–30). Lexington, MA: Lexington Books.

Deloitte, Touche and Tohmatsu, (1998). *Executives Living Aground: Guide to Tax Planning in 66 Jurisdictions* (New York: Deloitte, Touche and Tohmatsu, 1633 Broadway, New York 10019).

Hamel, G. (1991). Competition for competence and inter-partner learning within international strategic alliances. *Strategic Management Journal, 37* (4), 83–103.

Jossi, F. (1997). Mentoring in changing times. *Training, 34* (8), 50–54.

Lublin, J. S. (1996, January 29). An overseas stint can be a ticket to the top. *Wall Street Journal*, pp. B1, B5.

Mills, R. W., & Chen, G. (1996). Evaluating international joint ventures using strategic value analysis. *Long Range Planning 29* (4), 552–561.

Osborn, R. N., & Baughn, C. C. (1990). Forms of interorganizational governance for multinational alliances. *Academy of Management Journal, 33* (3), 503–519.

Parker, C., *Borg-Warner Chemicals* (A). (1989). IMD International Case, OB185, 1980, and Borg-Warner Chemicals Negotiation Exercise, IMD International Case, OB209, IMD International, chemin de Bellerive 23, CH-1007, Lausanne, Switzerland.

Parker, G. M. (1994). *Cross-functional teams.* San Francisco: Jossey-Bass.

Parker, V. A., & Kram, K. E. (1993). Women mentoring women: Creating conditions for connection. *Business Horizons, 36* (2), 42–51.

Parkhe, A. (1991). Interfirm diversity, organizational learning and longevity in global strategic alliances. *Journal of International Business Studies, 22* (4), 579–602.

Ragins, B. R. (1997). Diversified mentoring relationships in organizations: A power perspective. *Academy of Management Review, 22* (2), 482–521.

Ragins, B. R., & Scandura, T. A. (1994). Gender differences in expected outcomes of mentoring relationships. *Academy of Management Journal, 37*, 957–971.

Scandura, T. A., Tegeda, M. J., Werther, W. B., & Lankau, M. J. (1996). Perspectives on mentoring. *Leadership & Organization Development Journal, 17* (3), 50–56.

Shelty, Y. K. (1991, November/December). Strategies for US competitiveness: A survey of business leaders. *Business Horizons*, pp. 43–38.

Tallman, S. B. (1994). *Managing international joint ventures in the modern economy.* Unpublished paper, David Eccles School of Business, University of Utah, Salt Lake City, UT 84112; tel. 801-581-8774.

Tallman, S. B., & Shenkar, O. (1994). A managerial decision model of international cooperative venture formation. *Journal of International Business Studies, 25* (1), 91–113.

Van Collie, S.C. (1998). Moving up through mentoring. *Workforce, 77* (3), 36–42. *World Competitiveness Report.* (1997). IMD International, chemin de Bellerive 23, CH-1007, Lausanne, Switzerland.

Related Readings

New Career Dynamics

1. Webber, A. M. (1993, January/February). What's so new about the new economy. *Harvard Business Review,* pp. 4–12.
   A classic on the new economy. The article argues that knowledge, residing in people and technology, is the new competitive advantage. How to effectively manage knowledge workers is key.
2. Hall, D. T., & Mirvis, P.H. (1996). The new proteam career: Psychological success and the path with a heart. In D. T. Hall (Ed.), *The career is dead: Long live the career* (pp. 15–45). San Francisco: Jossey-Bass.
   Wonderful chapter on the new career contract, why an individual perspective on careers is essential in the new world of work, and the implications of the new world of work on careers.
3. Mirvis, P.H., & Hall, D.T. (1996). New organization forms and the new career. In D. T. Hall (Ed.), *The career is dead: Long live the career* (pp. 72–101). San Francisco: Jossey-Bass.
   Considers the impact of flexible organization, parallel structures, boundaryless, and virtual forms of organization on career development practices.
4. Kotter, J. P. (1995). *The new rules: How to succeed in today's post-corporate world.* New York: Free Press.
   Kotter describes the post-corporate world and why it happened, then advocates careers in small entrepreneurial businesses as future prototypes. He stresses lifelong learning.

Mentoring

1. Clawson, J. G. (1996). Mentoring in the information age. *Leadership & Organization Development Journal, 17* (3), 6–15.
   Discusses expected changes in the mentoring process as a result of transitions from the bureaucratic age to the information age, including heterogeneous, team-based, and peer relationships; focuses on life issues, customer service, and finding protégés.
2. Dansky, K. H. (1996). The effect of group mentoring on career outcomes. *Group & Organization Management , 21,* 5–21.
   Develops a new construct called group mentoring that is defined as an alternative substitute to interpersonal mentoring; psychosocial and career support may be provided by the group dynamics of professional associations.
3. Forret, M. L., Turban, D. B., & Dougherty, T. W. (1996). Issues facing organizations when implementing formal mentoring programmes. *Leadership & Organization Development Journal, 17* (3), 27–30.

Based on interviews with training and development directors in five large organizations, the authors discuss who should receive mentoring and how to pair mentors and protégés, train participants, handle supervisor conflicts and ineffective relationships, and evaluate formal programs.

4. Hurley, A. E., & Fagenson-Eland, E. A. (1996). Challenges in cross-gender mentoring relationships: Psychological intimacy, myths, rumors, innuendoes and sexual harassment. *Leadership & Organization Development Journal, 17* (3), 42–49.

Develops a continuum of sexuality and intimacy in cross-gender mentoring relationships (nonsexual psychologically intimate, perceived sexually intimate, sexually intimate); discusses how organizations might manage sexuality and intimacy in cross-gender relationships.

CHAPTER 12

Useful Concepts

Because of his language skills and international experience, Matt becomes the key link between Plasmatec and Groupe Techno-Sang (GTS) in France. He spends most of his time commuting between France and Santa Cruz, trying to do two jobs at once. He soon finds himself exhausted and unable to focus on either his new responsibilities or his family.

Meanwhile Jan is becoming more successful in her career at the law firm. However, the fact that she has to rely more and more on the babysitter and housekeeper to keep the family going plays on her conscience. She espouses, eventually, more of a balance in her life. Ironically, in one of her monthly lunches with her friend, Heather confesses her jealousy of Jan's "perfect" life with her family.

Just when Jan and Matt seem to be reaching high points in their careers, Matt is being pushed to take the position as manager of the new joint venture in France. Plasmatec wants Matt there to bridge the gap between the two companies. At the same time, Jan is offered the chance to become a full-time member of her firm, which she has been working for on a free-lance basis. Both Matt and Jan have mutually exclusive offers that could help them advance their careers, but one of them will have to accommodate the other. After much discussion of how it would eventually affect them and their family, they agree the move to France is what the family needs to pull them all back together.

Two critical international issues common to relationships, especially in two-career marriages, are confronted in Chapter 12. The first is how to manage the two-career partnership when one partner must travel internationally, there are children, and the couple must decide whether or not to renegotiate their relationship contract and relocate overseas. The second, although more general, is deciding individually and as a couple what constitutes career success and happiness. Pre-departure preparation is a third concern for individuals and families moving abroad.

Managing the Dual-Career Partnership

It is difficult to juggle the demands of work, family, and self-development in the best of two-career marriages. The Halls (1976) maintain that when both work requirements and family role definitions are inflexible and demanding, the couple can become "adversaries" who compete for time, reliable transportation, psychological, and even physical space (a home office) and less taxing and time-consuming chores at home. The couple are "allies" if there is either more flexible role requirements at home or more flexible requirements at work (or both) and it is easier to juggle the various demands. The problems are exacerbated when there are children who bring their own demands, even their own careers (e.g., music lessons, a sports team), to the situation. The more children, the more complex.

Financial resources are also important because some of the tensions can be resolved when others help with cleaning, laundry, child care, food preparation, yard and home maintenance, and when newer and more reliable cars and home appliances are available.

Sekaran (1986, pp. 84–85) maintains that a dual-career partnership can work well if the following guidelines are in place:

- the spouses are clear about their career goals and enjoy mutual love, respect, support, and courtesy for each other as individuals
- a strong team spirit allows the couple to collaborate emotionally, professionally, and domestically
- there exists flexibility and a willingness to adjust to various crises and situations
- there is a sense of fair play and equity so that both partners share the workload
- the definition of success (financially, career-wise, at home) is continually debated and redefined so there are mutually compatible goals
- the couple learns over time when to act independently (as an individual), when to be in a dependent mode, and when to be interdependent (as a couple)
- the couple develops excellent listening, communication, problem-solving, and conflict management skills
- they learn to manage time effectively
- they learn to effectively make the transition from work space to home space and vice versa
- there exists a high level of motivation to make the marriage/family work given this very complex lifestyle

On another level, Carlson, Kaemar, and Stepina (1995) uncovered in their research that the degree of work/family conflict depends on the amount of time spent at work and the extent of work identity. Internal conflict occurs when more time is required for working than there is work identity to merit such away-from-home time. Internal conflict also occurs in reverse when one has more work identity than is fulfilled by the extensive time spent at home. Did Jan start to push the limits in her own life in the right balance of work/home time with which she was comfortable? Did Matt?

On the issue of accommodating one's work to the marriage, as Jan does, the following is an excerpt from Professor Lotte Bailyn (1980, pp. 90–101) in her study of MIT alumnae about accommodation:

> Small as these numbers are, the differences among these groups are suggestive. Eliminating those alumna with no career involvement, we see a characteristic difference in how the married and the single alumna view the midcareer period of their lives. Asked to give their perceived success at work both now and at the height of their careers, all the single women perceived themselves to be on a plateau. In particular, all of those with full career involvement saw themselves on a rising career trajectory.

Perceived Success at Height of Career as Compared with Now	Full Career Involvement		Accommodative Involvement
	Single (N = 3)	Married (N = 4)	(N = 4)
Same (equal to now)	3	0	2
Going up (higher than now)	0	4	2

This is not caused by a ceiling effect. None of these women puts her current success at the top of the scale; all of them could have perceived their success as still rising. See Table 12.1.

It is the distinction between the married and the single alumna with full career involvement that is most relevant. All three single alumna followed traditional, linear careers: two in engineering and one in architecture. Though they all changed jobs and organizations at least once, they worked continuously and remained committed to their original career choices. The only real shift that occurred was the move on the part of the architect from working as an employee to establishing an independent practice, a move she made about five years after graduating from the Massachusetts Institute of Technology.

TABLE 12.1
Career and Work Attitudes (mean scores)

	Full Career Involvement		Accommodative Involvement
	Single (N = 3)	Married (N = 4)	(N = 4)
Career certainty	2.7	4.8	3.8
Career aspirations	4.0	4.2	3.7
Job satisfaction	3.3	4.0	4.5
Success now	3.7	3.2	3.5
Success at height	3.7	4.8	4.0
Work orientation (a)	3.3	3.9	3.1
Professionalism (b)	3.3	4.3	2.6

(a) Based on the average of five items dealing with the extent of involvement with one's work.
(b) Based on three items dealing with the extent of professional activity: for example, belonging to a professional society, going to meetings, publishing.

Note: These scores are based on self-ratings on a scale from 1 to 5, where 1 is low and 5 is high. All scores, except where otherwise noted, are based on single items.

These linear careers, so typical of the traditional male career pattern, contrast sharply with those of the married women alumna with full career involvement. All but one had a slow period in her career history, a period in which she pursued an accommodative rather than a fully committed career. All but one had to leave a job because of a family move prompted by a husband's relocation. Also, only one has stayed in the same career throughout this period. One shifted, six years after receiving her Ph.D., from a research job in a laboratory to a teaching position in a technical institute. Another left her technical job as an engineer in a university research group and shifted to a business function in industry. Finally, one alumna made a dramatic career shift; nine years after graduating from the Massachusetts Institute of Technology she entered graduate school to obtain a Ph.D. in an entirely new field.

These interruptions—some prompted, as indicated, by family changes in response to a husband's career needs—have not been detrimental to these women. All see themselves on a rising career trajectory and anticipate greater success at work in the years ahead. In general, their reactions to their careers and to their work are consistently more positive, as shown in Table 12.1, than are those of the single alumna whose careers have followed more traditional lines. Further, as is indicated by the last two items in Table 12.1, they are more involved with their work and are more professionally established.

This small group of married women seems to have been able to reach, at midlife, a work situation that fits their lives and that would seem to be an appealing one to their employers. Yet none moved into her present position in a traditional manner. On the contrary, these alumna had slow periods in their careers and modified their initial career lines to some extent. Though admittedly limited, these data show that organizational careers can survive slow starts, late entrances, and midcourse changes in direction, and may indeed benefit from such unorthodoxies. They lend some credence to the viability of slower, apprenticeship career routes.

A final word on these data. It is clear that these women were free to pursue their less orthodox careers by the fact that they were not tied to being the economic providers in their families. But with the increasing number of dual career marriages, this freedom is being given also to many more men. It has already been shown that a certain amount of financial stability at midcareer is a necessary accompaniment to career changes at that time (Robbins, 1978). With two-earner families, both partners will have the opportunity also during the early years to choose slower and less involving (and hence less economically rewarding) work options.

What Is Career Success Anyway?

Matt and Jan go off to Carmel to sort out whether or not Matt should take the position in France or Jan should once more put her career on hold. Jan's previous conversation with Heather underlies Matt and Jan's discussions in Carmel and brings up the question of what constitutes career success.

The instructor will probably ask you to complete the Career Success Map questionnaire at the end of this chapter. A discussion in class will help you both analyze Matt and Jan's situation and ascertain your own career success orientation profile.

Pre-Departure Training

Following is an excerpt from Mendenhall and Oddou (1995, p. 212) on the subject of pre-departure training programs. Unless there is such systematic training or information sharing for the expatriate and the spouse/family, the parties are left, as Jan was, to collecting various perceptions.

> Firms vary in the type of training they offer executives. A few firms have an intensive month-long training session, while others hand the executive a few brochures just before he or she boards the plane.

> The content also differs widely. Those firms who understand that working abroad is more than solving a technical problem cover a much wider range of topics: foreign customs, thinking patterns, societal values, language, the organizational culture, environmental factors, support systems, and so forth. Other firms simply rely on the brochures they hand the executive to cover the necessary material. While brochures are sometimes quite informative, they do not treat factors that will directly facilitate adaptation.

> When an executive is sent to a culture that closely resembles his or her own, information is probably sufficient. However, for the executive (and family) going to Malaysia or Japan, where the cultures differ significantly from the U.S., information might not be enough. Training should include role playing, culture confrontation, and behavioral situations. Only in behavioral situations is an individual forced to deal with the emotions that result from misunderstandings, frustration, and differences in customs and courtesies. The executive will confront these same emotions overseas. It is far better to try to understand and deal with them before leaving to reduce the amount of culture shock.

> Finally, since the top reason for early returns is the spouse's inability to adapt, the wise firm will include the spouse and any other family members in their teens and older in the training. In fact, such training is actually more important for the spouse than it is for the executive. Although the executive changes job locations, often the exact nature of the job itself may not change drastically. It is the spouse who experiences extreme changes: a postponed career, a different language, different stores and shopping habits, a lack of friends and family upon which to rely, and so on.

> An extensive cross-cultural training program reflects a firm's commitment to you and your success overseas. Chances are that such a firm also forecasts its worldwide human resource needs months in advance and strategically values its overseas operations. If the training also includes your spouse and older family members, your probability of success abroad is much higher. If the assignment fits into your personal career plans, you should probably accept it.

> On the other hand, if you are headed to Japan and are handed brochures as you are boarding the plane, you should probably hope there is one domestic stop before reaching the foreign country. If so, deplane and tell your firm you changed your mind.

CAREER SUCCESS MAP QUESTIONNAIRE

Basic talents, values, and motives have an impact when decisions are made about careers. The following survey is designed to help you understand your career orientation. You cannot fail this test; there are no right or wrong answers.

Each item contains two statements. Choose the one you feel more accurately reflects you or is more true of you. You must choose one of the statements, even though you may not like either or you may like both of them. Do not skip any pair of statements or circle both alternatives in one set. Circle the letter corresponding to the one sentence you select as the most reflective of you. Do not spend a lot of time weighing your answers.

Circle one letter in each pair.

1. (A) I like to organize myself and others to win. V
   (B) I like to do my own thing in an organization. X

2. (A) Work must be balanced by time for leisure and the development of significant relationships. Y
   (B) Personal needs must be subordinated for me to get ahead. V

3. (A) I would like to work in an organization which rewards hard work, loyalty, and dedication. W
   (B) I like setting my own goals and accomplishing them at my own pace and in my own way. X

4. (A) I am aggressive and have good analytical and people skills. V
   (B) I am able to keep a good perspective between the needs of my work and the needs of my family. Y

5. (A) I want to work independently. X
   (B) I like being a company person. W

6. (A) I enjoy working as a consultant or "trouble shooter" and getting turned on by an exciting project. Z
   (B) I enjoy working in a situation where I am the leader and am responsible for achieving certain objectives. V

7. (A) My spouse/partner is as important to me as my career. Y
   (B) My spouse/partner takes a back seat to my work when I am in the middle of a very exciting project. Z

8. The most important thing to me is:
   (A) Freedom X
   (B) Maintaining work/life perspective Y

9. (A) I am competent, loyal, trustworthy, and hard-working. W
   (B) I am politically skillful, a good leader, and a good administrator. V

I CAN BE DESCRIBED AS:

10. (A) Self-reliant   X

    (B) Balanced   Y

11. (A) One who gets "turned on" by exciting projects.   Z

    (B) One who likes to be his/her own boss.   X

12. (A) In equilibrium but divided.   Y

    (B) Imaginative, enthused.   Z

13. (A) Self-reliant, self-sufficient.   X

    (B) Imaginative, enthused.   Z

14. (A) Stable and tenacious.   W

    (B) Independent and self-directed.   X

15. (A) One who plans and organizes extremely well.   V

    (B) One who analyzes situations and develops creative new solutions. Z

16. (A) An expert in my field.   Z

    (B) A solid citizen.   W

17. (A) Able to modify my own goals to accommodate to organizational   W
        goals and leaders.

    (B) Intent on finding a way to make the organization's goals and my Y
        own "personal" goals converge.

A PERSONAL GOAL IS TO:

18. (A) Control my own destiny.   X

    (B) Not let work interfere with the needs of my personal life.   Y

IT IS IMPORTANT TO:

19. (A) Have a job where there is security and a sense of belonging.   W

    (B) Be able to devote time to family and other personal activities. Y

I PREFER:

20. (A) A career with potential for promotions.   V

    (B) The opportunity to tackle challenging problems or tasks.   Z

21. (A) I like being at the center of influence.   V

    (B) I value long-term employment, acceptance, and being valued by   W
        the organization.

22. (A) I view knowing the right people and making the right friends as V
        important to career advancement.

    (B) I view being able to develop my career along my own areas of   X
        interest as the critical factor.

23. (A) The bottom line for me is gaining a sense of balance between work and private life.   Y

    (B) The bottom line for me is stability, appreciation, and having a secure place in the organization.   W

24. (A) I would like a position with maximum self-control and autonomy.   X

    (B) I would like to be in the inner circle.   V

25. (A) The bottom line for me is stability, appreciation, and a secure place in the organization.   W

    (B) The bottom line for me is advancing up the organization.   V

26. (A) I view financial success and increased power and prestige as important measures of career success.   V

    (B) I view success in my career as having equal time for work, family, and self-development.   Y

I WOULD RATHER:

27. (A) Excel in my field.   Z

    (B) Be considered dependable and loyal.   W

I PREFER:

28. (A) Working with a team on a long-term and steady basis.   W

    (B) Working with a task force or project group on a fast-paced and short-term basis.   Z

29. (A) Professional development and continued training are important for their own sake.   Z

    (B) Professional development is important as a means to the end of becoming an expert and gaining more flexibility and independence.   X

30. (A) The bottom line for me is to seek an equilibrium between personal and professional life.   Y

    (B) The bottom line for me is excitement and stimulation.   Z

References

Bailyn, L. (1980). The slow burn way to the top. In C. B. Derr (Ed.), *Work, family and the career* (pp. 94–105). New York: Praeger.

Black, J. S., Gregersen, H. B., & Mendenhall, M. E. (1992). *Global assignments*. San Francisco: Jossey-Bass.

Carlson, D. S., Kaemar, K. M., & Stepina, L. P. (1995). An examination of two aspects of work-family conflict: Time and identity. *Women In Management, 10* (2), 1725.

Carter, N. (1997). Solve the dual-career challenge. *Workforce, 2* (4), 21–22.

Derr, C. B. (1986). *Managing the new careerists.* San Francisco: Jossey-Bass.

Derr, C. B. (1987, June). What value is your management style? *Personnel Journal,* pp. 74–83.

Derr, C. B. (1989). *Career success maps.* San Francisco: Jossey-Bass Audio Books.

Feldman, D. C., & Thomas, D. C. (1992). Career management issues facing expatriates. *Journal of International Business Studies,* second quarter, 271–293.

Frazee, V. (1996, October). Expert help for dual-career spouses. *Global Workforce,* pp. 25–28.

Hall, F. S., & Hall, D. T. (1976). *The two-career couple.* Reading, MA: Addision-Wesley.

Harvey, M. (1996). Addressing the dual-career expatriation dilemma. *Human Resource Planning, 19* (4), 18–39.

Harvey, M. (1997). Dual-career expatriates: Expectations, adjustment and satisfaction with international relocation. *Journal of International Business Studies, 28* (3), 627–658.

Mendenhall, M., & Oddou, G. (1995). The overseas assignment: A practical look. In M. Mendenhall and G. Oddou (Eds.), *Readings and Cases in International Human Resource Management* (pp. 206–216). Cincinnati: Southwestern.

Michaels, B. (1996, April). Work/family programs throughout the world: How other countries help workers balance obligations. *ACA News,* pp. 20–21.

Morris, B. (1997, March 17). Is your family wrecking your career? *Fortune,* pp. 70–90.

Morris, B. (1997, March 17). Home office heaven—and hell. *Fortune,* p. 82.

Sekaran, U. (1986). *Dual-career families.* San Francisco: Jossey-Bass.

Solomon, C. M. (1996). One assignment, two lives. *Personnel Journal, 75* (5), 36–38.

Swaak, R. A. (1995, January-February). Today's expatriate family: Dual careers and other obstacles. *Compensation and Benefits Review,* pp. 21–26.

Related Readings

Dual-Career Issues

1. Carter, N. (1997). Solve the dual-career challenge. *Workforce, 2* (4), 21–22.
   New issues for HR personnel have surrounded the increase of dual-career couples in the workplace. Human Resources (HR) professionals should be aware of the difficulties for dual-career couples and be willing to work to alleviate these. One important issue concerns the employee who has been asked to relocate (particularly for international moves). Some companies offer a spousal assistance program in order to make the transition more smooth. Spouses should be reminded of the many opportunities available with an international assignment.
2. Harvey, M. (1997). Dual-career expatriates: Expectations, adjustment and satisfaction with international relocation. *Journal of International Business, 28* (3), 627–658.
   In order to retain repatriated employees, HR professionals should take into consideration the following concerns impacting dual-career couples: (1) provide employment opportunities for the spouse; (2) provide commuting allowances for employees geographically separated from their spouse during an expatriate assignment; (3) provide assistance for the spouse in obtaining employment; (4) assist in obtaining the

necessary documents for the spouse to work; (5) encourage spouse to further education during their international assignment; and (6) provide additional resources in order to take the place of the spouse's previously earned income.

3. Solomon, C. M. (1996). One assignment, two lives. *Personnel Journal, 75* (5), 36–38.
   The number of dual-career couples is increasing. Managers may turn down an otherwise attractive expatriate assignment now because of concerns about the career of their spouse. HR personnel need to take a proactive stance on preparing expatriate spouses for their experience abroad. This includes more than just the pre-departure training of expatriate and spouse, but also might include more in-depth language training, assistance locating suitable employment for the spouse (possibly even steering the spouse toward volunteer work), providing additional resources in order to help the spouse make the adjustments, or putting the spouse in touch with a group of people with similar backgrounds and interests with which to share experiences.

4. Swaak, R. A. (1995). Today's expatriate family: Dual careers and other obstacles. *Compensation and Benefits Review, 27* (3), 21-26.
   International experience is becoming more important both for individuals and for their companies as dual-career couples increase. As a result, many employees whose spouses work are either missing opportunities or experiencing great hurdles at managing both careers. The three main reasons for employees not taking international assignments is because of the spouse's work, needs of the children, or responsibility for parents and grandparents.

   Companies are starting to offer assistance for employee spouses who prefer to work, through formal employment support, career services, and income replacement programs. The most difficult task in placing or assisting spouses in locating employment is obtaining a work visa. This is not insurmountable, but can be time consuming and difficult.

CHAPTER 13

USEFUL CONCEPTS

After much discussion of how it would eventually affect them and their family, Matt and Jan agree to move to France for Plasmatec. Having already experienced compensation problems at MedTech, however, they are committed to proceeding differently this time, and this attitude is encouraged by Plasmatec's CEO, Tom, who is so desperate for Matt to go and run the new joint venture that he tells Matt he can "write his own ticket." Following general advice from Professor Karl Davidson, Matt seeks the counsel of an international tax specialist and an international compensation expert. When Matt comes back to Tom with his agreement to go to France as president of Transfusions, he puts forward a specific and expensive proposal.

This brief chapter discusses international compensation issues. Three key subtopics are as follows:

- the international compensation package
- international tax issues
- future trends in managing expatriate costs

The International Compensation Package

Following are most of the various overseas allowances that might be negotiated in an expat compensation package.

Foreign service premium: This premium is paid to families to compensate for the inconvenience of living with foreign customs, transportation, language, housing, and so on. The amount is in the range of 10 to 25 percent of base pay, frequently with a ceiling of $40,000 to $60,000. The 1990 survey found that 78 percent of the more than 250 multinational companies (MNCs) surveyed pay a foreign service premium.

Hardship allowances: This is paid (in addition to the foreign service premium) to compensate an expatriate for especially adverse living conditions such as primitive isolation, personal risk, political instability, poor economic conditions, or extreme climates. Black et al. (1992, p. 185) cite use of both internal and external market tests to derive a fair hardship allowance. The external test involves benchmarking similar firms. The internal test is a market supply and demand test, assessing how much one must pay to attract quality applicants or employees to the difficult site.

Cost savings on hardship allowances are achieved by questioning the status quo. If a once primitive or dangerous city is now technologically up-to-date, clean, and boasts increased security, then promote the newer, attractive image for that location and decrease or eliminate the hardship allowance.

Rest and relaxation (R&R) allowances: Often associated with the hardship allowance, the R&R allowance provides for the family to get away periodically from the assignment and recuperate; they often make purchases or receive medical attention not available in the host country.

Cost of living allowances (COLAs): This allowance is paid to compensate for the imbalance in the cost to maintain equal standards of living across international borders. In general, if it costs more in the assignment country to maintain an equivalent standard of living than it does in the home country, a COLA is provided. The survey found that 91% of the MNCs in the study pay COLAs. In the case that the equivalent standard of living costs less in the assignment country than in the home country, negative adjustments are rarely made. Note that inflation and exchange rates can have a great impact on this allowance. Because both inflation and exchange rates can fluctuate wildly in some countries, this allowance is subject to review and adjustment on a daily, weekly, monthly, quarterly, or annual basis, depending on the range of fluctuations. If inflation is so rampant that an expatriate's actual spending power is affected weekly, then adjustments should be made weekly.

Relocation allowances: This allowance provides for miscellaneous expenses and inaccurate predictions of other allowances related to moving. It is generally a fixed amount equal to one month's salary, with a cap of $5,000. The survey found that 43% of the MNCs surveyed pay a flat sum both at the beginning and the end of the assignment.

Housing allowances: Just as a mortgage is generally any homeowner's single, largest monthly expense, so is the housing allowance usually the single largest item in an expatriate's compensation. Three varieties of housing allowances are discussed.

- *A flat allowance* may be provided; giving the expatriate a fixed housing allowance. The expatriate may spend more or less than the allowance and pocket or pay for the difference. The amount is often based on status within the organization and size of family.
- *A differential allowance* may be provided; giving the expatriate the difference between (equal) housing costs at home and abroad if the expenses abroad are higher.
- *A rental fee* may be charged to employees in the case where the employer provides housing.

Utility allowances: Companies may provide this allowance to cover utilities in the house abroad. Two types of utility allowances are discussed.

- *A fixed allowance* may be provided. Similar to the flat housing allowance, the expatriate may spend more or less than the allowance and pocket or pay for the difference. Companies are careful to determine accurate utility rates and average usage in order to establish a fair allowance.
- *A differential allowance* works similarly to a differential housing allowance, paying the expatriate the difference between utility costs at home and abroad if the expenses abroad are higher.

Furnishing allowances: This allowance assists the expatriate family in furnishing their home abroad. The alternatives are discussed.

A *shipping allowance* may be allocated with which to ship the family's belongings to the new country. Limits are generally based on a maximum weight limit with the expatriate paying for any shipping in excess of around 15,000 pounds. Although this type of an allowance is appealing to families who prefer to have the familiarity of their own furnishings, it is very expensive, and lost or damaged articles cause stress and frustration for the family.

A *goods or rental allowance* actually provides the family with furniture that has been purchased or rented by the company. This is generally accompanied by a limit on the personal shipping allowance to 1,000 pounds or less. Additionally, the company usually pays for storage of the family's own furnishings while they are abroad. Care must be taken to store furnishings in an environment safe from human or environmental damage.

A *lump sum allowance* of $8,000 to $10,000 is sometimes offered to families who are then free to purchase their own furnishings abroad or ship their own furniture. This is a fixed allowance. If expenses are less than the allowance, the expatriate pockets the difference. If expenses exceed the allowance, the expatriate is responsible for the difference. Cost savings are generally recognized by the company that provides a lump sum allowance. This fixes the company's liability and is usually even less expensive than rental if the expatriate is expected to stay abroad for three or more years. Note that very short assignments of one or two years can justify only rental expenses.

Education allowances: This allowance for children's education assists expatriates, who generally do not want their children to attend local schools abroad. The allowance helps cover the costs of "international" schools, tutors, or boarding schools.

Home-leave allowances: This is generally a cash payment to the expatriate to cover airfare for annual family visits to their home country. The company gives the expatriate the amount equal to the airfare (generally business class) and usually is not concerned with how the money is spent, leaving the expatriate and family free to seek budget airfares or visit an alternate destination.

Medical allowances: Companies generally pay 100 percent of medical expenses for expatriate families, including all expenses not covered by insurance. In assignment countries where medical care is subadequate this may include airfare to a more advanced country. Dental and optical expenses are often excluded in this allowance.

Automobile allowances: Most companies provide a differential automobile allowance, paying the expatriate the difference between the owning and maintenance costs at home and those abroad if the expenses abroad are higher. Senior-level executives may be provided with a car and chauffeur, depending on the benefits provided to their counterparts in the assignment country. The study found that 67 percent of the MNCs surveyed provide company cars to expatriates only when it is essential to do so, and 22 percent provide a car to all expatriates.

Membership in clubs allowances: In countries where club memberships provide vital opportunities for business contacts, companies pay for the membership. Frequently club membership is also the only way for expatriate families to have access to recreational facilities. The study found that 42 percent of multinational companies surveyed pay for such memberships on a case-by-case basis, and 6 percent pay for it in all cases.

Foreign country social allowances: Some caution that although base salaries may appear low in some countries, social allowances may make up the differences. Socially inclined countries often have triple or quadruple standards, providing additional allowances for single parent, head of household, or other social responsibilities.

Pension: Compensation experts maintain that pensions should be tied to the location where they will ultimately be spent in order to account for fluctuating currencies, local inflation, and changes in local living standards. However, because pension plans are determined by local laws, it is administratively complex to calculate currency differences and pension credits. The assistance of an internationally experienced actuary is advised.

Managerial pay—United States versus France: French CEOs only make an average 45 percent of the total compensation (salary, bonus, benefits, perquisites) of their U.S. counterparts. But the French director of finance makes 53 percent, the sales director, 73 percent, and the HR director, 74 percent of the compensation of a comparable American executive (Parker-Pope, 1996).

According to a Towers-Perrin survey in 1993, an American middle manager made $159,575 in total compensation, whereas a comparable French manager made $190,354. The Frenchman's salary was lower but the benefits considerably higher. Matt is the managing director, or PDG (président et directeur général) of Transfusions in France but only a middle-level manager in Plasmatec, USA.

International Tax Issues

Expatriates should receive personal advice from tax professionals who have experience with cross-border compensation packages. When choosing such a professional, be alert to the following issues (Black et al., 1992, pp. 191–192):

Tax protection: Under this policy, firms reimburse employees for taxes paid in excess of what they would have paid if they had remained in the country of origin.

- Many expatriate allowances increase the employee's taxable income, thereby increasing the tax liability.
- The additional allowance paid to the employee to cover the increase in taxes is also taxed, increasing the total tax liability.
- In cases when the host country taxes are actually lower than the home country taxes would have been, companies generally allow the employee to pocket the difference.

Tax equalization: The objective here is to see expatriates pay no more and no less than they would have paid in the home country. The tax expatriates would have paid (at home) is subtracted from their salary. The firm then pays all actual taxes that expatriates owe in the home and the host country. Ninety percent of the MNCs surveyed use tax equalization because of these advantages:

- This method actually reduces the total tax liability because taxable income is reduced. The savings go to the company.
- Repatriation problems are reduced in cases (Saudi Arabia) where the host country virtually takes no personal taxes. If expatriates kept the entire tax-free income, they would experience a 30 to 50 percent drop in disposable income upon repatriation.
- Tax equalization makes it easier for an expatriate in a low-tax host country to move to a high-tax host country because expatriates experience no difference in take-home pay.

To attract and motivate high-potential, high-quality employees to take international assignments, U.S.-based MNCs must use taxation strategies that both entice expatriate employees but also are cost effective for the firm. Thus it is important to understand the different types of compensation normally associated with an overseas assignment. In addition to a negotiated base salary, expatriate employees normally contract for and receive the types of compensation and benefits cited here, which are included in what U.S. taxation experts call "gross income."

Foreign earned income exclusion: One of the greatest tax benefits available to U.S. employees who relocate overseas is the foreign earned income exclusion. In order to help multinational businesses compete in the international labor market and to encourage them to employ U.S. citizens in their foreign operations, U.S. tax law through section 911 has given this special exclusion to expatriates who have made permanent tax homes outside the United States. The exclusion from U.S. taxation applies to self-employment income or to compensation earned in a foreign country and can exclude up to $70,000 from being taxed each year. This exclusion benefit must be prorated daily for employees who are overseas for a portion of the year. The 911 exclusion is not available to U.S. government employees such as diplomatic officials or military personnel. However, other special tax laws allow these expatriates to reduce their taxes by other means not available to other U.S. taxpayers.

Foreign housing exclusion or deduction: In addition to the foreign earned income exclusion of $70,000 per tax year, expatriates may be entitled to deduct or exclude their foreign housing costs in excess of a prescribed base amount. The housing cost exclusion is for reimbursed expenses from the employer. Alternatively, the deduction would be for costs that are not reimbursed. The base amount is calculated by taking 16 percent of the annual salary of a GS-14, step 1, U.S. government employee. For 1990 the salary of a GS-14 employee was $48,592, making the base housing amount for that year $7,775. For 1993 the salary was $54,607, making the base $8,737 for 1993. Expatriates may deduct or exclude their qualified housing expenses that are in excess of this amount.

Future Trends in Managing Expatriate Costs

For corporations, the root of the international management compensation problem is cost. Most companies estimate that it costs $250,000 to $400,000 just to send a mid-career employee with a family abroad. Derr and Oddou (1993) surveyed large American and European MNCs on this issue and discovered that in light of the concern about cutting the costs of expatriate compensation packages, it was useful to examine more carefully this most frequently used method of internationalizing managers. Many now involved in the expatriation/repatriation process are junior managers being consciously trained for future positions in the company. Expatriation and repatriation are part of their development as high-potential future executives.

An interesting modern trend is the career stage itself. During the 1970s and 1980s, international assignments typically came eight to twelve years into a manager's career; but they are now increasingly occurring at a younger stage and at more junior levels. Volkswagen Automobiles AG, for example, is one company that identified early international experience for high-potential young managers as its most important activity in developing a cadre of international managers. Many companies studied by Derr and Oddou (1993) focused on expatriating younger managers—age 26 to 32—for very practical reasons:

1. Because these individuals are at such early career stages, they are psychologically flexible. They haven't yet set up rigid categories of the "right" way or "appropriate" activities. It is hoped they will perceive many ways as "right" through this early exposure to pluralism and, what is more, remain permanently flexible and broadly based as they become middle- and senior-level managers.
2. These younger managers are freer for international assignments. Often they are not married. If partnered they either have no children or very young children. Hence they are more mobile. Transplanting an older manager often means he or she has a working spouse and children in school, both conditions that make high-potential candidates reluctant to accept transfers. Furthermore, older managers often require extensive amenities such as private schools for the children, executive search firms for working spouses, large houses, elaborate furniture, the need to move a large number of personal belongings, and a living standard that requires expensive housing and exclusive neighborhoods. These very real financial savings to the company make a broader use of young expatriate transfers possible.

References

Benders Federal Tax Service. (1995). M:7-20-7-302.

Black, J. S., Gregersen, H. B., & Mendenhall, M.E., (1992). *Global Assignments* (San Francisco: Josey-Bass Publishers). Brooks, J. (1993, April). Relocating employees overseas. *The Tax Advisor,* p. 207.

Deloitte, Touche and Tohmatsu. (1997). *Executives living abroad: Guide to tax planning in 66 jurisdictions.* Deloitte, Touche and Tohmatsu, 1633 Broadway, New York, NY 10019.

Derr, C. B., & Oddou, G. (1993). Internationalizing managers: Speeding up the process. *European Management Journal, 11* (4), 432–435.

Esquenazi-shaio, C. (1996, April). Compensating managers abroad is tough. *International Business*, pp. 31–36.

Gould, C. (1997, July). What's the latest in global compensation. *Global Workforce,* pp. 17–21.

Healey, A. M. (1996, July-August). Managing compensation in a global marketplace. *ACA News,* pp. 15–17.

Helms, M., & Crowther, M. (1995). International executive compensation practices. In M. Mendenhall & G. Oddou (Eds.), *Readings and cases in international human resource management* (pp. 394–404). Cincinnati: Southwestern.

Holleman, W. J. (1991, March-April). Taxation of expatriate executives. *International Executive,* pp. 70–74.

Parker-Pope, T. (1996, April 11). Executive pay: So far away. *Wall Street Journal,* p. R12.

Stone, R. J. (1986, January). Pay and perks for overseas assignments. *Personnel Journal,* pp. 64–67.

Swaak, R. A. (1995, November-December). Expatriate failures: Too many, too much cost, too little planning. *Compensation and Benefits Review,* pp. 47–55.

CHAPTER 14

USEFUL CONCEPTS

This chapter covers the Sumner family moving to a suburb of Grenoble, France. At first they are thrilled with the charm and newness of it all. They then experience culture shock, as do most expatriate families when establishing themselves abroad. Matt becomes increasingly involved at work while Jan and the children are left at home (also a normal state of affairs). Jan perceives that learning French, both for her and the children, is the most critical survival skill. The children, especially Jeffery, have a hard transition, and all of them become aware of adaptation problems. The extra time for family life, the financial remunerations, and the personal learning and growth eventually make the international move worthwhile for the whole Sumner family.

Matt also comes face to face with French culture at the office. He learns the importance of philosophical alignment before taking action. He comes to understand how the French view the role of "boss," and the importance of food and relationship building as part of task accomplishment.

This chapter focuses on several cultural issues. First, there is the question of culture shock and the Sumners' family adjustment. Second, there is an attempt to better understand France and French culture, both at the office and at home.

Expatriate Family Adaptation

Consult the culture shock material again in Chapter 5. In her research on expatriate families, Haour-Knipe (1990) points out several contextual factors related to family adaptation once overseas: (1) the push/pull factors (what family members expected and what they perceived they were leaving behind); (2) the involvement of family members in the decision (did the spouse and, to a lesser extent, the children really decide to move or was it forced on them or just happened?); (3) if there was previous cross-cultural experience and whether or not it was positive; (4) the extent to which the family has chosen to be more rooted or more mobile; and (5) whether or not important family issues were considered and at least emotionally resolved (such as the spouse's career, the children's friendships, the quality of educational opportunity in the new location, etc.).

Haour-Knipe distinguishes five qualitatively different types of family moves: (1) the "transfer move" in which families go along with the company's decision, (2) the "lifestyle move" with its basis in the family's belief that they will improve their quality of life by going to the new location, (3) the "experience move" where the major motivation is growth and learning, (4) the "ambition move" designed to support a career-oriented family member in getting ahead, and (5) the "mission move" driven by a strong sense of purpose and need to contribute.

In general, but depending on the contextual factors described earlier, transfer and ambition moves are associated with less well-adapted families. Moves in which the family, especially the spouse, actually chooses to go for lifestyle, mission, or experience, as just described, are normally a better match. An issue for companies is how to support family dynamics and encourage joint decision making, the setting of realistic expectations, helping the family to make the choice to go abroad for adaptive reasons (lifestyle, experience, mission) rather than simply for work-related reasons and, where possible, helping with education, dual-career, and child care issues.

Tung (1987) gives seven common reasons for expatriate failure or returning home early:

1. Inability of the manager's spouse to adjust to a different physical or cultural environment.
2. The manager's inability to adapt to an environment.
3. Other family-related problems.
4. The manager's personality or emotional immaturity.
5. The manager's inability to cope with the responsibilities posed by overseas work.
6. The manager's lack of technical competence.
7. The manager's lack of motivation to work overseas.

French Culture

France. See the map of France and the culturgram. Find Grenoble on the map.

French culture is introduced in the chapter about the Sumners' experience. Using the cultural frameworks, France is high on individualism. Michel Crozier (1964) sums it up in his classical study of French culture:

> Face-to-face dependence relationships are . . . perceived as difficult to bear in the French cultural setting. Yet, the prevailing view of authority is still that of universalism and absolutism . . . the two attitudes are contradictory. However, they can be reconciled within a bureaucratic system since impersonal rules and centralization make it possible to reconcile an absolutist conception of authority and the elimination of most direct dependence relationships. (p. 222)

There is also a high or large power distance between superiors and subordinates in France. Hofstede (1993, p. 84) also comments on French culture:

> In France, the principle is the honor of each class in a society which has always been and remains extremely stratified, in which superiors behave as superior beings and subordinates accept and expect this, conscious of their own lower level in the national hierarchy but also of the honor of their own class. The French do not think in terms of managers versus nonmanagers but in terms of cadres versus non-cadres; cadres have the privileges of a higher social class, and it is very rare for a non-cadre to cross the ranks.

Départments of France

P1. Hauts-de-Seine
P2. Seine-saint-Denis
P3. Val-De-Marne
P4. Ville-De-Paris
1. Pas-de-Calais
2. Nord
3. Somme
4. Ardennes
5. Aisne
6. Oise
7. Seine-Maritime
8. Eure
9. Calvados
10. Manche
11. Orne
12. Eure-et-Loir
13. Yvelines
13a. Val D'oise
14. Essonne
15. Seine-et-Marne
16. Marne
17. Meuse
18. Meurthe-et-Moselle
19. Moselle
20. Bas-Rhin
21. Vosges
22. Haute-Marne
23. Aube
24. Yonne
25. Loiret
26. Sarthe
27. Mayenne
28. Ille-et-Vilaine
29. Côtes-du-Nord
30. Finistère
31. Morbihan
32. Loire-Atlantique
33. Maine-et-Loire
34. Indre-et-Loire
35. Loir-et-Cher
36. Cher
37. Nièvre
38. Côte-D'Or
39. Haute-Saône
40. Haut-Rhin
41. Belfort
42. Doubs
43. Jura
44. Saône-et-Loire
45. Allier
46. Indre
47. Vienne
48. Deux-Sèvres
49. Vendée
50. Charente-Maritime
51. Charente
52. Haute-Vienne
53. Creuse
54. Puy-de-Dôme
55. Loire
56. Rhône
57. Ain
58. Haute-Savoie
59. Savoie
60. Isère
61. Haute-Loire
62. Cantal
63. Corrèze
64. Dorclogne
65. Gironde
66. Lot-et-Garonne
67. Lot
68. Aveyron
69. Lozère
70. Ardèche
71. Drôme
72. Hautes-Alpes
73. Alpes-Maritimes
74. Alpes-de-Haute-Provence
75. Vaucluse
76. Gard
77. Tarn
78. Tarn-et-Garonne
79. Gers
80. Landes
81. Pyrénées Atlantiques
82. Hautes-Pyrénées
83. Haute-Garonne
84. Hérault
85. Bouches-du-Rhône
86. Var
87. Aude
88. Ariège
89. Pyrénées-Orientales
90a. Haute-Corse
90b. Corse-du-Sud

France

- ⊛ National Capital
- • City
- — International Border
- — Department Border

0   25   75km
0   25   50   75 mi

Paris
Department boundaries

Culturgram™ '98

Boundary representations are not necessarily authoritative.

France
(French Republic)

BACKGROUND

Land and Climate

Slightly smaller than Texas, France covers 211,208 square miles (547,030 square kilometers). The terrain is varied, from plains to mountains and forests to farmland. Mountains stretch along the borders with Spain, Italy, and Switzerland. France boasts Europe's highest peak, Mont Blanc (15,771 feet or 4,807 meters). The Rhine *(Rhin)* River forms part of the border with Germany; the northern border with Belgium is a flat plain with rolling hills. The southern climate is Mediterranean, with warm, moist winters and hot, dry summers. The north is temperate and prone to rain. The west is also rainy and is influenced by the Atlantic, which moderates winter temperatures. The central east and upland areas have a continental climate, with fluctuating temperatures; in the mountains, thunderstorms are prevalent in summer. French sovereignty extends to the island of Corsica as well as ten overseas *départements* and territories.

continued

History

By 51 B.C., the Romans had conquered the area's Celtic inhabitants, the Gauls, who then adopted the Romans' customs, language, and laws. Clovis I, king of the Franks, defeated the last Roman governor in A.D. 486. In the late eighth century, France was just one part of the vast empire ruled by Charlemagne. In 987, France emerged as one of the empire's successor kingdoms. The following centuries brought intermittent conflict, particularly with the English, including the Hundred Years' War from 1337 to 1453. In 1429, after 80 years of war, Joan of Arc led the French to victory over the English. Later burned by the English (1431), she remains a French heroine today.

By the late 1600s, France dominated Europe. Under Louis XIV (the Sun King), the movement toward centralized government reached its peak. His palace at Versailles was the envy of the continent. But by 1789, royal extravagance and defeats in foreign wars resulted in the French Revolution. The monarchy of Louis XVI was toppled and the country entered the "reign of terror." Despite the conflict, the French Revolution marks a milestone in world history: the general movement toward democratic government. After a decade of instability, Napoleon Bonaparte took power, declaring himself emperor in 1804. Napoleon conquered most of Europe before embarking on a disastrous campaign in Russia in 1812. In 1814, Austrian and Prussian forces seized Paris and Napoleon was exiled. He returned in 1815 for the Hundred Days' War, which ended in his defeat by the English at Waterloo.

The monarchy was restored but was followed by the Second Republic (1848–52) and then the Second Empire (1852–70) under Napoleon III. Defeat at the hands of Germany led to the Third Republic in 1871. France was a major battleground during both world wars. It was occupied by the Germans between 1940 and 1944 and is famous for the D-Day invasion that turned the tide of World War II in favor of the Allies. In 1946, the Fourth Republic was declared, and after a referendum in 1958, a new constitution for a Fifth Republic was approved. Charles de Gaulle became president. France was a founding member of the European Community and is a central force in European Union (EU) politics today.

In 1968, students and workers protested over poor working conditions and a rigid educational system, resulting in lasting social change. The 1968 events were still fresh in the public mind when students in the early 1990s took to the streets, protesting conditions in public schools and proposed changes in wage laws. The social unrest and economic difficulties led three successive prime ministers to resign before a conservative was given the job in 1993. Early elections in June 1997 backfired on conservatives, as voters, weary of high unemployment and recent austerity measures, returned leftist Socialists to power.

THE PEOPLE

Population

France's population of 58.3 million is growing annually at 0.3 percent. Three-fourths of the population live in urban areas. Greater Paris claims eight million inhabitants and Marseilles one million. Ethnically, the French have a Celtic heritage that has mixed with various other European groups (Latin, Nordic, Teutonic, Slavic, and others) over the centuries. Immigrants and descendants of immigrants from France's old colonial possessions also inhabit France. These include North Africans (Algerians, Tunisians, and Moroccans), West Africans, Caribbean peoples, and Asians from the former Indochina region. Although they have integrated into French society, the various ethnic groups generally do not mix with one another. North Africans remain the most separate because of their Islamic religion.

The French enjoy a high standard of living. France's Human Development Index value (0.946) ranks it second out of 175 countries, indicating most people benefit from economic prosperity and the country's strong social welfare programs. Adjusted for women, the index value (0.926) ranks France sixth out of 146 countries.

Language

French is an important international language. It is an official language of the United Nations and is second only to English in use between nations for communication, business, and diplomacy. The French government has stressed the language so much that almost everyone in France speaks French, despite the different nationalities represented. Even regional dialects have lost their importance in recent years.

Despite the prominence of French, France has recognized its citizens' need to learn other languages. In 1992, it announced that traditional language learning in school will start earlier (age nine) and that all students will be required to learn a second foreign language beginning at age thirteen. In addition, past emphasis on grammar and theory will be replaced by a focus on communication skills. English is the most common foreign language. Even before 1992, children were learning English outside of school. Despite this move toward other languages, the French government resists the inclusion of foreign words and phrases in the French language.

Religion

The majority of the French (nearly 90 percent) are Roman Catholic and practice their faith by celebrating the various religious holidays and attending mass once or twice a year. While regular attendance at mass is increasingly rare, many people visit places of special devotion, such as shrines, to worship. A small percentage of the people belong to other Christian churches (2 percent), the Jewish faith (1 percent), and Islam (1 percent). About 6 percent claim no religion.

General Attitudes

The French believe success is judged by educational level, family reputation, and financial status. They are extremely proud of their culture, heritage, and way of life. They are among the most patriotic people in the world, which is illustrated by their attempts to limit the influence of other cultures in France. This patriotism includes a general expectation that visitors have some knowledge of French and show appreciation for French culture. While French attitudes have traditionally been dominated by Paris, there seems to be a growing decentralization in administration as well as attitudes. The French are reserved and private, and people tend to be more hospitable outside Paris. Politeness is valued in human interaction, and *s'il vous plaît* (Please) is a valued phrase.

Political and social trends have caused the French to reexamine their national identity. Society seems divided over issues related to the central government's structure, education, immigration, economics, and even language.

This introspection has led some to predict that French society will experience fundamental change during the next generation.

Personal Appearance

In general, the French take great care to dress well and fashionably, whether they are wearing formal or casual attire, and they feel more at ease with visitors who show the same degree of attention to appearance. Paris is the home of many of the world's leading fashion designers. Professional attire, depending on the business and location, tends to be formal. Parisians dress more formally than people in other cities. In the southern sunbelt, dress is more casual but not less stylish.

References

Black, J. S., Gregersen, H. B., & Mendenhall, M. E. (1992). Appraising: Determining if people are doing the right things. 162–182.

Brewster, C. (1991). Monitoring performance—and coming home. In *The management of expatriates* (pp. 79–83). Issues in Human Resource Management Series, Monograph 5. London: Kogan Page.

Cauchon, S. (1992, July 6). Surviving cross-cultural shock. *Industry Week*, pp. 35–38.

Channon, J., & Dakin, A. (1995, June 15). Coming to terms with local people, *People Management*, pp. 24–29.

Crozier, M. (1964). *The bureaucratic phenomenon.* (Chicago: University of Chicago Press, 1964).

Haour-Knipe, M. (1990). *Deciding to move abroad: Juggling family and career.* Unpublished paper, Department of Sociology, University of Geneva, Geneva, Switzerland.

Hofstede, G. (1984). *Culture's consequences: International differences in work-related values.* London: Sage.

Hofstede, G. (1993). Cultural constraints in management theories. *Academy of Management Executive, 7* (1), 81–94.

Laurent, A. (1992). The cross-cultural puzzle of global human resource management. In V. Pacik, N. M. Ticky, & C. K. Barnett (Eds.), *Globalizing management* (pp. 174–184). New York: Wiley.

Levinson, H. (1976, July-August). Appraisal of what performance? *Harvard Business Review*, pp. 30–48.

Platt, P. (1995). *French or foe: Getting the most out of visiting, living and working in France.* Cincinnati: C. J. Krehbiel.

Shilling, M. (1993, July). Avoid expatriate culture shock. *HR Magazine*, pp. 58–63.

Solomon, C. M. (1994, April). Success abroad depends on more then job skills: Personal and family needs. *Personnel Journal*, pp. 51–60.

Stuart, K. D. (1992, March). Teens play a role in moves overseas. *Personnel Journal*, pp. 72–78.

Tung, R. L. (1987). Expatriate assignments: Enhancing success and minimizing failure. *Academy of Management Executive, 1* (2), 117–125.

Related Readings

1. Solomon, C. M. (1994). Success abroad depends on more than job skills. *Personnel Journal,* pp. 51–60.
   HR personnel should (1) Allow employees to make a pre-assignment trip, in order to familiarize themselves with the country and make arrangements that will assist in making the transition smoother. (2) Offer a manual outlining the process of expatriate assignment. This will help the employees and their families understand the procedure, but will also make the process more equitable for all employees. (3) Prepare employees and their families for the inevitable period of adjustment that will occur after arrival in the new country. (4) Be aware of the needs of the families. (5) Assign a mentor to keep in touch with expatriates and to act as an advocate for their needs at the home office.
2. Stuart, K. D. (1992). Teens play a role in moves overseas. *Personnel Journal,* 71–78.
   Discusses the importance of involving teenage children of expatriates in their international assignments. Teenagers should receive cross-cultural training, in addition to the employee and spouse. Language training is especially important for teenagers. Allow plenty of time for the family to explore the country and enjoy new opportunities. Make sure the family can make arrangements for schooling, which can be available in a variety of forms.
3. Platt, P. (1995). *French or foe: getting the most out of visiting, living, and worship in France.* Cincinnati: C. J. Krehbiel. This is a delightful French culture primer used by the U.S. State Department to introduce its French Embassy employees to France and French culture.

CHAPTER 15

USEFUL CONCEPTS

Part of Matt's career development plan depends on excellent performance reviews (PRs) in Grenoble. Here we touch on an issue of great concern to most expatriate employees: how to demonstrate excellent performance and "global competence" to those back home. For most companies this is done via the annual performance review and/or the potential appraisal. The important caveat for overseas employees, however, is that their PRs are usually completed at least in part by their overseas bosses or, in the case of 360-degree feedback, their overseas colleagues and boss. Why should this create problems? Key points from the article by Oddou and Mendenhall (1993) point out problems inherent in appraising an expatriate's performance:

- *The expatriate is evaluated by a local manager from that manager's cultural framework.* The Dutch, for example, are known in Europe as very tough appraisers. As one high-level manager in a well-known Dutch multinational put it, "On a 1 to 5 scale where 5 is high, we only use 1 to 4; 2 is average, 3 is good, 4 is excellent, and 5 is reserved for God." This may not be the same as a back-home American perspective.
- *Some of the most important learning while abroad may not be visible and appraised back at the home office.* Learning how to work cross culturally, being able to implement business decisions in a complex situation, being flexible, being open to new methods and thinking and taking more overall responsibility for the business—many of these competencies may not show up when looking only at domestic measurement criteria such as profit margin and market share.

  When being evaluated by both a distant home office and a domestic foreign office, expatriates may experience a *double communication bind.* They may experience a communication gap by being separated from the home office by distance, time zones, and communication infrastructure. They may experience a similar communication gap with the foreign domestic office because of its lack of international experience and corporate culture.
- *It takes more time to learn an international job,* given language and cultural challenges and, therefore, it may not be fair to appraise expatriates on the same schedule as home-based employees.
- *The stakes are very high for an expatriate.* The performance appraisal while overseas will probably influence the positions or assignment when one returns home.

References

Black, J. S., Gregersen, H. B., & Mendenhall, M. E. (1992). Appraising: Determining if people are doing the right things. 162–182.

Brewster, C. (1991). Monitoring performance—and coming home. *The management of expatriates* (pp. 79–83). Issues in Human Resource Management Series, Monograph 5. London: Kogan Page.

Gabarro, J. J., & Hill, L. A. (1995). Managing performance. Harvard Business School Note 9-496-022, 1–7.

Gregersen, H. B., Hite, J. M., & Black, J. S. (1996). Expatriate performance appraisals in U.S. multinational firms. *Journal of International Business Studies, 27* (4), 711–738.

Harvey, M. (1997). Focusing the international personnel performance appraisal process. *Human Resource Development Quarterly, 8* (1), 41–62.

Levinson, H. (1976, July-August). Appraisal of what performance? *Harvard Business Review,* pp. 30–48.

Oddou, G., & Mendenhall, M. (1993). Expatriate performance appraisal: Problems and solutions. In M. Mendenhall & G. Oddou (Eds.), *Readings and cases in international human resource management* (pp. 383–393). Cincinnati: Southwest.

Related Readings

1. Black, J. S., Gregersen, H. B., & Mendenhall, M. E. (1992). *Global assignments: Successfully expatriating and repatriating international managers.* San Francisco: Jossey-Bass.

   The purposes of performance appraisals, evaluation and development, may often be in direct conflict. The authors describe the challenges to international performance appraisal as (1) invalid criteria, which may not work in the international setting. The raters must take into consideration certain environmental factors that would influence the "numbers" resulting from a manager's performance; (2) rater competence, which reflects not just the ability of the rater to evaluate fairly but also the possible lack of exposure to the ratee. In this way, the rater may not be closely familiar with the specific accomplishments of the job; and (3) rater bias, which can play into the evaluation of employees across cultures.

   The authors suggest three questions that should be answered in order to resolve these challenges:
   a. What should be evaluated? (This can only be decided after careful review and analysis.)
   b. Who should do the evaluating? (Authors suggest multiple raters who are familiar with the performance of the specific employee, namely on-site supervisors, peer managers, subordinates, clients, and global managers.)
   c. When should appraisals be done? (More frequently than once or twice a year.)

3. Brewster, C. (1991). *The management of expatriates.* London: Kogan Page.
   See the chapter on performance appraisals. The author looks at the difficulty of making comparisons of international performance appraisals because of (1) cultural differences, including the increased use of group work in some cultures, which can make it difficult to evaluate individuals, differing expectations of work, and difficulty with the more traditional, U.S. form of performance appraisal, specifically dealing with criticism from supervisors; (2) lack of information in the home country about the specific accomplishments of the employee. For example, what influence did the environment play in the results experienced by the expatriate manager? and (3) the objectives of each expatriate assignment may not be the same. If this is the case, requiring

certain "numbers" or targets may get in the way of accurate performance appraisals. The expatriate manager may be making progress in the country, but the numbers may not reflect that progress accurately, especially in comparison to managers in other countries or in the home country.

4. Gregersen, H. B., Hite, J. M., & Black, J. S. (1996). Expatriate performance appraisal in U.S. multinational firms. *Journal of International Business Studies, 27* (4), 711–738.
Performance appraisal practices for expatriates in multinational firms. Frequency and the use of multiple raters were found to be important in the accuracy of performance appraisals. Companies should use raters from within the host country, as well as those from the home country. In this way, employees are given a greater opportunity to be evaluated more completely on their performance. One of the suggestions is to customize the performance appraisal instruments for expatriates. In this way, they will not be held to targets or goals that may not be possible in their expatriate assignment. Those that implement customized performance appraisals should be cautioned that this policy will make it difficult to compare with the evaluations of other employees.

5. Harvey, M. (1997). Focusing the international personnel performance appraisal process. *Human Resource Development Quarterly, 8* (1), 41–62.
Emphasis is on recognizing the diversity of employees, not simply expatriates, but also local employees (from the host country) and also those from developing countries. The ideas and beliefs about leadership, control, participation, authority, communication, and evaluation probably differ for each country, which may get in the way of an accurate performance appraisal. The use of additional raters can give a more balanced view of an employee's performance. The authors suggest that performance appraisals should include some qualitative information because holding managers to specific goals or targets may not reflect their accomplishments accurately. Performance appraisals for international personnel can be very time consuming for several reasons, namely, the use for multiple raters, the geographic distance between the rater and the employee, and the increased use of a more qualitative nature. All of these issues add to the difficulties of international performance appraisal procedures for human resource personnel.

6. Vance, C. M., McClaine, S. R., Boje, D. M., & Stage, H. D. (1992). An examination of the transferability of traditional performance appraisal principles across cultural boundaries. *Management International Review, 32* (4), 313–357.
Compares performance appraisals in the United States, Indonesia, Malaysia, and Thailand. Many managers assume the management styles and systems are the same between the United States and these countries, and these systems can be transported directly into working situations there. Yet the styles that work in the United States do not necessarily work in Pacific Rim countries.

CHAPTER 16

USEFUL CONCEPTS

After joining Plasmatec and a brief stint in the marketing department, Jennifer Stewart is labeled a "high potential," or HIPO. For her further development, Jennifer is assigned to work at Transfusions, the Plasmatec joint venture with GTS in France, and help Matt develop new business ideas for Europe, the Middle East, and Africa. It's clear that part of Matt's performance review depends on how well he trains and develops Jennifer.

After the initial excitement and the normal adjustments, Jennifer struggles with French culture. What she encounters is the "deep culture" in which her basic assumptions about cross-gender collaborations, office politics, femininity, sexual relationships, and equality are all challenged. Jennifer comes at it from the perspective of a young, educated, professional American woman, and she encounters the differences between her and Carine, a young, educated, professional French woman. She gets support from Matt and understanding from Jan. Mostly, Jennifer's perspective is forever changed by coming up against new cultural values and another point of view.

The issues in this chapter are as follows:

- high-potential management
- internationalizing managers
- women working abroad
- confronting the "deep culture" of a country

High-Potential (HIPO) Management

Derr's research (1987, 1988) in large companies reveals that HIPOs often have the following characteristics:

1. The potential to assume critical leadership positions and reach the top management group.
2. Although not necessarily fast trackers, they change roles and move faster than their peer group.
3. All others are told to manage their own careers but HIPOs' careers are influenced and even managed by the company.
4. They are usually recognized by the company as having high potential and this recognition is kept quiet, perhaps kept on a secret list by the company's management development committee.
5. They have often had or are scheduled to have at least one meaningful expatriate assignment.
6. Being a HIPO requires dedication, flexibility, stamina, and a willingness to make the necessary personal sacrifices in order to become a company leader.

Jennifer's Résumé

RESUME

NAME: JENNIFER STEWART

EDUCATIONAL BACKGROUND:

- Georgetown University, BS in Political Science, 1990

- University of California at Berkeley, MBA, 1994

WORK HISTORY:

- Summer Intern, The State Department, 1989

- Congressional Liaison Office, Department of Commerce, 1990-91

- The European Desk, The State Department, 1991-92

- Plasmatec, Marketing Specialist, 1994-96

- Plasmatec, New Business Development Specialist, Europe, 1996-present

INTERESTS:

- Travel (speak some French)

- Art

- Hiking and backpacking

RECOGNITIONS:

- Phi Beta Kappa, Georgetown

- Winning Student Team in Marketing Competition '91, UC Berkeley

- New Employee Recognition Award, Plasmatec, 1993

LANGUAGE

- Latin (4 years)

- French (2 years)

Many talented HIPOs voluntarily withdraw (turn down the next developmental assignment) when the personal costs get too high.

In Derr's et al.'s 1988 research in American corporations, respondents were queried about obstacles they encountered in the optimal development of high-potential employees. A majority of these obstacles derived directly from conditions in a particular market or from a particular practice by the company. However, generic obstacles perceived by many management development directors in the diverse sample of companies were as follows:

- The company has a HIPO groomed for a particular position but the position is not available because of internal politics, slow growth, or lack of coordination between development and succession planning (28 percent of the companies reported this).
- Some managers are not willing to identify their best people as HIPOs and allow them to move on to the next assignment. To do so would have a negative short-term impact on the manager's productivity because of the loss of a key employee (28 percent).
- Defining and measuring potential is a difficult, subjective, and sometimes controversial process (16 percent).
- Too rapid movement creates such problems as the lack of accountability and failure to learn well any one part of the business (13 percent).
- We invest in HIPO development and then lose them. This is expensive (10 percent).
- Lack of adequate funding to train, develop and relocate HIPOs (9 percent).

Important characteristics or competencies of these future leaders include such attributes as:

- good interpersonal skills
- excellent oral and written communication
- leadership ability
- the ability to learn quickly from experience
- high intelligence
- knowledge of the company's products, markets, and policies
- the ability to organize, plan, and set agendas
- strategic ability
- technical competence
- team building
- the ability to deal with stress and ambiguity
- drive and perseverance
- the ability to select and develop a staff
- general management skills

Derr and Briscoe (1998) have completed a recent study in which ten bellwether American companies were asked about newer trends in high-potential management. Although most of the same knowledge and methods developed over the years and explained here still apply, the rapidly changing organizations of the 1990s also note some modifications.

First, global and technological changes are so rapid it is difficult to forecast the future and ascertain what kind of future managers or which competencies are most needed and most highly valued. Second, the shift from more long-term employment and hierarchical organization to more market-driven employment and flatter and more flexible organizations makes formal long-term succession planning obsolete. The focus is on training a "pool" of talent rather than a "stream" of successors. Third, flatter organizations are typically lean and have undergone radical restructuring. HIPOs are very busy, even overloaded, and very much needed in their current positions. A greater emphasis is being placed on on-the-job training and development as opposed to frequent job rotations across different parts of the business and job-away training.

Internationalizing Managers

In coming years, large companies will almost certainly become more global in their perspective. They will be more concerned about selecting, training, and developing global managers who understand the worldwide ramifications of their business and who can operate effectively around the world. The research of Derr and Oddou (1993) and of Oddou, Derr, and Black (1995) underscores that almost certainly large multinational enterprises will continue to expatriate home nationals while giving increasing attention to selecting them at a younger age and to training them and their families to operate effectively in their new setting.

It is safe to predict that companies will also become better at managing the repatriation transition. Instead of the mixed review young managers now give to international assignments, it may well be that they can report an experience which was personally developmental and professionally beneficial. A respondent from Citicorp Europe pointed out, "The corporate philosophy is that a successful career is best achieved by really mobile people. Young managers need to go abroad and senior managers with limited international experience will in the future be less valued." (Derr and Oddou, 1993, p. 441)

Developing greater global awareness and competency in senior personnel presents new challenges. An international Swiss bank respondent identified the problem:

> Expatriation has always been important for management development. . . . Junior expatriate programs will increase in importance. The issue is: Is expatriation enough? How does a firm internationalize senior managers who may have never worked abroad, or who had the experience twenty years earlier? And how does a firm manage mid-level executives—who are reluctant to accept an international assignment because of the spouse's career or the children's education? What options exist beyond expatriation and repatriation? (Derr & Oddou, 1993, p. 438)

To understand how the companies studied by Derr and Oddou (1993) conceptualized internationalizing senior managers, it is necessary to consider possibilities in this management process that go beyond expatriation and repatriation. Listed here are processes other than expatriation that are currently in vogue.

- *Importing Foreign Expertise*—bringing foreign nationals into the head office for a one- to three-year assignment that would involve them in decision making, provide a forum in which they could share their more global perspectives, and expose more nations to international views and values.
- *"Long" Business Trips*—typically, a mid- or senior-level manager would spend three to six months abroad conducting business, perhaps at a single regional or company headquarters office or perhaps at several different locales within a region. As more strategic business units and companies within the larger corporation locate their head offices away from corporate headquarters, more business has to be conducted at those locales.
- *International Task Forces*—working in international project groups is an excellent way to accomplish needed and important tasks; internationalization is a side benefit. Eighty-four percent of those queried by Derr and Oddou predicted that such task forces would increase in the years ahead.

  For two decades, Philips Electronics has used cross-national teams (the "octagons") as part of its managerial training and development. After a two-week seminar in Eindhoven, senior management presents a number of important global projects; each group chooses one. The task force participants devote about 20 percent of their time to these projects, meeting regularly in various European locations. At the project's end, the group presents its report to Philips's top-level managers, who consider carefully the possibility of implementing their recommendations. In a significant number of cases, the work of the octagons has become the basis for important new directions and emphases at Philips.
- *Attending Cross-Cultural Seminars*—a significant number of companies plan in-company seminars and external training sessions for their managers that constitute, in effect, cross-cultural classrooms. Such cross-cultural training is part of the training. One of the most telling results of the Derr and Oddou survey was the fact that over half of the respondents said younger managers would need a global orientation and international sophistication to make it to the top. In response to this statement, "In our firm, international assignments are now mandatory to reach senior management positions," 36 percent of respondents in these multinational companies answered "always," 21 percent replied "often," 13 percent specified "sometimes," 3 percent answered "rarely," and 27 percent answered "never." In other words, 57 percent of these bellwether multinationals always or often consider international experience "mandatory" for senior executives.

Women Managers Working Abroad

Nancy Adler (1995) points out in her extensive study of the role of North American women experiencing expatriation in Asia that important myths or beliefs about women working overseas are untested. One of these myths is that "women do not want to be international managers." Another is that "foreigners' prejudice against women renders them ineffective, even when the women are interested and are sent."

Addressing the first myth, Adler discovered that of the 1,129 MBAs she surveyed in the United States, Canada, and Europe, 84 percent of both men and women wanted an international assignment during some part of their career and there was no significant statistical differences between men and women MBAs.

Addressing the other myth, Adler found that 75 percent of the companies she studied believed that foreign customers in Asia would be biased against North American women. Adler interviewed 52 female expatriate managers, all of them having worked in male-dominated Asian settings, to further test the myth. Of these, 97 percent believed their experiences abroad were successful: 42 percent of the women believed being female was an advantage, and only 20 percent said it adversely impacted doing business abroad.

The most important findings in Adler's study was that foreigners are viewed as foreigners in Asian culture. Women expatriates are viewed as foreigners, not as local women, and the norms and rules for local women do not strictly apply to expatriate women.

References

Adler, N. J. (1995). Pacific Basin managers: A gaijin, not a woman. In M. Mendenhall & G. Oddou (Eds.), *Readings and cases in international human resource management* (pp. 128–148). Cincinnati: Southwest.

Bennett, A. (1993, March 15). GE redesigns rungs of the career ladder. *Wall Street Journal*, p. B3.

Burke, R., & Weir, T. (1977, November). Why good managers make lousy fathers. *Canadian Business*, pp. 1–7.

Crompton, R. (1996). Paid employment and the changing system of gender relations: A cross-national comparison. *Sociology: The Journal of the British Sociological Association, 30* (3), 427–441.

Dailey, R. (1995). Developing the Euro-manager: Managing in a multi-cultural environment. *European Business Review, 95* (1), 13–15.

Dalton, G. W., & Thompson, P. H. (1986). *Novations: Strategies for career management.* Glenview, IL: Scott Foresman.

Davis, S. M. (1984). *Managing corporate culture.* Cambridge, MA: Ballinger.

Deal, T. E., & Kennedy, A. A. (1982). *Corporate cultures.* Reading, MA: Addison-Wesley.

Derr, C. B. (1987). Managing high potentials in Europe: Some cross-cultural findings. *European Management Journal, 5* (2), 72–80.

Derr, C. B., & Briscoe, J. (1998). *Managing high-potentials: Practices in the United States.* Unpublished paper, David Eccles School of Business, BUC 401, University of Utah, Salt Lake City, UT 84112.

Derr, C. B., Jones, C., & Toomey, E. L. (1988). Managing high-potential employees: Current practices in thirty-three U.S. corporations. *Human Resource Management, 27* (3), 273–290.

Derr, C. B., & Oddou, G. R. (1991). Are multinationals adequately preparing American leaders for global competition? *European Management Journal*, pp. 227–244.

Derr, C. B., & Oddou, G. (1993). Internationalizing managers: Speeding up the process. *The European Management Journal, 11* (4), 435–441.

Douglas, M. (1982). Cultural bias. In M. Douglas (Ed.), *In the active voice* (pp. 183–254). London: Routledge.

Durham, C. A. (1995). At the crossroads of gender and culture: Where feminism and sexism intersect. *The Modern Journal, 79*, 153–165.

Ellement, G., & Moznevski, M. (1990). Ellen Moore (A): Living and working in Bahrain. Case 90-C019, Richard Ivey School of Business, University of Western Ontario, London, Ontario, Canada N6A3K7.

Hesterley, W., & Derr, C. B. New theories of leadership development, in Bournois, F. & Roussillon, S. (1998). "Préparer tes Futurs Leaders" (Paris: les Editions d'Organisation).

Magretta, J. (1997, March-April). Will she fit in? *Harvard Business Review,* reprint 97208.

Mainiero, L. A. (1994). Getting anointed for advancement: The case of executive women. *Academy of Management Executive, 8* (2), 53–63.

Oddou, G., Derr, C. B., Black, J. S., (1995). "Internationalizing Managers: Expatriation and Other Strategies," in J. Selmes (Ed.). *Expatriate Management* (New Haven, Conn.: Quorum Books).

Rosener, J. B. (1990, November-December). Ways women lead. *Harvard Business Review,* pp. 119–125.

Schwartz, F. N. (1989, January-February). Management women and the new facts of life. *Harvard Business Review,* pp. 65–76.

Schwartz, F. N. (1992, March-April). Women as a business imperative. *Harvard Business Review,* pp. 105–113.

Scott, J., Alwi, D. F., & Braun, M. (1996). Generational changes in gender-role attitudes: Britain in a cross-national perspective. *Sociology: The Journal of the British Sociological Association, 30* (3), 471.

Smircich, L. (1983). Studying organizations as cultures. In G. Morgan (Ed.), *Beyond method* (pp. 160–173). Beverly Hills, CA: Sage.

Spreitzer, G. M., McCall, M. W., & Mahoney, J. D. (1996). *Early identification of international executives.* Unpublished paper, School of Business Administration, University of Southern California.

Useem, J. (1995). Exporting American culture. Harvard Business School Case 9-396-055, pp. 1–18.

Westwood, R. K., & Leung, S. M. (1994). The female expatriate manager experience: Coping with gender and culture. *International Studies of Management and Organization, 24* (3), 64.

Related Readings

Managing High Potentials

1. Spreitzer, G. M., McCall, M. W., & Mahoney, J. D. (1996) The early identification of executive potential. Unpublished manuscript (Los Angeles: The Center for Effective Organizations, University of Souther California).
   Describes "Prospector," a measurement tool for identifying high-potential international executives. The 14 dimensions of "Prospector" are grouped into four sections:
   a. Ability to attract attention within the company. Potential executives need to first stand out in a positive way.

b. Taking opportunities for learning about the organization, other cultures, themselves, and the environment.

c. Responsive to learning opportunities. Employees must take responsibility for their own actions and show a commitment to others, which, in turn, allows greater opportunities. A particularly important point is being open to differences and learning from those differences.

d. Change as a result of experience shows a willingness to use information to make the changes necessary for more effective work.

2. Bournois, F., & Roussillon, S. (1998). *Préparer tes futurs leaders.* Paris: Editions d'Organisation.
New book to be published in 1998 in France promises a global perspective on this subject. Chapters about HIPO management in the United States, the United Kingdom, France, Germany, Italy, Poland, Japan, and China are included.

3. Derr, C. B., Jones, C., & Toomey, E. L. (1988). Managing high-potential employees: Current practices in thirty-three U.S. corporations. *Human Resource Management, 27* (3), 273-290.
Lays out general principles and a model of high-potential management.

4. Derr, C. B. (1987). Managing high-potentials in Europe: Some cross-cultural findings. *European Management Journal, 5* (2), 72–80.
Points out salient cross-culture differences among French, British, German, Swiss, and Swedish companies.

International Moves

1. Derr, C. B., & Oddou, G. (1993). Internationalizing managers: Speeding up the process. *European Management Journal, 11* (4), 435–441.
An article about the most recent trends for internationalizing managers. Summarized above, the article more fully discusses company alternatives to expatriation.

2. Oddou, G., Derr, C. B., & Black, S. (1995). Internationalizing managers: Expatriation and other strategies. In J. Selmer (Ed.), *Expatriate management.* New Haven, Conn.: Quorum Books.
Treats the same material but also includes Japanese companies.

3. Boyacigiller, N. (1995). The international assignment reconsidered. In M. Mendenhall & G. Oddou (Eds.), *Readings and cases in international human resource management* (pp. 149–156). Cincinnati: Southwestern.
Presents an informative and insightful company perspective.

4. Mendenhall, M., & Oddou, G. (1995). The overseas assignment: A practical look. In M. Mendenhall and G. Oddou (Eds.), *Readings and cases in international human resource management* (pp. 206–216). Cincinnati: Southwestern.
Presents the problem from an individual point of view. There are still career dangers associated with an international move.

"Core Culture" or Deep Culture

1. Schein, E. (1985). *Organizational culture and leadership.* San Francisco: Jossey-Bass.
Edgar Schein's classic book on the three levels of culture creates a three-tier model

for understanding culture: artifacts is the most superficial level of culture, norms and values is a deeper level, basic assumption or "deep culture" is the deepest level of culture and the most difficult.
2. Derr, C. B., & Laurent, A., (1989). The internal and external career: A theoretical and cross-cultural perspective. In M. B. Arthur, B. S. Laurence, & D. T. Hall, (Eds.), *Handbook of career theory* (pp. 454–471). New York: Cambridge University Press. Builds on Schein's work and extends it to differentiating between national and organizational culture.

Women Working Abroad

1. Crompton, R. (1996). Paid employment and the changing system of gender relations: A cross-national comparison. *Journal of the British Sociological Association, 30* (3), 427–445.
   Compares employment patterns for women in France and Britain, particularly looking at the government policies in both countries that have historically affected the employment of mothers. For example, women in France are generally viewed as both mothers and workers, whereas in Britain, women are typically viewed as mothers, and only rarely, workers. Because of this view, France has instituted paid maternity leaves and offers publicly funded child care, which is rated one of the best in Europe, and Britain offers the lowest level of child care in Europe.
2. Scott, J., Alwin, D. F., & Braun, M. (1996). Generational changes in gender-role attitudes: Britain in a cross-national perspective. *Journal of the British Sociological Association, 30* (3), 471–492.
   Compares the gender-role attitudes of men and women in Britain, the United States, and Germany. The findings show close similarities between the United States and Germany, but Britain shows a slower, less consistent rate of change. This change has slowed down even more in the 1990s. The authors believe this may be in part because relatively more women work part time in Britain, which provides a different view for both men and women.
3. Westwood, R. I., & Leung, S. M. (1994). The female expatriate manager experience: Coping with gender and culture. *International Studies of Management and Organization, 24* (3), 64–85.
   The authors studied the experience of female expatriates in Hong Kong, which is a patriarchal society. Overall, the women generally evaluated their experiences as positive and felt they were effective. Certainly there were problems, but these women felt they were able to adapt to the work and the environment. These findings support the notion that companies should not allow gender to be an issue when identifying those who would perform well in expatriate assignments.

CHAPTER 17

USEFUL CONCEPTS

This chapter discusses the cultural differences Jennifer encounters while pursuing new business leads in Germany, Russia, and Burkina Faso. It undertakes a country and cross-cultural analysis and evaluates Jennifer's new business proposals.

The culturgrams on Germany, Russia, and Burkina Faso provide basic country information. Cultural information is included in the chapter, plus the cultural frameworks are applicable. References and additional information on Germany are in Chapter 10.

New Business Development in a Global Company

Here are some excerpts from readings that Jennifer's assistant provided and that she is considering as she prepares for her new business development trip.

Purchasing Research and Development from Foreign Countries (Jeannet and Hennessy, 1992, pp. 371–372)

Instead of developing new products through its own research and development personnel, a company may acquire such material or information from independent outside sources. These sources are usually located in foreign countries that have acquired lead market status. Managers commonly read literature published by lead markets. Also, through regular visits to foreign countries and trade fairs, managers maintain close contact with their lead markets. Increasingly, however, these ad hoc measures are becoming insufficient for maintaining the necessary flow of information in rapidly changing markets.

For companies without immediate access to new technology embodied in new products, the licensing avenue has been the traditional approach to gain new developments from lead markets. U.S. technology has been tapped through many independent licensing arrangements. Japanese companies have made extensive use of the licensing alternative to acquire technologies developed in countries that were lead markets from Japan's point of view. In the early 1960s, several Japanese manufacturers of earth-moving equipment signed licensing agreements with the U.S. manufacturers to obtain expertise in hydraulic power shovels. Although some Japanese companies attempted to develop a new product line from their own internal resources, it was Komatsu who, based on a licensing agreement with a U.S. company, achieved leadership in Japan. By 1989, Japanese companies manufacturing earth-moving equipment owned some 21 facilities abroad, some partly owned and others fully owned. Many firms that were originally licensers to those Japanese firms are no longer independent or have even become Japanese partners, joint ventures, or subsidiaries. Although the advantage of licensing lies in its potential to teach new product technologies, there are typically some restrictions attached, such as limiting the sale of such products to specific geographic regions or countries.

A variation of the licensing agreement is the technology assistance contract with a foreign company, allowing a constant flow of information to the firm seeking assistance. Such agreements have been signed by several U.S. steel companies. Japanese steelmakers have achieved world leadership. Consequently, steel companies all over the world, Americans among them, have tapped the former's knowledge and experience. Sumitomo Metal signed contracts with clients in 19 countries, including U.S. Steel, for steelmaking, plate rolling, and pipe manufacturing. Other U.S. companies purchasing from Japanese companies included Armco, from Nippon Steel; Inland Steel, from Nippon Kokan; and Bethlehem Steel, from Kawasaki Steel.

Importing as a Source of New Product Technology (Jeannet and Hennessy, 1992, p. 373)

Some corporations have decided to forgo internally sponsored research and development, importing finished products directly from a foreign firm. Sometimes the importer assumes the role of an original equipment manufacturer (OEM) by marketing products under its own name. Some agreements made between Japanese suppliers and European and U.S. manufacturers serve to illustrate this strategy.

When IBM was looking for a small desktop copier to fill a gap in its product line, the company turned to a Japanese supplier, Minolta Camera Co., Ltd., instead of developing its own machine. IBM's product line included photocopying machines ranging from $6,000 to $40,000, after it dropped an older model that had sold for $4,000. But in 1980 the company opened its first retail outlets, which were targeted at small businesses. The need for a small desktop model became apparent and had to be filled quickly. The Minolta-supplied model was sold as the IBM Model 102 and resembled the Model EP-310, which was marketed by Minolta in the United States through a network of independent dealers.

Although the importing method gives a firm quick access to new products without incurring any research and development expenditures, a company could become dependent and lose the capacity to innovate on its own in the future. As was the case with General Electric's color TV production, economic changes can lead to reversals later on. GE had stopped production of color TV sets in the United States in the mid-1970s and sourced all such products from Matsushita in Japan. When the value of the yen rose to record levels in 1986, GE switched back to U.S. sourcing. This move was made possible because the company had earlier acquired RCA, which still operated a color TV plant in the United States. Consequently, such a strategy of importing new products should be pursued with great care and possibly only in areas that do not represent the core of the firm's business and technology.

Acquisitions as a Route to New Products (Jeannet and Hennessy, 1992, pp. 373–374)

To acquire a company for its new technology or products is a strategy many firms have followed in domestic markets. To make international acquisitions for the purpose of gaining a window on emerging technologies or products is developing into an acceptable strategy for many firms.

  Following is a list of important characteristics of target firms. It provides categories of competitive advantage Jennifer can consider (Yip, 1995, p. 240):

- Patents
- Research capability
- Development capability
- Product or service quality
- Alignment of offerings with critical needs of customers
- Breadth of product line
- Customer relationships
- Access to lower cost or more effective factors of production
- Location of manufacturing near customers or sources of supply
- Unique manufacturing technology
- Vertical integration
- Operating efficiency
- Access to distribution channels
- Physical distribution capability
- Marketing skills
- Reputation of company
- Strength of brand name
- Sales force effectiveness
- Technical support strength
- Customer service
- Government support or protection
- Size of business
- Superior financial resources
- Lower cost finance
- Cross-business synergy
- Corporate support

Culturgram™ '98

Germany

(Federal Republic of Germany)

Boundary representations are not necessarily authoritative.

BACKGROUND

Land and Climate

Covering 137,803 square miles (356,910 square kilometers), Germany is just smaller than Montana. There are four main geographic zones: the broad lowlands in the north; the central uplands, including various small mountain ranges; the wide valley and gorge of the Rhine River in the southwest; and the forested mountains and plateaus of the south. About 40 percent of Germany is forested. The Rhine, Danube, and Elbe Rivers flow through Germany. The climate is generally temperate and mild, with warm summers and wet winters.

History

Before becoming a nation-state in 1871, Germany was divided into a patchwork of small separate principalities and was once part of the Holy Roman Empire. Through three wars (1864–70), Prussian leader Otto von Bismarck united Germany into a powerful, industrialized nation. In World War I (1914–18), Germany allied with Austria and Turkey. In 1917 the United States joined

continued

Britain, France, Russia, Italy, and Japan to defeat the German Empire. Germany was made to pay huge reparations, admit guilt for the war, and cede about one-tenth of its territory. A democratic government, known as the Weimar Republic, was established in 1918.

The country's humiliation was made worse by the economic depression of the 1930s and a lack of support for Weimar leaders. Germany's distress gave rise to Austrian-born Adolf Hitler and his National Socialist (Nazi) Party. In 1933, President von Hindenburg named Hitler chancellor after the Nazis emerged as the dominant party in elections. In 1934, the day after von Hindenburg died, the posts of president and chancellor were combined, and Hitler declared himself *Führer* (leader) of the Third Reich. He soon embroiled Germany and the world in World War II. Before being defeated by the Allied forces in 1945, the Nazis occupied much of the continent, killing many, including six million Jews.

Germany was split into occupation zones to facilitate disarmament and organize a democracy. When the Soviet Union did not comply with the agreement, the zones occupied by the Western Allies became the Federal Republic of Germany (FRG), a democratic nation. The Soviets in turn created out of the eastern zone the German Democratic Republic (GDR), which followed the Soviet model of development. When thousands of people fled the east, the GDR built the Berlin Wall (1961) to shut off access to West Berlin. The wall remained a symbol of the Cold War until late 1989 when it was opened to traffic on both sides. The wall was eventually torn down and the two nations became the reunified Federal Republic of Germany on 3 October 1990. Berlin regained its status as the country's capital, but the actual transition from Bonn to Berlin will not be complete until the year 2000.

(Western) Germany was a founding member of the European Community, now known as the European Union (EU). It joined the North Atlantic Treaty Organization (NATO) in 1955, but German troops were restricted by constitution to German soil. In 1993, policy changes allowed troops to participate in United Nations relief operations in Somalia. The continued cost of German reunification, record-high unemployment, public attachment to generous social benefits, and meeting EU convergence criteria for a single currency continue to challenge Chancellor Helmut Kohl as he seeks reelection in 1998.

THE PEOPLE

Population

Germany's population is about 83.5 million and is growing at 0.7 percent annually. About 86 percent of all Germans live in urban areas. The population is primarily ethnic German. Non-citizen minorities from Turkey, the former Yugoslavia, Italy, Greece, and other nations live in Germany as guest workers (*Gastarbeiter*). They comprise up to 20 percent of some western metropolitan populations. In western states, numerous political refugees from the Middle East, India, Africa, and Asia receive room and board until their applications for asylum are processed. A small Slavic (Serbian) minority resides in the east, and a Danish population lives in the north. Many ethnic Germans from eastern European nations have emigrated to Germany to find work. The much-publicized violence against immigrant groups reflects the feelings of only a small minority of Germans. Most Germans do not support such activity but do support stemming the flow of "economic" refugees. New laws restrict the definition of a valid asylum seeker and limit other forms of immigration.

Germany's Human Development Index value (0.924) ranks it 19th out of 175 countries. Adjusted for women, the index value (0.886) ranks Germany 16th out of 146 countries.

Opportunities for personal advancement are available to most people, but in varying degrees, according to region and socioeconomic status.

Language

German is the official language. However, the German taught in school and used in the media often is not the German spoken daily. Various dialects are used in most areas. In fact, a German from Bonn or Hannover may have trouble understanding a person from München (where Bavarian is spoken) or Halle (Saxon). While the dialects are mostly verbal, they are part of folk literature and music and are also written. English, widely understood, is a required school subject. Many Germans in eastern states know Russian.

Religion

Germany is essentially a Christian, but secular, society. About 35 percent of the population belongs to the Roman Catholic Church, 36 percent is Protestant (mostly Lutheran), and 2 percent is Muslim. A number of other Christian denominations are active throughout the country. About 25 percent of the people have no official religious affiliation. Historically, entire towns and regions belonged to one faith, according to the local ruler's choice. These lines are still visible today, as Catholics reside mostly in the south and west and Protestants in the north and east.

General Attitudes

Germans are industrious, thrifty, and orderly. They appreciate punctuality, privacy, and skill. They have a strong sense of regional pride, a fact that the federal system of government recognizes and accommodates. World War II broke down class distinctions because most people lost their possessions and had to start over again. Germany emerged as a land of freedom and opportunity. Germans appreciate intelligent conversation but are often wary of unfamiliar or different ideas. Many are also prone to pessimism. Most Germans have a strong classical education because of the nation's rich heritage in music, history, and art, and they expect others to appreciate that background. Former East Germans share this approach to culture and are proud of how they have nurtured their cultural heritage through the performing arts and museums. After four decades of life under communism, however, it is not surprising that those in the east have somewhat different attitudes toward daily life and work.

Tensions exist between people in the west and east over matters relating to reunification. Easterners feel they are treated as second-class citizens, receiving lower salaries, getting blamed for tax hikes, and being ridiculed by their western counterparts. Westerners resent the economic burden of rebuilding the east; they believe easterners are less capable and unrefined. Such tensions will continue to exist at least until living standards in the east more nearly equal those in the west. Despite the emotional divisions, reconstruction and revitalization are building a united Germany.

Personal Appearance

Germans follow European fashion trends and take care to be well dressed in public. Sloppy or overly casual attire is inappropriate. Shorts and sandals are common leisure wear in summer. Women wear cosmetics sparingly. In southern Germany (mostly southern Bavaria), traditional clothing such as *Lederhosen* (leather pants, either short or knee-length), *Dirndlkleider* (dresses with gathered waists and full skirts, worn with an apron), Bavarian suits, and alpine hats may be part of one's modern daily wardrobe. Traditional costumes of other regions are worn during festivals and celebrations.

Culturgram™ '98

Russia
(Russian Federation)

Boundary representations are not necessarily authoritative.

BACKGROUND

Land and Climate

Russia is the largest country in the world. At 6,592,734 square miles (17,075,200 square kilometers), it is nearly twice the size of the United States. Four of the world's largest rivers (Lena, Ob, Volga, and Yenisey) and the world's deepest freshwater lake (Baikal) are in Russia. Much of Russia is covered by great plains, but a large frozen tundra dominates the extreme north. Much of western Russia is covered by forests. The low Ural Mountains divide Russia's smaller European side from its larger Asian regions. Siberia is mostly steppe (dry, treeless grasslands) and taiga (conifer forests). Russia's climate varies considerably by region. Russian winters last from November to March except in Siberia, where winter can last nine months.

History

Slavic people settled in eastern Europe during the early Christian era. Many converted to Christianity in the ninth and tenth centuries. In 988, Prince Vladimir declared Christianity the state's official religion. Early in the 13th century, Mongols conquered the Slavs and ruled for 240 years. The Slavs finally defeated the Mongols in 1480 to regain their sovereignty. In 1547, Ivan the Terrible (1533–84) was the first Russian ruler crowned Czar of Russia. He expanded Russia's territory, as did Peter the Great (1682–1724) and Catherine the Great (1762–96). The empire reached from Warsaw in the west to Vladivostok in the east. In 1814, Russian troops that had defeated France's Napolean marched on Paris, and Russia took its place as one of the most powerful states on earth.

When Czar Nicholas II abdicated because of popular unrest during World War I, Vladimir Lenin, head of the Bolshevik Party, led the 1917 revolt that brought down the provisional government and put the Communists in power. Lenin disbanded the legislature and banned all other political parties. A civil war between Lenin's Red Army and the White Army lasted until 1921, with Lenin victorious.

In 1922, the Bolsheviks formed the Union of Soviet Socialist Republics (USSR) and forcibly incorporated Armenia, Azerbaijan, Georgia, Ukraine, and Belarus into the union. During Lenin's rule, which ended with his death in 1924, many died as a result of his radical social restructuring. Lenin was followed by Joseph Stalin, a dictator who forced industrialization and collective agriculture on the people. Millions died in labor camps and from starvation. Germany invaded the Soviet Union in 1941, and World War II (the "Great Patriotic War") eventually took more than 25 million Soviet lives.

Nikita Khrushchev, who took over after Stalin's death in 1953, declared he would build real communism within 20 years. Hardliners opposed to his reforms and policy of détente with the West replaced Khrushchev in 1964 with Leonid Brezhnev. Until his death in 1982, Brezhnev orchestrated the expansion of

Soviet influence in the developing world, ordered the invasion of Afghanistan, and built up the Soviet nuclear arsenal. When the next two leaders died in quick succession, a younger man rose to power in 1986: Mikhail Gorbachev.

Gorbachev soon introduced the reform concepts of *perestroika* (restructuring) and *glasnost* (openness). Despite some new freedoms, many of the reforms failed—exposing in the process inherent weaknesses in the Soviet system. The union quickly unraveled in 1991 after several republics declared independence. Russia's leader at the time was Boris Yeltsin.

In 1993, after Yeltsin dissolved a combative parliament, his opponents voted to impeach him and seized the "White House" (parliament building) in an attempted coup. Following street riots, the showdown turned violent and militants were forced from the building by tank fire. That victory and the approval of Yeltsin's new constitution were two highlights of an otherwise difficult term in office. Communists and ultra-nationalists mounted a strong challenge to him in the 1996 elections. Despite poor health, Yeltsin prevailed in the balloting to become Russia's first ever freely elected president.

A violent 21-month war with separatists in the Chechnya region tarnished Yeltsin's image at home and abroad. Finding a solution was complicated by internal rivalries, rebellious military commanders, and Yeltsin's failing health. Tens of thousands died before a ceasefire finally restored peace in August 1996. Russia withdrew its troops in 1997 and Chechens elected their own local leaders. They have de facto control over internal affairs until 2001, when the two parties make a final decision on Chechnya's bid for independence.

In 1996, Russia and Belarus agreed to closely linking their societies without actually merging. The presidents of each nation then signed a union charter in 1997 outlining,

continued

among other things, how Russia and Belarus would cooperate and what infrastructure they would share. Also in 1997, Russia made peace with Ukraine over ownership of the Soviet Union's Black Sea naval fleet, helped negotiate a peace agreement in Tajikistan, participated in international summits, and announced it would no longer target nuclear weapons at former Cold War enemies.

THE PEOPLE

Population

Russia's population of 148 million is shrinking annually by 0.7 percent. Of 120 different ethnic groups in Russia, most are small. Ethnic Russians form 82 percent of the entire population. Other groups include Tartars (4 percent), Ukrainians (3 percent), Chuvashes (1 percent), Byelorussians (almost 1 percent), Udmurts, Kazaks, Buryats, Tuvinians, Yakutians, Bashkirs, and others. The capital and largest city is Moscow, with a population of more than 10 million. Other large cities (one to three million residents each) include St. Petersburg, Novosibirsk, Nizhniy Novgorod, Yekaterinburg, Saratov, and Samara. Most Russians still live in rural areas, but young people are moving to the cities. Russia's Human Development Index value (0.792) ranks it 67th out of 175 countries. Serious gaps between rich and poor, skilled and unskilled, and healthy and ill are widening and threatening Russia's future development. Women earn only one-fifth of the nation's income.

Language

Russian is the official language. It uses the Cyrillic alphabet, which consists of 33 letters, many of them unlike any letter in the Roman (Latin) alphabet. Non-Russians also usually speak Russian, especially in urban areas. Rural minorities more often speak their own languages at home or within their ethnic groups. For example, Tartars speak Tartar, Chuvashes speak Chuvash, and Udmurts speak Udmurt. These individual languages are only taught at schools in areas where the ethnic group is prominent. Ethnic Russians are not required to learn other local languages, but students are increasingly studying foreign languages (especially English, French, German, and Spanish).

Religion

The Russian Orthodox Church is the dominant religion. After the October Revolution (1917), the Communists separated the church from the state (which were previously tightly bonded) and discouraged all religious worship. Many churches were forced to close under Lenin and Stalin. Mikhail Gorbachev was the first Soviet leader to officially tolerate—even support—religion. Yeltsin also embraced the church, which is rapidly regaining its influence. Churches other than the Russian Orthodox are scarce in rural areas, but nearly every major religion and many Christian churches have members in cities. Some Tartars and Bashkirs are Muslim, and some Tuvinians and Buryats are Buddhist.

General Attitudes

In Russia's long history of totalitarianism, its inhabitants had few opportunities to make their own decisions, whether ruled by a Czar or the Communist Party. Personal initiative, personal responsibility, and the desire to work independently were suppressed by the state, and one was expected to conform to official opinion and behavior.

In the current climate, Russians are searching for new social values. The resulting confusion and chaos have led some to wonder whether the old ways weren't better—as evidenced in the Communists' strength during 1996 elections. Many Russians are not happy with their rapidly changing society, characterized by high prices, increasingly violent and rampant crime, unemployment, and a reduced quality of life. Some feel unprepared to pay such a high price for future economic benefits. Others, especially the younger generations, are eagerly taking advantage of the open environment. Indeed, Russians are learning the value of discussion and compromise, personal creativity, and risk-taking. This long-term process carries hard lessons such as financial loss, political polarization, economic instability, and social disruption.

Friendship is extremely important in Russia. Russians are warm and open with trusted friends. They rely on their network of friends in hard times and will go to great lengths to help friends whenever possible.

Although intensely proud of "Mother Russia" and its achievements, Russians are basically pessimistic and usually do not express much hope for a better life in the future (except among the youth). Even generally happy and optimistic Russians might not show their true feelings in public but rather express frustration with everyday life. A general feeling in Russia is that the "soul" of Russia is different from that of other countries, that development cannot take the same course as it has in Europe, for example. Russians often believe they must find a different path that takes into account their unique historical heritage and social structure. In general, Russians desire to be remembered not for the negative aspects of the Soviet period and its aftermath but for Russian contributions to world literature, art, science, technology, and medicine.

Personal Appearance

Russians, especially women, like to be well dressed in public. Urban people prefer European fashions. More young people are wearing shorts in warm weather; young women like short skirts. Jeans are popular among most age groups, except older women. The fur hat that many Russians wear in winter is called a *shapka* or *ushanka*.

Culturgram™ '98

Burkina Faso

Boundary representations are not necessarily authoritative.

BACKGROUND

Land and Climate

Burkina Faso's name means "the land of upright and courageous people." This landlocked nation covering 105,869 square miles (274,200 square kilometers) of West Africa is somewhat larger than Colorado. The mostly flat northern quarter is characterized by sand dunes and a dry climate. Half the nation is covered by the central plateau, and forests are most common in the fertile south. Burkina Faso's highest elevations include Mount Tenakourou (2,300 feet or 750 meters) and Mount Naouri (1,372 feet or 447 meters). Formerly known as the Black, White, and Red

Voltas, the country's main rivers are the Mouhoun, Nakambe, and Nazinon. Winter (November–March) is generally warm and dry, cooled by a consistent harmattan wind. March through May is typically hot and dry, but the rainy season follows from June to October. Daytime temperatures average 85°F (30°C) but can soar to 110°F (43°C) in the summer.

History

Before the colonial period, the region was dominated by several powerful kingdoms, the most important of which were the Mosse, Gurma, Emirat of Liptako, and Guriko. These kingdoms reached their zenith by the turn of the 11th century. Although Portuguese explorers named the three rivers, it was the French who conquered and colonized the land in the late 19th century. In 1904, the Burkinabè (Bur-keen-ah-BAY) territories became attached to the High Senegal–Niger French Colony until it dissolved in 1919. The territories then became a colony called Upper Volta.

The French dissolved Upper Volta in 1932 and distributed its territory among Côte d'Ivoire (Ivory Coast), French Sudan (currently Mali), and Niger. However, the French reestablished Upper Volta in 1947 and a peaceful struggle for independence was waged throughout the 1950s. Two rival leaders emerged from that movement. One of them, Daniel Ouezzin Coulibaly, died in 1958 and his opponent, Maurice Yameogo, then reconciled himself to the African Democratic Rally (RDA), of which Coulibaly had been a prominent member. Yameogo was subsequently chosen as the country's first president upon independence on 5 August 1960.

Yameogo's regime was viewed as corrupt and undemocratic and he was overthrown after a trade union uprising in the 3 January 1966 military coup. Lieutenant Sangoulé Lamizana took power as president. During the 1970s, Upper Volta's four trade unions were among the most powerful and independent in Africa and thus were often able to force political reform. For example, after a nationwide strike in 1980, Lamizana was overthrown in a coup. The coup leader was, in turn, ousted in 1982 by Commandant Jean-Baptist Ouedraogo. However, his supporting officers were divided in their opinions, which led to a 1983 coup by Captain Thomas Sankara.

For many, the charismatic Sankara soon became (and remains) a hero. He changed the country's name to Burkina Faso in 1984 and changed the flag colors from black, white, and red (for the three rivers) to red (blood of mar-

tyrs) and green (richness of agricultural potential) with a gold star (guide of the democratic and popular revolution). He made peace with Mali over a territorial dispute and espoused a socialist ideology. Sankara believed the people should be self-sufficient and not rely on Western aid, and he developed policies toward the goal. Yet in 1987, Sankara's closest associate, Captain Blaise Compaoré, staged a bloody coup in which Sankara and 12 other leaders were killed.

Despite Sankara's popularity, few Burkinabè protested the new coup in light of Compaoré's strength. Although some dissenters were punished, an armistice with opponents soon followed and a new constitution was issued in 1990. Presidential elections were held in December 1991 and legislative elections followed a few months later with 27 parties participating. Compaoré was elected president. Democratization then proceeded slowly but in a stable atmosphere. Compaoré was constitutionally prohibited from seeking a second term in 1998; however, parliament amended the constitution in 1997 to allow a sitting president to seek unlimited terms.

THE PEOPLE

Population

Burkina Faso's population of 10.6 million is growing annually at 2.5 percent. Eighty percent of all inhabitants live in rural areas. The two largest cities are the capital, Ouagadougou (population 800,000), and Bobo Dioulasso (400,000). The capital's name is often abbreviated as Ouaga. Nearly half of the population is younger than age 15. In past years, many men went to work in neighboring countries and sent their wages home to relatives in Burkina Faso, but the migration trend has slowed considerably. Burkina Faso's Human Development Index value (0.221)

continued

ranks it 172d out of 175 countries. Adjusted for women, the value (0.206) ranks Burkina Faso 144th out of 146 nations. These figures reflect the country's limited infrastructure, which contributes to the people's lack of access to resources and opportunities that would allow for personal advancement.

The Mossi (about 55 percent of the population) inhabit the central plateau. A number of smaller groups comprise the remaining 45 percent of the population, including the Fulani (15 percent) in the north; the Gurmantche or Gurma (10 percent) in the east; the Bissa and Gourounsi in the southeast; the Lobi and Dagari in the southwest; and the Bobo, Bwaba, Samo, and Senoufo in the west.

Language

More than 60 languages are used in Burkina Faso, but the most widely spoken are Mooré, Diula (a trade language used by many different groups, including the Bwaba, Bobo, and Senoufo), Fulfuldé (by the Fulani), and Gurmantchéma (by the Gurma). French is the official language of government and education but is only spoken by 15 to 20 percent of the people. People use Diula and Fulfuldé to communicate with ethnic groups in neighboring countries. These languages and Mooré are taught at the university level and are used in some television and radio broadcasts.

Religion

Both Muslims and Christians inhabit Burkina Faso, interacting on each other's holidays and respecting their traditions and beliefs. People from all ethnic groups belong to each religion, although Fulani are less likely to be Christians. Estimates differ as to how many people belong to each group, but Muslims comprise at least 30 percent of the population. Christians (15–20 percent) are most often Roman Catholic, but Protestant groups are also active. Christians tend to have Christian first names and Muslims use Islamic names.

Traditional animist belief systems are practiced exclusively by up to half of all people, who retain their Burkinabè names. Animist traditions act as unifying factors in Burkina Faso's tolerant religious climate, as many Muslims and Christians combine animist practices with their religion. It is not uncommon for them to consult a diviner or to participate in ritual dances. Masks play an important part in animist rituals. For example, dancers wear them to ward off bad luck or in performing agricultural rites. The shape and color of a mask depend on the ethnic group and purpose of the wearer.

General Attitudes

Burkinabè are warm, friendly, and generous. They have strong family values centered on respect for customs and tradition. A financially successful individual is responsible for the rest of the extended family. Humility and generosity are the most desired personal traits, while individualism and bragging are least tolerated. Although family ties are strong, people actually are quite independent. Moving into one's own home, even if it lacks running water or electricity, is an important goal; renting is considered a temporary situation.

Personal Appearance

Burkinabè wear both African and Western clothing. In rural settings, men wear a Muslim robe (*boubou*) while women wear a blouse (*camisole*) and a wraparound skirt (*pagne*). In cities, women wear elaborate, colorful African outfits made of locally designed or imported fabrics. Men usually wear the *tenue de fonctionnaire* (civil servant suit, with shirt and pants made of the same cloth). Both rural and urban dwellers buy used clothing imported from Europe, Asia, and the United States. Lately, however, with politicians and civic leaders calling for consumption of local products, embroidered traditional outfits have become more popular attire for social events.

Although on the decline, traditional face scarring is still practiced in rural areas by some (among the Mossi and Bwaba, for example) to distinguish between ethnic groups.

References

Baxter, J., & Somerville, K. (1989). Burkina Faso. In B. Szajkowski (Ed.). *Benin, The Congo, and Burkina Faso: Economics, Politics, and Society.* (London: Pinter Publishers).

Dulworth, S. (1995, November). Working in Russia: Yesterday, today, tomorrow. *Risk Management,* pp. 22–25.

Englebert, P. (1996). *Burkina Faso: Unsteady statehood in West Africa.* Boulder, CO: Westview Press.

Engberg-Pedersen, P., Gibbon, P., Raides, P., & Udsholt, L. (1996). *Limits of adjustment in Africa.* Copenhagen, Oxford, and Portsmouth, NH: Centre for Development Research.

Jeannet, J. P., & Hennessy, H. D. (1998). *Global marketing strategies* (2nd ed.). Boston: Houghton-Mifflin.

Klitgaard, R. (1990). *Tropical gangsters: One man's experience with development and decadence in deepest Africa.* New York: Basic Books.

Lamb, D. (1987). *The Africans.* New York: Vintage Books.

Puffer, S. M., & Shekshnia, S. V. (1996, March-April). The fit between Russian culture and compensation. *The International Executive, 38,* 217–241.

Skinner, E. P. (1989). *The Mossi of Burkina Faso: Chiefs, politicians, and soldiers.* Prospect Heights, IL: Waveland Press.

Thach, L. (1996, July). Training in Russia. *Training and Development,* pp. 34–37.

Yip, G. S. (1995). *Total global strategy: Managing for worldwide competitive advantage.* Englewood Cliffs, NJ: Prentice Hall.

Related Readings

1. Cosgrove, M. (1991). Roadblocks to new business development. *Journal of Business Strategy, 12* (3), 53–57.
   Case study of a major international oil company's experience with new business development. Upper-level management must treat new business development as a high priority. If not, day-to-day business activities will take precedence and new business development will not get the time, attention, and financial resources it needs in order to succeed.

2. Bakker, H., Jones, W., & Nichols, M. (1994). Using core competencies to develop new business. *Long Range Planning, 27* (6), 13–27.
   Incorporation of new business development depends on managing three domains successfully: (1) search and development of new ideas and businesses; (2) internal or within-company acceptance; and (3) statelholder or external acceptance. Using the core competence concept explained by the authors helps companies identify those areas that offer potential growth, thereby increasing the probability of success.

Chapter 18

Useful Concepts

This chapter deals almost exclusively with acculturation issues and, to a lesser extent, the effects of expatriation on one's career. Both of these topics have been dealt with to some extent in Chapters 5 and 14. However, in both of these chapters, the perspective was on Matt and Jan as expatriates, not as repatriates. Further, the focus was much more on acculturation than on the career effects of expatriation. Reentry has long been known as a critical juncture in the expatriate's life (and the family's if there is one). This is often the point at which the expatriate quits the firm for lack of an appropriate position available, stays only a short time to try to fit in, or remains with the firm for an indeterminate period of time. This section deals in part with reentry issues and the implications for repatriate management.

In addition, up to this point in the story, Matt has had two international assignments. The assignment to Japan was a result of a specific need for MedTech to have representation in Japan. The assignment was not given or accepted as a developmental assignment. Nor was it a part of a larger human resource effort to address strategically the needs of individuals identified as high potentials and the needs of those firms as well. The assignment to France, however, was of the latter type.

Because Matt was not sent to Japan as a high potential, neither was his return to Japan linked to his career development. His return from France was, however. These two types of situations represent much of the contrast in the career effects of international assignments. The effects are largely linked to the reason the person is assigned internationally: circumstances or identification as a high potential.

Thus in addition to addressing some reentry issues, this section also examines some typical effects on expatriates' careers.

Reentry Issues for Expatriates

At least two aspects of reentry are important to deal with here:

1. How firms help the expatriate (or don't) in the repatriation process.
2. The acculturation issues expatriates and families face upon reentry.

How Firms Help Expatriates Upon Reentry

Based on research cited earlier (Oddou, 1991), two "best practices" are performed by firms reputed to exemplify excellent human resource management practices:

- A position search *is undertaken* about six months before the reentry date.
- A strategic effort is made to reposition expatriates in a position that will utilize the skills and perspective they have gained in the international setting.

In Matt's situation, he went to France as a high potential. As a result, Plasmatec had already defined a career path for him. Although every position cannot be predictably vacant at the end of an expatriate's term, if the firm's entire upper management scheme is based on high potential identification and grooming, such coordination is easier. In Plasmatec's case, the position Matt took upon reentry was a natural advancement for him because of his preparation and his perceived competence.

Acculturation Issues Expatriates and Families Face upon Reentry

Expatriates and accompanying family members face essentially the same issues upon reentry as they do going to the foreign site. Although they are returning to their native culture, for many the transition is very problematic. It is most difficult under the following conditions:

1. Those who "left their hearts" in the foreign country.
2. Those who are returning to a different location from the one they left.
3. Those returning after being absent for a lengthy period, usually three or more years.
4. Those returning under very different organizational conditions from those under which they left.

In general, the same model of acculturation presented in Chapter 5 can be applied to reentry.

Career Effects of International Assignments

The career effects of international assignments tend to be directly related to the category of expatriate. For high potentials, it is a career-developing assignment, and these individuals typically return to a promotion or at least another position that is typed as development. In any case, the long-term prospects are upward advancement.

For non-high potentials (i.e., the technical and functional experts), reentry can represent a very mixed situation. Using one model of career stages (Dalton & Thompson, 1986), one study (Oddou & Mendenhall, 1991) showed a clear move toward an advanced career stage when moving from one's domestic position to the foreign country. However, upon reentry, there was some advancement but some reverse movement also. When asked the specific question whether the expatriate was promoted or demoted upon return, 26 percent reported they were promoted and 20 percent reported a demotion.

Further, there are other indications that reentry can be psychologically problematic for expatriates. For example, 66 percent reported experiencing greater independence upon expatriation; half that reported experiencing greater independence upon repatriation. Sixty-seven percent reported having a greater impact on the firm at the international site and only 13 percent said they had less. Upon repatriation, a little over half reported having a greater impact on operations, but 33 percent reported having less.

Other data reveal consistent results with the preceding picture. Only 29 percent said that expatriation was helpful for their careers when they returned. Thirty-nine percent said firms utilized their new skills and international perspective when repatriated. Finally, only 12 percent said their international assignment was better for their professional careers than for their personal development.

This data must be viewed in light of other findings about how these repatriates evaluated the usefulness of their international assignment:

- Nearly 90 percent said their assignment significantly increased their global perspective of their firm's operations.
- Over 85 percent felt they could better communicate with people of diverse backgrounds.
- Almost 80 percent said they can conceptualize and comprehend business trends and events better from their exposure to contrasting cultural, political, and economic systems.
- Nearly 60 percent reported they are better motivators as a result of working with culturally diverse personnel.

In summary, expatriate assignments are clearly professionally beneficial for high potentials. For non–high potentials, this is not clearly the case. However, despite the frustration expatriates in the non–high-potential category experience, the overwhelming majority said they were glad they took the assignment because of the clear personal development they and their families experienced.

What is not clear is the long-term prospects of career development for the non–high potentials. In today's increasing global marketplace, international experience will likely be a greater asset than it has been in the past.

References

Dalton, G., & Thompson, P. (1986). *Novations: Strategies for career management.* Glenview, IL: Scott Foresman.

Oddou, G., & Mendenhall, M. (1991). Succession planning for the 21st century: How well are we grooming our future business leaders? *Business Horizons, 34* (1), 26–34.

CHAPTER 19

USEFUL CONCEPTS

This chapter focuses on global strategy, the role of a senior manager in charge of global operations, and critical international issues of concern to top management. Matt struggles to develop a global strategy that gives direction and is not simply reactionary. Based on several models and other cases he's known, he comes up with a strategy that is broad, flexible, and rewards local initiative within corporate guidelines but nevertheless allows for a sense of corporate control and directionality. It depends, in large measure, on successful international management development and teaching corporate culture, as well as a clear corporate vision or sense of direction.

Many companies go global to grow economically, leverage globally, enhance their position in financial markets, and become more competitive. They worry about how to develop expertise, information systems, partnerships with other companies, and an organization that can exploit their new opportunities. It seems like a challenging and complex yet necessary and potentially profitable undertaking. However, many business leaders remain skeptical about aggressively pursuing such opportunities.

Here are some overall guidelines a company strategist like Matt might consider, plus some data supporting his ideas about reorganizing his function, going into emerging markets, and focusing on internationalizing managers.

Strategic Guidelines for "Managing Across Borders"

Companies today must optimize efficiency, responsiveness, and strive for total success and competitiveness. However, these qualities are difficult to attain in the international sphere because of the following:

1. Companies must add geographically oriented management.
2. A three-way balance of organizational perspectives and capabilities among product, function, and area must be reached.
3. Operating units are divided by distance, time, culture, and language.

To successfully meet these challenges, global companies might pursue policies similar to those outlined below. This is a summary of Bartlett and Goshals (1989) recommendations.

I. From Unidimensional to Multidimensional Capabilities
   A. Unidimensional approach
      1. Build multiple strategic capabilities in complex organizations (forces managers to make dichotomous choices).
      2. Pursue a strategy of national responsiveness, instead of global integration.

3. Debate centralization or decentralization of key assets and resources.
4. Acknowledge need for strong central control versus subsidiary autonomy.

B. Multidimensional approach

1. New competitive challenge forces managers to achieve global efficiency and integration. To achieve this, three general areas must be covered:

a. Strong geographic management—essential for development of dispersed responsiveness; worldwide companies to respond to the needs of different national markets.

b. Business management— rationalization, product standardization, low-cost global sourcing.

c. Functional management—organizations to build/transfer core competencies, knowledge, and skills to apply to worldwide operations.

II. Overcoming Simplifying Assumptions

A. Three assumptions block necessary organizational development from uni- to multidimensional:

1. Roles of different organizational units are uniform and symmetrical, all managed in the same way.

2. Company creates internal interunit relationships on patterns of dependence and independence, assuming they will be clear and unambiguous.

3. Corporate manager's principal task is to institutionalize clearly understood mechanisms for decision making and to implement simple means of exercising control.

B. To create successful multidimensional organizations, managers must work against these assumptions by:

1. differentiating tasks and responsibilities.

2. managing interdependence among different company units.

3. coordinating and coopting instead of controlling; having a shared vision of company's strategic task.

III. From Symmetry to Differentiation

Instead of simplistic dichotomies (e.g., global vs. domestic businesses) companies should create different levels of influence from different people and duties. Case studies of Unilever and Procter & Gamble show such an evolution.

IV. Independence to Interdependence

A. New strategic demands make organizational models of simple interunit dependence or independence inappropriate.

B. Independent units are threatened by global competitors who:

1. cross-subsidize local markets from global firms.

2. integrate research, manufacturing, other scale-efficient operations in home markets.

C. Dependent units are threatened by a central-unit risk of being unable to respond to national competitors or sense important local markets.

D. Achieving an "integrative organization"
1. Must change basis of relationship among product, function, geographic management groups to one focused on interdependence, collaboration, integration.
2. Example: Procter & Gamble has formed Eurobrand teams for developing product-market strategies for different product lines. Success of each team depends on support of other subsidiaries. The interdependencies of this setup foster teamwork that is driven by individual interests.
E. Three factors are at the core of organizational relationships:
1. Product interdependence—specialized worldwide manufacturing operations while retaining flexibility locally. The result is a flow of parts, components, finished goods to increase interdependencies.
2. Resource interdependence—flow of funds, skills, and other scarce resources.
3. Informational interdependence—flow of intelligence, ideas, and knowledge.
V. From Control to Coordination and Cooperation
Simplifying assumptions of symmetry and dependence leads to simple controls in the management, allowing tight operational controls in subsidiaries dependent on the center and a looser system of administrative controls in decentralized units.
A. Need for coordination in management, involving:
1. committees, task forces.
2. broadening of administrative processes.
3. socialization processes for knowledge flows (e.g., transfer of people, informal communication channels, forums to facilitate interunit learning).
B. Usage of new coordinating methods
1. Distinguishing between where tasks are to be formalized and managed through systems and where social linkages are to encourage informal agreement and cooperation.
2. Differentiating the way product, functions, and geographic units are managed.
3. Differentiating roles and responsibilities within the organization.
4. Implementing cooption—the process of uniting the organization with a common understanding of, identification with, and commitment to the corporation's objectives, priorities, and values.
5. Make control less dominant by the increased importance of interunit integration and collaboration.
VI. Sustaining a Dynamic Balance: The "Mind Matrix"
A. The organization must possess a differentiated influence structure. Roles must change continually with changing environment. The key word here is "flexibility."

   B. Previous tools for flexible management
       1. formal structure to shift roles over time.
       2. prevent multidimensional perspective from atrophying by rebalancing power relationships.
       3. prevent the establishment of entrenched power bases.
   C. Successful approaches to management
       1. companies aiming to develop multidimensional perspective and flexibility at the level of the individual manager.
       2. understanding of the need for multiple strategic capabilities.
       3. view problems from both local and global perspectives.
       4. "create a matrix in the minds of managers."

Yip provides some additional guidelines and ideas for implementing a global strategy (1995, p. 236).

1. Do not assume "it cannot happen here." Almost any industry has the potential for globalization and global competition.
2. Global industries are not born but are created by global companies. The rewards of globalization go to the first movers.
3. Globalization requires a clear vision of the firm as a global competitor. It also requires a long-term time horizon and a commitment from top management.
4. Globalization is not all or nothing. A business can be global in some elements of its strategy and not in others.
5. Shift the burden of proof from assuming that strategy should be local unless proven otherwise to assuming the strategy should be global unless proven otherwise. In deciding on product and program adaptation, search for what is really necessary rather than assuming the local managers know best.
6. Be careful to match strategy changes with the necessary organization and management changes.
7. Globalization should not be a religion but a philosophy.
8. The slogan "Think global, act local" is wrong. It should read, "Think and act global and local."

The Head Office International Organization

Key elements of the global organization are outlined in Yip's book (1995, p.56):

> Four factors and their individual elements determine the crucial organization forces that affect a company's ability to formulate and implement global strategy:
>
> - *Organization structure* comprises the reporting relationships in a business—the "boxes and lines."
> - *Management processes* comprise the activities such as planning and budgeting that make the business run.

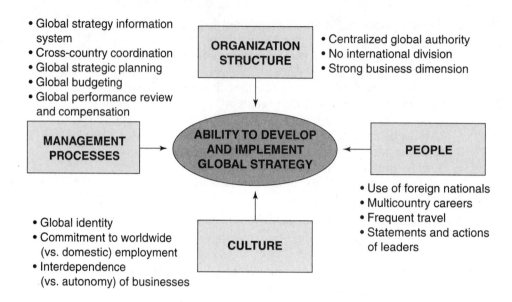

- Global strategy information system
- Cross-country coordination
- Global strategic planning
- Global budgeting
- Global performance review and compensation

ORGANIZATION STRUCTURE

- Centralized global authority
- No international division
- Strong business dimension

MANAGEMENT PROCESSES

ABILITY TO DEVELOP AND IMPLEMENT GLOBAL STRATEGY

PEOPLE

- Use of foreign nationals
- Multicountry careers
- Frequent travel
- Statements and actions of leaders

- Global identity
- Commitment to worldwide (vs. domestic) employment
- Interdependence (vs. autonomy) of businesses

CULTURE

- *People* comprise the human resources of the worldwide business and include both managers and all other employees.
- *Culture* comprises the values and unwritten rules that guide behavior in a corporation.

Each of these factors directly affects the others and the use of global strategy. Each operates powerfully in different ways. A common mistake, in implementing *any* strategy, is to ignore one or more of them, particularly the less tangible ones such as culture. A blockage in even one dimension of organization can severely cramp the ability to think and behave globally. Figure 19.1 lists the key factors and their key elements (Yip, 1995, p. 56).

Yip also elaborates how to evaluate the international organization (1995, pp. 213–214)).

Measuring Global Organization

Measuring the extent to which management and organization help global strategy involves more subjectivity than measuring industry globalization potential and the use of global strategy levers. Because the effects of organization are so specific to individual companies, corporate managers might find it particularly helpful to measure global organization in their different worldwide businesses. They are likely to find that some elements are common across businesses and others differ. Then they can investigate if these differences have helped or hurt the globalization efforts of each business. These measures are as follows:

Organization Element	Measure
Organization Structure	
One global head	Whether there is one person whose primary job it is to be head of the worldwide business
International division	Whether there is an international division that does not contain the domestic business
Functional line heads	Whether there is a single head with line authority for each function
Functional staff heads	Whether there is a single staff coordinator for each function
Strength of business dimension	In a matrix structure, the strength of the business dimension relative to the geographic and functional dimensions
Management Processes	
Global strategic information system	Extent to which the business collects strategic information such as market share and competitor data, from around the world in a consistent format on a regular basis
Cross-country coordination	Extent to which the business has processes for coordinating strategy across countries—*sharing information, negotiating plans, clearing plans with headquarters,* and *direction by headquarters*
	Frequency of *global meetings*
	Use of *global teams*
	Number of *global product managers or global account managers*
Global strategic planning	Extent to which the business uses an effective strategic planning process that integrates across countries rather than just adding up the national plans
Global budgeting	Extent to which the business has global budgets that are used for global programs, as opposed to national budgets for national programs
Global and performance review and compensation	Extent to which senior managers are evaluated and compensated on the basis of global and not just regional or national performance; percentage of compensation tied to global performance

People

Foreign nationals in home country	Percentage of senior managers in home country who are foreign nationals
Home country nationals in other countries	Percentage of senior managers in other countries who are home country nationals
Foreign nationals in other countries	Percentage of senior managers in other countries who are non–home country foreign nationals

Culture

Global culture	Extent to which corporate or business culture is global rather than national
Interdependent culture	Extent to which culture favors interdependence rather than autonomy

Emerging Markets

Conclusion: Over the next two decades the greatest opportunities for U.S. exports will be the 10 Big Emerging Markets (BEMs):

Transition: Matt is considering whether and how much to expound Plasmatec sales into the emerging or under-developed economies. Following is U.S. Department of Commerce data about the importance of emerging economies for economic growth.

1. Chinese Economic Area (Hong Kong, Taiwan, China)
2. South Korea
3. Indonesia
4. India
5. Poland
6. Turkey
7. South Africa
8. Mexico
9. Brazil
10. Argentina

Value: U.S. exports to BEMs in 1993 were $113 billion, expected to exceed exports to Japan and Europe by 2010.

1993 Department of Commerce Report; February 15, 1995, letter from Secretary of Commerce

International Recruiting Intentions

% of Companies in Agreement

Statement	American MNCs	European MNCs	Japanese MNCs
We will, in the future, recruit for international potential	51%	44%	21%
We will, in the future, train our people to think and act internationally	78%	75%	65%
We will expatriate more home country personnel to worldwide foreign operations	43%	49%	49%

Oddou, Derr, Black, & Gregersen, 1998.

Future International Field Experience

% of Companies in Agreement

Statement	American MNCs	European MNCs	Japanese MNCs
Extensive travel will be more important in the future	53%	56%	90%
International task forces and project teams will be increased in the future	82%	80%	53%
More foreign nationals will be coming to work in domestic offices in the future	49%	70%	3%
Increasing future use of "long" business trips (3–6 months) working abroad without dependents	Frequent	Frequent	Frequent Use
Future employees must learn to think and act globally	78%	75%	65%

Oddou, Derr, Black, & Gregersen, 1998.

References

Adler, N. J. (1991). *International Dimensions of Organizational Behavior.* Boston: P.W.S. Kent.

Allard, L. A. C. (1996, May). Managing globe-trotting expats. *Management Review,* pp. 39–43.

Baird, L., Briscoe, J., & Tuden, L. (1993). Globalizing management to meet the challenges of global business. Unpublished *Executive Development Roundtable Report.* Boston: University School of Management.

Bartlett, C., & Goshals, S. (1989). *Managing across borders.* Boston: Harvard Business School Press.

Bird, A., & Dunbar, R. (1991, Spring). Getting the job done over there: Improving expatriate productivity. *National Productivity Review,* pp. 145–156.

Derr, C. B., & Oddou, G. R. (1991). Are US multinationals adequately preparing future American leaders for global competition? *International Journal of Human Resource Management, 2* (2), 222–244.

Derr, C. B., & Oddou, G. (1993). Internationalizing managers: Speeding up the process. *European Management Journal, 2* (4), 435–432.

Fatehi, K. (1996). Development of international corporate structure. In K. Fatehi (Ed.), *International Management* (pp. 90–105). Upper Saddle River, NJ: Prentice-Hall.

Garten, J. E. (1997, May-June). Troubles ahead in emerging markets. *Harvard Business Review,* reprint 97302.

Geo-JaJa, M. H., & Mangum, G. (1997). *The Foreign Corrupt Practices Act's consequences for U.S. trade: The Nigerian example.* Working paper, Center for International Business Education and Research (CIBER), David Eccles School of Business, University of Utah, Salt Lake City, UT 84112.

Goold, M., & Campbell, A. (1987, November–December). Many ways to make strategy. *Harvard Business Review,* pp. 70–76.

Klaus, K. J. (1995, Spring). How to establish an effective expatriate program. *Employment Relations Today,* pp. 59–70.

Moore, M. T. (1996, February 8). New breed CEO markets locally—worldwide. *USA Today,* pp. 1–2B.

Oddou, G., Derr, C. G., Black, J. S., & Gregersen, H. B. (1998). *Building global leaders: Strategy differences among European, U.S. and Japanese multinationals.* Unpublished paper. Write Professor Gary Oddou, College of Business, San Jose State University, San Jose, CA 95213.

Odenwald, S. (1993, July). A guide for global training. *Training and Development,* pp. 23–31.

O'Donnell, S., & Roth, K. (1995). *Implementing lateral centralization at the foreign subsidiary: The role of compensation and reward systems.* Unpublished working paper D-95-17, Center for International Business and Research (CIBER), College of Business Administration, University of South Carolina, Columbia, SC 29208.

Phillips, M. M. (1998, January 26). U.S. firms may lose labor cost advantage. *Wall Street Journal,* New York, January 26, 1998, p. A1.

Porter, M. (1985). *Competitive advantage.* Boston: Harvard Business School Press.

Solomon, C. M. (1994, October) How does your global talent measure up? *Personnel Journal,* pp. 96–108.

Yip, G. S. (1995). *Total global strategy: Managing for worldwide competitive advantage.* Englewood Cliffs, NJ: Prentice-Hall.

Related Readings

1. Amin, S.G., and Hagen, A.F. (1998). Strengthening American international competitiveness: A recommended strategy. *American Business Review, 16* (1), 94–104.
   U.S. businesses have become less competitive in the global market. The authors describe seven areas in which U.S. companies may be experiencing difficulties: (1) productivity, (2) investment, (3) international trade, (4) technological development, (5) product quality, (6) educational system, and (7) political-legal environment. Many of these areas have seen a decrease within the United States at the same time that other countries have increased or improved in these areas.

   The authors suggest ten segments of a macro-level plan to upgrade the ability to compete with other countries: (1) develop programs to look at the internal organization of industries within the United States; (2) establish financial programs that will encourage greater investment; (3) commercialize advancements in technology; (4) improve worker skills; (5) emphasize quality issues; (6) target specific industries and geographic markets; (7) establish national standards for education; (8) increase focus on customer satisfaction; (9) create a more healthy corporate environment; and (10) take international competition seriously and learn from other countries.

2. Baird, I. S., Lyles, M. A., & Orris, J. B. (1994). The choice of international strategies by small businesses. *Journal of Small Business Management, 32* (1), 48–59.
   The focus of this article is on small businesses. As small companies venture into international markets, they may find their lack of knowledge and experience hinders their ability to succeed. Companies can choose to pursue international strategies that are either competitive or cooperative. For most small companies, cooperative strategies tend to work better because of the opportunity to share risk, knowledge, and resources. In this way, they may be able to avoid some of the problems associated with limited background and resources. Although establishing an international strategy may be difficult, it is imperative for those companies that are pursuing international markets in any way.

Credits

Culturgrams on pages 33, 80, 121, 141, 144, 148

 © 1998. Brigham Young University's David M. Kennedy Center for International Studies, Publications Division, PO Box 24538, Provo UT 84602-4538. Culturgrams © are available for more than 165 areas of the world. For more information, please call 800-528-6279.

page 57

 Reprinted with permission of Academy of Management, PO Box 3020 Briar Cliff Manor, NY 10510-8020. "Expatriate Adjustment Model," Black, Mendenhall & Oddou, *Academy of Management Review* 1991, vol. 16 no. 2, pp. 291-317. Reproduced by permission of the publisher via Copyright Clearance Center, Inc.

Index

Page numbers in this index refer to Part II of the book.